To Doug
with hopes
that we might
eventually do
something together
in this general
area

J.

# SOCIOLOGICAL

# PERSPECTIVES ON

# LABOR MARKETS

This is a volume of
*Quantitative Studies in Social Relations*
Consulting Editor: Peter H. Rossi, University of Massachusetts,
Amherst, Massachusetts
A complete list of titles in this series appears at the end of this volume.

# SOCIOLOGICAL PERSPECTIVES ON LABOR MARKETS

Edited by

## Ivar Berg

*Department of Sociology*
*University of Pennsylvania*
*Philadelphia, Pennsylvania*

**ACADEMIC PRESS**

*A Subsidiary of Harcourt Brace Jovanovich, Publishers*

New York    London    Toronto    Sydney    San Francisco

ACADEMIC PRESS, INC.
111 Fifth Avenue, New York, New York 10003

*United Kingdom Edition published by*
ACADEMIC PRESS, INC. (LONDON) LTD.
24/28 Oval Road, London NW1 7DX

Library of Congress Cataloging in Publication Data
Main entry under title:

Sociological perspectives on labor markets.

   (Quantitative studies in social relations)
   Includes bibliographies and index.
   1. Labor supply--Social aspects--United States--
Addresses, essays, lectures. 2. Industrial sociology--
Addresses, essays, lectures. I. Berg, Ivar E. II. Series.
HD5724.S624        306'.3        81-3656
ISBN  0-12-089650-8              AACR2

PRINTED IN THE UNITED STATES OF AMERICA

81 82 83 84    9 8 7 6 5 4 3 2 1

*To William Form, Charles Killingsworth, and Delbert Miller, whose scholarly urges over many years are reflected in these pages*

# Contents

## Chapter 3
## An Outline of a Theory of the Matching of Persons to Jobs    49

*AAGE B. SØRENSEN AND ARNE L. KALLEBERG*

## Part II
## FIRMS, OCCUPATIONS, AND LABOR MARKETS

## Chapter 4
## Economic Organization of Firms and
## Labor Market Consequences:
## Toward a Specification of Dual Economy Theory    77

*MICHAEL WALLACE AND ARNE L. KALLEBERG*

## Chapter 5
## Firms, Occupations, and the
## Structure of Labor Markets:
## A Conceptual Analysis    119

*ROBERT P. ALTHAUSER AND ARNE L. KALLEBERG*

# Part IV
# DISCRIMINATION IN LABOR MARKETS

## Chapter 9
## Female Underemployment in Urban Labor Markets    251

*ALICE ABEL KEMP AND E. M. BECK*

## Chapter 10
## Assessing Trends in Occupational
## Sex Segregation, 1900–1976                           273

*PAULA ENGLAND*

## Chapter 13
## Toward Model Specification in the Structural Unemployment Thesis: Issues and Prospects

# List of Contributors

*Numbers in parentheses indicate the pages on which the authors' contributions begin.*

ROBERT P. ALTHAUSER (119), Department of Sociology, Indiana University, Bloomington, Indiana 47405

E. M. BECK (251), Department of Sociology, University of Georgia, Athens, Georgia 30602

IVAR BERG (1, 347), Department of Sociology, University of Pennsylvania, Philadelphia, Pennsylvania 19104

ROBERT BIBB (347), Department of Sociology, Vanderbilt University, Nashville, Tennessee 37235

DANIEL B. CORNFIELD (219), Department of Sociology, Vanderbilt University, Nashville, Tennessee 37235

PAULA ENGLAND (273), School of Social Sciences, University of Texas—Dallas, Richardson, Texas 75080

T. ALDRICH FINEGAN (347), Department of Economics and Business Administration, Vanderbilt University, Nashville, Tennessee 37235

MARK GRANOVETTER (11), Department of Sociology, State University of New York at Stony Brook, Stony Brook, New York 11794

*ARNE L. KALLEBERG* (49, 77, 119), Department of Sociology, Indiana University, Bloomington, Indiana 47405

*ALICE ABEL KEMP* (251), Department of Sociology, University of Georgia, Athens, Georgia 30602

*ROBERT K. MILLER, JR.* (297), Department of Sociology and Anthropology, University of North Carolina at Wilmington, Wilmington, North Carolina 28406

*TOBY L. PARCEL* (187), Department of Sociology, University of Iowa, Iowa City, Iowa 52242

*PAUL G. SCHERVISH* (153), Department of Sociology, Boston College, Chestnut Hill, Massachusetts 02167

*AAGE B. SØRENSEN* (49), Department of Sociology, University of Wisconsin—Madison, Madison, Wisconsin 53706

*TERESA A. SULLIVAN* (329), Department of Sociology, The University of Chicago, Chicago, Illinois 60637

*MICHAEL SWAFFORD* (347), Department of Sociology, Vanderbilt University, Nashville, Tennessee 37235

*MICHAEL WALLACE* (77), Department of Sociology, Indiana University, Bloomington, Indiana 47405

# Preface

This volume's origins are traced in Chapter 1, and a brief statement is made about the main differences between the contributors' perspective on labor market phenomena on the one hand, and a far more familiar perspective on the other. The book's genesis and its authors' aspirations need not detain us, therefore, in this brief preface.

This volume may be viewed in the larger context of research interests common to sociologists and economists. Growing numbers of sociologists are broaching issues that they had long regarded as belonging in the economist's realm. At the same time, economists are seeking to augment their familiar "marginalist" schema, long dominant in economics, and are increasingly turning their attention to issues that can be effectively joined only by attending to institutional arrangements, demographic developments, political questions (concerning equity, especially), and to what they term *nonallocative sources of efficiency in organizational settings.* As mathematical problems pertaining to quantitative research began to tax imaginations in both disciplines, a need to share investments in the development of techniques arose. There has, correlatively, been a certain sharing in the exploitation of the methodological infrastructures in the disciplines.

Consider, in this larger context, that a well-received quantitative study of economic development is likely to accord as much attention to the work of noneconomists as to that of economists: see *Society, Politics, and Economic Development* by Irma Adelman and Cynthia Taft Morris (1971), for example. The single most influential body of studies of the correlates of industrialization was undertaken by a consortium of social scientists whose efforts are conveniently summarized by John Dunlop and his associates (1975). One of the most influential clusters of studies of the sources of efficiency contains what is, in good measure, an inventive recasting by Harvey Liebenstein (1960, 1979), an economist, of materials to be found in sociologists' studies of organizations since 1929. Sociologists have even joined in economists' efforts to divine the logics to be inferred from research on the evolution of what is termed *the world-system*. One of the most provocative studies of post-World War II monetary developments, written in the so-called neo-Marxist perspective, is by a sociologist (Block, 1977). A brief discussion of the most relevant overlap, that existing in the study of labor markets, is the subject of Chapter 1 of this book.

One could easily continue listing the overlaps to which I here allude. Investigators in the two disciplines regularly encounter each other, coming and going, at funding agencies, symposia, demography centers, survey institutes, before national commissions and congressional committees, and, not least frequently, at the bins from which computer printouts are collected for use in studies of income distribution, "relative deprivation," poverty, mobility, educational investments, and economies of families, economic growth, mortality and morbidity rates, and education. This volume's title, an imperialistic one, is reasonably descriptive, however—the shared interests of innumerable economists and sociologists and the contributions of T. Aldrich Finegan, an economist, notwithstanding. The title is appropriate not because it proclaims that the contributors speak for sociology, but because these chapters present marked variations on a widely heralded perspective on human resources, known in sociological circles as *status attainment theory*. This perspective has much in common with an equally heralded one among economists, known as *human capital theory*. But more of that in Chapter 1.

It remains to be said in this preface only that we invite our readers to regard the chapters herein as working papers or as exercises in the quantitative study of the structures and functionings of diverse types of markets in the United States. In these markets, employed Americans, their job-seeking peers, and the employers who hire, promote, lay off, and discharge them enter into arrangements whereby they adapt their exchanges, bargains, and agreements. My collaborators join me in inviting others to correct our mistakes, sharpen our analytical wits, and elaborate on those of our conceptualizations that offer promise. We thank the many colleagues, identified and otherwise, who have read and criticized early drafts of our work.

Special thanks, finally, go to those who have helped with the book's preparation (Joanie Prior, Winifred Berg, and Terry Ezekiel, particularly); to those who encouraged us (Peter Rossi, especially); and, inevitably, to audiences that favored us with their questions and suggestions when seven of these chapters were first presented as papers.

## References

Adelman, Irma, and Cynthia Taft Morris
  1971   *Society, Politics and Economic Development: A Quantitative Approach.* Baltimore: Johns Hopkins Univ. Press.
Block, Fred
  1977   *Origins of International Economic Disorder: A Study of U.S. International Monetary Policy from World War II to Present.* Berkeley: Univ. of California Press.
Dunlap, John T., *et al.*
  1975   *Industrialization and Industrial Man Reconsidered.* Princeton: The Inter-University Study of Human Resources in National Development.
Liebenstein, Harvey
  1960   *Economic Theory and Organizational Analysis.* New York: Harper.
  1979   "X-efficiency: From concept to theory," *Challenge* 22 (4), 13–22.

# SOCIOLOGICAL

# PERSPECTIVES ON

# LABOR MARKETS

# Chapter 1

# Introduction

*IVAR BERG*

The publication in 1979 of *Who Gets Ahead?*, the second of two reports by teams under Christopher Jencks's direction, marks, rather appropriately, the end of two decades of intensive research into the distribution of incomes and statuses in America, during which such inquiries have been dominated by human capital theory and status attainment theory. The names Dennison, Schultz, Becker, Mincer, Hansen, and Taubman—among innumerable economists—and Blau, Duncan, Coleman, Featherman, Hauser, and Jencks—among a host of sociologists—come most immediately to mind.

There have, of course, been other efforts to divine the logics by which Americans are aligned among and assigned or consigned to their occupations. Thus, there has been something of a renaissance on the social sciences' left flank, for example, complete with journals and professional associations, in accord with which older ideas about class and production relations are reformulated by a new generation of Marxian revisionists to fit the facts of what they term *postindustrial society.*

Studies have also appeared by a number of program-oriented liberals responsive to leaders in foundations, Congressional study committees, and the subsidiaries of a few federal agencies, such as the Office of Education, who seek to improve the proximal experiences and opportunities of students, job applicants, and jobholders. While it must be acknowledged that status

1

SOCIOLOGICAL PERSPECTIVES ON
LABOR MARKETS

attainment and human capital theorists do not own a monopoly in the stratification studies industry, it will not likely be denied that the most influential work in this broad field over the past 20 years is that done by scientists at work on the elaboration of these closely parallel theories.

It is also the case that proponents of these theories are receiving aid, if not necessarily comfort, from a new wave of would-be geneticists and eugenicists. The evidence of human capital and status attainment theorists' influence, meanwhile, is plentiful. Their data, like Schultz's, help win Nobel medals; like Coleman's, they help school busing protagonists win Supreme Court cases; like Jencks's, they help win prized space in widely read book reviews; and, like Blau and Duncan's and Becker's, they help reap endless mentions in the intimidating columns of the *Social Science Citation Index* and valued places in course lists in hundreds of universities.

It is of immediate relevance, given their influence, to note that the overwhelming emphases in these studies are upon identifying different combinations of backgrounds, exposures, aptitudes, abilities, and personality traits that "effect"—the word is basic coin of these theorists' realm—the occupational, income, and life chances of labor force participants. These theorists seek to discover the attributes, in short, that determine the "quality" of the republic's labor supply.

One cannot avoid the suspicion that the popularity of these studies in scientific, intellectual, and public policymaking circles derives, in very substantial measure, from the fact that the favored apparatus rests upon a foundation of agreeable assumptions about the great significance, to differentially well-situated peoples' careers, of factors under their genes', their families', their schools', and, otherwise, under their own essential control, an idea about individual responsibility whose time came long ago in our republic. Additional orders of popularity attach to such a model (*a*) among many gratified educators who apparently augment earners' abilities, shape their personalities, and affect their beliefs and values in what many social scientists take to be "functional" ways; (*b*) among rational decision-making employers who are obligated in their respective markets to search for and hire only the "best persons" for their job vacancies; (*c*) among social scientists, Left and Right, whose paradigms require that employers "exploit surplus value" and turn "well-deserved profits," respectively; and (*d*) by many of those, obviously, who are themselves more successful in their careers and who choose to credit their circumstances to the superiority of their chromosomes, their backgrounds, their admirably judicious husbanding of their personal human capital, their sacrifices, their abilities, and their amiable personalities.

The theoretical linchpin, in view of the generally high associations between schooling, attitudes, abilities, and personalities on one side, and successes (or failures) on the other, is wrought of an assumption that favorable traits generate productivity increases, increases that unfavorable traits do not generate. The higher productivity associated with the superior traits, in turn, is deserving of higher rewards. The higher returns to the better educated, for example, are thus routinely taken to be persuasive—if indirect—evidence of the productivity of better educated workers. This marginalist model thus quickly converts measures of employers' demand into measures of supply. The tautological character of the logic adumbrated here is generally overlooked, however, in recognition of (*a*) the difficulties, or impossibilities, of measuring directly the actual productivity differences of survey and census respondents possessing different traits or combinations thereof; and (*b*) employers' putative obligations to protect themselves from the chill winds of the marketplace that are seen, literally, to force them, eyes on bottom lines, to reward productivity.

## Sociological and Institutional Perspectives on Labor Markets

An appreciation of the recent accomplishments and the influential character of an analytical social science model that can so easily transmute complex supply and demand questions into simpler questions of supply *alone* need not, however, obscure—as the transmutation most assuredly does—the unattended questions of employers' actual ways.

Indeed, there have been many efforts, over many decades, to introduce corrections that add greater model specifications to the parsimonious and problematic marginalist model. In modern times these efforts, often militant, have lead to raging debates between marginalists, on one side, and what Fritz Machlup (1967) called the "managerialists" and "behaviorists," on the other. Machlup's reference, in a "revisit to the battleground," was to a number of investigators, reaching back to John R. Commons, Stanley B. Mathewson, Chester Barnard, Elton Mayo, and an earlier generation of labor economists, "before human capital," led by Richard Lester, John Dunlop, Sumner Schlichter, E. Robert Livernash, Arthur Ross, and many others; to students of bureaucracy and organization; to "plant sociologists" like Melville Dalton, Leonard Sayles, Donald Roy, and William Whyte; and to students, like Herbert Simon and James March, of decision making. These scholars pointed, collectively, to the wide degrees of managers' freedom, in an economy whose markets were rife with imperfections, to act in ways other than those delineated for them by marginalists in the theory of the firm. While many would recognize John Dunlop's name, only a few specialized social scientists would likely know of the ideas and investigations of the others; hardly a contemporary reader of *The New York Times Book Review*, *The New York Review of Books*, *Commentary*, *The New Republic*, *The Wall Street Journal*, and *Business Week*, meantime, could have failed to be treated to thoughtful discussions of the two Jencks teams' studies and the Coleman report (1966). And Herbert Simon's Nobel medal came only long after the marginalists, with Simon's help, discovered that "satisficing behavior" was really only a special—if significant—case of the marginal theory of demand by which attention, ricochet fashion, bounces back to supply problems, through the artful use of indirect measures of demand.

Machlup, himself an active combatant in the war he described, agreed with the foregoing view, if not precisely with the intonations, as he wrote charitably but condescendingly of the contributions to economists' forecasting efforts of the work of the ragtag army of antagonists who sought to bring the demand for labor in firms and in the economy to front and center, antagonists who sought to expose this demand to direct scrutiny rather than to postulate demand exclusively in terms of payments made to the factors of production.

My own interests, meanwhile, have fallen on what is here denoted as the actual demand side—the development of direct methods for studying the realities of demand and for "decomposing" employers' ways. While admiring the marginalists' model, and learning a great deal from the human capital and status attainment theorists, I have long hoped for renascent efforts by nonmarginalists, not in anticipation that marginalist theorists' work could be subverted, but in hopes that supply and demand issues could be distinguished and then simultaneously—and more truly—joined. My hope, in fine, has been for an *entente cordiale*, not a reversion to the war between the estates of the arts, as Machlup limned them in 1967 in his Presidential Address to the American Economic Association. To put it in trade terms, I believe that the human capital and status attainment theories have taken us a long way in our sociological and economic studies of welfare, resource allocation, stratification, and distribution. These studies' recent efforts appear to be moving further and further from substantive questions however, and are becoming more and more the grist for methodologists' mills; while one can readily applaud such developments for purposes of abstract theory building, one also senses a need to move, on other fronts, to add demand-related specifications to the favored theorists' model with its supply-related specifications and its truncated character.

Given these interests, I was delighted to receive three papers on the direct roles of "demand side" factors that appear to influence the fates of labor market participants in systematic ways, among 30-odd submissions for a session I was asked to organize on "Economy and Society" at the 1979 meetings of the American Sociological Association. These papers highlighted the fact, among others, that similar traits are rewarded quite differently in different labor market contexts, in different industries, and even within firms. A fourth paper, cast in theoretical terms, offered a perspective within which the better-known "supply studies" and the far lesser-known "demand studies" could be integrated such that the large unexplained residual variances in human capital and status attainment studies could be retrieved from the "luck" or "chance" rubic, a kind of social science limbo to which these variances are not uncommonly consigned. I was pleased, a few months later, to receive three additional papers by authors interested in research on demand among several papers submitted for a session on "Labor Markets" at the 1980 meetings of the Southern Sociological Society. The authors of this second set of papers agreed to join with the earlier authors in the present publication venture. Three additional papers, two of which were coauthored by one of the first group's authors, were added because they helped greatly to extend the reach of the volume.

It is of interest to note that, at this writing, only three members of the entire group are what, these days, are called senior colleagues; all the others are members of a generation of sociologists whose training in labor market studies began when there were virtually no modern studies like those they have undertaken, and when the human capital and status attainment investigators were putting their rather different intellectual machinery into high gear.

There is no need to rehearse in this brief introduction what my colleagues report upon in the pages that follow; the chapters speak very well for themselves. As Mark Granovetter and Teresa Sullivan suggest in their separate chapters, with caution and with polite respect for the work of those whom I have termed *supply investigators*, the time is ripe for preliminary efforts to draw the strands together and to encourage interested theorists in the economic and sociology professions to begin to think in more systematic ways about a better specified model of labor market processes, mobility phenomena, and stratification, and of the uses, abuses, and misuses of human resources in advanced societies. Such efforts can only be aided by an appreciation of the results of the types of studies represented herein by what looks to be a new breed of social scientists who, not unlike many of Machlup's erstwhile antagonists, are at home with critically relevant scholarship in each of two rather widely separated disciplines whose previously interdisciplinary exchanges have generally been confined to studies of development and modernization and to comparative analyses of industrialism and industrial man.

It is also tempting, if marginally immodest, to suggest that my collaborators' work herein is responsive to urgings by John Dunlop (1977), formerly Secretary of Labor and an old-line institutionalist, who praises students of aggregate supply for their intellectual derring-do but deplores their inability to link their work to a host of policy problems. It is his judgment that vexed problems, in both policy and program terms, of unemployment, training, inflation, and the rest are simply not addressed in the otherwise intriguing regressions reported in supply studies. Certainly these problems are not addressed in the Jencks teams' admirably executed second study of supply, in which liberals' interventions on behalf of "wars against poverty" or "equal opportunity" are essentially written off: "If we wish to redistribute income," they report, "the most effective strategy is probably still to redistribute income [1979, p.311]." While there are hints of a concern about demand factors in such a formulation, they are not very revealing ones—as Jencks would readily admit. One must, in fact, have friendly knowledge of Jencks's avowed preference for socialist modes of distribution to infer what "redistribution" might entail and whereof it involves "demand policies."

I would like to suggest that while Dunlop's urges and the lacunae in our knowledge about the demand side are not met and filled, respectively, by my collaborators, the many well-articulated hints in these chapters will help us move into the new decade with some confidence that policy lessons can be derived from sound empirical inquiries into human resources problems that derive from the same concerns and research designs as those by the Doeringers and Piores and, earlier, by Dunlop himself.

I would not, of course, like to suggest that the demand-centered focus in this volume is the only useful sociological perspective on labor markets. There are able scholars working in the field of the sociology of education, for example, on what seem to be noneconomic schooling effects on school processes, governance, and organization, and on pupils' and students' own "inputs," work that needs to be incorporated in both supply- and demand-centered studies given the association between education, achievement, and income. One of the reasons for the significance of these studies is that studies of this sort are, in many ways, remarkably like studies of employers and employees in their work settings; the methods and findings in school studies thus help to open one's eyes to research possibilities regarding the production process in general and the roles of organizational attributes in this process. These education studies, like those in progress at the University of Chicago under Robert Dreeben's direction, also help us to move, expeditiously, to clearer conceptualizations of precisely what it is we really are trying to say about schooling and education, in both supply and demand terms.

My own substantive contribution to this volume and to the discussions I hope it will help inform must, of needs, be negligible; I am, in company with Robert Bibb, T. Aldrich Finegan, and Michael Swafford, all of Vanderbilt University, in the very early stages of an effort designed to afford prospective readers with a better-specified model of unemployment than, we believe, is presently available. While we cannot yet offer any findings, the questions we are addressing are closely related to many raised in my colleagues' articles in this volume. In place of the obligatory statement of the research agenda suggested by my coauthors, I will instead exploit an editor's privilege to make choices and outline the rationale for our investigation, which points to a number of items in a research agenda to which my colleagues' efforts in the present volume direct attention. This outline will be found at the volume's end, together with the chapter by Teresa Sullivan, the discussant at both of the panels mentioned earlier, in place of the usual roundup of closing thoughts about policy implications and further research. Our readers will see that this closing chapter picks up on the brief comments in this introduction on differences between supply and "indirect demand" studies on one side and supply and "direct demand" studies on the other. The exercise is intended only to add a note to the burden of one of the main arguments in the chapters that precede it: that there we are in an increasingly better position to pick up on the leads of those whose efforts Machlup could treat so patronizingly in 1967 and, thus, to effect some useful adjustments in the orthodoxies of the 1960s and 1970s. As these orthodoxies are joined by would-be geneticists (ecologists, more properly), the arguable need for "interindustry" competition in the stratification studies industry grows appreciably.

## Acknowledgments

I am pleased to express my thanks to my colleagues for their interest in pooling the efforts herein, to Terry Ezekiel for initial editorial counsel on manuscript details, and to Joanie Prior and Wynn Berg for help in manuscript preparation.

## References

Coleman, J. S., E. Q. Campbell, C. J. Hobron, J. McPartland, A. M. Mood, F. Weinfield, and R. L. York.
    1966   *Equality of Educational Opportunity.* Washington, D.C.: US Govt Printing Office.
Dunlop, J.
    1977   "Policy decisions and research in economics and industrial relations." *Industrial and Labor Relations Review* 30(April):275–282.
Jencks, C., S. Bartlett, M. Corcoran, J. Crouse, D. Eaglesfield, G. Jackson, K. McClelland, P. Mueser, M. Olneck, J. Schwartz, S. Ward, and J. Williams
    1979   *Who Gets Ahead?* New York: Basic Books.
Jencks, C., M. Smith, H. Acland, M. J. Bane, D. Cohen, H. Gintis, B. Heyns, and S. Michelson.
    1972   *Inequality.* New York: Basic Books.
Machlup, F.
    1967   "Theories of the firm: Marginalist, behavioral, managerial." *American Economic Review* 62(March):1–33.

# Part I

# "MATCHING" PERSONS AND JOBS: THEORETICAL PERSPECTIVES

# Chapter 2

# Toward a Sociological

# Theory of

# Income Differences[1]

*MARK GRANOVETTER*

In recent years the prosaic but basic question of why different people have different incomes has increasingly occupied social scientists. Most such attention focuses on earned income, and this chapter similarly limits itself. I contend that the main need in this area is not for further empirical research but for deeper and broader theoretical development. There is no shortage of theories on income differences, but the existing traditions are narrowly focused and tightly encapsulated from one another.

Any attempt at theoretical progress must overcome the current fragmentation of ideas. Some of the fragmentation lies within disciplines; this is especially true for economics, despite some sociologists' image of that field as monolithic. This chapter will focus more on the barriers that separate economic from sociological ideas. While sociologists and economists have become increasingly aware of one anothers' ideas, this has not led to genuine integration. When sociologists claim to be making use of economic theory, it is usually either lip service or some superficial version; similarly, when

[1] An earlier version of this chapter was delivered at the 1979 meetings of the American Sociological Association. The paper was begun at the Center for Advanced Study in the Behavioral Sciences, Stanford, California, where my stay was supported in part by the National Science Foundation and the Andrew Mellon Foundation. Partial support was also received from the University Awards Council of the State University of New York.

SOCIOLOGICAL PERSPECTIVES ON
LABOR MARKETS

economists refer to sociological ideas, these are typically simplistic and often out of date.

My aim here is to sketch what a broad sociological theory of income differences would look like, one that took economic arguments seriously but put them in a broader framework. I think of this broader framework as sociological, but this may be only a disciplinary conceit and thus inessential to the argument. My plan is as follows: I will first raise some broad sociological questions that will lead to a classification of those factors that are important determinants of income. I will then use this classification as a device for comparing existing theories of income determination. Finally, I will discuss some of the ways economic and sociological ideas could benefit one another, by citing specific examples of research within each of the disciplines that is in some serious way incomplete because of disciplinary blinders. As this brief outline already makes clear, the theory I am working "toward" will not appear in this chapter, which may be viewed instead as a preliminary exercise that aims to reorient the way questions about income differences are asked.

## Some Broad Sociological Questions

Being as simpleminded as possible leads, I believe, to the conclusion that three main factors contribute to earned income: (a) the characteristics of the job and employer; (b) the characteristics of the individual who occupies the job; and (c) how a and b get linked together—what I will call *matching processes*. For analytical purposes, I want to argue that it makes sense to think of each of these as exerting a separate and independent influence on earnings and that, furthermore, each is related to fundamental social structural characteristics of the society in which income is earned.

Begin with job characteristics. The idea that there exist "jobs" whose identities are independent of incumbents, and that such positions are the economic norm, is relatively recent. The ideal type of such positions is perhaps best defined in Max Weber's discussion of bureaucracy (1921/1968, 956–1005), where the independent existence of positions depends on and is defined by their place in a technically rational division of labor. It is that place which determines the rewards allocated to the position, rather than any special characteristics of incumbents. This idea is so familiar that some well-known analyses of stratification implicitly assume that all positions have rewards independent of their holders; functionalist arguments (that unequal rewards are necessary because some positions in society are more important than others) and most Marxist arguments (that positions must be unequally rewarded because of their different relationships to the ownership and control of capital) have in common the assumption that the characteristics of incumbents have no impact on the rewards of positions held (see Davis & Moore, 1945; Wright, 1979, chap. 2).

We may pose as an empirical question whether there actually are circumstances where the nature of a position alone determines rewards. It is plausible that this is the case to the extent that socioeconomic roles are closely defined—that is, that there is little leeway for different results based on who performs the given role. It would follow that the extent and location of such leeway ought to be an important focus of study in the comparison of reward structures across socioeconomic systems. The Weberian analysis would suggest that the more modernized the society, the more roles are so closely structured that rewards are preset. Whether or not this is correct, it is clear that *some* roles in our society have this characteristic: that while performance must not fall below some minimal level, beyond that level the role is so closely defined and interdependent with other roles that additional skill, charm, talent, or diligence not only cannot improve the outcome, but may even worsen it. Where diligence is at issue, such an event is called *rate-busting*; where skill is involved, we hear of *overqualification* for the position. Both are considered disruptive influences precisely because they involve an attempt to redefine the position of a role within a division of labor in a way that is not considered feasible.

Assemblyline jobs are perhaps the prototypes of such positions; attempts to speed up would only throw the entire productive system out of kilter. But many other jobs share similar features: most secretarial jobs, for example, and probably even some executive positions, especially in stable and predictable industrial environments.

At the other extreme, we may imagine systems where only personal characteristics, and not at all those of roles, determine economic outcomes. In such systems, the usual sociological conception of "role" would hardly seem applicable, since there would be so little of the stylized reciprocal expectations we associate with this idea (e.g., Berger & Luckmann, 1967). And so it is in those systems anthropologists call *prestige economies*, where economic rewards are determined mainly by personal prestige, gained by force of personality and skill at assembling a following—as for the Melanesian Big Men so well described by Douglas Oliver (1955). Such tribal economies do not indeed have stable roles; when one Big Man is eclipsed or dies, there is no well-defined slot that others believe needs to be filled.

In modern economies such as ours, some individuals continue to be rewarded according to this older pattern (i.e., mainly as a result of their personal characteristics). As Weber might have predicted, this is most obvious for the self-employed, such as doctors, lawyers, and writers, who operate outside of bureaucratic structures. But it extends as well to people employed by firms insofar as their value to the firm depends on their building up a following (e.g., professional entertainers, athletes, and salespersons).

In a system where rewards were determined entirely by personal characteristics, income differences could naturally be understood by studying only those characteristics. But as soon as the features of jobs start to exert an influence on rewards, so that these are determined for most people by some mixture of individual and job characteristics, a third factor becomes central: matching—how do individuals with certain characteristics get matched up with jobs of certain types? To the extent that individual and job characteristics determine wages jointly, this matching question is theoretically urgent. Yet, in both sociology and economics, analyses of the matching between specific individuals and roles are rare. Both functionalist sociologists and Marxist economists believe, for example, that inequality is due to the variation in rewards attached to different roles, but neither pays much attention to how individuals get linked to such roles. Yet it is hardly informative to say that someone earns a high income as the result of holding a high-wage job; one needs an account of what determines who *comes* to hold jobs with high or low wages, that is, an account of matching processes.

I argue, then, that in modern economic systems, with few exceptions, one's earnings are determined by three factors: personal characteristics, characteristics of the job or role occupied, and processes that match these two. Existing theories of income differences can be categorized by how much attention they pay to each of these. Whereas an adequate theory would need to consider and integrate all three, most existing ones pay them unequal attention, and can, in fact, usually be seen as focusing almost exclusively on one.

## A Review of Existing Theories of Earnings Differences

### Status Attainment and Human Capital Theories

The two traditions that dominate current research in sociology and economics—status attainment research and human capital theory, respectively—are curiously similar in their nearly exclusive attention to characteristics and decisions of individuals and their neglect of the nature of jobs and matching processes.

In sociology, since Blau and Duncan's *The American Occupational Structure* (1967), empirical work has focused heavily on structural equation models, most of which have asserted that the "attainment" of status or income is caused mainly by background, personal characteristics, and levels of achievement. (Note the implicit individual-level bias of the word *attainment*; the use of such language both reflects and reinforces the underlying assumptions.) Sewell and Hauser's statement is representative; "We postulate that socioeconomic background affects mental ability, that background and ability affect educational attainment, that background, ability and education affect occupational achievement, and that all of the preceding variables affect earnings [1975, p.50]." Furthermore, this model "is basic . . . because it exhausts the influence of fundamental conditions of ascription and achievement. . . . Consequently factors of luck or chance are implicated in the process of achievement to the extent of indeterminacy in the outcomes of our basic model [1975, p.184]."

This tradition pays little attention to employers and jobs or to matching processes. The question of how individual characteristics actually generate income differences is addressed only by citing the path decomposition of particular effects. Having found, for example, that "a year of educational attainment is worth just over $200 in annual earnings," Sewell and Hauser add the explanation that "of this effect, just over half is explained by the higher status jobs open to better educated men; even for men with jobs of equal status, an additional year of schooling is worth $97 [1975, p.84]."

Fägerlind attempts to provide a theoretical framework for such assertions, in explaining results for his large sample of Swedish students: "The resources the individual has access to in early childhood, mainly family resources and personality assets, are converted into 'marketable assets' mainly through the formal educational system [1975, p.78]." But the central question of how such "resources" are "converted" to income is here merely begged, and we are left with the assertion that individual-level characteristics generate income.

Writers in this tradition, of course, probably do not believe that structures of employment and matching are infinitely malleable to the distribution of individual characteristics nor that the partial regression slopes on which the conclusions rest are timeless. But even those who are clearly aware of this (e.g., Jencks *et al.*, 1979) do not analyze what economic or labor market conditions have brought these slopes to their present values or which conditions might change them. Without a more explicit theory of how these individual-level variables have their effects, it is difficult to form any opinion about how long they can be expected to persist (cf. Granovetter, 1976).

Some revisionism has recently appeared within the status attainment tradition, edging it away from its highly individualistic assumptions. In most cases this trend has consisted of assertions that slopes of individual-level variables will differ according to context; depending on the writer, the context is said to be occupation, industry, firm, or social class (e.g., Beck,

Horan, & Tolbert, 1978; Bibb & Form, 1977; Stolzenberg, 1975; Talbert & Bose, 1977; Wright & Perrone, 1977). While this new emphasis is salutary, it is not theoretically coherent; its mode of formulation continues to give explicit causal priority to individual-level variables, without attempting to integrate these in any theoretical detail with the characteristics of jobs or of matching processes.

Some such revisionists describe their problem as one of determining whether the "rates of return" to individual-level variables (as measured by regression slopes) vary importantly by context (e.g., Beck *et al.*, 1978). I argue, however, that to cast the question in this way accepts too easily the idea that there is an uncomplicated relationship between such variables as education and income—that the statistical correlation does not reflect complex processes of negotiation or structural influences, but rather a direct translation of a "resource" into money. This view, as well as the "rate of return" language, is taken over from human capital theory in economics.

Despite criticism (e.g., Blaug, 1976), human capital theory remains the dominant tradition in current labor economics. Its rise to this position can only be understood via a brief history of economic theories of wages in the twentieth century. At least since the turn of the century, the theory of wages has been treated by economics as simply a special case of the theory of commodity prices. Underlying ideas have changed little since Hicks's classic 1932 exposition:

> The theory of the determination of wages in a free market is simply a special case of the general theory of value. Wages are the price of labor; and thus, in the absence of control, they are determined, like all prices, by supply and demand. . . . The demand for labor is only peculiar to this extent: that labor is a factor of production, and is thus demanded . . . not because the work to be done is desired for and by itself, but because it is to be used in the production of some other thing which is directly desired [1932/1964, p.1].

First consider demand. For most productive processes, holding constant the amount of capital employed, the value of the product generated by each additional unit of labor eventually declines (i.e., diminishing marginal returns to labor). In competitive markets, firms are assumed to be *price-takers*—they face a market wage for labor that they cannot affect. Given this fixed wage, therefore, a rational (i.e., profit-maximizing) firm would add workers only until the point where the value of the additional product produced as a result of having hired the last unit of labor equaled the wage of that unit; diminishing returns implies that hiring beyond that point would reduce net revenues. (Note that the wage of the last unit is the same as the wage of any other unit—the given market wage.) Thus, for any wage, there is a determinate number of labor units that a rational firm would demand; graphing together all such points (wage, number of labor units) generates the demand curve for labor. But by hypothesis, the wage is the same as the value of product added by hiring the last unit of labor—that is, any market wage is the same as the *marginal product of labor*. Thus, the demand curve for labor is identical to the curve that would be gotten by graphing the marginal product of labor against the number of labor units in use. The point where this curve is then intersected by the supply curve of labor is, in the usual way, the equilibrium price of labor.

Each unit of labor is thus paid the marginal product of labor. The argument is hence sometimes thought of as the *marginal product theory of wages*. This shorthand is deceptive, however, as it seems to imply that workers are paid as a result of those personal characteristics that make them more or less productive. Three points need to be made here about the notion of the marginal product of labor.

1. For any given industry, the amount of product resulting from a given number of labor units results from the nature of the existing technology—in economic language, from the production function. It follows that workers in an industry with backward technology will have lower marginal products for this reason alone; characteristics of the job rather than workers' skill levels determine this.

2. Marginal product is also determined by product price, since the demand for labor is derived from the demand for the product it produces—the number of physical units of product added by bringing in one more labor unit must be multiplied by product price to get the marginal (value) product used in this theory. It follows that if consumers change their demand in such a way as to want less of a product at any given price (i.e., if the product demand curve shifts to the left), the marginal product of labor is again reduced, with no relation to workers' skill.

3. The marginal product is determined in part by the supply schedule of labor; if it shifted to the right (i.e., more workers available at any given wage), more workers would be hired at a lower wage—that is, the marginal product would have declined, again for reasons unrelated to workers' skills.

It is important, therefore, to remember that to say workers are paid the marginal product of labor is to say much more than that they are paid according to ability and experience.

Though abstractly reasonable, this neoclassical argument about wages tells us only what a rational firm pays a "unit" of labor. In other words, the theory works because it makes the simplifying assumption that labor is infinitely divisible into homogeneous units, as well-behaved neoclassical commodities are supposed to be. Labor, or course, is not well behaved and comes instead in inconvenient lumps called workers. The artifice adopted to deal with this problem as far back as Marx and Ricardo, and carried through by Marshall and modern economists, has been to imagine that there exists some fundamental minimal unit of labor, sometimes thought of as an entirely unskilled worker, and that other more skilled workers can be considered to present some multiple of this basic unit (see, e.g., Rees & Shultz, 1970 p.6). Since the marginal product of labor is a feature of the basic unit, wage differences among workers would then explained by differences in the number of units presented. But this then throws the explanation of inequality back on the question of what explains such differences, an issue not addressed by the original theory. The recognition that neoclassical theory thus had little to say about workers' wage differences led to the dominance in the 1940s and 1950s of labor economics by "an institutionalist tradition . . . whose intellectual roots lay in the law and a sociological rather than an economic theory [Rees, 1973, p.viii]."

Human capital theory has changed this situation. In this fully neoclassical account, workers are seen as rational individuals who attempt to maximize their lifetime income by investing in their productive capacities (Becker, 1964; Mincer, 1974). Education is the prototypical investment, but the theory applies also to any other investment, such as health or on-the-job training, that can yield a return in income. Income differences are seen, then, as differing returns to different initial and continuing investments.

The theory, however, pays little attention to the mechanisms by which investments generate a stream of income. (For further comments on this theme, see Granovetter, 1977.) Responding to a deficiency in neoclassical theory in the analysis of labor supply, human capital ideas overreact by imagining that the supply side is *all* that need be analyzed to understand income differences. The imbalance is quite similar to that of status attainment arguments, which also assume that worker characteristics are sufficient to explain inequality. But this is implausible; it implies, for example, that wages would increase indefinitely if only individuals kept investing more in their productivity. Sørensen comments that some "basic predictions from the theory do not square well with reality; . . . one would predict that changes in the distribution of education would alter the distribution of incomes [1977, p.966]"; but empirical evidence since World War II does not support such a prediction.

The difficulty is that whether one's "investment" pays off depends on whether there is demand for what one's acquired skills can produce (i.e., on the characteristics of available jobs) and on whether one will be in a position to help meet that demand (i.e., on matching processes). It is naive to see productivity as a matter of individual skills and is, in fact, less theoretically sophisticated than the older neoclassical arguments on marginal productivity, which, whatever their shortcomings, at least recognized that wages are generated not only by skills but by skills in conjunction with consumer demand, technology, and a work position.

## Institutional Economics: Wage Structures, Segmented Labor Markets, and Labor Queues

The classical assumption of infinitely divisible commodities, when applied to labor, is unable to deal efficiently with the existence of workers, who come only in inconvenient lumps. This supply-side deficiency gave rise to human capital theory. The same assumption makes the existence of jobs, a demand-side lumpiness, equally difficult to analyze. Yet, the empirical observations of institutional economists in the 1940s and 1950s, of whom John Dunlop is the best known, made clear that the wages of a job often depended crucially on where it stood in a structure of jobs. The inability of the standard neoclassical analysis to cope with such observations led in this case to a tradition that, unlike human capital theory, has diverged markedly from neoclassical assumptions.

Dunlop and his students stressed the concept of "wage-structure": "the complex of rates within firms differentiated by occupation and employee and the complex interfirm rate structures [J. Dunlop, 1957, p.128]." The problem of wage determination, for this group, was to determine how a particular *job* comes to have the wage it has. This is accompanied by seeing where the job fits in relation to other jobs and the firm in relation to other firms. Well-defined systems of jobs and firms comprise the wage-structure. Certain jobs, for example, are central—"key jobs"— in that if their wages change, this will set off a chain reaction of other changes in associated jobs that all together make up a "job cluster." Among firms, a "wage contour is defined as a stable group of wage-determining units . . . which are so linked together by 1) similarity of product markets, 2) resort to similar sources for a labor force or 3) common labor-market organization (custom) that they have common wage-making characteristics [J. Dunlop, 1957, p. 131]."

The ideas of job clusters and key jobs led directly to Doeringer and Piore's concept of the *internal labor market:* "an administrative unit, such as a manufacturing plant, within which the pricing and allocation of labor is governed by a set of administrative rules and procedures," in contrast to the labor market of conventional theory, "where pricing, allocation and training decisions are controlled directly by economic variables [1971, pp. 1–2]." In such tightly closed systems of jobs, they argue, wages are based mainly on job characteristics, with careful attention to consistency within the hierarchy. For example, jobs "which involve wide contacts with other workers acquire a strategic position in the internal wage structure which makes it impossible to change their wages without adjustments throughout the system [1971, p.89].[2]

This stream of literature, then, takes for granted that jobs have well-defined identities independent of incumbents and that this, plus how the overall structure of jobs fits together, is what determines wages. Like human capital theory, which responded to a supply-side deficiency in neoclassical wage theory and ended analyzing *only* supply, this line of argument responded to difficulties in the analysis of demand and ended up attributing wages only to demand-side factors. Unlike human capital theorists, however, these authors did not claim to explain inequality by recourse only to one set of factors. They recognized that to argue that a job's wage is determined by its characteristics and its position in a system of jobs does not explain how particular individuals get linked up with high- or low-wage jobs, which one needs to know to understand wage differences among actual workers.

Attempts to explain this better led to what was first called *dual* then *segmented* labor market theory. (See the useful though skeptical review in Cain, 1976; a more sympathetic account is Gordon, 1972.) This argument, propounded especially but not exclusively by radical economists, asserts that internal labor markets are only one kind of work setting and offer to those in them, substantial advantages, such as built-in career ladders and mobility opportunities—hence the designation of such markets as *primary*. Other workers are said to be confined to *secondary* labor markets, which are "composed of workers, especially women, blacks teenagers and the urban poor, who follow a much more random series of jobs and are generally denied opportunities for acquiring skills and advancement [Edwards, 1975, p.16]."

Empirically, there is some argument about the actual extent of confinement. Here I need only to point out that if workers are not actually confined to one such market segment, then the theory does not explain wage inequality except in the very short run. On the other hand, to the extent such confinement operates, the real causes of inequality lie in the matching processes that lead to this immobility in low-wage jobs.

But in practice, segmented labor market theorists pay little attention to matching processes. Instead they argue that confinement occurs because workers lack stable work habits. This surprising reductionism to the causal level of individual attitudes by scholars, many of whom are Marxist and might thus be expected to lean toward more structural explanations, is justified by the claim that secondary employers "do not expect, may even

---

[2] Notice that *strategic* is defined here not with reference to a rational position in the division of labor, but rather by an implicit social psychological argument that workers are more likely to compare their wages to those of positions they frequently interact with. This argument is made explicit in an imaginative empirical study by Gartrell (1979).

discourage and therefore fail to elicit stability [Edwards, 1975, p.16]." I believe that this superficial treatment of *confinement* is closely related to the general failure of Marxist analysis to take seriously the question of how individuals and socioeconomic roles are matched up.

Beyond this, the theory has a curiously static and atomistic flavor. The economy is imagined to be cut up into some small number of separate markets (three in Piore's 1975 analysis—hence the shift to the *segmented* designation; more in other analyses) that are semi-impermeable to one another and have little mutual influence. Even if we could accept the notion that two, three, or six segments were enough to explain income inequality (unlikely in light of the finding of Jencks *et al.* that, when we divide workers into 435 detailed occupational categories, nearly two-thirds of income variation is still *within* occupational groups (1972, pp.226, 225 n61)), we would want to understand much more about the possibility of personnel flows among segments and other ways they could influence one another.

The original emphasis of scholars such as Dunlop and Livernash on how wage-structures were interdependent in complex ways—related to networks of economic complementarity and social relations within and between firms—seems to have been lost track of here as "sectors" of the market have been given the bulk of the explanatory attention. It has been assumed that within sectors, uniformity of wage-setting practices exists, so that the task to be accomplished is to show that such practices are demonstrably different across some definition of sectors. In practice this is achieved by regressing earnings on various variables separately in each sector (as, e.g., in Osterman, 1975) and looking for differences in slopes. Insight into interactions and mobility among sectors or into matching processes is precluded by such a procedure.

A different attempt to show how workers end up in jobs whose incomes are more or less predetermined is made by Thurow (1975). Like wage-structure and segmented labor market theorists, he argues that a wage is determined mainly by the job rather than by the incumbent; his justification for this assertion is different, however, resting on the claim that "marginal products are inherent in jobs and not in individuals [1975, p.85]." His solution to the question of how workers are matched with jobs at any given salary level is the idea of a *labor queue*; workers are said to be arranged by employers on such a queue in order of their *trainability*—the cost of training them for such jobs. If there are more workers at a given level of trainability than jobs that demand that level, some workers will get worse jobs than they "deserve" by this criterion: "In effect, they will participate in a lottery [1975, p.92]."

Two comments are apt. First, the idea of trainability depends so heavily on workers' background characteristics and educational achievement

(Thurow, 1975, pp.86–88) that the labor queue idea is empirically difficult to distinguish from human capital or status attainment ideas of income causation. More importantly, the idea of such a queue, while perhaps more flexible than that of fixed labor market segments, hardly takes the complexity of matching processes seriously; it is radically inconsistent with both theoretical and empirical accounts of the matching of workers to jobs (see Granovetter, 1974).

## Information and the Matching Problem

Analysis of theories preoccupied with the demand side of the labor market—those arguing that jobs' or industries' characteristics mainly determine wages—led me to pinpoint neglect of the matching between workers and jobs as the main defect in such arguments. It has taken economists longer to address the matching problem than to address other shortcomings in the neoclassical theory of wages. This may be because the matching problem is more subtle: In neoclassical markets there is no such problem—supply and demand are brought into balance and the market cleared by the movement toward equilibrium prices. For this movement to occur, however, market participants must have full knowledge of the market situation.

Local labor market studies from the 1930s on showed repeatedly, however, that information was highly imperfect; formal and easily accessible means of job placement, such as employment agencies and newspaper advertising, accounted for only a small proportion of actual hires. Most placements were mediated instead by information gotten from friends and relatives or by "blind" applications—a privatization of information radically at variance with the assumption of widespread or perfect knowledge. (See Granovetter, 1974, pp.5–6, for a summary of the empirical studies.) This situation was generally considered by economists as reflecting workers' irrational behavior; the solution repeatedly prescribed was expansion of state and federal employment services and the implementation of computerized matching of workers to jobs.

This situation changed in the 1960s when economists began to integrate information considerations into standard theory. Stigler's 1961 formulation is quite general, pointing out that information is a scarce commodity, whose acquisition requires expenditures of time, effort, and money. It is thus a proper subject of economic analysis: Producers or consumers seeking information will incur the required costs only up to the point where these are outweighed by benefits—the standard maximizing assumption of marginal analysis.

Though this point applies in principle to information in all commodity markets, the great bulk of literature on the economics of information has referred to labor markets. Stigler initiated the analysis from the supply side in his 1962 article; not until the 1970s did economists pay serious attention to the employer's information problem, in theories of *signaling* or *screening*. As of 1981, little has been done in the way of meshing these two sides of the information problem, though I will argue that this is the crux of the matching process. I shall briefly review the supply- and demand-side analyses in turn.

On the supply side, first Stigler (1962) and later McCall and others (e.g., Lippman & McCall, 1976; McCall, 1970), though their models differ in certain important ways (Lippman & McCall, 1976, is a useful literature survey), all conceive of workers as engaged in a process called *job search*, which is conducted in a rational manner. My study of a random sample of job changers in a Boston suburb added a sociological dimension to this discussion and highlights certain inadequacies in the economic notion of job search (Granovetter, 1974). I pointed out that workers (as well as employers) prefer information derived from their personal contacts. This preference is neither accidental nor irrational: Such information is less costly and of better quality than that obtained from impersonal sources. "[A] friend gives more than a simple job-description—he may also indicate if prospective workmates are congenial, if the boss is neurotic, and if the company is moving forward or is stagnant. . . . Similarly, . . . evaluations of prospective employees will be trusted better when the employer knows the evaluator personally [Granovetter, 1974, p.13]." Income is closely related to these considerations: Nearly half of those using contacts to find a new job reported 1969 incomes over $15,000, whereas the corresponding proportion for those using agencies and ads is under one-third and for direct application under one-fifth (1974, p.14).

The problem for economic models of job search is not that workers act irrationally in their acquisition of job information but rather that, empirically, it is often difficult to accept the implicit assertion that information results from "search." Fully 29% of my respondents denied having carried out any active search before taking their present job (see similar figures in U.S. Department of Labor, 1975); more significantly, this figure was strongly related to income: Whereas 21.0% of those reporting an income of $15,000 or less said they had not searched, 40.2% of those with incomes over $15,000 made this assertion. For those with incomes of $25,000 or more, over 55% said that information about the job taken did not come from a search they had undertaken (Granovetter, 1974, pp.32–36). There are two reasons for these findings. One is that some jobs are found as the result of employer searches, rarely represented in job-search models; I will comment further on this later. Another is that job information is deeply imbedded in other social structural processes, in a way that makes it difficult to assert even that workers act *as if* they were conducting a rational search (the usual response of economists to assertions that economic actors do not empirically *report* rational market behavior). By this I mean that information, unlike most other commodities, may often be acquired as the by-product of other activities. A prototype of such a situation is learning about a new job at a party or in a tavern. It strains credulity to assert that the costs of having attended such occasions ought to be called a cost of job search and that one could expect workers to equate, either consciously or unconsciously, the marginal costs and benefits of such "search." More generally, there are few business-related activities that cannot be the occasion for information about new job opportunities to be acquired, whether or not this is the intent of the actors involved. When people transacting business know one another, as is typical in any regularized transactions, the social amenities of such acquaintanceship include inquiries about one's general satisfaction with one's situation and gossip about corporate and personal events. The typical assertion of job-search models, that search takes place from a position of unemployment, excludes such circumstances; this is highly unrealistic for populations such as the professional, technical, and managerial personnel that I studied. (Some further comments of mine on models of job search are reported in Petersen, 1980).

On the demand side of the labor market, the main work has come in the 1970s as theories of "signaling" or "screening," (e.g., Spence, 1974; Stiglitz, 1975a), which take as their main problem "the uncertainty of the employer, which stems from the fact that he does not know, prior to hiring, how productive a particular employee will turn out to be; this is because the employer cannot directly observe productivity prior to hiring. [Spence, 1974, p.6]." The emphasis has been on how workers might invest in various kinds of certification devices, especially education, which employers can then read as signaling some level of productivity. The models entail that workers investing in such signals will receive a higher income, net of investment costs, than if they had not, since there would otherwise be no economic motive for investment. But the argument has become controversial in economics since, though posed in a way that is quite consistent with neoclassical assumptions, it opposes directly the human capital account of why education is related to income: not necessarily because it makes workers more productive, but only because it certifies them as such, without necessarily increasing productivity at all (cf. Berg, 1970; Blaug 1976, pp.845–849).

In my view, the signaling argument is more sophisticated than that offered by human capital theory, because it allows the relation between signals and productivity to be an empirical question, rather than one which is decreed a priori. Two aspects of this literature, however, seem unrealistic. One is the exclusive concentration on the demand side. Spence points out that when "the employer and potential employee confront each other in the market . . . neither is certain about the qualities of characteristics of the service which the other is offering for sale [1974, p.6]." But his models treat only the employer's, not the employee's, uncertainty. It seems highly likely that employers also invest in signals meant to show that they are progressive and provide a pleasant working environment. (In some locales, such investment seems a major support for the landscaping industry.) But these investments are not treated in the literature, perhaps because they are less easily quantified than is education. Yet, given my earlier comments on the complex nature of "marginal productivity," it does seem mistaken for signaling theorists to talk, as human capital theorists also do, as if productivity resides only in workers. It would make as much sense to spin theories about how employers try to show that their jobs are productive (consistent, for example, with Thurow's argument that marginal productivity resides in jobs). Neither seems adequate to me, as both neglect the matching of the two sides of the market; marginal productivity results only from a combination of a worker with a job.

Furthermore, my empirical work suggests that the signal chosen in the usual models—education—is not actually the main conveyer of information in labor markets. It is true that most jobs have clear-cut educational requirements, such that employers assume workers lacking them to be ipso facto unqualified. This is, however, a crude screen indeed, and if used alone, would leave the employer still with a large and unmanageable information problem. On paper, there are few jobs for which large numbers of people are not qualified; in practice, employers use a more refined and differentiated signal than educational qualification: They use the recommendations of people personally known to both them and prospective employees. Similarly, prospective employees know better than to rely on landscaping or other signals put out by employers and attempt, instead, to find out the inside story from their contacts. Such facts are massive in their familiarity. Readers are invited to recall how they found a doctor, dentist, plumber, or electrician when first moving to their present locale.[3] Yet they are absent from economic models of screening, perhaps because of the difficulty of imagining how to analyze "investment." One has some control over the amount of education acquired (provided, that is, perfect capital markets). One has less control over who will form good opinions of oneself and repeat them to others; there is even less control over which people these opinions

---

[3] For application of these ideas to the difficulties experienced in placement by institutions that rehabilitate handicapped or disabled workers, see Granovetter, 1979.

will be repeated to. There is little way of knowing who is known personally to people one meets; the amount of information required to be accurate about this is stupendous.

Systematic study of social structure is required for such analysis and does suggest some leads. I found, for example, that workers' acquaintances were more likely than their close friends to be instrumental in linking them up to new jobs, and argued that this was not accidental but resulted from the social structural fact that one's close friends are more likely than acquaint-ances to know the same people one already knows, hence less likely to be sources of information not already available (Granovetter, 1974, chap. 3; see also Granovetter, 1973; these findings are amplified with a different sample in Lin, Ensel, & Vaughn, 1979).

Can economic models be constructed that take such facts into account? Respondents in my study seemed surprised when, after reviewing their careers, they recognized the central role played by acquaintances in job mobility. Poor investment "choices," showing ignorance of these principles, were clear in some cases—such as for workers who remained for many years in firms where other co-workers also did so, with the result that, when the firms were bought out in conglomerate mergers, they knew no one personally in other firms and consequently had great difficulty moving (Granovetter, 1974, chap. 6). On the other hand, one does hear talk about "investing" in one's reputation and "cultivating" contacts, especially those who are "well placed." Thus, there may be some scope for rational models. Boorman (1975) has followed up the weak-tie, strong-tie distinction pro-posed previously, and constructed an interesting and complex economic model of investment in contacts; the purpose assumed is not signaling but simply acquisition of information about jobs, so that this belongs more properly with the discussion of job search: It could, however, be adapted to the purposes of signaling. Whether empirical work could mesh with such models remains an open question.

I have discussed theories of job search on the supply side of the labor market and those of signaling on the demand side; in both cases I have commented that such theories ought properly to apply to both sides of the market. Employers as well as employees search, and employees as well as employers try to read signals from the other side of the market. The one-sidedness of both sets of ideas precludes sophisticated approaches to the question of how employers and employees are matched. Furthermore, an adequate theory would have to incorporate both searching and signaling, whereas present theories consider these as sequential activities. Spence, for example, comments that when "the employer and potential employee con-front each other in the market (the confrontation may be preceded by a considerable amount of search by either party or both) neither is certain about the qualities . . . the other is offering for sale [1974, p.6]." But such a version implies that employers and employees first conduct a search in which *only the identities* of the others are learned and no signals read until the next stage of the process. In practice this seems highly unlikely.

Beyond these points, theories of search and signaling, as presently constituted, implicitly assume that only an information problem requires solution. There exists a distribution of workers on the one side and vacant jobs on the other that need only to be matched up. Two facts contradict this simple version and lead to a need for more emphasis on matching processes. First, many workers who move to new jobs have no interim period of unemployment; in my random sample of professional, technical, and managerial job changers, 89% of respondents fell in this category (Granovetter, 1974, p.44). This means that it may often not be obvious to employers who, exactly, is "in the market." Correspondingly, workers may take new jobs not previously held by anyone, so that no "vacancy" can be said to have existed. In my sample, about 45% of new jobs filled could be called well-defined vacancies; 20% were jobs where no vacancy existed but where the job was essentially similar to other jobs of its kind already existing in the firm; and 35% of jobs were created de novo, in the sense that either the work was not being done or the tasks had not previously been combined into one position. Those finding jobs via personal contacts were twice as likely to have taken this last category of job (Granovetter, 1974, pp.14 15). Interviews showed that in many cases, the job was created only because employers had come across a person whose characteristics and skills they considered particularly appropriate for this work—even when they had not actively searched for such a person. Any firm has a variety of projects on the back burner that may or may not come to fruition; the information and personnel pool it is linked up to may determine which of these are pursued. A complex process of negotiation between firm and prospective employee, in which the exact details, work, and salary of such jobs are hammered out, constitutes the matching process here. Search, signaling, and job creation are all inextricably intertwined, in a way that cannot be well captured by models more appropriate to situations where consumers are surveying department stores for the range of refrigerator prices or used car lots for an appropriate vehicle.

Thus, informationally based theories, mostly in economics, sometimes address the characteristics and decisions of workers, sometimes those of employers, but not both; and, as with other theories surveyed thus far, the mechanisms by which these two sides are matched are neglected. Like status attainment and human capital theories, and arguments from institutional economics, these models founder on their failure to give balanced attention to the three factors outlined at the beginning of this chapter.

## Integration of Sociological and Economic Conceptions of Income Determination

To this point, I have argued that various extant theories fail to give a rounded picture of the determination of earnings. I believe that a necessary (though perhaps not a sufficient) condition for overcoming this narrowness is an integration of sociological and economic ideas about income. For this to occur will require that the two disciplines pay more detailed attention to one anothers' efforts than is customary. In this section, therefore, I will develop examples of the ways in which sociological ideas may inform even the most orthodox economic efforts and vice versa.

### Sociological Contributions to Economic Arguments

Sociology and economics differ markedly in their stance toward formal models. In sociology, such models are assumed false unless proven otherwise. In economics, by contrast, it is mainly elegant formal models that are rewarded; arguments not embodied in such models are not so much disbelieved as ignored. This prejudice is so ingrained that even well-known empirical facts have been neglected for many years, until they finally were incorporated into models, whereupon they suddenly became the focus of attention. Such has been the case with worker productivity differences, imperfect information, and the existence of hierarchy in organizations. Because most economists imagine sociological variables to involve nonrational behavior of the sort that impedes market processes, and since such behavior is not easily modeled, sociological forces are usually written off as frictional drags or residual influences; explanation of economic events by such forces is considered a last recourse, and a tautological one at that.

I will argue, by contrast, that this vision of what sociology is about is greatly mistaken and that, even if orthodox neoclassical wage theory were substantially correct, sociological analysis could still illuminate labor market processes. Two aspects of the theory seem particularly suited to such illumination: (a) the determinants of supply and demand; and (b) the determinants of temporary disequilibrium. I will treat these in turn.

#### DETERMINANTS OF SUPPLY AND DEMAND

Suppose a situation where wages for any given type of work were completely determined by supply and demand. Full explanation of wage differences would still await understanding of why these differed among types of work. Consider first supply. Economists' attention to labor supply questions has focused mostly on labor force participation and level of training or skill (the subject of human capital theory). Rees points out that, by comparison, the number of hours people are willing to work is a "somewhat neglected aspect of labor supply" and "still more neglected" is the amount of effort expended (1973, p.4). I believe it is no coincidence that neglect is concentrated in those topics where causal factors are most sociological. Four decades of industrial sociology have made clear, for example, that the amount of effort, and consequently output, generated by work groups depends not only on the technical and economic situation but also on informal agreements within the groups about what is the "proper" amount of output and what constitutes rate-busting. It is also well known that the extent of such output restriction depends heavily on the social structure of work groups—on, for example, the extent to which such groups are close knit and in constant contact (e.g., Dalton, 1959; Homans, 1950; Sayles, 1958).

It seems likely that occupations and industries vary systematically in the social structure of work groups, hence in the extent of output restriction; a simple supply–demand argument indicates that, where such restriction is more common or extensive, the supply curve for labor is shifted leftward and wages correspondingly raised. In any comparison of occupational or industrial groups, this should account for part of the wage variation. Though none of this contradicts in any fundamental way the standard explanation of wages, no economist seems to have studied the social dynamics of output restriction or used the vast sociological literature on the subject in any explanation of wages. It may be that this literature is not known to economists, but I think the problem to be more one of an ingrained reluctance to appeal in any way to sociological determinants. Even Leibenstein, who means to break decisively with neoclassical theory and who makes effort level an important part of his "new foundation for microeconomics," does not ever seriously consider the ways in which the social structure of work groups affects effort; instead, he sees his task as one of developing "new psychological postulates" that better describe worker decision making than do the standard maximization ones (1976, chaps. 6–7). In so doing, he remains firmly within the atomized decision-maker framework of classical economics.

On the demand side, economists content themselves with the marginal productivity argument: that the number of labor units demanded at a particular wage is precisely the number that makes the wage equal to the value added by the last unit. Hidden in this formula is the fact that "value added" is found by multiplying the number of physical units of the product by the market price for each such unit. But this is crucial, since it shows that the marginal product of labor is due *not* simply to labor efficiency, as often assumed, but also to the extent of demand for the particular product. Neglecting this central fact leads to serious difficulties. Fogel and

Engerman, for example, have been criticized for asserting that slave production of cotton was more efficient than free production of wheat. They based this calculation on the value of the product produced by each type of labor; but a boom in the demand for cotton had pushed up its price and therefore slaves' marginal products. Thus, the efficiency claim is more complex than at first glance (see David & Temin, 1976, pp.218–223).

An increased demand at all prices for some product (i.e., a rightward shift of the demand schedule) will lead to increased marginal products and thus wages for those producing it. Hence patterns of product demand in a society are important determinants of wage differentials; yet economists rarely study directly the factors leading to demand shifts, or their impacts on inequality. Such study would involve sociological analysis of life-style changes, mobility, and the diffusion of innovations. Supply forces are charted more easily, from demographics and individual decisions, and have been paid more attention by economic historians. Thus, in a study of inequality trends in American income distribution from 1896 to 1948, the economic historian Williamson notes that large wage differentials from 1896 to 1914 have commonly been attributed to the influx of European immigrants but that this assertion has not been systematically tested. His econometric model, by contrast, suggests that in this period, as later, demand forces were more significant and that "demand seems to be the dominant force behind America's 20th century distributional trends [J. Williamson, 1976, p.395]."

It will not be enough simply to chart the sociology of demand shifts: The mechanisms by which these have their effects must also be attended to. In 1955, the economist Reder noted that demand shifts do not always operate in the straightforward manner of classical theory. Taking seriously the independent importance of workers and jobs, Reder points out that the "wage rates paid for particular jobs are not analogous to factor prices. The skill and other characteristics of workers who apply for given jobs vary with the state of the labor market, and the wage rates paid on given jobs are therefore affected by 'quality' variations in the job applicants [1955, p.834]." Consequently, "variations in relative scarcity of job applicants can be met by varying either (or both) of two determinants of hiring policy; i.e., employers may adjust 1) wage rates; 2) hiring standards; or some combination of the two [p.835]."

In particular, Reder considers the effects of economic booms, such as those associated with wars, in which "a general increase in demand for all grades of manual labor [is] of such size that . . . labor slack is eliminated from the market [p.837]." What would be the impact on the *skill margin*— that is, the difference in wages between skilled and unskilled workers? Skilled workers, like other manual workers, would be put in short supply by such a boom, and one might expect to see the wages of all types of workers bid up in the classical manner, leaving the skill differential unchanged. Instead, Reder argues, the option of "quality changes" may now be used by employers. Rather than raise the wages of skilled workers, employers could now upgrade workers of the next lower skill grade, giving them a wage higher than they could previously obtain but lower than the going wage for skilled labor; furthermore, this eliminates the necessity for a general increase in skilled labor wages. The substitution could be made feasible by some combination of training and alteration of production processes.

This upgrading, however, leaves a shortage in the next-to-highest skill category, which is met by substitution from the group below that, and so on. When eventually, workers from the lowest skill category are upgraded and no new labor supply is forthcoming from outside the labor force, the resulting shortage in the bottom category must then result in the wages of that category being bid up; hence, "wage rates paid on the lowest grade of jobs would rise proportionately more than the rates on others [Reder, 1955, pp.837–838]," thus reducing the skill differential.

This interesting argument has not, so far as I know, been pursued in detail by economists; I believe this is because the conceptual apparatus required to do so is sociological. The argument is different from most economic accounts in taking seriously the distinct characteristics of workers and jobs and stressing the complexities of matching between the two. In particular, Reder's argument requires detailed attention to the structure of connections among different sets of jobs as a determinant of mobility. There is a striking resemblance to the sociologist White's later (1970) model of mobility through *vacancy chains*, where the vacating of one job sets off a cascade of mobility through the system of jobs. One of the factors creating vacancies in White's analysis is the creation of new jobs, related to Reder's shifts in demand. White also gives equal importance to rates of retirement and new labor force entrants, which suggests that Reder's model could benefit from more attention to labor supply. What is important is that White's argument provides a technology and associated social structural ideas needed to study, empirically, *indirect* effects such as the ones described by Reder.

More generally, such an argument could be seen as a way of helping to explain changes in relative wages among *any* sets of jobs linked to one another by the relation of substitutability. To understand which sets of jobs *are* so linked is not merely a straightforward economic–technical question but rather requires considerable sociological analysis. The issue is one of what labor pool is available to employers who have particular openings to fill. This is a matter that turns out empirically to depend heavily on the structure of personal, organizational, and professional contact networks, as I have described in some detail in an earlier monograph (Granovetter, 1974). Where this pool is confined only to workers in the same firm, one may wonder whether the effects of substitution could be as strong as Reder suggests. The extent to which interfirm mobility is common or likely may thus be a crucial element in this argument (cf. Granovetter, 1974, pp.73–117).

Note also the potential connection of this argument to segmented labor market analysis. Segmented labor market theorists argue that confinement to one segment can be a reason for low wages but they specify poorly the reasons for confinement and offer little operational methodology for investigating it. The Reder argument, amplified by the sociological concepts I have described, suggests a way to study the circumstances under which the so-called primary and secondary labor markets are linked up, both with personnel flows and wage influences across the boundaries. This amplified argument implies that under certain conditions unskilled workers can be integrated into broader mobility flows and connected to job ladders ordinarily closed to them. Even those workers who remain in the unskilled category would benefit from their reduced supply.

The extent to which such events actually occur must be, of course, an empirical question. I assert here only that the Reder argument, as augmented, could be useful in pursuing that question. The combination of sociological and economic concepts suggested, unfortunately, is difficult for most analysts to assimilate, given the strong resistance of members of each discipline to seriously using concepts from the other. Even economists whose ideas predispose them to break out of this dilemma do not make contact with the relevant sociological traditions. Piore, for example, wants to formalize the "intuitive notion that socioeconomic movement . . . is not random but tends to occur in more or less regular channels. These channels are such that any given job will tend to draw labor from a limited and distinct number of other particular points. As a result, people hold jobs in some regular order or sequence. We shall term such a sequence a *mobility chain* [1975, p.128]." But the close relation of this idea to sociological work on vacancy chains, interorganizational relations, and contact networks is not explicitly recognized or pursued.

I have concentrated so far on effects of shifts in the absolute level of supply or demand. But such effects are also determined by the shapes of supply–demand schedules and especially by their elasticities, defined as the proportionate rate of change in labor demanded or supplied divided by the proportionate rate of change in wages. More intuitively, elasticity is a measure of how responsive labor supply or demand is to changes in wages. Where supply and demand have very different elasticities, the result is that one has much more impact on wages than the other. Consider, for example,

Case 1, Figure 2.1a, where demand is highly inelastic but supply is elastic; here shifts in the demand schedule will have little effect on wages since the flat supply curve can intersect all possible demand curves only over a narrow range of wages. Such a situation was assumed in one or another form by Ricardo, Malthus, and Marx, all of whom believed that any wage increases would be eaten up by resulting inflows to the labor market, driving wages back down. Demand was therefore irrelevant to wage analysis. On the other hand, if supply were inelastic and demand highly responsive to wage differences (Case 2, Figure 2.1b), then wages would be determined almost exclusively by demand—that is, by the point at which the demand curve intersects the nearly vertical supply curve. Here, "marginal product" is really the main determinant, and supply can be neglected. Where both supply and demand are highly elastic (Case 3, Figure 2.1c), both are important determinants of wages, but the flatness of both curves holds possible wage shifts in a narrow range; correspondingly, where both are steeply sloped (inelastic, as in Case 4, Figure 2.1d), shifts in either curve will generate large changes in equilibrium wages, and the basic wage situation is unstable. Thus, certain occupations or industries may have a highly stable wage structure as the result of high elasticity of both supply and demand, and others an unstable one for the opposite reason. Then an increase in national aggregate demand, as in an economic boom, will raise wages much more in the latter than in the former, leading to wage differences attributable not to characteristics of individuals or of jobs, but to this complexity in the matching process.

What determines the elasticities of supply and demand? Some of the factors are no doubt technical and economic. But also crucial must be such sociological considerations as the comparative attractiveness of industries and occupations, the ease of movement from one to another (mediated in part by contact networks), and commodity substitutability (mediated by tastes and trends and the diffusion of innovations). Thus, to the extent that wage inequality among groups is the result of such differences in supply–demand elasticities, considerable sociological analysis would be needed to provide a full account of the causes.

In the preceding comments, I have intentionally neglected long-run equilibrating forces. It may well be, for example, that an occupation facing a short-run inelastic labor supply, which experiences a large wage increase, will eventually generate new labor supplies as new generations of potential workers see the advantage to be had (cf. Freeman, 1971). But in the long run, as Keynes remarked, "We are all dead"; inequalities occur in the here and now, and it can be little consolation to those suffering them that they might ultimately be ironed out.

DETERMINANTS OF TEMPORARY DISEQUILIBRIUM

Economists admit that while the "tendency" of market prices (including wages) is "toward" equilibrium, actual markets are often temporarily in disequilibrium. Hicks, in his classic *Theory of Wages*, remarks that, while workers may well not be paid the marginal product at any given time, "any such difference if it is maintained for long slowly bends wages to meet the new situation [1932/1964, p.86]." The problem is that the forces leading to equilibrium may move so slowly that existing disequilibria account for a substantial amount of inequality. Many of the factors generating such disequilibria are sociological: information gaps, resistance to migration, power differentials, shifts in consumer preferences; these impediments to speedy market reactions have historically been viewed by economists as frictional drags rather than as central objects of study.

An example is the situation of rapidly expanding industries with short-run inelastic labor supply—the situation of Case 4, Figure 2.1d, if we imagine that the demand schedule shifts to the right. Hicks comments that the

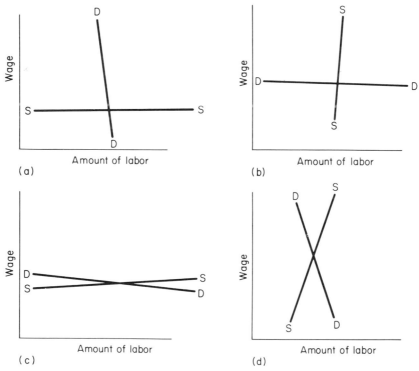

**Figure 2.1.**  Variations in the elasticity of demand and supply for labor. (*a*) Case 1: Elastic supply, inelastic demand. (*b*) Case 2: Inelastic supply, elastic demand. (*c*) Case 3: Supply and demand both elastic. (*d*) Case 4: Supply and demand both inelastic.

level of wages which is needed to attract labor quickly into an expanding trade is . . . higher than that which is required to maintain the larger labor force; but having once risen, the differential does not fall back easily. It is therefore highly probable that actual wage-systems are full of differentials that have lost their economic function being (as it were) the fossilised remains of historical shortages [1932/1964, p.320]

This raises the interesting possibility that some wage inequality results from the recent history of differential industry expansion. Increased wages are needed initially because of short-run inelastic labor supply; eventually, when this increase results in more elastic supply, the wages in such an industry will increase more slowly than in others and general equilibrium of wages will in time be attained. But in the middle period, significant inequalities may obtain. This could be studied with data on industrial history, wage trends, labor flows, and shifts in consumer demand and organizational expansion. But the 17 years since Hicks's suggestion have seen little pursuit of these more or less sociological themes.

Another interesting example of disequilibrium is substantial differentials in wages by city size, which persist even after corrections for such obvious intervening variables as cost of living and distribution of education (Fuchs, 1967). Fuchs suggests as one possible explanation the

existence of a disequilibrium in the supply of labor and capital. Surplus labor from agriculture may tend to move first to the small towns, and then later to the larger cities. Capital may be more readily available in the large cities. It there is a disequilibrium, we should observe a tendency for labor to migrate from small to large cities, and for industry to move in the opposite direction [1967, p.34].

Again, this interesting suggestion has not been pursued by economists, perhaps because determinants and patterns of migration are more typically a sociological concern.

In both of these cases—expanding industries and city-size differentials—disequilibrium occurs because matching processes occur that are far more complex than those envisioned in the standard theory. The existence of wage differentials among industries or occupations, or among cities of different sizes, for comparable work, "should" be eliminated by workers' flowing from lower to higher wage locations. Reluctance to analyze matching processes in detail makes such disequilibrium difficult to explain. Unlike Hicks and Fuchs, most economists when faced with such differentials will not admit the existence of disequilibrium but argue instead that they are "compensating differentials"—that higher wages in one situation than in another must reflect nonmonetary disadvantages suffered by the higher-paid workers, such as work in a less desirable location—or alternatively that the workers are not really of equal quality (e.g., Rees & Shultz, 1970, Rottenberg, 1956). Such an explanation is thought more parsimonious than the assertion of disequilibrium, which appears ad hoc to most economists. From the perspective of a noneconomist, however, the notion that systems are more likely than not to be in equilibrium is what seems difficult to credit.

It is thus not surprising that power differentials which artificially restrict supply to certain occupations, raising the wage beyond what the equilibrium level would be, are not seriously analyzed by economists. Reynolds comments on the most obvious example, that of physicians. "There are strong indications that the market for medical practioners is out of equilibrium. . . ." One indication of this is the "widening earnings differential [between physicians and other occupations]. It is true that training costs have been rising, as a growing percentage of doctors enter specialities requiring some years of apprenticeship beyond medical school. This might warrant some widening of the earnings gap, but scarcely at the rate observed in recent years [1974, p.286]."

But the study of such entry restriction is not congenial to economists. It involves not only the question of power differentials, but the nature of professionalization, the organization of interest groups and lobbies, the nature of occupational information networks that encourage some and not other students to choose this or that occupation, the maintenance of occupational mystiques, and other topics of sociological import. (For a sociological treatment of some of these issues, with historical perspective, see Collins, 1980.) The recent strong influence of human capital theory, with its sense that investment in skills somehow automatically yields returns, has created an atmosphere even more hostile to such subjects than previously existed.

Sociological analysis, then, can be seen as a useful adjunct to economic models. On the supply side, decisions of workers are seen more clearly by sociologists than by economists to be embedded in noneconomic aspects of social reality, hence not likely to be made by isolated, atomized individuals uninfluenced by those around them. The discussion of work groups' output restrictions and that of restriction of physician supply are examples. On the demand side, I have stressed that patterns of product demand (from which labor demand is derived) are not merely the result of "tastes" that arrive mysteriously on the scene, but rather can be understood in terms of social structure, mobility, and innovation diffusion. Perhaps the most significant contribution that can be made by sociological analysis lies in the understanding of matching processes, as I have argued for the Reder upgrading model, the meshing of supply–demand elasticities, the Hicksian expanding industries effect, and the city-size wage differential noted by Fuchs.

Much of this may not sound like sociology to economists: One reason for the neglect of such analysis is exactly that most economists think of sociology as being mainly the study of ingrained custom and habit. The economist Duesenberry, for example, has commented that "economics is all about how people make choices; sociology is all about how they don't have any choices to make [1960, p. 233]." In this vision, sociologists are supposed to imagine a world of actors so constrained by their values and ideas about what is proper that they move through life like automatons, playing out their pre-programmed roles. No wonder this is seen as inconsistent with rational behavior! Phelps Brown, discussing the "sociologist's approach to pay determination," comments that the sociologist sees people as acting "in certain ways because to do so is customary, or an obligation, or 'the natural thing to do', or right and proper, or just and fair [1977, p. 17]."

It may be a law of (academic) nature that every discipline sees every other discipline as it actually was 15–20 years earlier. In the 1950s, when sociological theory was dominated by Talcott Parsons, some justification could be offered—though even then it would have been a gross oversimplification—for the view that sociology concerned itself mainly with values and culture. This view is badly out of date in the 1980s, when sociologists are much more interested in social structure, flows of information and influence, networks of social relations, and the exercise of power. None of these concerns is inconsistent with the notion of rational choice; each, rather, is concerned with the complex and restrictive framework within which such choice must be made (see, e.g., Heath, 1976; Tilly, 1979). The time is thus ripe for a reconciliation and synthesis of the two disciplinary perspectives.

## Economic Contributions to Sociological Arguments

If sociologists took economic theory more seriously, much of this section would merely repeat the previous one, since they are the logical ones to execute the research I have faulted economists for missing. Sociologists, however, generally have no clearer notion of economics than economists have of sociology; they assume that the two disciplines are engaged in a zero-sum game and that, if economic arguments are valid, they are ipso facto out of business. This misconception depends on certain stereotyped images of economic theory: that it always assumes systems to be at equilibrium; that individuals are always assumed to be paid according to ability—where ability is equivalent to marginal product; that every waking moment is assumed to be spent in pursuit of the maximization of something—usually lifetime income.

Just as there are some sociologists who fulfill the economists' stereotype of what sociology is about, there are also some economists who write as if these assumptions are accurate. (For a merciless parody, by an economist, of the overapplication of human capital theory, see Blinder's *The Economics of Brushing Teeth* [1974].) But by and large, economic theory is more sophisticated than these stereotypes. Disequilibrium is a matter of increasing interest and has always been theoretically admissible; marginal product, as I have pointed out, is, even in the earliest formulations, a complex construct depending not only on ability but also on technology, work processes, and underlying product demand.

In my view, then economic theory usefully describes forces that operate even when the idealized conditions that would produce a speedy equilibrium are weak or absent. Even if the theory were entirely correct, however, it could never be more than a highly incomplete account of the forces impinging on earnings; thus, if sociologists were to do the sort of research described in the previous section, it would in no way reduce them to an ancillary role. Moreover, a broader use of economic theory would allow sociologists to refine and enrich the research they currently do. Here I offer only a few examples of cases where even simple ideas about supply, demand, and marginal productivity could better inform sociological analyses of wages.

Two empirical studies concern themselves with male–female wage differentials. Bibb and Form explain womens' low wages by showing that women are disproportionately located in peripheral industries that are "inefficient and marginally profitable [1977, p.992]." They counterpose two possible explanations: one "sociological" and one "economic." The sociological account is based on the idea that firms are stratified so that peripheral industries, being weaker, are less able to pay high wages; the economic account is specified as human capital theory—that is, that education and experience should explain earnings differentials. They find that these human capital variables explain less variance in income than those associated with the "stratification of firms" and hence conclude that this sociological explanation is superior to the economic.

This conclusion is possible because they take human capital ideas as the essence of the economic theory of wages and thus assume that marginal productivity is an attribute of the worker. But a broader neoclassical perspective would suggest that working in a "peripheral" industry yields low pay because such industries are less productive than are "core" industries. In this situation, the skill or talent of workers may be only weakly related to output, since the rudimentary technology and unreliable product demand—characteristics of the job—establish such low ceilings on what can be accomplished. Such an argument is also more consistent with the neoclassical theory of the firm, which asserts that, since rational employers would not pay wages higher than they needed to, a firm's profits and wages should be uncorrelated. This account, which uses a more fully rounded notion of marginal productivity than does human capital theory, has quite different implications than the one proposed. The issue can probably not be settled with these data.

In another study, Talbert and Bose (1977) expect and their data confirm that "sales clerks located in departments with homogeneously high-status clientele will receive higher rewards because of the store's dependence on these customers. We include among high-status departments those which sell high-cost products such as furniture and appliances, since they also tend to attract customers with relatively high purchasing power [p. 410]." Furthermore, an important part of womens' lower wages results from their underrepresentation in such departments. Talbert and Bose interpret the higher wages in such departments as the result of "organizational adaptation to environmental complexity and uncertainty [p. 407]." Organizations are said to implement a strategy that "allows for differential treatment of environmental elements. Units managing environmental segments representing high organization dependence are likely to receive a disproportionately high share of organizational resources, including wages [p.407]." Furthermore, "such informal stratification is a primary basis of power dynamics among organizational elites [p.407n]." An alternative explanation is simpler: Clerks in high-status departments who successfully sell big-ticket items add more to the revenues of the store than do clerks in other departments; their marginal product is higher, and standard economic theory thus unambiguously predicts their higher pay. In this case, marginal product seems some combination of the attributes of the job and those of the worker—whatever attributes make a successful salesperson.

In both cases—peripheral industries and high-status departments in stores—the marginal product interpretation suggests a shift in emphasis: Rather than arguing that observed wage differentials result from power plays or strategic manipulation, it indicates that they are more straightforwardly attributable to ordinary rational economic behavior. This does not rule out sociological explanations of inequality but rather shifts our interest away from the question of how a particular job's wage is determined to that of how it is determined who is *matched* with jobs that have high earnings potential. As I have argued throughout, sociological analysis can make its most distinctive and powerful contribution by aiding our understanding of this matching problem.

Sociologists need not believe, of course, that workers are always paid labor's marginal product. In recent years even economists have displayed increasing doubt that this is the case and offered data (e.g., Medoff &

Abraham, 1979) and models attempting to explain such divergences (e.g., Lazear, 1979; Lazear & Rosen, 1979). In fact, Medoff and Abraham, using one of the rare data sets that includes measures of worker performance, reach the startling conclusion that over time, "for those persons not changing grade, relative within-grade performance appears to remain stable or deteriorate while relative within-grade salary rises substantially [1979; p. 46]."

The sociologist Pfeffer (1977), though his language is not economic, in effect offers some interesting hypotheses on this subject. He argues that some work settings make productivity more difficult to assess than others and that in such settings one can expect a greater influence on wage of social status background and contact networks. These settings are identified as staff (rather than line) positions, small (rather than large) organizations, and nonmanufacturing firms (finance, banking, insurance, and real estate). His data confirm the hypotheses. This analysis of matching processes could profitably be combined with recent economic theorizing on similar subjects. Implicitly, Pfeffer argues here that social status and contact networks are used as screens or signals because the nature of the work makes direct observation of productivity difficult. If this is correct, there may be evidence here for the notion, which I suggested earlier, that individuals can rationally invest in contract networks and perhaps even in the accoutrements of social status groups, such as "exclusive" clubs, the "right" clothes, language, and manners, and other subtle indicators that clearly mark off higher social classes to those properly attuned. Combining the sociological insights here with the rigor of economic models could produce an analysis more sophisticated than either currently offers.

## Limitations and Prospects

A chapter of this length cannot adequately treat all factors impinging on earnings. In this section I mean not to repair the various omissions, but only to identify them and suggest how they relate to what has been discussed. Perhaps most glaring is the absence of any discussion of discrimination. I have neglected this important aspect of matching processes in part because it is already widely recognized and discussed and in part because proper perspective would have required too extensive a discussion for the present format. Instead, I chose to highlight less commonly analyzed issues.

It is time also to say that, while the tripartite division of causal factors into those of personal and job characteristics and matching processes has been a useful initial probe into the literature and a serviceable sorting device, it has certain limitations. In particular, it has some of the atomistic flavor I have criticized in other contexts. To take this classification literally entails the implicit assumption that workers and employers enter the system that determines earnings as individuals, without significant interaction and organization beyond this individual level. This is a gross oversimplification. Workers interact extensively with one another in an attempt to influence earnings. They do so by means of organizations of various kinds, the most obvious of which are trade unions. A recent review article concludes that the "ability of unions to extract wage gains over and above what could have been achieved in their absence is generally an accepted fact in academic literature. . . . Debate instead has focused on the magnitude and nature of such effects [Parsley, 1980, p.1]." Correspondingly, employers, especially though not exclusively in oligopolistic industries, combine both informally and in formal trade associations whose operations may have effects on wages.

Furthermore, most individuals are employed not in a one-on-one situation with an employer, but rather in an organization whose structure has some impact on earnings (see, e.g., Baron & Bielby, 1980). One central organizational feature in most firms, for example, is the existence of clear-cut hierarchies with well-defined levels. One of the reasons that wage changes for one job frequently entail wage changes in others is the need to maintain consistency among such levels (Doeringer & Piore, 1971). Simon (1957) has even suggested that the number of such levels may be the main determinant of the wages of those at the top of the pyramid in industrial firms (see also Lydall, 1968, pp. 127–133). Yet, there is considerable dispute in the literature on the question of exactly why firms typically have such hierarchies. The Weberian notion that a clear chain of command is efficient has been amplified in various ways by economists who argue that a rational firm requires hierarchy in order to minimize various costs that would otherwise be faced, such as transaction costs (O. Williamson, 1975) or the costs of acquiring information on employee productivity (Stiglitz, 1975a). Marxists, on the other hand, have argued that hierarchies have no economic function but rather are required in order to prevent workers from developing autonomy or an integrated understanding of the productive process, either of which would generate threats to capitalist hegemony (Marglin, 1974; Stone, 1975). White (1978) suggests a third view, that hierarchies may be the more or less adventitious result of ordinary productive and marketing activities, required neither for efficiency nor for repression. This debate is one example of the complexity of collective processes that have important impacts on earnings but are currently poorly understood. As with other issues discussed in this chapter, a confrontation of organizational ideas from sociology with efficiency considerations from economics and political ones from Marxist thought may help generate more sophisticated analysis.

The extent to which wages are influenced by interactions that take place in a network of firms is also an issue that requires a less atomistic paradigm than the one I have employed here. Dunlop's notion that there exist *wage contours*—sets of firms whose wages influence one another—and that such influence may be highly asymmetrical (e.g., Eckstein & Wilson, 1961), would repay further analysis. Developments in interorganizational analysis (summarized by Aldrich, 1979) could help clarify this situation.

Finally, an important omission from the present chapter is any discussion of the impact of macroeconomic forces on earnings differences. This is a complex subject on which clear positions have not been staked out by economists; hence existing schools of thought on wage differences tend to revolve mostly around microeconomic analysis. This is the case despite the fact that levels of employment and the "stickiness" of prices, including wages, in the face of demand and supply changes have been central issues in macroeconomics. Recent ferment and revisionism in this area (e.g., Eichner, 1979; Leijonhufvud, 1968) lead, however, to the hope that more systematic consideration of how this larger framework relates to inequality will soon come to occupy considerable attention.

## Summary

It will be clear by now to the reader that the exercise I have indulged in here is not a theory, but rather the statement of a puzzle and a display of many of the pieces. In an area where intellectual interchange has been extremely fragmentary, this seems to me a necessary first step. More generally, I believe that a number of difficult problems lie on the border of sociology and economics and consequently receive more narrow and less sophisticated treatment than they require. Ultimately, both sociological and economic theory need to be reconstructed and integrated in ways that will yield a far more powerful apparatus than either now offers. Such a task is unlikely to be achieved as the result of purely abstract considerations, but rather step by step in the course of attacking specific problems. One such problem is that of earnings differences, and my main purpose here is to encourage the integration described by focusing attention on an issue that is of compelling theoretical as well as practical significance.

## Acknowledgments

I am indebted to Mitchel Abolafia for his comments and his valuable literature review. The following individuals make up an incomplete list of those who have been extremely generous with their comments: Howard Aldrich, Daniel Cornfield, William Form, Christopher Jencks, Arne Kalleberg, Susan Mueller, John Padgett, Charles Perrow, James Rule, and Robert Willis.

# References

Aldrich, H.
 1979  *Organizations and Environments.* Englewood Cliffs, New Jersey: Prentice-Hall.
Baron, J. and W. Bielby
 1980  "Bringing the firms back in: Stratification, segmentation and the organization of work." *American Sociological Review* 45(October):737–765.
Beck, E. M., P. Horan, and C. Tolbert
 1978  "Stratification in a dual economy." *American Sociological Review* 43(October):704–720.
Becker, G.
 1964  *Human Capital.* New York: Columbia Univ. Press.
Berg, I.
 1970  *Education and Jobs: The Great Training Robbery.* New York: Praeger.
Berger, P., and T. Luckmann
 1967  *The Social Construction of Reality.* New York: Doubleday.
Bibb, R., and W. Form
 1977  "The effects of industrial, occupational and sex stratification on wages in blue-collar markets." *Social Forces* 55(June):974–996.
Blau, P., and O.D. Duncan
 1967  *The American Occupational Structure.* New York: Wiley.
Blaug, M.
 1976  "The empirical status of human capital theory: A slightly jaundiced survey." *Journal of Economic Literature* 14(September):827–855.
Blinder, A.
 1974  "The economics of brushing teeth." *Journal of Political Economy* 82(July–August):887–891.
Boorman, S.
 1975  "A combinatorial optimization model for transmission of job information through contact networks." *Bell Journal of Economics* 6(spring):216–249.
Cain, G.
 1976  "The challenge of segmented labor market theories to orthodox theory." *Journal of Economic Literature* 14(December):1215–1257.
Collins, R.
 1980  *The Credential Society.* New York: Academic Press.
Dalton, M.
 1959  *Men Who Manage.* New York: Wiley.
David, P., and P. Temin
 1976  "Slavery: The progressive institution?" In P. David, H. Outman, R. Sutch, P. Temin, and G. Wright (eds.), *Reckoning with Slavery*, London and New York: Oxford Univ. Press.
Davis, K., and W. Moore
 1945  "Some principles of stratification." *American Sociological Review* 19(April):242–249.
Doeringer, P., and M. Piore
 1971  *Internal Labor Markets and Manpower Analysis.* Lexington, Massachusetts: Heath.
Duesenberry, J.
 1960  Comment on "An Economic Analysis of Fertility." In Universities-National Bureau Committee for Economic Research (ed.), *Demographic and Economic Change in Developed Countries.* Princeton: Princeton Univ. Press.
Dunlop, J.
 1957  "The task of contemporary wage theory." In G. Taylor and F. Pierson (eds.), *New Concepts in Wage Determination.* New York: McGraw-Hill.

Eckstein, O., and T. Wilson
  1961   "The determination of money wages in American industry." *Quarterly Journal of Economics* 76(August):379–414.
Edwards, R.
  1975   "The social relations of production in the firm and labor market structure." In R. Edwards, M. Reich, and D. Gordon (eds.), *Labor Market Segmentation*. Lexington, Massachusetts: Heath.
Eichner, A., Ed.
  1979   *A Guide to Post-Keynesian Economics*. White Plains, New York: M. E. Sharpe.
Fagerlind, I.
  1975   *Formal Education and Adult Earnings*. Stockholm: Almqvist and Wiksell.
Freeman, R.
  1971   *The Market for College-Trained Manpower*. Cambridge, Massachusetts: Harvard Univ. Press.
Fuchs, V.
  1967   *Differentials in Hourly Earnings by Region and City-Size, 1959*. Occasional Paper 101, National Bureau of Economic Research. New York: Columbia Univ. Press.
Gartrell, D.
  1979   "The social evaluation of compensation: Public employees in Cambridge, Massachusetts." Unpublished doctoral dissertation, Harvard University.
Gordon, D.
  1972   *Theories of Poverty and Underemployment*. Lexington, Massachusetts: Heath.
Granovetter, M.
  1973   "The strength of weak ties." *American Journal of Sociology* 78(May):1360–1380.
  1974   *Getting a Job: A Study of Contacts and Careers*. Cambridge, Massachusetts: Harvard Univ. Press.
  1976   Review of Sewall and Hauser's *Education, Occupation and Earnings*. *Harvard Educational Review* 46(February):123–127.
  1977   Review of Mincer's *Schooling, Experience and Earnings*. *Sociological Quarterly* 18(Autumn):608–612.
  1979   "Placement as brokerage: Information problems in the labor market for rehabilitated workers." In D. Vandergoot, R. Jacobsen, and J. Worall (eds.), *Placement in Rehabilitation: A Career Development Perspective*. Baltimore: University Park Press.
Heath, A.
  1976   *Rational Choice and Social Exchange*. London and New York: Cambridge Univ. Press.
Hicks, J. R.
  1964   *The Theory of Wages*. New York: St. Martin's. (Reprint of 1932 edition, with 1964 supplement.)
Homans, G.
  1950   *The Human Group*. New York: Harcourt.
Jencks, C., S. Bartlett, M. Corcoran, J. Crouse, D. Eaglesfield, G. Jackson, K. McClelland, P. Mueser, M. Olneck, J. Schwartz, S. Ward, and J. Williams
  1979   *Who Gets Ahead?* New York: Basic Books.
Jencks, C., M. Smith, H. Acland, M. Bane, D. Cohen, H. Gintis, B. Heyns, and S. Michelson
  1972   *Inequality*. New York: Basic Books.
Lazear, E.
  1979   "Agency, earnings profiles, productivity and layoffs." Report 7945, Center for Mathematical Studies in Business and Economics, University of Chicago.
Lazear, E., and S. Rosen
  1979   "Rank-order tournaments as optimum labor contracts." Working Paper 401, National Bureau of Economic Research, Cambridge, Massachusetts.

Leibenstein, H.
1976   *Beyond Economic Man: A New Foundation for Microeconomics.* Cambridge, Massachusetts: Harvard Univ. Press.

Leijonhufvud, A.
1968   *On Keynesian Economics and the Economics of Keynes.* London and New York: Oxford Univ. Press.

Lin, N., W. Ensel, and J. Vaughn
1979   "Social resources, strength of ties, and occupational status attainment." Department of Sociology, State University of New York at Albany. (Mimeo)

Lippman, S., and J. McCall
1976   "The economics of job search: A survey." *Economic Inquiry* 14(June):155–189.

Lydall, H.
1968   *The Structure of Earnings.* London and New York: Oxford Univ. Press.

Marglin, S.
1974   "What do bosses do? The origins and functions of hierarchy in capitalist production." *Review of Radical Political Economics* 6(Spring):60–112.

McCall, J.
1970   "Economics of information and job search." *Quarterly Journal of Economics* 84(February):113–126.

Medoff, J., and K. Abraham
1979   "Can productive capacity differentials really explain the earnings differentials associated with demographic characteristics? The case of experience." Working Paper 363, National Bureau of Economic Research, Cambridge, Massachusetts.

Mincer, J.
1974   *Schooling, Experience and Earnings.* New York: Columbia Univ. Press.

Oliver, D.
1955   *A Solomon Island Society.* Cambridge, Massachusetts: Harvard Univ. Press.

Osterman, P.
1975   "An empirical study of labor market segmentation." *Industrial and Labor Relations Review* 28(July):508–523.

Parsley, C. J.
1980   "Labor union effects on wage gains: A survey of recent literature." *Journal of Economic Literature* 18(March):1–31.

Peterson, J.
1980   "An agenda for socioeconomic life-cycle research." *Journal of Economics and Business* 32(winter):95–110.

Pfeffer, J.
1977   "Toward an examination of stratification in organizations." *Administrative Science Quarterly* 22(December):553–567.

Phelps Brown, E. H.
1977   *The Inequality of Pay.* Berkeley: Univ. of California Press.

Piore, M.
1975   "Notes for a theory of labor market stratification." In R. Edwards, M. Reich, and D. Gordon (eds.), *Labor Market Segmentation.* Lexington, Massachusetts: Heath.

Reder, M.
1955   "The theory of occupational wage differentials." *American Economic Review* 45 (December):833–852.

Rees, A.
1973   *The Economics of Work and Pay.* New York: Harper.

Rees, A., and G. Shultz
1970   *Workers and Wages in an Urban Labor Market.* Chicago: Univ. of Chicago Press.

Reynolds, L.
    1974    *Labor Economics and Labor Relations* (6th ed.). Englewood Cliffs, New Jersey: Prentice-Hall.
Rottenberg, S.
    1956    "On choice in labor markets." *Industrial and Labor Relations Review* 91(January):183–199.
Sayles, L.
    1958    *Behavior of Industrial Work Groups.* New York: Wiley.
Sewell, W., and R. Hauser
    1975    *Education, Occupation, and Earnings.* New York: Academic Press.
Simon, H.
    1957    "The compensation of executives." *Sociometry* 20(March):32–35.
Sørensen, A.
    1977    "The structure of inequality and the process of attainment." *American Sociological Review* 42(December):965–978.
Spence, M.
    1974    *Market Signaling.* Cambridge, Massachusetts: Harvard Univ. Press.
Stigler, G.
    1961    "The economics of information." *Journal of Political Economy* 69(June):213–225.
    1962    "Information in the labor market." *Journal of Political Economy* 70(October, Pt.2):94–105.
Stiglitz, J.
    1975a    "Incentives, risk and information: Notes towards a theory of hierarchy." *Bell Journal of Economics* 6(autumn):552–578.
    1975b    "The theory of 'screening', education and the distribution of income." *American Economic Review* 65(June):283–300.
Stolzenberg, R.
    1975    "Occupations, labor markets and the process of wage attainment." *American Sociological Review* 40(October):645–665.
Stone, K.
    1975    "The origins of job structures in the steel industry." In R. Edwards, M. Reich, and D. Gordon (eds.), *Labor Market Segmentation.* Lexington, Massachusetts: Heath.
Talbert, J., and C. Bose
    1977    "Wage-attainment processes: The retail clerk case." *American Journal of Sociology* 83(September):403–424.
Thurow, L.
    1975    *Generating Inequality.* New York: Basic Books.
Tilly, C.
    1979    *From Mobilization to Revolution.* Reading, Massachusetts: Addison-Wesley.
U. S. Department of Labor
    1975    *Jobseeking Methods Used by American Workers.* Bureau of Labor Statistics Bulletin 1886. Washington, D. C.: US Govt Printing Office.
Weber, M.
    1968    [*Economy and Society*] (G. Roth and C. Wittich, Trans.). Totowa, New Jersey: Bedminister Press. (Originally published, 1921.)
White, H.
    1970    *Chains of Opportunity.* Cambridge, Massachusetts: Harvard Univ. Press.
    1978    "Markets and hierarchies revisited." Department of Sociology, Harvard University. (Mimeo)
Williamson, J.
    1976    "The sources of American inequality, 1896–1948." *Review of Economics and Statistics* 58(November):387–397.

Williamson, O.
  1975   *Markets and hierarchies.* New York: Free Press.
Wright, E. O.
  1979   *Class, Crisis and the State.* New York: Schocken.
Wright, E. O., and L. Perrone
  1977   "Marxist class categories and income inequality." *American Sociological Review* 42(February):32–55.

# Chapter 3

# An Outline of a Theory

# of the Matching of

# Persons to Jobs[1]

*AAGE B. SØRENSEN*

*ARNE L. KALLEBERG*

Much recent research in sociology has focused on labor market processes. These concerns include analysis of the processes that produce variation in individual earnings by characteristics of people and their jobs; the analysis of career patterns and job mobility processes; and the analysis of employment and unemployment patterns of various population groups. Sociologists share many of these concerns with economists, and there is much overlap in research topics among sociologists and economists.

Despite similarities in methodology and research design, the research traditions in sociology and economics have quite different intellectual backgrounds. Most empirical research on labor market processes in economics is guided by the dominant school of labor economics—the neoclassical theory of wage determination and labor supply, with marginal productivity theory accounting for the demand side and human capital theory taking care of the supply side. In contrast, sociological research on labor market phenomena has its origin in research describing socioeconomic attainment and social mobility processes for various population groups. Sociological

[1] This research was supported in part by funds granted to the Institute for Research on Poverty at the University of Wisconsin by the Office of Economic Opportunity pursuant to the provisions of the Economic Opportunity Act of 1964. The conclusions expressed herein are those of the authors.

SOCIOLOGICAL PERSPECTIVES ON
LABOR MARKETS

research on attainment and mobility has not employed an explicitly stated conceptual apparatus that informs the choice of variables and the interpretation of parameters. Although there is a growing body of findings about the magnitude of the influences of various variables on the outcomes of labor market processes, particularly income attainment, there are few efforts by sociologists to identify the mechanisms that create the influences of personal and job characteristics on income and earnings or on the other labor market outcomes.

There is no need for sociologists to develop a unique theory of labor market processes if the neoclassical economic theory adequately accounts for the findings of empirical research. With respect to a favorite variable of both economists and sociologists—that is, education—human capital theory does provide an interpretation of results. However, the economic theory does not provide a rationale for the sociological concern for occupational attainment. Job characteristics, including those presumably captured by the Socioeconomic Index (SEI) or prestige scores of occupations, play little or no role in the orthodox economic theory. Still, occupational status accounts for a substantial fraction of the explained variance in sociological income attainment models.

The amount of variance added to income attainment models by occupation is not necessarily a strong argument for replacing or supplementing the economic theory. Sociologists have not been able to account for very much variance in income attainment. Research informed by human capital theory (e.g., Mincer, 1974) has in fact been able to do as well or better without including occupation. A measure of occupational status must necessarily show some relation to income, reflecting the between-occupation variance in income that it captures. An observed effect of job characteristics on income or earnings may be attributed to a misspecification of sociological models, both with respect to functional form and omitted variables, and need not be considered a challenge to the economic theory.

There are, however, other reasons for critically evaluating the neoclassical or orthodox economic theory. The economic theory is powerful, and numerous predictions can be derived from it regarding the earnings attainment process and other labor market processes, particularly labor supply. (A list of such predictions is presented by Becker, 1964.) Some of these predictions are borne out by empirical observations; some are not. Thurow (1975, pp.56–70) presents a list of deviations from the theory, pertaining to such issues as the relationship between wages and unemployment, changes in the distribution of earnings, and the relationship between the distribution of education and the distribution of income. Numerous others have identified features of the earnings attainment process and of labor markets that deviate from the assumptions and predictions of the neoclassical theory.

A review of these challenges to orthodox theory has been presented by Cain (1976). Particularly important are those critiques that argue that labor markets are segmented and that stress the differences between either so-called primary and secondary jobs (cf. Doeringer & Piore, 1971); or monopoly, competitive, and state economic sectors (cf. Averitt, 1968; Bluestone, 1970; O'Connor, 1973); or wage competition and job competition sectors (Thurow, 1975); or internal and external markets (Doeringer & Piore, 1971; Kerr, 1954). These critiques all observe that jobs and job structures differ, contrary to the assumption about the homogeneous nature of labor markets made by the economic theory. They stress qualitative differences among jobs relevant for employment and earnings processes and claim to be able to account for the observations that deviate from the orthodox economic theory, as well as to provide different explanations for labor market processes that also can be explained by the orthodox theory. An example of such an alternative explanation is Thurow's (1975) interpretation of the relationship between education and earnings.

Most of the criticism comes from within economics, though there are examples of research and conceptual elaboration by sociologists pertaining to the issues raised by the segmented labor market theory (Sørensen, 1977; Spilerman, 1977; Stolzenberg, 1975). The issues are clearly relevant for sociological research, and more so since the alternatives to the neoclassical theory provide a rationale for introducing job characteristics sociologists are likely to continue to emphasize.

The classical sociological theorists did not leave labor market analysis to economists. Marx and Weber spent lifetimes analyzing the relation between economy and society, and their concerns in many ways parallel the issues raised in recent controversies. Marx's analysis of capitalist society is an analysis of the implications of the fundamental condition of capitalist production: Labor is treated as a commodity bought and sold freely in a market. This conception of the labor market, we shall argue in the following pages, parallels the conception of the orthodox economic theory.

Marx treated labor in capitalist society as a homogeneous abstract category, and though there are occasional remarks concerning deviations from this model of labor as a commodity and their relevance for class conflict (e.g., Marx, 1961, Vol. 1, chap. 14), no systematic analysis of alternative labor market structures is presented. Weber's long analysis of the sociological categories of economic action (Weber, 1947, Pt. I, chap. 2) provides, in contrast, numerous concepts relevant for the analysis of labor market structures (including nonmarket relationships), particularly in the sections on the social division of labor. The concepts are highly relevant for the issues raised by the challenges to orthodox economic theory, and some of Weber's basic concepts will be used extensively in this chapter.

The following pages provide a conceptual framework for the analysis of labor markets. Labor markets are arenas for the matching of persons to jobs. The conditions that determine the earnings outcome of this matching process are of primary interest here, particularly the identification of what determines the influence of job and personal characteristics on earnings. The purpose of this chapter is not to show the neoclassical theory to be wrong, but rather to identify the conditions for the emergence of the matching process associated with the labor market structure assumed in the orthodox economic theory. It will be argued that the conditions for the emergence of this matching process are not present in some segments of the labor market. The absence of these conditions leads to alternative matching processes, and a model of one important alternative matching process will be presented. The two contrasting matching processes will be shown to have very different implications for the earnings determination process and for other labor market processes.

## Basic Concepts

The theory proposed in this chapter will rely on Weber's notion of open and closed social relationships (Weber, 1947, p.139) to identify different job structures characterized by different matching processes.[2] The degree of closure, in turn, is seen as determined by the bargaining power of employers and employees. We shall, therefore, refer to the employment relationship as the crucial determinant of the notion of the matching process and its earnings outcome.

Employment relationships are social relationships created in the production of goods and services between an employer (or his agent) and an employee. We concentrate on employment relationships typical of capitalist production in which the employer appropriates the output from the production process and has complete possession over the nonhuman means of production. Our analysis will focus on the consequences for the earnings

---

[2] The definitions are given in paragraph 10 in the section on "Basic Concepts" in *Economy and Society*, Volume 1. "A social relationship . . . will be known as 'open' to those on the outside, if . . . participation . . . is . . . not denied to anyone who is inclined to participate and is actually in a position to do so. The relationship will be known as 'closed' [if] participation of certain persons is excluded, limited or subject to conditions [Weber, 1947, p. 139]." Weber argues that market relationships are open and gives as an example of a closed relationship the "establishment of rights to and possession of particular jobs on the part of the worker ]Weber, 1947, p.141]." This identification of open relationships with market relationships (for the exchange of labor for wages) and of closed relationships with control over the job by the worker (and the absence of market relationships) will be relied on heavily in this chapter.

determination process and other labor market processes of variation in control over the job by the employer versus the employee. Two aspects of control over the job may be distinguished. One is control over the activities of the job, resulting in more or less autonomy for the employee; the other is control over access to the job, resulting in a more or less closed employment relationship. These two dimensions may vary independently. Particularly, control over access to the job will be considered crucial, because it influences the nature of competition among employees.

The degree of control over access is a continuum. At one extreme, the employee "owns" the job and no one else can get access unless the current incumbent voluntarily leaves it and a vacancy is established. The length of the employment is then completely controlled by the employee, and the employment relationship is closed to outsiders. At the other extreme, the employer may replace the incumbent at any time. The employment contract is reestablished in every short interval of time, and the employment relationship is completely open to outsiders.

The employment relationship is established in a process assumed to involve purposive actors as employers and employees where both parties are attempting to maximize earnings. The earnings of the employer are determined by the value of the product of the job–person combination in relation to costs of production. The value of production is a question of prices of products and quantity produced. Quantity produced in turn reflects the performance of the employee and the technology used, including the technical division of labor adopted. For purposes of this analysis, the main variable of interest is the performance of the employee and the main costs of production of interest are the wages paid to the employee and the costs of supervision.

The performance of employees or the quantity of labor supplied will be taken as determined by such attributes of the employees as their skills, abilities, and effort. The employer's return from production evidently depends on his or her ability to obtain the highest output at the lowest costs. While numerous factors may influence the overall level of wages, the employer's ability to minimize costs of production depends not only on the overall level of wages but also on the ability to tie variations in wages paid to variations in the employee's productivity. The main argument of this chapter is that the mechanisms the employer can use to relate wages to performance depend on the employment relationship, particularly the employee's control over access to the job, and that these different mechanisms identify important differences in labor market structures relevant also for labor market processes other than earnings.

The orthodox economic theory identifies a particular set of mechanisms for relating the productivity of employees to their earnings. We shall first consider these mechanisms and the employment relationships needed for these mechanisms to be effective.

## The Neoclassical Theory of Earnings Determination

In the economic theory, a wage rate is generated by a labor market as a result of the demand and supply schedules of labor. Demand for labor varies with the derived demand for products, as reflected in their value. The link between wages and the value of products is established through the concept of marginal productivity, since profit-maximizing firms will be in equilibrium when the value of the marginal product equals the marginal cost or price of labor as a factor of production. This should produce different wage rates for identical labor supply because of differences in demand. However, the neoclassical theory emphasizes supply differences as a source of differences in wage rates and earnings, in particular those supply differences resulting from different skills and other individual characteristics related to an employee's productive capacity.

Differences in skills, according to human capital theory, determine different levels of productive capacity resulting in different wage rates. If skills were acquired at no cost, those wage differentials would soon lead to equalizing skill acquisition. But skills are acquired at costs. These costs are partly direct in the form of tuition and living expenses and partly opportunity costs in the form of earnings foregone. No one should undertake training if the returns from this training, in the form of increased earnings accumulated over the working life, are not at least equal to the costs of training.

If only skills acquired through training are relevant, earnings differentials would be exactly off-setting the differences in training costs. However, it is usually recognized that earnings differentials also capture variations in ability, where ability is used to refer to such characteristics as IQ, motivation, and creativity. Ability may be incorporated in the theory by recognizing that persons with different abilities have different investment costs and hence need different earnings to induce the undertaking of training. In addition, some aptitudes may be innate and scarce; these will command a rent because of their fixed supply. Finally, some variation in earnings can be attributed to different opportunities for financing training, particularly as a result of the unequal distribution of parental wealth in combination with the unwillingness of lenders to take collateral in human capital.

The basic proposition derived from the neoclassical theory is then that differences in earnings reflect differences in the productive capacity of persons as a result of their training, abilities, and training opportunities. There may be transient variations in earnings as a result of differences in derived demand in combination with market imperfections, but the basic source of inequality in earnings is unequal endowments in productive capacities among persons. In other words, identical persons are assumed to obtain almost identical earnings, regardless of the characteristics of the jobs they are in.

This theory can be used to account for a number of features of observed earnings attainment processes. Most importantly, it provides an explanation for the relation between education and earnings that interprets education as a source of marketable skills. Also, the theory predicts growth patterns for earnings, where earnings increase rapidly in the younger years and then gradually reach a stable level, with growth after entry into the labor market explained by investment in on-the-job training. Empirically, the theory fares well in accounting for variations in earnings among persons, using schooling and time in the labor force (as a proxy for on-the-job training and experience) as the main independent variables (Mincer, 1974).

The economic theory also emphasizes supply in accounting for other market processes. Most importantly, unemployment is seen as mostly voluntary, except in certain population groups (youngsters, blacks) where minimum wage laws make it impossible for employers to pay the market wage.

The focus in human capital theory on the supply side—that is, on characteristics of persons—reflects the job structure assumed in the theory—that is, one of a competitive and perfectly functioning labor market. These and other characteristics assumed in the scenario presented by the neoclassical theory are discussed next. To distinguish the neoclassical theory of the earnings determination process from the alternative model of the matching process that will be formulated later in the chapter, we will refer to the neoclassical theory as the *wage competition* model (following Thurow, 1975) to emphasize the focus on competition among employees for wages.

## Conditions for the Neoclassical Theory to Apply

The neoclassical world assumed in deriving the theory of wages is one where individuals engage in purposive behavior; that is, each individual has an ordered set of preferences and chooses the most preferred position available. Certainty about income, prices, and quality of goods is assumed, as is a competitive and perfectly functioning market. In the derivation of the theory, this market for labor is assumed to be like a market for any other good.

Of these various assumptions, not all imply the orthodox theory. The assumption of purposive behavior is a necessary but not a sufficient condition for marginal productivity theory to apply. The assumption about certainty (i.e., full information) is important, and we will argue that uncertainty about productivity leads to matching mechanisms different from the one predicted by marginal productivity theory. However, certainty is not the most crucial assumption, for uncertainty does not necessarily lead to a violation of basic principles of the economic theory.

The most important assumption is that of a market for labor with properties similar to those of a competitive market for consumer goods. Three features of markets for consumer goods are particularly salient:

1. In a market for goods, the seller completely relinquishes control over the use of the goods to the buyer.
2. Goods are supplied with well-defined properties, so that comparisons of prices and properties of goods can be made.
3. Goods are divisible, so that any quantity can be bought and sold.

Of these, the first assumption will be held to be the most crucial.

In labor markets, workers supply their labor/power in exchange for wages. However, the employer does not always gain complete control over what is bought. If employers have complete control over access to the job, they indeed have complete control over the commodity (labor power) being bought. If, on the other hand, the employee has control, the employee retains bargaining power over the employment relationship. The situation corresponds to one that would prevail in the exchange of commodities if the buyer was forced to deal only with a single seller for a particular commodity. The exchange relationship would then be insulated from competition from other sellers of that particular good. In a parallel way, the employment relationship is insulated from competition from other workers if the employee has control over the job.

The crucial aspect of control over the job is control over access to the job. A competitive labor market that determines wage rates is one where employers make wage offers and workers bid for employment on the basis of their productivity. The match is made when the value of the marginal product demanded equals the wage rate of the employee. This presupposes that employees paid more than their value can be replaced by others who are willing to work at the wage rate that equals marginal productivity, whereas employees who are paid less than their value can get access to jobs where the wage rate reflects their productivity. Only when the employment relationship is completely open will such a clearing of the market through wage rates be possible. Closed employment relationships, where new recruits can only get access if the incumbent leaves, insulate incumbents from competition. Employers cannot resolve discrepancies between productivity and wage rates by threatening to replace or actually replacing the current employee by someone who is more productive at the same wage rate or who is willing to work at a lower wage rate.

It could be argued that the existence of closed employment relationships does not prevent the employer from relating wages to performance, even in the absence of the ability to replace an employee. Most importantly, the employer can use promotion schemes to reward performance and in this way obtain efficient production. This is correct. Our argument is not that closed employment relationships necessarily prevent efficient production, but that promotion systems represent very different mechanisms for relating wages to performance than the use of competition among employees in open employment relationships where employers make wage offers and employees bid for employment on the basis of their productivity. Promotions can take place only when there is a vacancy in a higher level job and are meaningless as rewards for performance unless jobs at different levels provide different wages so that wages become attributes of jobs rather than of people. Although a firm with closed employment relationships may operate efficiently because of the overall match between job assignments and performance of employees, the wages for individual employees will reflect the jobs they hold and therefore, not only their performance, but also the rate at which vacancies appear, the organization of jobs, and the seniority of employees. A very different labor market structure exists from the one assumed in the neoclassical theory when wages are tied to jobs and not to individual variations in performance. The consequences of this will be explored at length later in this chapter.

It should be noted that new recruits to closed employment relationships may engage in wage competition for the vacancies created when incumbents leave their jobs. But there will be great uncertainty about the labor performance of new recruits, and this will prohibit attempts to link the value of marginal products to wage rates for new recruits.

The uncertainty about the productivity of new recruits makes it impossible to measure productivity. Lack of measurability is another way that labor markets differ from markets for goods. As mentioned earlier, in markets for goods, comparisons of prices and properties of goods can be made. In calculations of marginal productivity, it is clearly necessary for outputs from jobs to be measurable. Further, the absence of measurability will be argued later to be one of the determinants of employee control over access to the job. However, measurability is not a sufficient condition for the marginal productivity theory to apply. Even if there is perfect measurability, closed employment relationships will not allow the employer to equate marginal products and wage rates at the level of individual employees.

The third feature stated earlier was that goods are divisible commodities. If this were true of labor, employers would be able to continuously adjust to changes in the demand and supply of labor and therefore be able to hire and fire any quantity of labor. This will not be possible when jobs are highly interdependent, since the removal or addition of single jobs is impossible.

Interdependent production systems may then lead to persistent inefficiencies. However, indivisibility is of little consequence when employment relationships are closed, because single employees cannot then be removed even if single jobs are removable. Hence, divisibility, like measurability, is less a fundamental requirement than a control over access to the job.

Control over access to the job determines whether competition among employees will take place and hence whether the job structure is as assumed in the neoclassical theory. We earlier identified another dimension of control over the job, that is, control over the activities of the job. However, if the employment relationship is completely open, there is less need to control activities, since the wage rate will reveal performance and the threat of dismissal will act as a disciplinary factor. Autonomy on the job is a problem for the employer in closed employment relationships, and we will return to this later.

The application of marginal productivity in determining wages and earnings ensures employers that they will operate at maximum efficiency, because wages paid directly reflect the productive capacity of the individual employee. The effort and motivation of the employee need not concern the employers, since they can rely on the competition among workers to ensure that any variation in performance is reflected in the wage rate. Clearly, it should be in the interest of the employer, other things being equal, to gain complete control over access to the job and thus ensure the existence of the job structure assumed in the neoclassical theory.[3]

As open employment relationships benefit the employer, a closed employment relationship is in the interest of the employee. If the employment relationship is completely open and supply–demand schedules (as well as the techniques) remain constant, wage gains can only be made by the employee increasing his or her productive capacity. This will usually involve training costs. Further, variations in earnings produced by changes in supply and demand, including decreases in earnings, will occur independently of the employee's actions. Closed employment relationships, on the other hand, insulate the earnings from changes in supply and demand. They assure the

---

[3] Marx has described this job structure as a characteristic of the highest development of capitalist society:

> The indifference to the particular kind of labour corresponds to a form of society in which individuals pass with ease from one kind of work to another, which makes it immaterial to them what particular kind of work may fall to their share. Labour has become here, not only categorically but really, a means of creating wealth in general and has no longer coalesced with the individual in one particular manner. This state of affairs has found its highest development in the most modern of bourgeois societies, the United States. It is only here that the abstraction of the category 'labour', 'labour in general', labour *sans phrase*, the starting point of modern political economy, became realized in practice [Marx, 1973, p.104].

employee that if there are opportunities for better jobs they can be utilized, while if there are no such opportunities, the status quo will at least be preserved.

Later in the chapter, we argue that closed employment relationships are empirically important. Hence, employees are able, under certain conditions, to realize their interest in control over access to the job. The sources of this control are both technological and social and are discussed in the next section.

## Sources of Employee Control over the Job

We have described the neoclassical model for matching persons to jobs and argued that open employment relationships are a fundamental characteristic of the job structure assumed in this theory. We also argued, other things being equal, that it should be in the employer's interest to have open employment relationships and in the employee's interest to have a closed relationship. The problem is then to determine under which circumstances employers will relinquish control over the job.

The legal system of capitalist society accords the employer the formal control over access to the job, reflecting the employer possession of the physical means of production and the right to dispose of output. It might be argued that no rational employer should relinquish possession of the job and insulate the employment relationship from competition. However, it is our intention to show, quite to the contrary, that under certain circumstances it is the goal of ensuring the highest possible revenue that makes it necessary for the employer to relinquish control over access to the job. The employment relationship is a power relationship, because each party controls something of interest to the other party. It will be our argument that technical and social aspects of the production process may accord the employee control over the employer's ability to realize the highest possible earnings or revenue—a control that can be used by employees to realize their interest in control over access to the job.

Training requirements of jobs, particularly the amount of on-the-job training that is needed, have been argued by Thurow (1975) in his job competition model and by the dual labor market theorists (e.g., Doeringer & Piore, 1971) to be of fundamental importance for the emergence of job structures similar to the one that we will argue may result from closed employment relationships. This is indeed a very important determinant; however, in this section we will argue for other causes as well. In addition to training requirements, we will emphasize (a) the degree of interdependence among jobs, and the existence of job ladders; (b) the measurability of the output from jobs and autonomy; and (c) the existence of collective action by employees. For reference, Figure 3.1 summarizes the relations among the various determinants of the emergence of closed employment relationships.

## Training Requirements

If no one outside a job has the necessary skills to perform adequately on the job, training must take place on the job. If employers pay for this training, they have made an investment in the employee, and the employee gains control over access to the job in proportion to the size of the investment.

Not all training on the job necessarily leads to greater employee control over the job. Within the neoclassical framework, Becker (1964) argued for the distinction between general and specific on-the-job training. General on-the-job training can be transferred to another job, in contrast to specific on-the-job training that produces skills usable only on the job where they are acquired. Employers would not pay for general on-the-job training, since it may increase the productivity of other firms not engaged in providing the training. Hence general on-the-job training should lead to lower earnings for the employee in the training period and higher earnings later on to compensate for the training costs incurred by the employee. Specific on-the-job training, on the other hand, is borne by the employer and, as we have argued, should lead to increased employee control over the job.

Becker relies on the orthodox labor market theory in deriving the general relationship between skills and earnings, but for the question of the allocation of costs, the theory is not necessary. One must assume purposive behavior of both parties. If employers paid for general on-the-job training, they would be subsidizing other firms regardless of how earnings are determined. Specific on-the-job training similarly represents a cost to the employer, regardless of how earnings are determined.

In the case of general on-the-job training, there is also a source of employee control over the job derived from the on-the-job training requirements. Training on the job is rarely a self-learning process—co-workers usually provide a large part of the training. This means that if wage competition prevails, these co-workers may be in competition with their trainees once the training is completed. Hence, competition among employees provides an incentive for employees not to provide training. Granting employees greater control over the job is a way for employers to secure that training can in fact take place. This, and not the degree of skill specificity, appears to be Thurow's (1975) major argument for the emergence of job competition, where employment relationships are closed. Doeringer and Piore (1971),

Technical division of labor

Employer-employee social relations

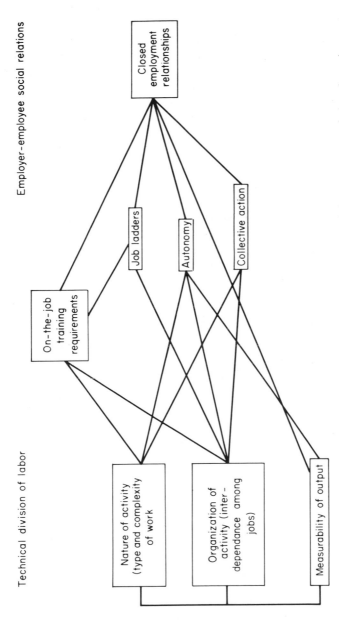

**Figure 3.1.** Interrelationships among the social and technical determinants of the emergence of closed employment relationships.

on the other hand, argue for the similar concept of primary jobs principally in terms of skill specificity.

Whether because of skill specificity or because of the necessity of having co-workers provide the training, the amount of training to be provided is the determinant of the amount of control gained by the employee. The amount of training required depends in turn on the complexity of the job and the amount of training provided by other agencies, for example, schools. Schools solve the need for general training without according employees control over the job. Schools cannot, however, provide training for specific jobs, nor can they provide training for jobs if the training requirements are unknown. Even if employers have the opportunity to transfer training to agencies outside the firm, such a move takes time; and, since training provided in schools is provided by teachers removed from the production process, the training provided will tend to be inflexible to technological and other changes in training requirements of actual jobs.

These are some of the most important variables related to training requirements of jobs that influence employer control over jobs. They are not however the only job characteristics relevant for the employment relationship.

## The Relation of Jobs to Other Jobs

Two aspects of the linkages among jobs can be identified: One is the degree of technical interdependence among jobs; the other is the linkages among jobs that form career trajectories. Both aspects of job structure have relevance for the employee's ability to realize his or her interests in gaining control over access to jobs.

Interdependence among jobs, created by the technical division of labor, implies that the existence of some jobs is necessary for the functioning of other jobs. The corresponding separation of the existence of the job from the jobholder is a necessary though not sufficient condition for the employee to gain control over the job.

The main impact of interdependence of jobs on the employment relationship is indirect. The degree of interdependence may affect the measurability of output and the likelihood of collective action among employees. Both measurability and collective action will be shown later to be important for the employment relationship.

The creation of highly interdependent jobs, however, has contradictory effects on employment relationships. Task interdependence usually results in less complex single tasks, and this may be a main motivation for the creation of such job structures. This should facilitate the creation of open employment relationships. At the same time, lack of measurability and collective action are sources of employee control over the job, creating a tendency toward closed-relationships. This is, of course, one important aspect of the contradictory nature of capitalist production as identified by Marx.

The existence of job ladders that form career trajectories will reinforce existing tendencies toward closed employment relationships. Even though employees are in closed relationships, serious business downturns and the like may force some employees out of jobs. Persons out of jobs who have spent part of their working career in closed employment relationships and who have obtained on-the-job training in these jobs may seem to constitute a threat to employee control over the job. However, their impact is reduced by two things. First, they usually constitute only a minority of job seekers. Second, the existence of job ladders in connection with closed employment relationships further reinforces employee control over the decision to leave.

Job ladders are introduced as a solution to the problem of creating incentives for performance in closed employment relationships, because career trajectories—represented by promotion opportunities to higher paying jobs— act to motivate workers who are insulated from competition with persons outside of jobs. However, in order to be effective, promotion opportunities must be available to all. They are not available to all if persons are hired into higher job ladders from the outside. Persons who have been forced out of job competition jobs will often be candidates for jobs at higher job ladders; but in order to keep promotion schedules intact, employers are unlikely to give them access to such jobs. Hence, they are only candidates for jobs at entry ladders, where the rewards provided are not likely to be attractive to job seekers who are already qualified. Even here, such job candidates are not attractive to the employers either, since they are likely to disturb training arrangements. Hence, the existence of promotion ladders provides a further insulation of employees against competition from the outside.

## Measurability of Output

Calculations of the value of marginal products assume that prices exist and quantities of output can be measured. Maximum efficiency may be obtained if outputs from single jobs can be linked to the value of total output. If prices do not exist, the value of total output is ambiguous; if, furthermore, the quantity of output from single jobs cannot be easily calculated, uncertainty about the value of marginal products of single jobs will exist.

Uncertainty about marginal products due to a lack of measurability should affect the employment relationships. Measurability is never completely nonexistent, or jobs would not exist. Indicators of productivity will be developed even for tasks where the output is impossible to quantify. These indicators are likely to be influenced by the employee's definitions of what are appropriate standards of job performance, since the employer will have to rely on information provided by the employee. The employee's control over information about the job thus represents a resource that may be used to further the employee's interest, and control over access to the job is in the employee's interest, as described earlier.

Measurability is, in general, more difficult with jobs where decisions constitute the output. Hence, certain white-collar and managerial employees should gain control over their jobs partly as a result of this lack of measurability. The exceptions are the very top managerial jobs, where the employee may be held accountable for a whole division of a firm or the whole firm. Employee control may then be less in such jobs, and involuntary terminations of employment relationships indeed appear to be more frequent in high managerial jobs than in middle-level jobs. On the other hand, such employees have command over substantial resources that may be used to further their interest versus the employer's.

## Collective Action

So far, we have discussed only sources of employee control over the job that are derived from intrinsic characteristics of jobs and the organization of jobs. Employees may, in addition, derive control over their jobs through some kind of collective action—in particular, unionization.

Unionization and similar forms of collective actions are confronted with a free-rider problem. As pointed out by Olson (1965), unions provide public goods that benefit even those who do not contribute to the provision of the good. This has a number of implications when such a good is likely to be provided (e.g., the influence of group size, use of nonvoluntary means of securing contributions); but most elementary, it is to be expected that the lower the cost of providing public goods, the more likely they will be provided, other things being equal. Employee control over jobs reduces the costs of engaging in collective action concerning employment relationships and the distributions of rewards. Hence, the ability to engage in collective action may derive from the same job characteristics that independently produce closed employment relationships, and the collective action then reinforces already existing tendencies.

However, even in cases where wage competition should be expected, collective action may occur; and, as a result of the increased bargaining power of employees, closed employment relationships may be instituted. Certain craft unions and professional organizations are able to control almost complete access to jobs by licensing and apprenticeship arrangements.

The benefits to employees of collective actions are greater in such jobs, and if various facilitating circumstances are present—such as high communication among workers, low upward mobility, and similar ideologies—unionization and other forms of collective action may emerge and higher employee control over jobs may be derived.

It is argued by the so-called radical critique of the neoclassical theory (e.g., Gordon, 1972) that the job structures that are argued here to emerge as a result of closed employment relationships are instituted by the employer to prevent the emergence of collective action on the part of employees. The logic is that the differentiation of workers into different job structures weakens worker solidarity and prevents class action by the working class as a whole. Though this may be the consequence of a differentiation of job structures, it is according the employers a great deal of enlightenment to attribute the emergence of closed employment relationships to the need to prevent class action.[4]

This section has focused on identifying the job structures where the neoclassical model should not emerge. The next section will outline the matching process we argue will result in closed employment relationships in production systems.

## Vacancy Competition

When employees have control over access to the job (as a result of the technical and social aspects of jobs structures identified in the preceding section), others can only get access to the job when incumbents leave. Hence, a vacancy must exist for a person to get access to a job. We will refer to the resulting matching process as *vacancy competition*. We do not wish to argue that this is the only alternative matching process to the wage competition model described by neoclassical economics. At least one other alternative employment relationship can be identified: This is the often met arrangement when employees are directly involved in the disposition of goods to the market, and the "salesperson" is paid some fraction of total earnings. But such relationships presuppose that jobs are not highly interdependent and that the salesperson is primarily involved in the disposition, rather than in the production, of goods.[5] Vacancy competition in contrast

---

[4] The argument assumes that capitalists are more interested in preventing class action than in maximizing profit. That capitalists are interested in preventing class action is not disputed; that they give higher priority to this goal than to efficiency implies that the capitalist relations of production are noncontradictory and hence static.

[5] A similar arrangement accounts for the apparent contradiction of the argument presented here exemplified by the existence of wage competition among faculty at elite universities despite

is likely to emerge in closed employment relationships where jobs are interdependent in a technical and social division of labor around production.

In vacancy competition, as in wage competition, employers are assumed to be concerned about hiring the most productive employee at the least cost. But because of the indeterminate length of the employment relationship and the lack of competition among employees over wages, it will not be possible for the employer to link marginal productivity to the wage rate. This has important consequences for (a) the determination of who should be hired; (b) the determination of earnings; and (c) the organization of jobs in job ladders. These consequences all follow from the employer's attempt to secure the highest possible return from production when faced with employee control over the job.

In wage competition, the employer can rely on the wage rate as a measure of a person's productive capacity. The employer need only be concerned that the value of marginal productivity equals the wage rate and can be indifferent to the relationship between personal characteristics of employees and their performances. In contrast, in vacancy competition, the employer should be very much concerned about the relationship between personal characteristics and productive capacity, because once hired the employee cannot be easily dismissed. Furthermore, it is a person's potential performance that will be of concern, including the person's ability to fulfill the training requirements of jobs. Previous experience, education, and such ascriptive characteristics as race and sex will be used as indicators of potential performance; the main requirements are that the indicators chosen are visible and in the employer's experience show some relationship to performance. Based on the information provided by these indicators, the employer will hire the most promising candidate among those available for a job. In other words, access to a vacancy will be determined by a ranking of job candidates. As proposed by Thurow (1975), the situation may be conceived of as one where a queue of job candidates is established for vacant jobs. A person's position in the labor queue will be determined, not by his or her absolute level of productive capacity, but by the rank order in relation to other job candidates according to characteristics deemed relevant by employers.

As there is a queue of persons for jobs, there will be a rank order or a queue of vacant jobs, where the rank order is established by the earnings provided by vacant jobs, the career trajectories they imply, and such other characteristics as status, pleasantness, and convenience. The matching pro-

tenure. Here the individual scholar, and not the employer (i.e., the university), disposes himself of the products (articles and other contributions) to a competitive market and obtains himself the returns from this activity (i.e., prestige in the profession).

cess, then, is a matching of the queue of persons to the queue of vacant jobs. The highest placed person in the labor queue will get the best job in the job queue. Changes in the supply of persons with certain characteristics (say a change in the distribution of education) and changes in the availability of jobs at different levels of rewards will change the rank orderings. As a result, whenever there is a change in the labor and job queues, persons with similar characteristics will tend to be hired into different jobs and persons in similar jobs may have different personal characteristics. The organization of jobs into career trajectories (discussed later) will further reinforce these tendencies.

Wage rates in vacancy competition are characteristics of jobs, not of persons. Because employers have no effective way of enforcing a translation of productivity variations into wage rates other than by promotions, wages will tend to become heavily influenced by such institutional forces as collective bargaining and employee desire to preserve traditional relative wage differentials. Internally, wage differentials will reflect the organization of jobs into job ladders.

The creation of job ladders in internal labor markets is, as already mentioned, a way for the employer to create an incentive structure in the absence of open employment relationships. The organization of jobs into promotion schedules further acts as a screening device, inducing low-performance employees to leave on their own decision by denying or delaying promotion in relation to other employees. To be effective, jobs at the same level in a promotion schedule should provide identical earnings, whereas jobs at different levels should provide a differential large enough to induce employees to compete for promotion opportunities. This further reinforces the tendency in vacancy competition for earnings to become a characteristic of jobs so that similar jobs provide similar earnings regardless of characteristics of the incumbents.

Actual promotion opportunities are created when persons leave the firm or a new job is added, setting in motion chains of vacancies (White, 1970). The number of job levels, the distribution of jobs at various levels, the seniority distribution of employees, and the demand for products influencing the creation of new jobs (or the elimination of jobs), all interact to produce promotion schedules governing the careers of employees. These promotion schedules will under certain conditions result in career lives that are similar to those predicted by human capital theory, even though the mechanisms are quite different (Sørensen, 1977).

In wage competition, employees can change their earnings only by changing their performance. In vacancy competition, changes in earnings are generated by moves in mobility regimes that are chains of vacancies in internal labor markets. There is, in vacancy competition, no automatic correspondence between the creation of promotion opportunities and whatever changes take place in a person's productive capacity. Employees may be promoted without a preceding change in productivity, and a change in productive capacity need not result in a promotion. This means that the cross-sectional association between personal characteristics and earnings will be attenuated, even though personal characteristics are crucial for access to jobs. (A formal derivation of this conclusion and an empirical illustration is presented by Wise, 1975).

In vacancy competition, variations in earnings reflect variations in job characteristics and the organization of jobs in internal labor markets. This is in contrast to the situation in the neoclassical model of wage competition, where the primary source of variation is the variation in personal characteristics that determine a person's productive capacity. Some implications of these effects of open and closed employment relationships will be discussed next.

## Implications

The utility of the theory outlined here of matching persons to jobs may be suggested by the implications for issues related to research and policy on inequality in society. Some of these issues will be discussed to indicate the kind of analysis suggested by the framework presented here.

### Constraints on Growth in Earnings

The two polar models of the matching process suggest different constraints on a person's ability to increase his or her earnings. In wage competition, earnings directly reflect performance and hence the skills and abilities of a person. Increases in earnings then are obtained by increasing the skill level of a person, and the major constraint on growth in earnings will be limitations on acquiring additional human capital. In wage competition markets, the amount of training that can be provided in jobs will be low, since on-the-job training, as argued earlier, is a major cause of the emergence of vacancy competition. Hence, the major source of income inequality among persons lies outside the labor market—that is, in the educational and other training institutions that produce skill differentiation.

In vacancy competition sectors, the major constraint on the attainment of income is access to jobs. If no job is available, a person will not be able to obtain earnings. Growth in earnings is produced by the utilization of opportunities for mobility to better jobs, and this opportunity structure, not changes in skills, governs the earnings variations over time. The major source of variation in earnings is then the restriction of access to jobs and the level of derived demand that determines the availability of jobs.

The different constraints on growth in earnings in wage competition and job vacancy competition jobs imply that quite different policies will have to be used in an attempt to increase pretransfer earnings of poverty groups. In wage competition sectors, policies aimed at increasing skill levels either through schooling or—for those already having entered the labor market— through various off-the-job training programs would presumably be effective. In vacancy competition sectors such policies would be quite ineffective since such training would not make jobs available.

The rather limited success of worker training programs suggests that job vacancy competition indeed is predominant in the U.S. economy. More correctly, the fate of such programs suggests that it is indeed difficult to prepare low-skilled workers for jobs that demand high skill levels, since such jobs, as argued earlier, tend to be vacancy competition jobs.

### Educational Attainments and the Labor Market

In wage competition, changes in the supply of skills will produce changes in wage rates. For example, if the supply of highly skilled persons increases and the supply of low-skilled persons decreases, the wage rate for highly skilled persons should go down and the wage rate for low-skilled persons should increase.

In the human capital literature, educational attainment is used as a measure of skill level. The growth in educational attainment witnessed in the 1960s produced a marked change in the supply of highly skilled versus low-skilled workers. In wage competition sectors, one should then expect a decrease in income inequality.

In vacancy competition sectors, changes in wage rates are not affected by growth in educational attainments leading to an equalization of the distribution of education. It is a person's relative position in the distribution of education that counts. Since parents presumably are concerned about securing at least the same position for their offspring as they have achieved, growth in education will feed on itself as more and more education is needed to secure the same relative position.

The 1970s would appear to have been a crucial period for testing the implications of the two models for matching persons to jobs. If wage competition jobs are predominant in the economy, the rapid growth in educational attainments in the 1960s should have been accompanied by a decrease in the demand for higher education. If vacancy competition jobs are predominant, no such decrease should be observed. The evidence is ambiguous, however. It has been argued that a decrease in the demand for higher education levels indeed takes place as a result of a smaller wage differential between high school and college graduates (Freeman, 1976). On the other hand, it can be argued that the decline in enrollments is only temporary and reflects the disappearance of the incentive to attend college produced by the war in Vietnam in the 1960s (Suter, 1976).

## Class Conflict

We have argued that the emergence of vacancy competition does not necessarily reflect a lack of purposive behavior—particularly profit-maximizing behavior—on the part of employers. Instead, this matching process emerges as a result of increased employee control over the job derived from the training requirements of jobs and other sources of control.

Even if vacancy competition is an accommodation of employers to the features of job structures inducing employee control, it does not follow that employers will not try to change the structure of jobs to reduce employee control and secure the highest possible profits. An analysis of changes in job structures to reveal the extent of this practice constitutes a lacuna in the literature. From a Marxist perspective, Braverman (1974) has, however, argued that such changes constitute one of the major dimensions of class conflict in capitalist society.

Braverman (1974) argues that, contrary to popular belief, there has not been an upgrading of skills in the labor force, but a degrading, since activities associated with single (artisan) jobs have been spread over many jobs, reflecting the capitalist attempt to reduce worker control over the production process and maximize profits. The logic of such a skill-stripping of jobs follows directly from the features of wage and vacancy competition we have outlined.

The evidence for Braverman's (1974) argument is somewhat impressionistic. Particularly, the rise of semiskilled occupations is used to support his thesis because these occupations are argued to require much lower skill levels than the label seems to indicate. The rise of such occupational categories is indisputable, though it is uncertain how much variance in skill levels exists among semiskilled jobs. Also, semiskilled jobs are exactly the jobs where training on the job is predominant. Finally, as we have argued, there are sources of employee control other than the skill requirements of jobs. Particularly, the interdependence among jobs created by decomposing jobs into simple routine tasks may act as a counterforce both because of the employer's reduced ability to eliminate single jobs and because of the bases for collective action created by the interdependence.

It should be the case, though, that profit-maximizing employers will attempt to change job structures whenever possible to reduce the chances for vacancy competition jobs to emerge. The main constraint on their ability to do so is the introduction of new technologies that create on-the-job training requirements and the other sources of employee control analyzed earlier. Any uniform trend toward either one of the two polar models of matching persons to jobs therefore is unlikely to occur.

The argument about skill stripping is based on the assumption of profit-maximizing behavior of employers in the short run so that the equalizing of marginal productivities and wage rates in each time period must be achieved through the elimination of employee control over the job. If employers are assumed not to be profit maximizing in the short run, but to be concerned about long-term growth and dominance in product markets, then a uniform trend toward closed employment relationships can be argued. The reason is that predictability of markets—in particular, labor markets—becomes a major concern. Closed employment ensures a stable labor force with mutual concern of employees and employers for the survival and continued growth of the firm. Though closed employment may be inefficient in the short run in comparison with more wage competitive job structures, the long-term gains will outweigh the costs.

## Conclusion

This chapter has identified what we argue is a basic determinant of the earnings determination process in the matching of persons to jobs: the degree of control exercised by the employer versus the employee in controlling access to the job. Concrete employer control has been argued to produce the job structure assumed in the neoclassical wage competition model for the earnings determination process. Employee control, in contrast, has been argued to produce a matching process referred to as vacancy competition. The two matching processes have been argued to have quite different implications for a number of issues relating to the study of inequality and attainment processes in society.

The sources of employee bargaining power over control of the job are partly technological and partly social. The technological sources, including the technical division of labor (which of course may reflect employer interest in dominating the labor process), lead to a differentiation of jobs with respect to training requirements, where particularly the on-the-job training requirements have been argued to be an important source of employee control over the job. Uncertainty about productivity and supervisory costs have further been argued to provide sources of employee control. The job structures that are likely to emerge when employees have control over the job—in particular, the formation of promotion ladders as incentive structures—further reinforce these tendencies toward employee control. The major social source of control is collective employee action in the form of unions. Though unions are argued to be more likely to emerge when technology and the technical division of labor already include employee bargaining power over the employment relationship, the gains from unionization are greatest when these technical sources are absent.

The job structures identified in this chapter have many similarities to the dual labor market conception of matching processes. Vacancy competition structures are likely to be similar to the job structures identified as primary jobs (e.g., Doeringer & Piore, 1971). However, the dualist literature has a very descriptive character, and there is also some confusion as to whether the labor market segmentation is a segmentation of jobs or of persons (blacks, poor, and women in the secondary sector, white skilled workers in the primary sector). The main conclusion derived from this literature is that there are good jobs and bad jobs. The analysis presented in this chapter proposes a conceptual framework that identifies where closed employment relationships are likely to emerge and the reasons they emerge. Also, we have mentioned that high-paying jobs are not necessarily all vacancy competition jobs; for example, wage competition may be likely to emerge among managers.

The notion of vacancy competition is, as mentioned, close to Thurow's conception of job competition. However, in contrast to the analysis proposed in this chapter, Thurow relies exclusively on training requirements as a cause of job competition structures. True to the economists' image of the world, the nature of skills and their relation to productivity, not the bargaining power of the two parties to the matching process, is seen as the fundamental source of variation in job structures. We argue that the bargaining power that determines the emergence of open and closed employment relationships has sources other than just skill and training requirements.

The research task identified by this chapter is twofold. One set of activities would test the various hypotheses of the sources of closed employment relationships by focusing directly on the technical and social determinants of job security, voluntary job mobility, etc. The other set of activities would focus on testing the different implications of the different job structures for the earnings determination process. The framework for such research is already available for the wage competition model in the form of the earnings functions suggested by human capital theory. The development of parallel models for the vacancy competition model has only recently begun (e.g., Sørensen, 1977, 1979).

# References

Averitt, R. T.
  1968    *The Dual Economy*. New York: Norton.
Becker, G. S.
  1964    *Human Capital*. New York: National Bureau of Economic Research.
Bluestone, B.
  1970    "The tripartite economy: Labor markets and the working poor." *Poverty and Human Resources Abstracts* (5 March–April):15–35.
Braverman, H.
  1974    *Labor and Monpoly Capital*. New York: Monthly Review.
Cain, G. G.
  1976    "The challenge of segmented labor market theories to orthodox theory: A survey." *Journal of Economic Literature* 14:1215–1257.
Doeringer, P. B., and M. J. Piore
  1971    *Internal Labor Markets and Manpower Analysis*. Lexington, Massachusetts: Heath.
Freeman, R.
  1976    *The Overeducated American*. New York: Academic Press.
Gordon, D. M.
  1972    *Theories of Poverty and Underemployment*. Lexington, Massachusetts: Heath.
Kerr, C.
  1954    "The Balkanization of labor markets." In E. W. Bakke, P. M. Hauser, G. L. Palmer, C. A. Myers, D. Yoder, and C. Kerr (eds.), *Labor Mobility and Economic Opportunity*. Cambridge, Massachusetts: Technology Press of MIT.
Marx, K.
  1961    *Capital* (Vol. 1–3). Moscow: Foreign Language Press. (Originally published in English, 1887)
  1973    *Grundrisse*. (M. Nicolaus, Trans.) New York: Vintage Books. (Originally published in German, 1939)
Mincer, J.
  1974    *Schooling, Experience and Earnings*. New York: National Bureau of Economic Research.
O'Connor, J.
  1973    *The Fiscal Crisis of the State*. New York: St. Martin's.
Olson, M.
  1965    *The Logic of Collective Action*. Cambridge, Massachusetts: Harvard Univ. Press.
Sørensen, A. B.
  1977    "The structure of inequality and the process of attainment." *American Sociological Review* 42:965–978.
  1979    "A model and a metric for the analysis of the intragenerational status attainment process." *American Journal of Sociology* 85:361–384.
Spilerman, S.
  1977    "Careers, labor market structure, and socioeconomic achievement." *American Journal of Sociology* 83:551–593.
Stolzenberg, R. M.
  1975    "Occupations, labor markets and the process of wage attainment." *American Sociological Review* 40:645–665.
Suter, L. E.
  1976    "Trends in college enrollment in the post-Vietnam era." Paper presented at the American Sociological Association Meetings, New York City, August.

Thurow, L. C.
  1975    *Generating Inequality*. New York: Basic.
Weber, M.
  1947    [*The Theory of Social and Economic Organization*] (A. M. Henderson and T. Parsons, Trans.). New York: Oxford Univ. Press.
White, H. C.
  1970    *Chains of Opportunity: System Models of Mobility in Organizations*. Cambridge, Massachusetts: Harvard Univ. Press.
Wise, D. A.
  1975    "Personal attributes, job performance and probability of promotion." *Econometrica* 43:913–931.

# Part II

# FIRMS, OCCUPATIONS, AND LABOR MARKETS

# Chapter 4

# Economic Organization of Firms and Labor Market Consequences: Toward a Specification of Dual Economy Theory

*MICHAEL WALLACE*

*ARNE L. KALLEBERG*

In recent years, persons concerned with the determinants of socioeconomic achievement have emphasized the importance of "positional" attributes (e.g., industries, occupations, firms, class) in explanations of individual inequality. As a result, there has been a renewed interest among stratification researchers in what Marx (1867/1975) recognized as the uneven development of capital and, further, in how such features of the macroeconomy affect conditions of employment for individuals. One mechanism of structural differentiation originally discussed by Marx is what may be classified generally as the economic organization of firms in the capitalist system.

A theoretical framework for examining the dynamics of the economic organization of firms, and centering on the unevenness of the capital accumulation process among different corporate entities, is dual economy theory. Although the modern variant of this perspective evolved from a body

SOCIOLOGICAL PERSPECTIVES ON
LABOR MARKETS

of theoretical traditions ranging from institutional economics (e.g., Averitt, 1968; Galbraith, 1967, 1973) to neo-Marxism (e.g., O'Connor, 1973), an underlying thread of unity ties all these literatures to Marx's classical distinction between "big capitals" and "little capitals." Dual economy theory posits that there has been an historical trend toward the development of a dichotomous industrial structure and points to various features of the economic and social organization of production as primarily responsible for this development. Importantly, this theory also argues that a consequence of this trend has been the segmentation of the labor force and labor market along various dimensions ranging from occupational markets (Osterman, 1975; Piore, 1975; Rosenberg, 1975) to class positions (O'Connor, 1973; Wright, 1976) to racial and sexual divisions (Bonacich, 1976; Edwards, 1979). The emphasis on the relationship between economic segmentation and fragmentation of the working class makes dual economy theory a potentially useful complement to individually based theories of socioeconomic achievement, since it focuses on the linkages between the organization of firms at the macro level and the experiences of individuals who contend for rewards in the economic system. However, this aspect of the theory has been lacking in specificity, leading some to characterize recent research as being mired in a circularity of reasoning (see, e.g., Hodson & Kaufman, 1981) regarding the proper role of labor market structures in a broader theory of capitalist economic organization.

The current state of dual economy theory as it relates to consequences for labor market participation is in disarray. The theory is poorly specified, and, therefore, its utility for quantitative analyses of individual outcomes is dubious. Several dichotomous operationalizations of "monopoly" and "competitive" sectors (e.g., Beck, Horan, & Tolbert, 1978; Bibb & Form, 1977; Hodson, 1978) and one continuous measure based on factor scores (Tolbert, Horan, & Beck, 1980) have appeared in the published literature, but these definitions diverge from each other and their differences have not been systematically studied. Further, approaches to this issue in which individuals are categorized as being employed in particular economic sectors present a number of difficulties for understanding *how* characteristics implied by dual economy theory affect inequality.

First, the use of a dichotomous measure of industrial structure to represent the dualistic nature of capitalist enterprises, especially in individual studies of income inequality, is very simplistic. Such an approach vastly underestimates the diversity of macroeconomic factors that may impinge upon individual outcomes. It essentially undermines the richness of dual economy theory for specifying relationships between firm characteristics and labor market structures (cf. Kaufman, Hodson, & Fligstein, 1980). While the emphasis of dual economy theory on the historical development of monopolistic capital markets alongside traditional competitive capital may be accurate, the existence of discrete economic sectors should be treated as an empirical question, not as an a priori assumption.

Second, operationalizations of dual economy theory (e.g., Tolbert *et al.*, 1980) confound features of the economic organization of firms (e.g., firm concentration, profits, capital intensity) with characteristics of the labor force and labor market (e.g., average or median earnings, race, sex). The rationale underlying these operationalizations is that dual economy theory implies a correspondence between aspects of firms' economic organization and labor force consequences. The problem with this assumption is that, while these concepts are related, their correspondence is far from perfect. Indeed, one sign of the maturation of dual economy theory is the recent recognition by some authors that there is a conceptual distinction between economic sectors and labor markets although, empirically, they may overlap (for arguments in support of this distinction, see Althauser *&* Kalleberg, this volume; Edwards, 1979; Hodson, 1978). This recognition represents a significant advancement over earlier developments of the notion of dualism, such as that of Bluestone (1970), in which firm characteristics and labor market attributes were used almost interchangeably in descriptions of economic sectors. Indeed, while Bluestone's early work was seminal in that it reopened dual economy theory as a means for investigating specific consequences of labor market participation (such as urban poverty), it also served as the source of much of the current confusion between firm characteristics and labor market consequences.

These two criticisms call into question the validity of empirical studies that utilize a unidimensional measure to operationalize the dual economy. Instead of the uncritical acceptance of a bimodal industrial distribution along some single dimension, further attention should be devoted to the study of the dimensionality of the dual economy itself. Several questions are broached by the dual economy literature but are in need of fuller examination: What variables represent the essential mechanisms that propel capital structures to ever-greater inequities in size and importance in the economy? What features of labor market organization (at an aggregate level) are likely to be associated with these macroeconomic processes? What, if any, are the mediating processes by which the economic organization of firms shapes diverse labor market structures?

We will attempt to address several of these questions in this chapter. With the presentation of a set of cross-sectional analyses, we attempt to overcome some of the limitations of previous work and to proceed toward a fuller specification of dual economy theory. Our analyses attempt to evaluate the dimensionality of concepts from the dual economy literature and to make preliminary statements about relationships between the economic organization of firms and some representative labor market consequences. We further assess how these relationships are mediated by occupational structures that, arguably, could provide an alternative explanation for some outcomes, such as higher earnings, racial or sexual composition, or job stability. We finally indicate future directions for research on the dual economy and relate our analyses to future studies of the impact of dual economy on individual achievement.

## Dual Economy Theory: Concepts and Issues

Dualistic explanations of the macroeconomy have proceeded at two related, but conceptually distinct, levels. First, there is the dual economy proper literature, which pertains directly to the organization of firms and industries. Second, there is that branch of dual economy theory more properly referred to as "segmented labor market theory," which focuses on the structure of jobs and the experiences of individuals in jobs (see Althauser & Kalleberg, this volume; Kalleberg & Sørensen, 1979 for reviews of this literature). The distinction between these two sets of concepts reflects the distinction made in this chapter between two types of industrial-level variables: (*a*) those pertaining to the economic organization of firms; and (*b*) those that describe labor force and labor market characteristics. We argue that features of the economic organization of firms are reflected in labor market outcomes, but the correspondence is not as strong as has often been assumed. Since most attempts to justify a relationship between dual economy and dual labor market theories have been unsystematic, the theoretical justification for relating features of firm organization to labor markets has been weak and its empirical basis has been virtually ignored. In this section of the chapter, we first review some of the theoretical literature referring specifically to the economic organization of firms. Next, we maintain that the struggle for control of the work process has been one important means by which the effects of economic organization have been translated into specific labor market structures and consequences for the labor force. Then we relate this literature to that on segmented labor markets.

### *Economic Organization of Firms and Industries*

That branch of dual economy theory that has been primarily concerned with the economic organization of firms posits that there has been an historical trend in the economy toward a dichotomous structure of firms and industries: Averitt (1968) speaks of "center" and "periphery" firms, Galbraith (1973) of "planning" and "market" systems, and O'Connor (1973) of "monopoly" and "competitive" sectors. Although these authors owe much to previous theoretical and empirical work (e.g., Baran & Sweezy, 1966; Berle & Means, 1932; Bluestone, 1970; Chandler, 1962, 1977), we choose them as representatives of the dual economy perspective on the economic organization of firms.

## AVERITT

While the trend toward monopolization and the concomitant social and political power of large corporations had been noticed much earlier (see, e.g., Berle & Means, 1932), it was only recently that this issue became a prominent topic in economic and sociological circles. Averitt (1968) was among the first to use the term *dual economy* to describe the fragmentation of the American economic structure into qualitatively different economic sectors. In so doing, he identified one of the central tendencies in advanced capitalism. Averitt asserts that the forces of corporate segmentation cut along three primary dimensions: (*a*) the distinction between center and periphery firms; (*b*) the prevailing technical system of production in an industry; and (*c*) location in key or nonkey industries. For Averitt, the most important distinction by far is that between center and periphery firms; the dichotomy between large firms with substantial market power and small, competitive firms is the fulcrum upon which American business dualism rests.

Center firms differ from periphery firms on almost every imaginable criterion: "economic size, organizational structure, industrial location, factor endowment, time perspective, and market concentration [Averitt, 1968, p.1]." Averitt argues that center firms' distinctiveness "stems from their size and independence [p.105]," but the logic of his discussion hints at multiple origins of dualism. The most fundamental requisite that an aspiring center firm must possess is the ability to successfully adapt to its changing environment (cf. Chandler, 1962). One factor in the environment that must be exploited to its fullest potential is the *technical evolution of production*— that is, the changing capacity to meet production demands in the most technically efficient way possible. As more capital investment is made in modern machinery and equipment and as different stages of the production process are successfully integrated under one corporate roof, larger economies of scale prevail. Larger economies of scale necessarily mean larger economic size (in terms of average sales or average profits) and, concomitantly, the erection of barriers to entry for smaller firms.

Inevitably, confinement to a single industrial market places upper limits on firm growth. This leads large firms to diversify their financial assets beyond their mother industry, resulting in the emergence of the modern conglomerate corporation that spans many different industries. Typically, conglomerate acquisitions involve movement into more competitive and, usually, unrelated product areas where prospects for economic expansion are most viable. The urgency for diversification by center firms lends importance to a long-term perspective and, relatedly, the rise to prominence of managerial expertise. An important managerial talent is the ability to allocate and redistribute financial holdings among a variety of subsidiaries and corporate divisions. Center firms thus put a premium on attracting the highest-quality managerial personnel available.

The most tangible consequence of the prominence of the center firm for purposes of social and political power (not to mention labor market consequences) is the development of a high degree of market power (e.g., concentration) in many industries. For Averitt, this applies not only to consumer markets but also to the various linkages between center and periphery firms via factor and product markets. Many periphery firms are "forward" or "backward satellites" of more powerful center firms, on whom they depend either as a supplier of materials or as an outlet for their own products. Thus, the market concentration of center firms has a strong bearing on factor costs (including labor costs) and, ultimately, on consumer prices in a variety of markets.

Put succinctly, "The center firm is all that the periphery firm is not [p.8]" and vice versa. Periphery firms conform more readily to the neoclassical model of competitive capitalism. They exercise no autonomous influence, either individually or collectively, over market prices. Typically involved in a single product line or a series of related product lines, their investment strategies are governed by short-term profit considerations. To the extent that long-term planning is invoked, it is to anticipate the future actions of their suppliers or buyers—generally center firms.

Averitt recognizes that the state has some role in the organization of production. Among other things, it is seen as a seller of services, a buyer of products, a subsidizer of economic sectors, a regulator of firms, a provider of collective goods, an underwriter of minimum welfare, and the overseer of aggregate economic activity (p.155). However, these functions receive inadequate attention from Averitt. He contends that the primary role of the state is that of "the manager of aggregate demand, the guardian of national prosperity [p.173]," which is carried out through fiscal and monetary policies. While the strong inference could be made that state policies tend to favor center firms, this argument is not forcefully made by Averitt. Ultimately, he maintains that relationships between the state and both economic sectors are overshadowed by the interlocking nature of center–periphery linkages.

## GALBRAITH

Galbraith's (1973) distinction between the planning and market systems, while similar in origin to Averitt's discussion of center and periphery firms, differs in several of its particulars. While still stressing that the large corporation is the quintessential actor in the economy, Galbraith is intensely aware of the indeterminacy of the economic processes that contribute to dualism: "The change of which the corporation is the driving force is a complex process in which many things are altered at the same time and in which cause becomes consequence and cause again. No description is uniquely correct; much depends on where one breaks into this matrix [p.38]."

The point at which Galbraith chooses to break into the matrix is with technology and its resultant impact on the organization of the firm. As technology advances, says Galbraith, a greater gestation period is required between initial investment and realization of profits from a final product. Such investments will not be made by competitive firms in the market system, however, unless intervening processes, particularly prices, can be brought under control. In short, the firm must possess some modicum of market power before it will ever venture into costly technologies, which illustrates the indeterminacy of these processes from Galbraith's viewpoint.

Whatever its origins, the option to follow a policy of technological innovation has transformative consequences for the organizational structure of the firm. For Galbraith, greater discretion is placed in the hands of technical and managerial personnel to the point that ownership of capital becomes a secondary basis for industrial authority. As the organizational structure of the firm becomes more elaborate, "authority passes to the organization of the firm—to the technostructure of the corporation [p.40]."

Firms in the planning system wield such disproportionate power that they effectively undermine the principle of the neoclassical model that production should respond to consumer preferences. Corporate decisions in the planning system are entirely self-serving; they are made in accordance with the firms' "own protective purposes" (i.e., the maintenance of financial solvency) and its "affirmative purposes" (i.e., the enlargement of its economic size). Strategies for the accomplishment of these goals are often in direct conflict with the profit-maximizing strategies of competitive firms. For instance, firms in the market system are constrained to operate at an optimally efficient level; to operate above or below that scale of production would be to give an advantage to the competition. Firms in the planning system, however, recognize no upper limit on economic size, because they have effectively insulated themselves from the challenges of a competitive market. This underscores Galbraith's contention that the primary goal of firms in the planning system is not the making of profits per se (although a high volume of profits is a frequent result) but the perpetuation of the organization. This coincides with Averitt's (1968) observation that the center firm has become an "eternal" fixture of the social structure.

For Galbraith, the relationship between the planning system and the state further contributes to the dualistic nature of capitalist production. While formally an arbiter of the public purpose, the state plays an ever-larger role in accomplishing the objectives of the planning system. First, the formal machinery of democracy is more accessible to firms in the planning system. Second, the state serves as a market for goods that provides a stable source of income and profits, especially for the planning system. Third, the state creates various regulatory mechanisms (i.e., formal regulatory bodies, antitrust laws, etc.) that divert, but seldom thwart, the growth of large firms. Thus, in contrast to Averitt, Galbraith attributes a more direct role to the state in the coordination of production.

### O'CONNOR

The importance of the state for facilitating economic segmentation is the central feature of O'Connor's (1973) conceptualization of the dual economy. Like Bluestone (1970), O'Connor adopts the view that the state constitutes a third sector of production alongside the monopoly and competitive sectors. He places a major emphasis on the state's role in facilitating the capital accumulation process, especially for firms in the monopoly sector, which increasingly are seen as the "engine" (p.23) of national prosperity. In broad terms, the state provides two supporting functions for monopoly capital: (a) the encouragement of the conditions where *accumulation* of capital is possible; and (b) *legitimation*, or the maintenance of social harmony among conflicting groups in society. These functions are served in various ways: the purchase of products (e.g., military goods) from private enterprises, the socialization of the costs of production through taxation policies, and moderate redistribution of income through a myriad of transfer programs.

For O'Connor, the role of technology is not as indicative of the centrality of the monopoly sector to the economic system as is the state's willingness to socialize many of the costs of expensive technology for the monopoly sector. One means of doing this is to guarantee a market for goods from high-technology, capital-intensive industries. Another is to finance much of the infrastructural investment (e.g., highways, energy development) in return for partial regulation in such industries as transportation and public utilities. Such regulation serves primarily a legitimation function, providing the state with some control over prices and market development. But it also serves an important accumulation function by raising barriers to entry for potential competitors, thus ensuring regional monopolies in many of these industries.

Unlike Averitt or Galbraith, O'Connor makes noticeable strides toward an understanding of the labor market segmentation that results from dualism in the private sector. For instance, he contends that the key to wage inequality is the high capital-to-labor ratio in the monopoly sector. Capital-intensiveness contributes to higher worker productivity, which, in the neoclassical sense, should translate into higher earnings. But there are other factors leading to higher wages in the monopoly sector. Because of greater market concentration, prices are not directly tied to costs of production but rather are in accordance with a certain desired level of profits (an observation also made by Galbraith). The discretion over prices possessed by monopoly firms means that wage increases can be passed on to consumers through higher prices. In addition, the desire for stable production schedules requires that monopoly firms make their peace with labor. Monopoly firms, then, have both the economic wherewithal and a pragmatic motive for not resisting a union movement—and subsequent higher wages—with greater fervor. Indeed, O'Connor asserts that large sections of organized labor have entered into a tacit coalition with the monopoly sector to accomplish the mutual objectives of stabilizing demand and employment.

While O'Connor makes some progress toward an understanding of the linkages between the economic organization of firms and labor markets, it is not the main purpose of his work to develop a theory of income inequality. He does outline some of the structural determinants of wage inequality among the monopoly, state, and competitive sectors but pays little attention to other aspects of labor market segmentation. In effect, O'Connor tacitly adopts Bluestone's (1970) early view that economic sectors and labor markets correspond in a virtually one-to-one fashion. While O'Connor's analysis is insightful and well suited for his purposes of developing a model of the fiscal crisis of the state, we have already suggested some of its limitations for a detailed analysis of labor market consequences. Ultimately, we must examine the corpus of literature dealing specifically with the issues of labor market segmentation in order to develop a well-rounded theory of the dual economy.

## Economic Segmentation and the Problem of Control

Edwards and his colleagues (Edwards, 1975, 1979; Reich, Gordon, & Edwards, 1973) have pursued a long-standing interest in issues of control in the work place. They see much of the evolution of job structures in capitalist enterprises as a response by capitalists to crises of worker discipline. Specifically, labor market institutions emerge largely from attempts by capitalists to maximize quantitative and qualitative efficiency (cf. Gordon, 1976) and the resistance by workers to such attempts. Many of the outcomes of the labor process can be viewed, directly or indirectly, as by-products of this struggle for control in the work place.

Edwards (1979) argues that, as the forces of centralization and concentration of capital have pervaded larger sectors of the economy, techniques of control have changed to accommodate the challenge to worker discipline. In the early entrepreneurial firm—and in its modern vestige, the firm in the competitive sector—techniques of control were simple, personal, and frequently exercised at the discretion of the establishment's owner. Because of the physical nature of output in these enterprises, the work was directly overseen by the entrepreneur or a member of his family. Productivity was easily gauged so a tangible criterion for evaluation was readily available to the capitalist.

With the centralization of capital and the concomitant growth in the economic and employee size of the firm, it became impossible for a single person to directly oversee the entire production process. This resulted in the implementation of a system of hierarchical control in which authority was vested in layers of foremen and supervisory personnel. This system was based on the principle that "each boss . . . would re-create in his shop the situation of the capitalist under entrepreneurial control [Edwards, 1979, p.31]." This organizational innovation ensured vertical lines of communication leading directly to the capitalist, though the different segments of the production process were often not well coordinated. The cutting edge of hierarchical control was not, however, increased efficiency of production but rather the maintenance of the status quo in capitalist–worker relations: "However irrational it was from the standpoint of efficiency, hierarchical control constituted a 'rational' framework for the regular and permanent delegation of the capitalist's powers [Edwards, 1979, p.33]."

The forces of centralization pushed forward, and as they did, larger plant sizes and economic scale dictated new forms of work organization that were *structural* in form. In manufacturing industries, this period was marked by the introduction of the assembly line system that, according to Edwards, was the epitome of technical control of work. This system tied the worker to the work process by assigning him a role in a technically interdependent system of production. This relieved supervisors of the need to directly oversee the production process and simultaneously offered the advantage to employers of being able to control the pace of work and monitor output.

While the introduction of technical control overcame some of the limitations of simple (i.e., entrepreneurial and hierarchical) control, it became the source of other contradictions. First, it was not directly applicable to many nonfactory settings that accompanied the rise of the service economy in the United States. Further, its arbitrary and obtrusive nature led to increasingly open conflicts between labor and the representatives of capital, particularly in the factory setting. These conflicts, along with the growing geographic concentration of the work force, led to the growth of a viable labor movement. All this occurred at a time when the monopoly sector could ill afford a breach in labor discipline. Because a growing share of productive activity in a given market was controlled by a few large firms, a disruption of production in a single firm could create a regional economic crisis. According to Edwards (1979), after various attempts to undermine labor militancy by such practices as "welfare capitalism" and "scientific management," the monopoly sector settled on a policy of bureaucratic control that has been pervasive since World War II. (For a somewhat different view of the role of scientific management in the organization of capitalist work, see Braverman, 1974.)

Bureaucratic control differed from previous forms of control in that it was vested in the formal structure of the firm. In contrast to simple control systems rooted in the personal relationships between workers and bosses:

> Bureaucratic control is embedded in the social and organizational structure of the firm and is built into job categories, work rules, promotion procedures, discipline, wage scales, definition of responsibilities, and the like. Bureaucratic control establishes the impersonal force of "company rules" or "company policy" as the basis for control [Edwards, 1979, p.131].

This observation more adequately specifies the relationship between the production process and the primacy of the organization discussed by Averitt (1968) and Galbraith (1973). However, where they see autonomy of the giant corporation as an outgrowth, at least in part, of the *technical* relations of production (Averitt calls it the "evolution of technology"), Edwards sees this transformation as a consequence of the changing *social* relations of production between capitalists and workers. While it is not possible to adjudicate these two views in this chapter, our assumption is that, ultimately, the evolution of labor market structures rests on a dynamic synthesis of *both* the technical and social relations of production (cf. Kalleberg & Griffin, 1980).

The purpose of bureaucratic control from the standpoint of employers was to enhance the stability of output while de-emphasizing the importance of maximum quantitative efficiency. In contrast to the entrepreneurial firm, which must maximize the marginal productivity of workers to remain competitive, the bureaucratically organized firm seeks to direct the activities of its workers in such a manner as to implement a "minimal acceptable performance" for all workers rather than eliciting "peak performances" (Edwards, 1979, p.146). In this way, employers are guaranteed a desirable volume of profits with the least resistance from their labor force.

This parallels Galbraith's (1973) argument, discussed earlier, that large firms are not as interested in minimizing costs of production and/or maximizing profits as they are in preserving the long-range conditions for business prosperity (cf. Averitt, 1968; O'Connor, 1973). Moreover, it lends supporting evidence to Braverman's (1974) argument concerning the detailed division of labor and the organization of work. Braverman asserts that the detailed division of labor, aside from degrading the quality of work and contributing to worker alienation, had the additional effect of erecting a transcendent system of authority relations in the capitalist enterprise.

## Labor Market Segmentation

The struggle for control of the labor process has had transformative consequences for the organization of work and the evolution of job structures. Several empirical studies have documented this process. In a case study of the steel industry, for example, Stone (1975) points to the creation of a variety of institutional structures designed to ensure labor discipline: "hierarchical job ladders, limited ports of entry, inducements to stay on the job, job-specificity of skills, and a sharp division between the physical and mental aspects of work [p.75]." Stone emphasizes the importance of internal labor markets as a means for stabilizing labor supply with the lure of advancement in wages and/or authority. Further, she reiterates Edwards's point about the efficiency of such an organization of work:

> The creation of the internal labor market throughout American industry was the employers' answer to the problem of discipline inherent in their need to exert unilateral control over production. Were it not for that, a system of job rotation, or one where workers themselves allocated work, would have been just as rational and effective a way of organizing work [p.77].

Thus, the emergence of internal labor markets, especially in the monopoly sector, is a tangible consequence of the historical emergence of monopolistic firms and resultant control-related problems.

The internal labor market (Doeringer, 1967; Doeringer & Piore, 1971) plays a central role in segmented labor market theories. For workers, it is a vehicle to both higher wages and greater stability of employment, two of the characterizing features of what Piore (1970, 1975) terms the primary labor market. In contrast, conditions of employment in the secondary market, which is marked by the absence of internal markets, tend to be low-paid, with little possibility of advancement, and poorer working conditions. Consequently, secondary jobs are associated with considerable instability among both jobs and workers. Further, the highly personal relationship between workers and supervisors "leaves wide latitude for favoritism and is conducive to harsh and capricious work discipline [1975, p.126]." Thus, work in secondary markets exemplifies the social relations of production that Edwards (1979) associates with "simple control systems."

Piore divides the primary market into upper and lower tiers. The upper tier is marked by the presence of a large degree of personal autonomy for its jobholders; this is often the result of the very nature of their occupational activities. This suggests that, to some extent, labor market segmentation is occupationally based and may be independent of firm characteristics. But this argument begs the question of what role the centralizing tendencies of capitalism have had in the emergence of technical and professional occupations that make up the upper tier. This question, important as it is, must go unanswered for now. It is sufficient to say that internal labor markets for much of the upper tier of the primary market derive from occupational power and may therefore cut across industrial boundaries. Internal labor markets for the lower tier of the primary market (mainly white-collar clericals and blue-collar craftsmen and operatives) are embedded in the organizational structure of the firm and, therefore, tend to be industrially based (for a fuller discussion of these different types of internal markets, see Althauser & Kalleberg, this volume).

The historical separation between the primary and secondary labor markets is a pervasive feature of the American stratification system. Persons who are habitually employed in the secondary market are denied access to the better jobs of the primary market. Several mechanisms combine to screen certain workers from advancement to the primary market: inadequate training (both general and specific training), erratic work histories, and the lack of applicable on-the-job experience. Persons characterized by these traits are viewed by employers as unreliable or transient, thus reinforcing those behaviors in their employment patterns (Gordon, 1972).

Unions minimize some of these effects and, thus, ensure stable, gainful employment for their members. Unions are instrumental in securing training programs for their members, monitoring regular career advancement through internal labor markets, and forestalling job displacement via the seniority system. For these reasons, unions are often viewed as vehicles toward more job security and higher earnings as well as a more equitable labor market system. Unfortunately, unions, like employers, have traditionally discriminated against persons whom they regard as unemployable. In previous decades, large numbers of blacks were relegated to less desirable employment in the secondary market, thus increasing income inequality between black and white workers. Women have had marginal success in cracking the primary market, but they are typically employed in white-collar clerical and semiprofessional positions outside of what Levinson (1967) calls the "unionized sector." As a result, while often achieving occupational status comparable to men, women have experienced severe discrimination in job stability and earnings.

On this basis, several writers (e.g., Bonacich, 1976; Edwards, 1979; Gordon, 1972) have concluded that racial and sexual divisions in the work force constitute crosscutting barriers to equality in addition to those imposed by primary and secondary markets. Others (e.g., Szymanski, 1976) have even asserted that racial and sexual discrimination are functional substitutes for the capitalist, each generating a reserve army of cheap, underemployed labor.

One final factor contributing to labor market segmentation, particularly as it relates to issues of control, is class. Traditionally, Marxists have conceived of class in terms of the ownership or nonownership of the means of production. This single distinction defined two specific classes: the bourgeoisie (owners of capital) and the proletariat (nonowners of capital). Moreover, these class relations have been viewed as unassailable; even the gross transformations in the structure of capitalist production have done little to alter this two-class dichotomy according to some Marxists.

Increasingly, however, this view has been challenged by Marxists and non-Marxists alike. As noted earlier, Galbraith (1973) argues that with the growth of the planning system, the basis of corporate authority has shifted from ownership of capital to organizational technocracy. Edwards (1979) also documents the shift to a bureaucratic system of control, but he does not abandon class, conceived in terms of relations to capital and control of labor power, as the essential dimension of corporate authority. However, he does not adequately account for the transformation of class relations that has transpired as a result of the emergence of monopoly capitalism.

Wright and others (Wright, 1976; Wright & Perrone, 1977) have specified a model of the class structure of advanced capitalism. Building on the separation of ownership and control that has been so frequently cited by some as a sign of the erosion of capitalist class relations (the most celebrated advocate of this position is Dahrendorf, 1959), Wright argues that there has indeed been a qualitative shift in the structure of class relations but that this shift has ultimately strengthened the position of capital vis-à-vis labor. The major change in capitalist class relations, says Wright, is the emergence of a manager class, which serves as an intermediary between capital and labor. Managers, like workers, do not own the means of production; but as persons who control the labor power of others, they are considered representatives of capital in the work place. Several studies (e.g., Kalleberg & Griffin, 1978, 1980; Wright & Perrone, 1977) have documented the fact that managers enjoy significantly greater job rewards than do nonsupervisory workers.

O'Connor (1973) observes a macrolevel shift in the nature of class relations that is an additional consequence of the historical tendency toward dualism. As large unionized sectors have achieved greater social and political power, many of their vital concerns about productivity and the business cycle have come into closer alignment with the views of firms in the monopoly sector. Increasingly, he argues, the axis of conflict has shifted from capital versus labor to *big* capital and *big* labor versus *little* capital and *little* labor. Increasingly, then, the proliferation of large monopolistic unions represents an additional dimension of labor market segmentation.

## Implications of the Literature for Empirical Research

This review of the relevant dual economy literature is not intended to be exhaustive, but it does suggest that the tendency toward dualism has a multidimensional undercurrent. First, at the level of the economic organization of firms, several variables appear essential: market concentration, economic scale, profits, process of production, capital intensity, economic growth and the expansion of markets, and the role of the state, which itself is multidimensional. The three key aspects of state activity in the dual economy appear to be (a) the purchase of goods, primarily from the monopoly sector; (b) the regulation of some industries in the monopoly sector; and (c) direct political access, through the lobby process, of the monopoly sector to the democratic machinery of the state.

Second, at the level of labor market consequences, there are at least four major dimensions of segmentation that have crosscutting ramifications: (a) segmentation by primary and secondary markets (including segmentation within the primary market); (b) segmentation by class; (c) segmentation by sex; and (d) segmentation by race. In addition, several processes contribute to or amplify these divisions, including membership in unions, educational preparation, access to internal labor markets, and applicable work experience. All of these processes are intermediate to the outcomes of primary concern: stable employment and an adequate level of earnings.

The linkages among these various attributes are very complex, and our ability to specify concrete relationships is relatively underdeveloped. In any event, the number and diversity of the concepts derived from the dual economy literature emphasize that it should be thought of as a focusing tool rather than a precise description of the structure of the American economy. The dualistic framework provides a means for clearer specification of empirical hypotheses; whether monopoly and competitive sectors exist as dichotomous, disparate units should be regarded as an empirical question. In our subsequent analyses, we seek to measure the concepts implicated in dual economy theory and to examine their interrelationships as well as their associations with previously suggested dichotomous definitions of these two sectors. Our analyses are limited by the inability to operationalize all the variables that we ourselves regard as important. Most notably, we are unable to accurately categorize industries according to process of production, which Averitt emphasizes, nor are we able to classify industries by every dimension of their relationship to the state. At the level of labor market consequences, we are unable to develop a meaningful indicator of the class structure as it interacts with industry according to Wright and O'Connor.

## Operationalization of Dual Economy Concepts

### Data

Data were collected from a variety of sources for 68 major industry groups that were based on the 1967 Standard Industrial Classification (SIC) two-digit codes (U.S. Bureau of the Budget, 1967). The 68 industries used in the analysis are shown in the Appendix. The 1967 classification was chosen for two primary reasons. First, SIC categories are the basis of classification for corporate income tax returns and other sources that were used in the construction of variables. Second, the 1967 SIC index is the most recent one before the 1970 Census of Population from which many of the labor market variables were developed. Our analysis converges on the year 1970, although, in some cases, indicators were only available for years shortly before or after that year.

We use industries as our units of analysis although many of the assumptions of dual economy theory rest on the centrality of the firm as the relevant social actor. We believe, however, that our choice of industry as the unit of analysis is justified by the argument that firms must operate within the context of industrial structure (see Blauner, 1964; O'Connor, 1973; and especially Hodson, 1978, for arguments to this effect). While we agree with Averitt (1968) that diversified corporate structures may crosscut industrial boundaries, we do not see this as a debilitating argument against our approach. Besides the theoretical considerations, the choice of industries offers many strategic benefits for an analysis of the dual economy. In particular, government agencies, economists, sociologists, and business organizations typically collect data on firms that are aggregated to the industry level. In addition, most national data sets identify an individual's industry but not the name of the employer. To the extent it is possible, we incorporate a consideration of the firm: Our analysis explicitly deals with the economic organization of firms, and our variables reflect average firm characteristics, such as profits, size, and utilization of capital.

The 1967 SIC index originally contained 78 industries. However, five of them—four public sector industries and one miscellaneous category—were excluded from the analysis because of the nonavailability of some industrial data. Five more industries were collapsed into other existing classifications. The remaining 68 industries represent the entire private sector of the American economy.

## Variables

Variables were constructed from the available data that reflect concepts in the dualistic literature for both firms and labor markets. Indicators used in the construction of our final variables had to meet two criteria. First, they had to be conceptually similar in order to be included in the same measure. Second, they had to load together with these variables in an exploratory factor analysis of all indicators taken separately. (This factor analysis is not presented.) Values for these constructed variables were finally assigned to each industry. Because the metrics of the indicators differed widely and because some variables combined two or more indicators, the variables were constructed using $z$ scores. This permitted easy addition or subtraction of multiple indicators to create a scale measuring the desired concept. For example, our concentration variable involves the addition of three $z$ scores; for each of these, the industry's value was deviated from the mean score and divided by the standard deviation for all industries. Variables used in the analysis as well as sources of data are described below.

### ECONOMIC ORGANIZATION OF FIRMS

Our survey of the relevant literature as represented by Averitt (1968), Galbraith (1973), and O'Connor (1973) suggests six variables that are both relevant and capable of being measured from existing data. They are concentration, economic scale (i.e., average assets, sales, and profits), firm size (i.e., number of persons employed), capital intensity, the role of the state as a market of goods, and the state as a regulator of industry. Measures for these variables are given in Table 4.1. Most of the measures are fairly straightforward, with the possible exception of the state as regulator variable. This variable reflects the fact that industries that experience heavy government regulation often do so in exchange for state protection of their monopoly status, a point alluded to earlier. Thus, the two indicators GOVTREG and PCTNLFIRM are negatively correlated, resulting in the latter being subtracted from the former to create our measure of the state as regulator

TABLE 4.1

Economic Organization of Firms: Variable Construction and Sources[a]

| Concept | Indicator | Description | Source |
|---|---|---|---|
| Concentration | ASSRECT | Sales receipts by firms with over $100 million in assets divided by total sales receipts (1970) | U.S. Department of Treasury, 1974 |
| | CONRECT | Sales receipts by firms with over $5 million sales divided by total sales receipts (1970) | U.S. Department of Treasury, 1974 |
| | FOURFIRM | Four firm concentration ratio (1966) | Shepherd, 1969 |
| Economic scale | AVGASSET | Average assets for all firms (1970) | U.S. Department of Treasury, 1974 |
| | AVGUPROF | Average undistributed profits per firm (1970) | U.S. Department of Commerce, 1976 |
| | AVGRECT | Average receipts for all firms (1970) | U.S. Department of Treasury, 1973 |
| Firm size | MEDESTAB | Median establishment size (1970) | Freedman, 1976 |
| | SIZE | Average size of all businesses (1970) | U.S. Department of Commerce, 1976 (employees); U.S. Department of Treasury, 1974 (businesses) |
| Capital intensity | CAPINT | (Total costs of sales and operations minus total labor costs) divided by (number of employees) | U.S. Department of Treasury, 1973 (costs of sales and operations and cost of labor); U.S. Department of Commerce, 1976 (employees) |

| | | | |
|---|---|---|---|
| State as market | PCTTOTAL | Percentage of total industry goods and services purchased by the state (1967) | U.S. Department of Commerce, 1974a |
| | | | U.S. Department of Commerce, 1974b |
| | PCTFINISH | Percentage of finished industry goods and services purchased by the state (1967) | U.S. Department of Commerce, 1974a |
| | | | U.S. Department of Commerce, 1974b |
| State as regulator | GOVTREG | Dummy variable indicating whether an industry is heavily regulated by the state (1970) | Scherer, 1970 |
| | (-) PCTNLFIRM | Percentage increase in new large (> $5 million in sales) firms in an industry from 1965 to 1970 | U.S. Department of Treasury, 1974 |
| | | | U.S. Department of Treasury, 1968 |
| Beck | MONSECTOR1 | Dummy variable indicating placement in monopoly sector (1970) | Beck et al., 1978 |
| Bibb -- Form | MONSECTOR2 | Dummy variable indicating placement in monopoly sector (1970) | Bibb & Form, 1977 |
| Hodson | MONSECTOR3 | Dummy variable indicating placement in monopoly or state sector (1970) | Hodson, 1978 |
| Tolbert | OLIGOPOLY | Continuous variable score indicating capacity for oligopolistic behavior (1970) | Tolbert et al., 1980 |

[a] A minus sign in parentheses (-) indicates that this indicator was subtracted from the preceding one to create a given variable.

concept. Also shown in Table 4.1 are the variables used for the designation of monopoly versus competitive sectors as given in four previously published definitions of the dual economy.

## LABOR MARKET CONSEQUENCES

Our review of the literature has pointed to the possibility of several important consequences for labor market segmentation. The labor market variables, measured for each of the 68 industries, are as follows: average earnings, job stability, work experience, training, unions, sexual composition, and racial composition. These variables measure, with mixed degrees of precision, the concepts implicated in the labor market segmentation literature. Job stability, for example, with its emphasis on full-time employment, is a fairly close approximation of the defining characteristics of the primary market. Indeed, one of the components of this variable is a percentage of primary market employees in an industry according to Rosenberg's (1975) classification. Work experience, we would argue, is a proxy for internal labor markets; one of the components, average length of tenure with an employer, directly suggests the existence of (especially firm-based) internal markets. The other measures—earnings, racial and sexual composition, and training requirements—are also key concepts in explanations of labor market segmentation. Details of the construction of the labor market variables are presented in Table 4.2.

The inclusion of unions in the labor market section of the analysis does not violate the assumption that unions represent an important intervening mechanism between the economic organization variables and such labor market rewards as earnings and job stability. For the purposes of representing the structure of the dual economy, unions play an important role in mediating the effects of economic segmentation on labor market outcomes (see Kalleberg, Wallace, & Althauser, 1981). However, the ambiguity surrounding the role of unionization has not been resolved in the literature. In a study examining the sectoral structure of American industry, for example, Kaufman *et al.* (1980) argue with some justification that unionization is one of the key components of capital structure in an industry (what we here refer to as the economic organization of firms). However, the logic of the dual economy literature, we believe, is more in favor of including unions as a consequence variable than as a variable reflecting the economic organization of firms.

## OCCUPATIONAL STRUCTURE

One reasonable argument for why economic segmentation might result in particular labor market consequences is the intervening impact of occupational structure. If industries require special types of occupations to

TABLE 4.2

Labor Market Segmentation: Variable Construction and Sources[a]

| Concept | Indicator | Description | Source |
|---|---|---|---|
| Job stability | FTFYR | Percentage of employees working full time, full year (at least 40 hours a week and 50 weeks a year) (1970) | U.S. Census, 1970 |
| | PRIMKT | Percentage of persons in an industry employed in occupations designated as primary-sector jobs (1970) | Rosenberg, 1975 |
| | (-) PARTTIME | Percentage of employees working less than 20 hours per week | U.S. Census, 1970 |
| Work experience | TENUREM | Average job tenure for males (1972) | U.S. Department of Labor, 1973 |
| | (-) UNDER 25 | Percentage of persons under 25 years old (1970) | U.S. Census, 1970 |
| | LABFEXP | Mean years of labor force experience after end of formal schooling (1970) | U.S. Census, 1970 |
| Training | EDUC | Average years of schooling (1970) | U.S. Census, 1970 |
| | VOCTR | Percentage of employees with some vocational training (1970) | U.S. Census, 1970 |
| | AVGGED | Average GED[b] score for industries | U.S. Census, 1970 |
| Unions | PCTUNION | Percentage of employees who belong to unions (1970) | U.S. Department of Labor, 1973 |
| | PCTAFLCIO | Percentage of employees who belong to AFL-CIO affiliated unions (1970) | U.S. Department of Labor, 1973 |
| Sex | WOMEN | Percentage of employees who are women (1970) | U.S. Census, 1970 |
| Race | NONWHITE | Percentage of employees who are nonwhite (1970) | U.S. Census, 1970 |
| Earnings | EARN | Average earnings for employees (1970) | U.S. Census, 1970 |

[a] A minus sign in parentheses (-) indicates that this indicator was subtracted from the preceding one to create a given variable.

[b] GED: General Educational Development scores are estimates of the relative cognitive development necessary to perform adequately the occupation activity (see Temme, 1975).

carry on production, labor market consequences may be largely the result of characteristics of these occupations rather than the features of economic segmentation we have discussed. To evaluate this argument, we introduce major occupational groups in the later stages of the analysis to determine the degree to which the impact of the economic organization of firms on labor force consequences is mediated by occupational structure. Our operational measure of the occupational structure is the percentage of the industry's work force employed in each of 10 major occupational classifications: professionals, semiprofessionals and technicians, managers, office clericals, nonoffice clericals, sales workers, craftsmen, operatives, service workers, and laborers. (Details of this classification may be found in Freedman, 1976).

## Analysis

### DIMENSIONS OF THE DUAL ECONOMY

Our first analysis examines the dimensionality of the concepts that we have identified from dual economy theory. This explicitly addresses the question of whether these concepts may be represented by a single factor, which the various unidimensional operationalizations of the dual economy have implicitly assumed. As a prelude to this analysis, we present in Table 4.3 a correlation matrix of all variables in the chapter (with the exception of the occupational variables, which are used as controls). There are several interesting bivariate correlations, none of which are drastically out of line with dual economy theory. It is important to note that the two size measures (economic scale and firm size) show a virtually zero correlation, attesting to their conceptual uniqueness. Interestingly, the two state measures show a moderate negative correlation, indicating they might be operative in different domains of the monopoly sector, as we suspect they should be. Four of the seven labor market variables—unions, work experience, average earnings, and job stability—show moderate to strong positive correlations with many of the economic organization variables. Sex and race composition and training show no consistent pattern of relationship with the economic organization variables, suggesting that differences on these dimensions may be due largely to occupational differences. In Table 4.4, we present the results from a series of factor analyses of the correlations among both sets of variables given in Table 4.3. In Panel A, we present the results of a factor analysis of both the economic organization and labor force variables. The results—a five-factor solution accounting for 78.3% of the total variance—suggest that the relationships among the dual economy concepts are considerably more complex than a simple unidimensional definition of monopoly versus competitive sectors would imply. Nevertheless, these factors are interpretable from the standpoint of dual economy theory as outlined earlier. For example, there is almost a perfect separation between economic organization variables and labor market variables. The only exception is the first factor, which shows unions and the state as a market for goods loading together. This is not so surprising, however, given O'Connor's (1973) arguments about the alignment of interests between monopoly firms and organized labor. One focal point for this alignment has been with regard to state fiscal policy that could simultaneously stimulate productivity and reduce unemployment. This is one of the vital functions of the state as a market for goods: It serves the interests of both big capital and big labor. (For an analysis of this process as it pertains to military spending by the state, see Griffin, Devine, & Wallace, 1981.)

Factors II and V represent labor market factors, one centering on the racial dimension of segmentation and the other on the sexual dimension. Factors III and IV represent dimensions of the economic organization of firms. Factor III suggests that monopoly sector firms tend to be highly concentrated, employ large numbers of workers, and are subject to some state regulation. Factor IV emphasizes the relationship between technology (i.e., capital intensity) and the economic size of the firm as measured by average profits, assets, and sales. Moreover, the factor correlations emphasize the interrelatedness of the dual economy. All three economic organization factors (Factor I included) are positively, but slightly, correlated (after correcting for the direction of the factor loading). The biggest correlation between any two factors (Factors III and V) is .406, which suggests that large firms in concentrated industries are associated with fewer numbers of females and higher earnings.

Since these results may be tainted by the inclusion of economic organization variables and labor market variables in the same analysis, we present the results of factor analyses of economic organization variables only (Panel B) and labor market consequence variables only (Panel C). The results of these two analyses virtually replicate the findings of Panel A.

The factor analysis of the economic organization variables only yields a three-factor solution in which 78.7% of the total variance is explained. The first two factors are identical to Factors III and IV in the previous analysis. These results suggest a stable distinction, among other things, between employee size of an organization (firm size) and its economic size (economic scale). These two dimensions thus might have unique or different implications for studies of individual outcomes in the labor market, a possibility that has been ignored in past research. Without qualification, the third factor represents the influence of the state on economic activity. However, it is important to note that the two concepts, state as a market and state

TABLE 4.3

Correlation Among Industry Variables, $N = 68$

| Variables | | $X_1$ | $X_2$ | $X_3$ | $X_4$ | $X_5$ | $X_6$ | $Y_1$ |
|---|---|---|---|---|---|---|---|---|
| $X_1$ | Concentration | --- | | | | | | |
| $X_2$ | Economic scale | .325 | --- | | | | | |
| $X_3$ | Firm size | .500 | -.035 | --- | | | | |
| $X_4$ | Capital intensity | .450 | .424 | .153 | --- | | | |
| $X_5$ | State as market | .144 | -.012 | .121 | .164 | --- | | |
| $X_6$ | State as regulator | .564 | .056 | .349 | -.034 | -.250 | --- | |
| $Y_1$ | Unions | .547 | .068 | .404 | .310 | .455 | .161 | --- |
| $Y_2$ | Work experience | .449 | .198 | .540 | .309 | .103 | .210 | .502 |
| $Y_3$ | Training | -.018 | .049 | .056 | -.080 | .268 | -.125 | -.133 |
| $Y_4$ | Sex (1 = female) | -.263 | -.024 | -.232 | -.265 | -.004 | -.261 | -.395 |
| $Y_5$ | Race (1 = nonwhite) | -.003 | .123 | .015 | .178 | -.102 | -.012 | -.005 |
| $Y_6$ | Job stability | .496 | .180 | .306 | .253 | .209 | .176 | .481 |
| $Y_7$ | Earnings | .468 | .237 | .366 | .242 | .326 | .127 | .480 |
| $Z_1$ | Beck et al. | .640 | .105 | .304 | .273 | .298 | .366 | .412 |
| $Z_2$ | Bibb--Form | .629 | .108 | .411 | .314 | .400 | .216 | .718 |
| $Z_3$ | Hodson | .608 | .278 | .277 | .327 | .305 | .240 | .337 |
| $Z_4$ | Tolbert et al. | .756 | .455 | .344 | .497 | .221 | .204 | .504 |

as regulator, load in different directions. This might suggest the contradictory nature of much state activity in the economy, as suggested by O'Connor's distinction between accumulation and legitimation. Again, the correlations among the three dimensions of economic organization are small and positive, although the correlation between Factors I and III is practically zero.

The results of the factor analysis of just the labor market variables are consistent with much of the literature on labor market segmentation. It is important to note that earnings and job stability, the two key variables in that literature, load on both factors. Both variables load highly and in the opposite direction from percentage female on the first factor, and highly (and opposite) from percentage nonwhite on the second factor. These results lend support to the argument that there are pervasive racial and sexual

| $Y_2$ | $Y_3$ | $Y_4$ | $Y_5$ | $Y_6$ | $Y_7$ | $Z_1$ | $Z_2$ | $Z_3$ | $Z_4$ |
|---|---|---|---|---|---|---|---|---|---|
| --- | | | | | | | | | |
| -.192 | --- | | | | | | | | |
| .151 | .174 | --- | | | | | | | |
| -.446 | -.455 | .178 | --- | | | | | | |
| .514 | .288 | -.579 | -.493 | --- | | | | | |
| .375 | .370 | -.475 | -.406 | .789 | --- | | | | |
| .416 | .267 | -.279 | -.141 | .485 | .466 | --- | | | |
| .537 | -.037 | -.573 | -.082 | .632 | .630 | .609 | --- | | |
| .383 | .099 | -.215 | -.039 | .467 | .400 | .609 | .514 | --- | |
| .568 | .147 | -.412 | -.054 | .655 | .545 | .710 | .661 | .675 | --- |

divisions in the labor market (Bonacich, 1976; Edwards, 1979). Moreover, they are consistent with, but of course do not confirm, Szymanski's (1976) argument that women and blacks often serve as functional substitutes as sources of low-paid labor. Additionally, the analysis suggests distinct bases of discrimination between women and nonwhites (mainly blacks). From Factor I, we suggest that women are excluded from "good" jobs on the basis of their relative (to men) lack of work experience and their relative exclusion from those sectors of the labor market that are highly unionized. These findings are consistent with arguments for the absence of internal labor markets or job shelters (Freedman, 1976) in sectors of the economy that employ large numbers of women. Blacks, on the other hand, appear from Factor II to be deprived of better jobs because of their relative (to whites) lack of training. Overall, these results suggest that blacks may be denied

## TABLE 4.4

Oblique Rotations of Factor Matrixes Produced by Principal Components Factor Analyses of the Correlation Matrixes for the Industry Variables, $N = 68$[a]

| Variable/factor | I | II | III | IV | V | $h^2$ | | Correlations among factors | | | | |
|---|---|---|---|---|---|---|---|---|---|---|---|---|
| | | | | | | | | I | II | III | IV | V |
| A. All industry variables | | | | | | | | | | | | |
| Concentration | --- | --- | -.757 | --- | --- | .758 | I | --- | | | | |
| Economic scale | --- | --- | --- | .762 | --- | .353 | II | -.124 | --- | | | |
| Firm size | --- | --- | -.548 | --- | --- | .521 | III | -.155 | -.015 | --- | | |
| Capital intensity | --- | --- | --- | .598 | --- | .475 | IV | .224 | .016 | -.199 | --- | |
| State as market | --- | --- | -.811 | --- | --- | .435 | V | -.240 | .070 | .406 | -.192 | --- |
| State as regulator | .582 | --- | --- | --- | --- | .581 | | | | | | |
| Unions | --- | --- | --- | --- | --- | .611 | | | | | | |
| Work experience | --- | --- | --- | --- | -.438 | .646 | | | | | | |
| Training | --- | -.753 | --- | --- | --- | .539 | | | | | | |
| Sex (1 = female) | --- | --- | --- | --- | .812 | .585 | | | | | | |
| Race (1 = nonwhite) | --- | .714 | --- | --- | --- | .547 | | | | | | |
| Job stability | --- | -.511 | --- | --- | -.645 | .827 | | | | | | |
| Earnings | --- | -.516 | --- | --- | -.400 | .722 | | | | | | |
| Eigenvalues | 4.28 | 2.09 | 1.48 | 1.24 | 1.08 | | | | | | | |
| Percentage total variance | 32.9 | 16.1 | 11.4 | 9.6 | 8.3 | | | | | | | |
| Percentage factor variance | 47.5 | 20.8 | 12.9 | 10.1 | 8.7 | | | | | | | |

B. Economic organization variables

| | I | II | III | | |
|---|---|---|---|---|---|
| Concentration | .810 | --- | --- | .655 | --- |
| Profits/scale | --- | .733 | --- | .250 | .181 |
| Firm size | .600 | --- | --- | .301 | .030 |
| Capital intensity | --- | .605 | --- | .331 | .113 |
| State 1 | --- | --- | .524 | .203 | |
| State 2 | .745 | --- | .591 | .518 | --- |
| Eigenvalues | 2.18 | 1.41 | 1.13 | | |
| Percentage total variance | 36.4 | 23.5 | 18.8 | | |
| Percentage factor variance | 55.6 | 28.9 | 15.5 | | |

C. Labor market variables

| | I | II | | |
|---|---|---|---|---|
| Unions | .670 | --- | .444 | --- |
| Work experience | .746 | --- | .575 | -.113 |
| Training | --- | -.730 | .534 | |
| Sex (1 = female) | -.661 | --- | .439 | |
| Race (1 = nonwhite) | --- | .694 | .493 | |
| Job stability | .776 | -.503 | .943 | |
| Earnings | .639 | -.508 | .741 | |
| Eigenvalues | 3.16 | 1.79 | | |
| Percentage total variance | 45.1 | 25.7 | | |
| Percentage factor variance | 68.2 | 31.8 | | |

[a]Factor loadings less than |.400| are not shown.

access to the entry-level positions in primary markets (Doeringer & Piore, 1971; Gordon, 1972), whereas women are denied the opportunity to advance once having gained entry.

Our results in this analysis can be compared favorably to one other factor analytic study of the dual economy. Oster (1979) factor analyzed 25 variables in an attempt (similar to ours) to determine the underlying dimensions of the dual economy. The factor analysis he presents, however, is more similar to the exploratory analysis that we used to construct variables. To be strictly comparable with our approach, it would have been necessary for Oster to use the results from his analysis to construct conceptually relevant variables and to enter these variables into a second-order factor analysis. This was the procedure used in the present analysis. Nevertheless, after entering variables measuring both the economic organization of firms and labor market consequences, Oster finds a three-factor solution. He interprets the first factor as a dual economy factor and the other two as sex and race factors, respectively. Oster's analysis further supports our hypotheses that economic segmentation is multidimensional and that labor market components are conceptually distinct from economic organization variables.

## COMPARING UNIDIMENSIONAL DEFINITIONS OF DUAL ECONOMY

In our next set of analyses, we examine three dichotomous definitions (Beck et al., 1978; Bibb & Form, 1977; Hodson, 1978) and one continuous measure of dual economy (Tolbert et al., 1980) with respect to the variables identified here as components of the dual economy theory. These all assume that the variables derived from dual economy theory may be represented by a single dimension; all three (with the exception of Hodson's) further assume that such a representation adequately taps the effects of industrial structure on income inequality. Hodson's (1978) classification, strictly speaking, is not a dichotomous scheme, since he explicitly places some traditional private sector industries in the state sector. We believe, however, that, without doing a disservice to his classification, it is safe to place such industries in the monopoly sector for purposes of the analyses in this chapter (especially since we include state influence variables explicitly as regressors in our models).

We first note (from Table 4.3) that the correlations among these three definitions across our 68 industries are considerably less than unity: The highest bivariate correlation between any two definitions is .710 (between Beck et al. and Tolbert et al.) and the lowest correlation is .514 (between Bibb–Form and Hodson). Further, all four definitions show moderate correlations with each of the six economic organization variables in addition to suspiciously high correlations with many of the labor market variables.

The differences among these definitions, however, caution us against accepting any of them uncritically and point to the need to examine which of the dual economy variables each definition is tapping. A criterion of what would constitute a good unidimensional definition of dual economy would be one that adequately taps all (or most) of the economic organization variables while not being too dependent on the labor market variables. Such a definition would be suitable for analyses of individual income inequality because it would be suggestive of the complexity of the macro forces in the industrial structure but not be contaminated by the labor market factors that are strongly correlated with individual earnings.

In Table 4.5 we present the regressions of each of these four definitions on (a) the economic organization variables; and (b) the economic organization variables *and* the labor market variables. As can be seen, none of the definitions meets the above criterion of adequacy if the goal is to create an encompassing unidimensional typology of the dual economy. However, there is some commonality among the definitions. All four measures appear to be tapping the concentration variable, and all, with the exception of Tolbert *et al.*'s continuous measure, implicate the state as a market for goods. At this point, however, the definitions diverge. The definitions of both Beck *et al.* and Tolbert *et al.* are heavily influenced by some of the labor market variables, especially training and work experience. Bibb–Form reflects earnings, sexual divisions in the labor market, and the impact of unions. Hodson's definition shows a positive effect of job stability and a negative impact of unions. Further, when controlling for labor market variables, three of the definitions (Beck *et al.*, Bibb–Form, and Tolbert *et al.*) reflect the impact of additional economic organization variables, but they are in the unexpected direction. Most of these additional effects are the opposite of what would be expected from looking at simple bivariate correlations (shown in Table 4.3).

The results in Table 4.5 indicate there is some shared notion that the dual economy centers on concepts of market concentration and the role of the state as a purchaser of goods. Hodson's measure comes closest to reflecting all (or most) of the economic organization variables without being too dependent on the labor market variables. But even it fails to tap several important dimensions of the dualist conception of economic segmentation. These results underscore the conclusions reached in the previous section: Dual economy theory implies a diverse and interrelated set of concepts that are not likely to be well represented by a single measure. For broad purposes of assessing macro trends in the evolution of American capitalism, the issues raised here are probably less important. However, if the goal is to assess the structural impact of economic organization on individual inequality (a purpose for which several of these measures have been used), a unidi-

TABLE 4.5

Standardized Coefficients From Regressions of Four Definitions of Dual Economy on Industry-Level Variables, $N = 68$

| Independent variable | Dual economy variable[a] | | | | | | | |
|---|---|---|---|---|---|---|---|---|
| | Beck et al. | | Bibb & Form | | Hodson | | Tolbert et al. | |
| Concentration | .594**** | .646**** | .614**** | .461**** | .574**** | .571**** | .807**** | .794**** |
| Economic scale | -.106 | -.199** | -.086 | -.073 | .097 | .058 | .195 | .175 |
| Firm size | -.074 | -.310*** | .097 | -.041* | -.023 | -.056 | .030 | -.113+ |
| Capital intensity | .024*** | .009* | .014**** | -.137*** | -.006*** | -.033*** | .033 | -.061 |
| State as market | .248*** | .152 | .274 | .178* | .221 | .308 | .032*** | -.004**** |
| State as regulator | .125 | .121 | -.090 | -.152* | -.026 | -.019* | -.264 | -.308 |
| Unions | | -.024**** | | .193 | | -.251 | | -.007*** |
| Work experience | | .413**** | | .052 | | .102 | | .217*** |
| Training | | .412**** | | -.046**** | | -.002 | | .258**** |
| Sex (1 = female) | | -.146 | | -.324 | | -.020 | | -.269**** |
| Race (1 = nonwhite) | | -.031 | | .107 | | .098* | | .084* |
| Job stability | | -.221 | | .069* | | .314 | | .181** |
| Earnings | | .054 | | .181 | | -.089 | | -.181 |
| Adjusted $R^2$ | .421 | .535 | .463 | .707 | .373 | .371 | .648 | .790 |

\* $p \leq .20$
\*\* $p \leq .10$
\*\*\* $p \leq .05$
\*\*\*\* $p \leq .01$

[a] Measures for Beck et al.; Bibb-Form; and Hodson coded 1 = monopoly sector, 0 = competitive sector. Tolbert et al. is a continuous measure, with high value being more oligopolistic.

mensional measure of dual economy does not sufficiently capture the complex interrelationships among these concepts. Moreover, there is a tendency for some of these measures to be highly associated with variables that refer to labor market consequences, particularly variables that are highly correlated with earnings, the dependent variable of major interest in most individual-level studies of socioeconomic achievement. This suggests that, indeed, many of these definitions are biased by a circularity of reasoning between economic organization variables and labor market variables (see also, Hodson & Kaufman, 1981).

## EFFECTS OF ECONOMIC ORGANIZATION OF FIRMS ON LABOR MARKET CONSEQUENCES

In the previous sections, we have investigated some of the issues concerned with the dimensionality of the dual economy. Briefly, our analyses have suggested that the dual economy implies a multidimensional set of concepts, some at the level of the firm or industry and others associated with segmentation of the labor market. Moreover, our analyses have suggested that any unidimensional definition of the dual economy is likely to be deficient in tapping all the relevant dimensions. Having made a conceptual distinction between the economic organization of firms and labor force consequences, we here investigate the impact of the former on the latter.

Before turning to these analyses, however, it is important to note the results of some analyses that are not reported in this chapter. We considered that one major intervening variable between the firm variables and labor market variables might be the occupational structure of an industry. Thus, we attempted to assess the impact of the economic organization of firms on occupational structure. First, we divided the occupational structure into the 10 major occupational groups discussed earlier in the chapter. Then, taking each of the three dichotomous measures of dual economy mentioned earlier (Beck *et al.*, 1978; Bibb & Form, 1977; Hodson, 1978), we assessed the distribution of occupations in monopoly and competitive industries according to all three definitions. Some occupational groups, such as technical workers, managers, clerical workers, and laborers, appeared fairly stable across sectors according to all three definitions. Professionals, sales workers, and service workers were more numerous in the competitive sector, whereas crafts and operative workers were more frequently represented in the monopoly sector.

In order to get a better understanding of these relationships, we examined the association between our occupational groups and the economic organization of firm variables. This was accomplished by regressing the percentage of workers in each occupational group for an industry on the economic organization variables. In general, the impact of our economic organization variables was surprisingly low, with $R$ squares for the occupational groups ranging from .046 for managers to .362 for sales workers. Overall, the results of these unreported analyses indicated that the economic organization of firms has a relatively trivial impact on the distribution of major occupations in an industry. We remain cautious in interpreting these results, however, as it is possible that the level of aggregation of our occupational groups and/or our SIC industrial groupings account for the weakness of these particular models. In any event, these analyses are not central to the theme of this chapter; our main purpose in introducing occupational structure is to use it as a control variable in assessing the net impact of the economic organization variables on various labor market outcomes.

In Table 4.6, we present (in Panel A) the standardized coefficients obtained from regressing each of the labor market variables on the economic organization measures. Panel B presents the standardized coefficients from equations that control for occupational differences by including as regressors the percentage of workers in 9 of the 10 major occupational groups (percentage of managers is the excluded category). The coefficients for the occupational categories are not shown. Differences in the coefficients in these two panels address the question of the degree to which the total economic organization effects are mediated by the occupational measures. Differences in the (adjusted) $R^2$s in the two panels indicate the increase in explained variance when the occupational groups are added as regressors.

Our findings are quite interpretable from the standpoint of dual economy theory. For average earnings, four of our economic organization variables have significant effects in the expected direction. Two of these effects, economic scale and firm size, become smaller and nonsignificant when occupational structure is controlled. This indicates—at least among industries—that the effects of firm and economic size on earnings are mediated by occupational structure. Two other effects, concentration and the state as a market for goods, remain strong even after controlling for occupation. The concentration effect supports previous research by economists (e.g., Dalton & Ford, 1977; Weiss, 1966); the effect of the state supports the expectations of (particularly Marxist) interpretations of the dual economy (e.g., Hodson, 1978; O'Connor, 1973). As shown by the increment to $R^2$, occupational distributions do explain a significant portion of the variance in average earnings.

Our measure of job stability, both theoretically and in its method of construction, can be viewed as a proxy for the primary labor market. Our analysis indicates that concentration has the strongest impact on job stability, both before and after controlling for occupation. This supports the argument of dual economy theorists that one of the by-products of market concentration is the desire of employers to secure stable factor and product

TABLE 4.6

Standardized Coefficients From Regressions of Labor Market Variables on Economic Organization Variables (Panel A) and Controlling for Occupational Structure (Panel B), $N = 68$

| Independent variable | Dependent variables | | | | | | |
|---|---|---|---|---|---|---|---|
| | Unions | Work experience | Training | Sex | Race | Job stability | Earnings |
| **Panel A** | | | | | | | |
| Concentration | .459**** | .132 | -.001 | .076 | -.177 | .496**** | .363**** |
| Economic scale | -.100 | .115**** | .147 | .104 | .081 | .036 | .159* |
| Firm size | .138 | .471 | .092* | -.122*** | .077* | .087 | .204 |
| Capital intensity | .068**** | .139 | -.201** | -.334*** | .233 | -.017 | -.057*** |
| State as market | .347 | -.002 | .266** | -.014** | -.114 | .102 | .235*** |
| State as regulator | -.052 | -.031 | -.105 | -.282 | .036 | -.111 | -.100 |
| Adjusted $R^2$ | .418 | .310 | .026 | .086 | -.028 | .205 | .267 |
| **Panel B** | | | | | | | |
| Concentration | .373*** | .251* | .153 | -.165 | -.020** | .423**** | .327*** |
| Economic scale | -.027 | .144**** | -.013 | .033 | .204** | -.015 | .107 |
| Firm size | .062* | .496**** | .010 | .010 | .198 | -.045 | .069 |
| Capital intensity | -.169**** | -.047 | .048* | .036 | -.006 | -.068 | -.088** |
| State as market | .346 | -.070 | .138 | -.021*** | -.035* | -.001 | .188 |
| State as regulator | -.024 | -.112 | .068 | -.256 | -.198 | .068 | .118 |
| Adjusted $R^2$ | .573 | .561 | .670 | .730 | .510 | .673 | .619 |

markets. This includes the desire to achieve a stable supply of competent labor, which is accomplished by providing inducements for workers to stay on the job. This analysis best addresses the issues concerning the overlap between sectors and markets. Our analysis suggests there is indeed an overlap between these two concepts, but nothing approaching a perfect correspondence.

The analyses involving unions suggest that the tendency of unions to locate in an industry is a consequence of two primary factors, concentration and the state as a market for goods. According to the increment to $R^2$, the relationship between occupational structure and unions is relatively weak (the main occupations that are unionized are crafts and operatives). These analyses indicate that, to the extent a unionized sector exists (Levinson, 1967), it is a consequence of prior structural arrangements in the organization of production.

Firm size (in terms of persons employed) has the strongest influence on work experience (which includes a component relating to average tenure with a given employer). This tends to implicate the existence of internal labor markets in large firms, supporting, for example, Stolzenberg's (1978) analysis at the individual level. Additionally, we find that when controlling for occupation, concentration and economic scale also have moderate impacts on work experience. Since many internal markets are occupationally based (Althauser & Kalleberg, this volume), the analysis in Panel B suggests that firms in concentrated industries and/or having a large economic size (economic scale) may be negatively related to occupational internal labor markets. Occupational structure thus suppresses the relationship between concentration–economic scale and work experience; controlling for occupation reveals these positive direct effects of concentration and scale on work experience. This finding, among others, would be obscured by the adherence to a single measure of dual economy.

Panel A of the regressions for training appears to indicate (by the low $R^2$) that economic organization has relatively little impact on training requirements. It does show, however, that industries that sell goods to the state recruit a more highly educated labor force than do other industries. Training requirements are also higher in industries that are not capital intensive. This probably reflects the fact that professional and technical workers, who are highly educated, tend to be employed in competitive industries with low capital intensity. In any event, when occupational structure is controlled (Panel B), the effect of capital intensity becomes nonsignificant. Only the effect of the state as a market for goods remains significant. The large increment to $R^2$ indicates that a good portion of the variance in training is explained by occupational structure, which conforms to the general wisdom of past stratification research.

As expected, both sexual and racial composition are largely dependent on occupational structure (as evidenced by the increments to $R^2$). Women tend to be excluded from work in capital-intensive industries (probably largely because of their historical exclusion from unions in the heavy manufacturing industries), whereas blacks tend to be more frequently employed in such industries. Women are also less frequently employed in monopolistic firms that are subject to heavy state regulation (a factor that contributes to lower proportions of both women *and* blacks after occupation is controlled). The effects of capital intensity for both women and blacks are mediated by occupational structure (Panel B). After occupation is controlled, the analysis indicates that women are less frequently employed in concentrated industries, which is consistent with much of the dual economy literature. Blacks, however, tend to be employed in firms that are large in both economic and employee size, which does not readily conform with dual economy theory. Our interpretation of this finding is that, while blacks may tend to be employed in large, profitable firms—a relatively surprising finding—this is somewhat offset by the existence of occupations in such firms that are not conducive to the employment of blacks.

To summarize the results in this section, we found that each of our economic segmentation variables has significant effects on one or more labor market outcomes that past research has seen as relevant. This attests to the importance and uniqueness of each of these concepts. Many of these effects remained strong after controlling for occupation, others were mediated through occupation, and still others are suppressed when occupation is not controlled. Importantly, training requirements, sexual composition, and racial composition vary greatly among occupational categories, as suggested by much of the literature. On the other hand, economic segmentation variables have strong and substantially unmediated effects on unions, work experience, job stability, and earnings. We interpreted work experience as evidence for the existence of internal labor markets and job stability as denoting the presence of primary labor markets. In this way, our findings have further implications for current stratification research on labor market segmentation and its impact on individual outcomes. Economic organization variables should be included alongside occupation and class as *separate* indicators of positional inequality in future studies of individual inequality.

## Conclusions

In this chapter we have attempted to deal quantitatively with several issues related to the specification of dual economy theory. We have examined the dimensionality of the concepts implied by the theory, evaluated existing unidimensional definitions of the dual economy, and assessed the relationships (controlling for occupational structure) between economic organization and labor market structures.

From this analysis we can draw several conclusions relevant for the utility of dual economy theory in future research. First, dual economy theory implies a multidimensional array of concepts that are causally interrelated. As would be expected from our survey of the dual economy literature, any attempt to portray the complexities of these processes with a single measure of monoploy–competitive sectors is likely to be incomplete. In order to optimize the utility of dual economy theory, researchers should look upon it as an agenda for analyzing the structural dynamics of firm organization and the resultant impact on labor market outcomes (see, e.g., Kaufman et al., 1980).

Second, while there is substantial overlap between the economic organization of firms and labor market consequences, this relationship is in need of further specification. It is clear that there is not a perfect correspondence between economic sectors and labor markets, as has been assumed in some past research. Some labor market variables, notably sex and race, exhibit much less dependence on industrial characteristics than the dual economy literature would suggest. Other consequences, such as earnings and job stability, are probably influenced by such intermediate labor market mechanisms as unions and internal markets.

Third, the major relationships between economic organization and labor market consequences hold even after the effects of occupational structure are controlled. This suggests that such variables as concentration, firm size, scale, and the role of the state might prove useful for studies of individual achievement, since they would complement the use of other positional variables (e.g., occupation, class) in such studies.

Finally, we note some of the limitations of our analyses in hopes of advancing future research in this area. We have used rather broad definitions of industry and occupation in order to accommodate the data that were available. Future research should attempt to analyze data at a more detailed level than the classifications used here. Further, we have not examined the causal relationships among the economic organization variables and/or the labor market variables. Analyses that further address the causes and consequences of concentration, for example, would provide greater insight into the origins and maintenance of the dual economy. Finally, we have limited our analyses to cross-sectional differences among industries. This approach was suitable for our purposes of assessing dimensionality and broaching preliminary hypotheses about the relationship between economic organization and labor force consequences. However, dual economy theory is an inherently dynamic model that necessitates longitudinal data for a more thorough analysis.

## Appendix A: SIC Classification of Industries

*SIC*
*code*     *Industry name*

| | |
|---|---|
| 01 | Agricultural production |
| 07 | Agricultural services and hunting and trapping |
| 08 | Forestry |
| 09 | Fisheries |
| 10* | Metal mining |
| 11* | Anthracite mining *and* |
| | Bituminous coal and lignite mining |
| 13 | Crude petroleum and natural gas |
| 14 | Mining and quarrying of nonmetallic minerals |
| 15 | Building construction—general contractors |
| 16 | Other construction—general contractors |
| 17 | Construction—special-trade constructors |
| 20 | Food and kindred products |
| 21 | Tobacco manufacturers |
| 22 | Textile mill products |
| 23 | Apparel and other fabric products |
| 24 | Lumber and wood products, except furniture |
| 25 | Furniture and fixtures |
| 26 | Paper and allied products |
| 27 | Printing, publishing, and allied industries |
| 28 | Chemicals and allied manufacturing |
| 29 | Petroleum and related manufacturing |
| 30 | Rubber and miscellaneous plastics |
| 31 | Leather and leather products |
| 32 | Stone, clay, glass, and concrete products |
| 33 | Primary metal industries |
| 34 | Fabricated metal products |
| 35 | Machinery, except electrical |
| 36 | Electrical machinery, equipment, and supplies |
| 37 | Transportation equipment |
| 38 | Professional, scientific, and controlling instruments |
| 39* | Miscellaneous manufacturing *and* |
| | Ordnance |
| 40 | Railroad transportation |
| 41 | Local and interurban transportation |
| 42 | Motor freight transportation and warehousing |
| 44 | Water transportation |
| 45 | Air transportation |
| 46 | Pipeline transportation |
| 47 | Transportation services |
| 48 | Communication |
| 49 | Electric, gas, and sanitary services |
| 50 | Wholesale trade |
| 52 | Retail—building materials and farm equipment |

* Two two-digit SIC industries have been combined into one classification.

| SIC code | Industry name |
|---|---|
| 53 | Retail—general merchandise |
| 54 | Retail—food stores |
| 55 | Retail—automotive dealers and service stations |
| 56 | Retail—apparel and accessory stores |
| 57 | Retail—furniture and home furnishings |
| 58 | Retail—eating and drinking places |
| 59 | Retail—miscellaneous stores |
| 60 | Banking |
| 61 | Credit agencies other than banks |
| 62* | Security and commodity brokers *and* Holding and other investment companies |
| 63* | Insurance carriers *and* Insurance agencies, brokers, and services |
| 65* | Real estate *and* Combinations of real estate, loan, and law offices |
| 70 | Hotels and other lodging places |
| 72 | Personal services |
| 73 | Miscellaneous business services |
| 75 | Automotive repair and services |
| 76 | Miscellaneous repair services |
| 78 | Motion pictures |
| 79 | Other amusement and recreation services |
| 80 | Medical and other services |
| 81 | Legal services |
| 82 | Educational services |
| 84 | Museums, art galleries, and zoological gardens |
| 86 | Nonprofit membership organizations |
| 88 | Private households |
| 89 | Miscellaneous services |

# Acknowledgments

We wish to thank the following persons for their helpful comments on previous versions of this paper: Howard Aldrich, Robert Althauser, James Baron, Daniel Cornfield, Larry Griffin, Randy Hodson, and Teresa Sullivan.

# References

Averitt, R. T.
  1968   *The Dual Economy: The Dynamics of American Industry Structure.* New York: Norton.
Baran, P., and P. Sweezy
  1966   *Monopoly Capital.* New York: Monthly Review Press.

Beck, F. M., P. M. Horan, and C. M. Tolbert III
  1978  "Stratification in a dual economy: A sectoral model of earnings determination."
        *American Sociological Review* 43:704–720.
Berle A. A., and G. Means
  1932  *The Modern Corporation and Private Property.* New York: Macmillan.
Bibb, R., and W. H. Form
  1977  "The effects of industrial, occupational, and sex stratification on wages in blue-collar
        markets." *Social Forces* 55:974–996.
Blauner, F.
  1964  *Alienation and Freedom.* Chicago: Univ. of Chicago Press.
Bluestone, B.
  1970  "The tri-partite economy: Labor markets and the working poor." *Poverty and Human
        Resources Abstracts* 5:15–35.
Bonacich, E.
  1976  "Advanced capitalism and black/white race relations in the United States: A split
        labor market interpretation." *American Sociological Review* 41:34–51.
Braverman, H.
  1974  *Labor and Monopoly Capital.* New York: Monthly Review Press.
Chandler, A. D., Jr.
  1962  *Strategy and Structure.* Cambridge, Massachusetts: MIT Press.
  1977  *The Visible Hand.* Cambridge, Massachusetts: Belknap.
Dahrendorf, R.
  1959  *Class and Class Conflict in Industrial Society.* Stanford, California: Stanford Univ.
        Press.
Dalton, J. A., and E. J. Ford, Jr.
  1977  "Concentration and labor earnings in manufacturing and utilities." *Industrial and
        Labor Relations Review* 31:45–60.
Doeringer, P. B.
  1967  "Determinants of the structure of industrial type internal labor markets." *Industrial
        and Labor Relations Review* 20:206–220.
Doeringer, P. B., and M. J. Piore
  1971  *Internal Labor Markets and Manpower Analysis.* Lexington, Massachusetts: Heath.
Edwards, R. C.
  1975  "The social relations of production in the firm and labor market structure." In R.
        Edwards, M. Reich, and D. Gordon (eds.). *Labor Market Segmentation.* Lexington,
        Massachusetts: Heath.
  1979  *Contested Terrain.* New York: Basic Books.
Freedman, M. K.
  1976  *Labor Markets: Segments and Shelters.* Montclair, New Jersey: Allanheld.
Galbraith, J. K.
  1967  *The New Industrial State.* Boston: Houghton.
  1973  *Economics and the Public Purpose.* Boston: Houghton.
Gordon, D. M.
  1972  *Theories of Poverty and Underemployment.* Lexington, Massachusetts: Heath.
  1976  "Capitalist efficiency and socialist efficiency." *Monthly Review* 28:19–39.
Griffin, D. J., J. A. Devine, and M. Wallace
  1981  "Monopoly capital, organized labor, and military expenditures: Military Keynesianism
        in the United States, 1949–1976." *American Journal of Sociology*, in press.
Hodson, R. D.
  1978  "Labor in the monopoly, competitive, and state sectors of production." *Politics and
        Society* 8:429–480.

Hodson, R., and R. Kaufman
    1981  "Circularity in the dual economy (Comment on Tolbert *et al.*)." *American Journal of Sociology*, 86:881–887.
Kalleberg, A. L., and L. J. Griffin
    1978  "Positional sources of inequality in job satisfaction." *Sociology of Work and Occupations* 5:371–401.
    1980  "Class, occupation, and inequality in job rewards." *American Journal of Sociology* 85:731–768.
Kalleberg, A. L., and A. B. Sørensen
    1979  "The sociology of labor markets." *Annual Review of Sociology* 5:351–379.
Kalleberg, A. L., M. Wallace, and R. P. Althauser
    1981  "Employer power, worker power, and income inequality." *American Journal of Sociology*, in press.
Kaufman, R., R. D. Hodson, and N. D. Fligstein
    1980  "Defrocking dualism: A new approach to defining industrial sectors." Paper presented at National Science Foundation Conference on the Structure of Labor Markets and Socioeconomic Stratification, University of Georgia, Athens, March 3–5.
Levinson, H.
    1967  "Unionism, concentration, and wage changes: Toward a unified theory." *Industrial and Labor Relations Review* 20:198–205.
Marx, K.
    1975  *Capital* (S. Moore and E. Aveling, trans.). New York: International Publishers. (Originally published, 1867).
O'Connor, J.
    1973  *The Fiscal Crisis of the State*. New York: St. Martin's.
Oster, G.
    1979  "A factor analytic test of the theory of the dual economy." *Review of Economics and Statistics* 61:33–39.
Osterman, P.
    1975  "An empirical study of labor market segmentation." *Industrial and Labor Relations Review* 28:508–523.
Piore, M. J.
    1970  "Jobs and training." In S. H. Beer and R. E. Barringer (eds.), *The State and the Poor*. Boston: Winthrop.
    1975  "Notes for a theory of labor market segmentation." In R. Edwards, M. Reich, and D. Gordon (eds.), *Labor Market Segmentation*. Lexington, Massachusetts: Heath.
Reich, M., D. M. Gordon, and R. C. Edwards
    1973  "A theory of labor market segmentation." *American Economic Review* 63:359–365.
Rosenberg, S.
    1975  "The dual labor market: Its existence and consequences. Unpublished doctoral dissertation, University of California.
Scherer, F. M.
    1970  *Industrial Market Structure and Economic Performance*. Chicago: Rand McNally.
Shepherd, W. G.
    1969  "Market power and racial distribution in white collar employment." *Antitrust Bulletin* 14:141–161.
Stolzenberg, R. M.
    1978  "Bringing the boss back in: Employer size, employee schooling, and socioeconomic achievement." *American Sociological Review* 43:813–828.

Stone, K.
  1975  "The origins of job structures in the steel industry." In R. Edwards, M. Reich, and
         D. Gordon (eds.), *Labor Market segmentation*. Lexington, Massachusetts: Heath.
Szymanski, A. J.
  1976  "Sexism and racism as functional substitutes in the labor market." *Sociological Quar-
         terly* 17:65–73.
Temme, L.
  1975  *Occupation: Meanings and Measures*. Washington, D.C.: Bureau of Social Science
         Research.
Tolbert, C. M., P. M. Horan, and E. M. Beck
  1980  "The structure of economic segmentation: A dual economy approach." *American
         Journal of Sociology* 85:1095–1116.
U.S. Bureau of the Budget
  1967  *Standard Industrial Classification Manual*. Washington, D.C.: US Govt Printing Office.
U.S. Department of Commerce
  1974a  *Input–Output Structure of the U.S. Economy, 1967*. Washington, D.C.: US Govt Print-
          ing Office.
  1974b  *U.S. Survey of Current Business* (February). Washington, D.C.: US Govt Printing
          Office.
  1976  *National Income and Product Accounts of the United States, 1929–1974*. Washington,
         D.C.: US Govt Printing Office.
U.S. Department of Labor
  1973  *Job Tenure of Workers*. Washington, D.C.: US Govt Printing Office.
  1976  *Handbook of Labor Statistics, 1976*. Washington, D.C.: US Govt Printing Office.
U.S. Department of the Treasury
  1968  *Statistics of Income: Corporation Returns, 1965*. Washington, D.C.: US Govt Printing
         Office.
  1973  *Statistics of Income: Business Returns, 1970*. Washington, D.C.: US Govt Printing Office.
  1974  *Statistics of Income: Corporation Returns, 1970*. Washington, D.C.: US Govt Printing
         Office.
Weiss, L. W.
  1966  "Concentration and labor earnings." *American Economic Review* 56:96–117.
Wright, E. C.
  1976  "Class boundaries in advanced capitalist societies." *New Left Review* 98:3–41.
Wright, E. C., and L. Perrone
  1977  "Marxist class categories and income inequality." *American Sociological Review*
         42:32–55.

# Chapter 5

# Firms, Occupations, and the Structure of Labor Markets: A Conceptual Analysis

*ROBERT P. ALTHAUSER*

*ARNE L. KALLEBERG*

Wage and income inequality and movement among jobs have long been of common interest to sociologists and economists. Until recently, though, most of the sociologists either concentrated on occupational stratification and mobility (e.g., Blau & Duncan, 1967) or tried to specify the hypotheses of classic stratification theories (Abrahamson, 1973; Broom & Cushing, 1977; Collins, 1971; Stinchcombe, 1963; Stinchcombe & Harris, 1969; Wright & Perrone, 1977). In contrast, economists debated the merits of neoclassical theories of marginal productivity and described the operation of neoclassical as opposed to institutional or segmented labor markets (Cain, 1976; Edwards, 1975; Kerr, 1950, 1954; Osterman, 1975; Thurow, 1975; Wachter, 1974). Sociologists paid only passing attention to labor markets (Caplow, 1954; Form & Huber, 1976; Stinchcombe, 1965), whereas economists largely ignored occupations (Stolzenberg, 1975).

Signs of a greater exchange between sociologists and economists are now apparent. Some economists (Osterman, 1975; Piore, 1975; Edwards, 1979) have incorporated conceptions of social class in their analyses. Sociologists (Stolzenberg, 1975, 1978; Bibb & Form, 1977; Spilerman, 1977; Beck, Horan, & Tolbert, 1978; Hodson, 1978) have operationalized and analyzed measures of economic sectors or labor markets and drawn, for hypotheses or interpretation of findings, on theoretical ideas developed by institutional econ-

SOCIOLOGICAL PERSPECTIVES ON
LABOR MARKETS

omists (Dunlop, 1957, 1966; Kerr, 1950, 1954), dual labor market theorists (Doeringer & Piore, 1971; Piore, 1975), dual economy theorists (Averitt, 1968; Bluestone, Murphy, Stevenson, 1973), and radical economics theorists (reviewed by Gordon, 1972b). This chapter will focus on such concepts as internal labor markets, primary and secondary labor markets, and core or center and periphery firms or economic sectors.

As new empirical work is organized around these concepts, two problems undermine the cumulation and corroboration of findings and the further development of theory: (a) inadequate definitions of concepts, particularly of internal labor markets; and (b) confounding different levels of labor market stratification—the levels of firms or economic sectors, job or labor markets, and demographic groups in the labor force (Gordon, 1972b, pp.134–135).

The first problem originates in the broad, multidimensional character of the definitions of internal, primary, and secondary labor markets so far adopted (Doeringer & Piore, 1971; Dunlop, 1957, 1966; Kerr, 1950, 1954). We show that widely adopted operational definitions of two of these concepts (internal labor markets = job ladders, seniority rights; primary markets = stable jobs) are inconsistent with the original, broad definitions. These inconsistencies accent the need to redefine these labor market types. In response we propose a typology of five labor markets. Each component market is defined and justified in view of the problems evident in a preceding discussion of literature.

The second problem originates in the largely unargued and unwise assumption that these three levels of stratification overlap nearly perfectly— that is, that center firms employ primary workers (prime-age white males) in primary jobs, while periphery firms hire secondary workers (minority group workers, teens, and women) for secondary jobs. This emphasizes the need to distinguish more precisely between the operation of diverse labor markets on the one hand and the impact of firm or economic sectors on the other. We propose a framework in which economic sectors and labor markets have origins and consequences largely independent of each other.

Finally, we explore briefly the implications of our theoretical arguments for future research, with emphasis on the location or measurement of types of labor markets and their consequences.

## Labor Markets: A Generic Concept

The use of the term "labor market" implies that there is enough uniformity of behavior among certain workers and among certain employers to warrant generalizations about the actions of each [Kerr, 1954, p.92n].

Writers have used the term *labor markets* to refer to such geographic areas as local, urban, or ghetto markets (see, e.g., Rees & Shultz, 1970; Vietorisz & Harrison, 1973), occupational groups (e.g., retail clerks in Talbert & Bose, 1977; Stolzenberg, 1975), and ethnic and racial groups (e.g., Bonacich, 1972, 1976). Their definitions may refer (*a*) to jobs with prevailing or at least comparable wage levels (see, e.g., Bonacich, 1976, p.36; Kerr, 1950, p.278); (*b*) to jobs in geographic, occupational, or industrial areas within which workers can move with comparative freedom; or (*c*) to both.

We prefer a more abstract definition. Labor markets are arenas (Freedman, 1976) in which one or more of the following are similarly structured: employment, movement between jobs, development and differentiation of job skills, or wages (in their own right or as functions of skills, social status, experience, and other determinants). The boundaries of markets depend on a writer's interests and theoretical perspective. That multiple markets exist, in contrast to a single national competitive labor market, is largely accepted and even consistent with opposing theoretical perspectives (e.g., neoclassical versus neoinstitutional economics) (Cain, 1976; Holt, MacRae, Schweitzer, & Smith, 1971; Wachter, 1974). Still, uniform terminology has been elusive so far, at least for the generic concept of labor market.[1]

## Definitions

### INTERNAL LABOR MARKETS

The concept of internal markets emerged from the postwar attempts by labor economists to articulate structured, institutional labor markets in contrast to classical or neoclassical models of perfect and imperfect markets (see Kerr, 1950). A market's structure or boundary was defined by institutional rules and administered by employers, craft groups, or unions that governed such employment relationships as recruitment, hiring, training, and pricing of workers.

Each structured market had within it an internal and external market (Kerr, 1954, p.101n), connected only by specific positions termed *ports of entry*. Workers in the external market could be viewed as residents of occupational or geographic arenas that supplied internal markets located in the same arena. Once part of an internal market, incumbents who moved

---

[1] Kerr (1950) distinguished two usages of the term *labor market:* wage market (characterized by similar wage rates) and job market (the area within which workers can change jobs). Although this chapter focuses on jobs and job structures, we wish to avoid the confusion that would result if we referred to markets defined by these characteristics as job markets. Hence we use the generic term *labor markets.*

beyond these entry ports (entry-level sales, clerical, union, or managerial jobs) enjoyed shelter from outside competition and, at most, limited competition from fellow workers. Subsequent job movement might be horizontal (e.g., members of some craft unions move across employers), vertical (up and down ladders of promotion within a firm), or a mixture of both.

Though incorporating many of the elements of internal markets, Doeringer and Piore (1971) elaborated further the concept of an internal labor market (ILM), drawing on their interviews with officials of 24 manufacturing concerns. Their stress on variation in the scope and structure of ILMs is significant for our purposes. They argued that ILMs vary in the degree of openness to the external markets as indicated by the number and location of entry ports and by more or less restrictive qualifications or requirements for entry. The typical plant confined entry jobs to a relatively few positions that required low levels of skill but ranged from entry through a single job (a *closed* ILM) to an extremely high proportion of entry jobs relative to all jobs in a market (an *open* ILM: examples are the men's garment and shoe industries; Doeringer & Piore, 1971, pp.42–43).

ILMs also have different internal structures, a fact that is indicated by the number of different levels of skills or responsibility encompassed in a *mobility cluster* (job ladders on which employees are promoted, demoted, transferred, or laid off; Doeringer & Piore, 1971, p.50) and by the breadth or range of jobs at a given level of skill within a cluster. Clusters may be either broad (e.g., plant-wide, industry-wide, or national in scope) or narrow (e.g., limited to a single department; some are limited to a single line of progression that is only one job classification wide; Doeringer & Piore, 1971, p.51).[2]

Finally, ILMs differ in the relative importance of seniority versus ability (or its surrogate) in determining different kinds of job movement (upward, downward, lateral, or layoff). Typically ILMs use both criteria. For promotions, ability is the most commonly used criterion; for layoffs, seniority is the most common (Doeringer & Piore, 1971, p.211; Wachter, 1974, p.647).

Doeringer and Piore (1971, pp.2–4) distinguished two different types of internal markets:

1. Jobs in a firm may constitute a single *enterprise market*, but in many instances, these broadly defined labor markets are further divided into internal *submarkets* (Doeringer, 1967, p.208; Dunlop, 1966, p.46) according to managerial, clerical, production, maintenance, and other occupational categories. Each is an internal market in its own right.

---

[2] Note that clusters of jobs may be defined differently for promotions, demotions, and lateral transfers (Doeringer & Piore, 1971, p.54). Our concern in this chapter is with the first type of job cluster (i.e., for promotions).

2. Yet some (managerial and craft) jobs are found in markets that may span more than one establishment. Managerial markets reach across several plants within a corporation. Craft markets, which represent the other *occupational internal labor markets* (Doeringer & Piore, 1971, pp.3–4) reach across employers, industries, and even geographic areas within the jurisdiction of a union.[3]

## PRIMARY LABOR MARKETS

Primary labor markets consist of a "series of internal markets" whose jobs "possess several of the following traits: high wages, good working conditions, employment stability and job security, equity and due process in the administration of work rules, and chances for advancement [Piore, 1970, p.55]." Piore broke down this market into two tiers (1975, pp.126–129). Mobility chains or job ladders along which employees progress toward jobs with higher pay and status are common to both tiers. Lower tier jobs are seen as routine and often repetitive and are associated with "elaborate . . . work rules and formal administrative procedures." In contrast, upper tier jobs offer more security and autonomy, higher pay and status, and greater opportunities for promotion; but they demand more initiative and creativity. A great deal of mobility and turnover is found here, but it is associated primarily with advancement.[4]

## SECONDARY LABOR MARKETS

In secondary labor markets, jobs "tend to involve low wages, poor working conditions, considerable variability in employment, harsh and often arbitrary discipline, little opportunity to advance [Piore, 1975, p.55]," and considerable turnover but no mobility chains or job progressions. Secondary markets are mixtures of ILMs and jobs outside ILMs (Doeringer & Piore, 1971, p.169). Three distinct employment situations define this market (Doeringer & Piore, 1971, pp.167–169): (*a*) completely unstructured competitive markets; (*b*) secondary ILMs (open markets with many entry ports and few, if any, steps on promotion ladders; examples include stitching and

---

[3] It is worth remembering the caveat offered by these authors: "Because the research upon which this volume is based focused primarily upon blue collar employment in manufacturing, the concepts and applications presented have particular relevance for this sector [Doeringer & Piore, 1971, p.2]." The extent to which these authors' conception of ILMs fits white-collar occupants of such markets is open to question.

[4] Piore also suggested that lower tier jobs entail learning processes confined to specific productive traits, whereas productive traits for upper tier jobs are deduced from general principles acquired from instruction. This argument is not essential to subsequent discussion here. He also associated middle-class membership with upper tier jobs, the working class with lower tier jobs, and the lower class with secondary market jobs. This argument appears entirely separable from his main line of argument (see Osterman, 1975, p.511).

pressing jobs in apparel factories);[5] and (c) jobs attached to internal labor markets that fall below the entry-level jobs of an ILM and are found in plants in which most of the remaining jobs are primary.

As Doeringer and Piore (1971, p.166) pointed out, the terms *primary* and *secondary* are poorly chosen, because most writers use them to distinguish "primary" workers (with major family responsibilities, who, thus, are seeking advancement, job stability, and higher pay) from "secondary" workers (who are not seeking permanent jobs and are indifferent to uninteresting or unattractive work). The parallel between jobs and workers is freely drawn by dual labor market theorists, because they stress the reciprocal causation between job characteristics and workers' attributes and attitudes. This argument supports a key assertion of the theory, namely, that many occupants of jobs in this market are trapped (Osterman, 1977, p.221) and unable to move into the primary market. Despite the parallel, we will use these terms to refer to characteristics of *jobs*, not workers. This treatment is consistent with dual labor market theory's stress on the distinction between "good" and "bad" jobs rather than on skilled and unskilled workers (Wachter, 1974, p.638).

## Concepts in Use: A Critical Review

We now turn to interpretations of these concepts in more recent works. We find that some writers narrow these broadly defined concepts by seeing a few selected features as essential or distinctive. This situation is unsurprising, because concepts invite such treatment when they are characterized by multiple attributes that are assumed to occur together.

What problems does this pose? In general, diverse interpretations of these concepts are logically inconsistent. Of course, explicit and deliberate departures of treatments from the broad concepts as originally developed may well be warranted. But the often subtle and implicit departures we will describe can grow through a chain of citations to unsubtle misrepresentations that are incoherent and increasingly inconsistent with each other and the original concepts.

### ILM = FIRM LABOR MARKET

Perhaps the most pervasive departure from the original equates an internal market with a labor market contained wholly within a firm. Some examples are explicit. Stolzenberg (1978, pp.817–818) stated that the "internal market exists entirely within a single firm" and that "internal markets

---

[5] Note that Gordon (1972a, p.204) describes these same jobs as illustrations of *secondary* blue-collar *work*.

can exist only in large organizations" (see also Edwards, 1975, p.5). Spilerman (1977) identified ILMs "with a situation in which seniority entitlements bind a firm to its workers and workers to the firm [italics, p.583]." Neoclassical writer Wachter (1974) blandly stated: "It is generally agreed . . . that the internal market consists of a set of structured employment relationships within a firm [p.642]." More often, the equation is left implicit.[6]

Yet for Doeringer and Piore, both enterprise and craft jobs could be associated with ILMs. Craft employment can span different employers and, as in managerial ILMs, different plants owned by a single employer. Dunlop (1966) spoke directly to this point: "All internal labor markets should not be presumed to be analogous to those in industrial plants [p.36]." In short, in the original conceptions some ILMs span single firms; others—submarkets within single firms—divide along occupational or functional (production maintenance) lines. Only in a few cases will all jobs in a single firm or plant comprise a single ILM.[7]

## ILM = JOB LADDER

Many writers have argued that the mobility cluster, or vertical job ladder of positions, is the distinctive internal, structural feature of ILMs. Policies of promotion from within require this feature. For Spilerman (1977, pp.560,583), *career lines* (defined as "collections of jobs in which there is a high probability of movement from one position to another") have the features of ILMs. Similarly, Williamson, Wachter, and Harris (1975, pp.256–276), following Doeringer and Piore (1971, pp.15–16), defined an ILM as a progression of jobs with complementarity of skills and experience. Idiosyncratic tasks[8] are a crucial feature of this complementarity. Such tasks

---

[6] For example, Robert Hall (1974, p.689) argues that mobility data provide evidence of entry into good jobs above the entry-level jobs of internal markets. This seems inconsistent with the ILM conception that access is restricted to entry-level jobs (and contrary, he suggests, to the hypothesis that secondary workers are trapped in their market). But the argument *assumes* that ILMs equal firm labor markets.

[7] Of course, this equation makes more sense if we consider Japanese ILMs. The broad conception of ILMs reviewed here generally differs from conceptions of ILMs in the literature on dual labor markets in Japan and in underdeveloped countries (Evans, 1973; see also Dore, 1974). Furthermore, the Japanese apparently have no counterpart to occupational *internal* labor markets to act as bridges between firms (Azumi, 1969, pp.44–45). At most, occupational labor markets (to be defined later) may exist and may act as bridges between small and medium-sized firms (Okamoto, 1974).

[8] More generally, there are "equipment idiosyncrasies, due to incompletely standardized, albeit common, equipment, the unique characteristics of which become known through experience"; communication idiosyncrasies with respect to information channels and codes that are of value only within the firm"; and others, all of which can provide present experienced

involve job-specific and hence firm-specific skills. This makes employee turn-over costly to employers.

The first difficulty with this equation of ILMs with job ladders is that the vertical dimensions of ladders vary. When they are long, then indeed jobs are "differentiated by levels of skill. . . . Work on one job develops the skills required for the more complex tasks on the job above it [Doeringer & Piore, 1971, pp.58–59]." But this line of progression is, after all, only *one* type of internal labor market structure (1971, p.58). Job ladders may also be short, as in the secondary ILMs (1971, p.167) or open ILMs of the garment and shoe industries, where the skills of each job are independent of other jobs' skills (1971, pp.58–59). Second, progressions up job ladders may have little to do with skill specificity, task idiosyncracy, or skill relationships between adjacent jobs on the ladder. Job ladders may be constituted for other reasons, such as reducing turnover costs regardless of skill specificity or interrela-tionships. In short, the Doeringer and Piore definition of ILMs is too broad to support a facile equation of ILMs with job ladders.

## ILM = SENIORITY ENTITLEMENTS

Employees and unions favor broad, not narrow, lines of progression, with "wide geographic and occupational coverage, entry confined to low-skilled jobs, and reliance upon uniform criteria such as seniority in the internal allocation of jobs [Doeringer & Piore, 1971, p.59]." It is not surprising, then, that some writers have interpreted seniority rights as the distinctive feature of ILMs (as Wachter, 1974, pp.647, claims dual labor market pro-ponents have).[9] For example, Reich, Gordon, and Edwards (1973) argued that unions, in response to the creation of job ladders, "sought freedom from the arbitrary discretionary power of supervisors by demanding a sen-iority criterion for promotion [p.362]." Similarly, Spilerman (1977) referred to "career-line paths" (p.583) or "orderly career lines" (p.578) as charac-terized by increasing age and earnings as individuals moved up job ladders.[10]

---

employees with a degree of monopoly over the technical knowledge and skill needed for their job (Williamson, Wachter, & Harris, 1975, pp.256–257).

[9] Even so, both Doeringer (1967, p.211) and Wachter have found that versions of merit and ability, and not seniority, dominate promotions and lateral transfers; in contrast, seniority is used almost exclusively in protecting employees from layoffs (see also Doeringer & Piore, 1971, p.34).

[10] In addition to orderly career lines, Spilerman (1977, p.582) identified chaotic lines (with no such progression) associated with jobs in the secondary labor market and craft and profes-sional career lines. Spilerman is unclear about whether the craft and professional lines are associated with internal labor markets. In contrast, such ladders are associated by others with the careers of many professionals (Edwards, 1979, p.176; Stinchcombe, 1979, pp.219, 225), thus implying either association with ILMs (Edwards, 1979, pp.181–183) or similarity (Stinch-combe, 1979, pp.239–241). See our discussion of occupational internal labor markets.

However, some positions in the primary labor market (dead-end jobs) have no prospects for advancement (p.583). It follows, then, that if "seniority entitlements bind a firm to its workers, . . . internal labor markets will exist even where the potential for earnings growth and promotion is no better than in the secondary sector [Spilerman, 1977, p.583]." Thus the defining criterion should be not earnings growth or employment stability[11] but "the degree to which workers accumulate nontransferable benefits [p.584]."

As a natural part of the tension between the interests of employees and the efficiency motives of employers, unions press toward an "increase in seniority as an allocative rule [Doeringer & Piore, 1971, pp.59, 191–192]." Thus, there are many reasons why either seniority rules or job ladders, but not both (as Spilerman's reasoning illustrates), might seem a dominant feature of ILMs. Yet seniority is not typically applied to promotions, and even when it is, promotion need not entail the progressive development of skill that is essential to an interpretation based on job ladders.[12]

## Why Redefine ILMs?

The original concept of an ILM featured breadth, as is evidenced by its multitrait or multidimensional character, and variety in each trait or dimension. Job ladders could have few, if any, or many vertical steps and could operate within either occupations or firms. Promotions might or might not be accompanied by progressively greater skill or knowledge, status, and pay and might be determined by ability, seniority rules, or a combination of the two. Such breadth and internal variation only increases the difficulty of generating a cogent theory of the consequences of ILMs for wages and employment patterns. The concept will prove far more useful if it is more carefully and less broadly defined than has been the case in the past.

## Various Concepts of Primary and Secondary Markets

### PRIMARY MARKETS = JOB STABILITY

Piore's (1970, p.55) definition of primary and secondary labor markets also exemplifies a broad composite concept. Nevertheless, Piore emphasized

---

[11] Spilerman associated Vietorisz and Harrison (1973) with this view, but we can find no statements to this effect in either this or their other writings.

[12] Kerr noted the same tension between craft-based internal markets and industrial unions' support for seniority rules: "Most labor market studies find the worker's chief attachment is to his occupation, yet the essence of the seniority approach is to create an employee largely devoid of narrow occupational attachment [1954, p.100n]."

employment stability (1975, p.126) above all other traits, and others have followed this lead. For example, Edwards (1975, pp.16–19) concluded that the principal difference between primary and secondary jobs was, indeed, work stability. Having rejected as too indirect the use of demographic groups (white males, teenagers, black females, all females over 15) as proxies for the particular market in which each group is heavily represented, Edwards recommended using measures of job tenure to divide respondents into primary and secondary sectors. Edwards also noted, though, that, because these measures are inversely related to movement up the job ladders of internal markets, they cannot represent the stability of employment within those markets (see also Gordon, 1972b, p.51).[13]

## SECONDARY MARKETS = FIRM–INDUSTRY MOBILITY

Taking an approach with analogous problems, Alexander (1974, p.66) associated (what amounts to) firm ILMs ("manorial markets") with low probabilities of leaving a firm in the preceding year, secondary markets with high probabilities of leaving both firm and industry, and craft ILMs ("guild structures") with large positive differences between the probabilities of leaving the firm and leaving the industry. But as Gordon would seem to suggest, secondary as well as primary market incumbents may not move between firms. Nor may they move between industries, following Spilerman's (1977, p.583) suggestion of occupational markets within the secondary market. Moreover, taking firm immobility as an index of firm labor market location assumes that all the jobs in a firm or industry belong within a single ILM. When these types of measures are operationalized at the higher level of aggregation consisting of four-digit industry groups (Alexander, 1974, p.67), an even rougher approximation of different markets results.

## SUMMARY

The association of primary and internal labor markets is qualified. Doeringer and Piore (1971, pp.167–168) did not argue that all internal markets are located in the primary sector. Instead, the secondary market contains secondary ILMs (examples are stitching and pressing jobs), and other secondary jobs occasionally are attached to ILMs in various firms.[14] The breadth of the concept of primary and secondary markets has prompted some to reduce the concept to a single dimension, such as job stability or high wage

[13] Taking a neoclassical view, Cain (1976, pp.1237–1239) also expresses reservations about the dual labor market theory's treatment of job stability or instability as the key characteristic dividing primary from secondary markets.

[14] As Doeringer and Piore (1971, p.169) point out, their views here are inconsistent with dual labor market theory's clear dichotomy between primary and internal labor markets and secondary markets, as found in Piore's (1970, 1975) definitions of these markets.

levels. However, the result usually is inconsistencies between market classifications in the original, broad definition and in the simpler operationalizations. Also, as with the concept of ILM, the breadth of definition may interfere with the development of theory to explain the origins or consequences of such markets. By definition the association of good jobs and high wages logically undermines theoretical and empirical exploration of the effects on wages of jobs in primary and secondary labor markets (especially when wage levels are used to classify jobs into markets; see Wachter, 1974, pp.648, 651–652 on this, and Andrisani, 1973, for an example).

The definitional association between the jobs in each market and demographic groups has similar unfortunate effects. Researchers define as secondary jobs those held mainly by minority group workers, women, and teens; and as primary, jobs held mainly by prime-age white males (Gordon, 1972b, p.52; see also Edwards, 1975, pp.16–19). Yet the parallel breaks down. Some prime-age white males remain employed in secondary jobs, and some nonwhites and females attain primary jobs. We cannot pursue explanations of this or other theoretical relationships between job markets and the employment of various demographic groups if groups and markets coincide by definition.

## A Different View of Markets

We have identified many types of ILMs. It is unlikely, then, that all have the same origins and consequences. The characteristics that differentiate the upper- from the lower-tier jobs are broad occupational categories (e.g., professional, managerial) and job characteristics (e.g., routine or repetitive work, autonomy) and not such structural relations as ladders or limited entry ports. Serious questions arise when we juxtapose these characteristics against other attributes supposedly common to each tier. Are the job progressions of managers and professionals fundamentally similar to those ascribed to some blue-collar workers? Similarly, what is the relation between seniority and job ladders? For many, seniority privileges convey the essence of the shelter provided by internal markets; yet they generally do not coincide with the structural relations among jobs. Therefore, our redefinition of ILMs features job ladders and not seniority rights net of job ladders as a key component.

Furthermore, both craft or occupational and firm markets have been regarded as ILMs even though the literature is mainly about firm markets. Some ILMs indeed may exist only within the confines of firms, but the definition of an ILM must specify precisely what all kinds of ILMs have in common and what features are unique to each type. Therefore, as two types of ILMs we propose: *firm internal labor markets* (FILMs), established by and confined to a single employer (organization, corporation), though not necessarily embracing all jobs in a firm; and *occupational internal labor markets* (OILMs), existing for incumbents of one occupation or of two or more associated occupations and not necessarily confined to a single employer.[15]

Because some jobs that are not ILMs enjoy the shelter of employment within the same organization, we propose *firm labor markets* (FLMs), which exist inside firms or organizations but lack the structural features that we associate with ILMs. Similarly, because some jobs or occupational groups enjoy some shelter from external competition because of the type of degree of skills required (Kerr, 1954, p.94; also Stolzenberg, 1975, p.647), we propose *occupational labor markets* (OLMs) as their location. All jobs not located in these four markets are in *secondary labor markets* (SLAMs).

## Internal Labor Markets

### REDEFINITION

The concept of an ILM should include any cluster of jobs, regardless of occupational titles or employing organizations, that have three basic structural features: (*a*) a job ladder, with (*b*) entry only at the bottom and (*c*) movement up this ladder, which is associated with a progressive development of knowledge or skill. Both FILMs and OILMs share these features, but they operate in distinctive ways that reflect their fundamental difference: that FILMs are controlled by employers, whereas OILMs are strongly influenced by the people who hold jobs in the occupation.

In FILMs, limited entry ports are a deliberate firm policy designed to support promotion from within. Equally deliberate are job progressions, sometimes entailing horizontal transfers between departments, that broaden and deepen firm- (and to some extent industry-) specific knowledge of employees. Movement up ladders is facilitated by varying combinations of formal and informal on-the-job training (OJT) and prior training or experience or education at entry.

---

[15] In literature on labor markets the words *firm* and *internal* in *firm internal labor market* are redundant, because the location of a market in a firm makes the market internal. We reject the redundancy, because we reject the usual equation of internal markets with firm markets. The term *firm internal labor market* (FILM) denotes a subcategory of ILM—one that is internal to a firm. The other subcategory is internal to occupations (OILM). Labor markets that lack ILM structures but exist within firms (FLMs, or firm labor markets) or within occupational groups (OLMs, or occupational labor markets) differ from ILMs, as discussed later.

In OILMs, senior incumbents influence entry in a variety of ways. By judging the ability of candidates to meet skill and entry requirements, they often have a decisive effect on how many applicants obtain jobs. Professional and union organizations may set entry-level standards and entry procedures that effectively restrict the supply of potential job applicants relative to the demand for their work. Quite apart from these restrictions, rapid growth of the demand for classes of workers relative to supply also may help to create an OILM. Although informal OJT facilitates movement up ladders, the progressive development of skill or knowledge usually requires a high degree of externally acquired (and often theoretical or general) knowledge or skill upon entry. The entry credentials usually suffice to postpone the eventual obsolescence of technical knowledge in the face of subsequent advances of knowledge or technique.

Several additional features of ILMs follow from their common structural skeleton: informal OJT of new employees by senior employees; little or no competition for other positions either from within or from outsiders; little competition from co-workers with equivalent experience and skills; considerable job security within the market; relatively little turnover, because of the prospect of starting over in entry-level jobs of other internal markets if an occupant of an ILM exits prematurely; and some control over the introduction of new knowledge and technology (Weinberg & Rothberg, 1957).

Our concept differs in several ways from earlier ones.

1. It excludes many markets and thus employees in them because they lack one or more of the three basic characteristics. Instead these are located in OLMs or FLMs, within which jobholders often continue to enjoy some of the benefits previously associated only with ILMs.
2. Neither job ladders per se nor job ladders with limited entry ports is the sole defining characteristic of an ILM; instead, the important criterion is the simultaneous combination of these two with a progressive development of skill or knowledge. Seniority rights are not necessary, though they sometimes accompany the markets that we define as ILMs.
3. The redefinition does not include references to high wages, employment of primary workers, or employment in particular economic sectors or industries.
4. ILMs have more structural homogeneity. Although the number of markets and their employees is lower than with the broader definition, ILMs will not necessarily include only small proportions of the labor force.
5. The concept anticipates patterns of exit from, and hence movement

among, ILMs and other markets. For example, some workers will progress to the top of middle-management FILMs, exit, and enter top-management OILMs, which span firms. Engineers may reach the top of an OILM and move into middle-management FILMs or top-management OILMs. Others, having failed to progress through a FILM, may exit not into other FILMs but into FLMs. Conversely, SLAMs may supply applicants for jobs in other markets, although we have not yet specified the conditions that would either foster or discourage these applicants.

## POSSIBLE CAUSES OF ILMs

According to Doeringer and Piore (1971, pp.13–17), skill and job specificity generates (broadly defined) ILMs for employers and employees alike. Specificity makes training costly to employers, who bear a larger proportion of the cost than employees do. Theoretically, though, employees cannot use their specific skills on other machines, in other firms or markets. Doeringer and Piore suggested that this feature could but would not necessarily generate ILMs with a progression of jobs at increasing levels of skill. Yet their argument—that ILMs reduce turnover and help recover some of the high cost of specificity—seems to assume an ILM structured according to our definition (see Doeringer & Piore, 1971, p.172).

Similarly, Doeringer and Piore (1971, pp.17–22) also argued that on-the-job training generates ILMs. They emphasize informal training by co-workers rather than formal programs of training. Yet only in some instances does OJT occur "along a promotion ladder in which work on the lower-level jobs develops the skills required for the higher level [p.19]." Again, the ILM-generating effect of OJT makes more sense when associated with ILMs as we have defined them. The progression of skill enables employees with more experience to train those with less, while the limitation of entry points to the bottom of the ladder provides job security for employees with experience (Doeringer & Piore, 1971, p.33; Williamson et al., 1975, p.257).

In OILMs, OJT may include self-training. For example,

> through frequent job changes, a [restaurant] cook can program his own on-the-job training, remaining in one establishment only so long as he has something to learn there. . . . These worker-initiated job changes generate the kind of exposure to new tasks and skills provided elsewhere by movement along an internal line of progression or by supervised rotation of work assignments [Taylor & Piore, 1971, pp.48,56].

Similar patterns apparently exist among some members of various professional, technical, and top-management occupations. For example some highly talented computer programmers and systems analysts frequently change employers after completing short-term projects.[16]

Many writers (Edwards, 1975; Marglin, 1974, p.63; Stone, 1975, pp.45–49; Wright &Perrone, 1977, pp.37–38) have associated hierarchical job and wage ladders with employer-run systems of control over work processes.[17] The prospect of movement up a ladder motivates the work performance of employees and undercuts any desire to combine against employers. Some writers believe that promotion to higher-level jobs has replaced monetary rewards (Gordon, 1972b, p.76).

To achieve control, employers must set up a hierarchy per se. Neither limited entry nor a progressive development of skill or knowledge is essential. Clearly, systems other than ILMs as we define them—for example, seniority ladders, promotions to higher jobs that do not depend on acquiring additional skill or knowledge—will accomplish employer control.

Nevertheless, limited entry would seem to enhance the appearance and practice of promotion from within that is associated with this use of job ladders, and progressive development of skill legitimizes the hierarchical structure of jobs. For example, in a firm a middle-management progression of jobs could be associated with increasing responsibility or authority (as in large urban banks).

Hierarchical job ladders also can give groups of employees (some unions) and senior incumbents of some occupations the means to control work processes. Again, a variety of structures may produce control. Nevertheless, limited entry is a prominent feature of some unions (crafts) and occupations (electricians, bricklayers), and the progressive development of skill and knowledge may offer a legitimation to the ladder that is even more valuable in OILMs than in FILMs. For example, in the U.S. Civil Service, engineers and technicians enjoy noncompetitive promotion from the GS–5 or –7 entry levels up to, but not including, the lowest supervisory level (GS–12), where promotion is competitive.

In sum, while job-specificity, OJT, and hierarchical approaches to control over work processes are said to generate broadly defined ILMs, we have seen that all three (a) can exist and operate outside of ILMs; and (b) make more sense as generators of ILMs as we have defined them.

---

[16] We learned of this pattern from both a large urban bank that employs computer personnel and from personnel at a university computing center. We make no claim that this pattern describes the experience of most or all programmers. Indeed, it may be the exception (Greenbaum, 1976).

[17] Marglin (1974, p. 81) makes the distinction between two aspects of worker's control of production: control over the product (its sale or distribution and profit) and control over work processes (the way work is done, the training and supervision of workers). Others (Wright, 1976) have suggested similar distinctions.

## Occupational Labor Markets[18]

Members of some occupational groups that do not inhabit OILMs have achieved by other means a significant degree of control over work processes. This is true even where a progressive development of skill or knowledge, job ladders, or a connection between ladders and such development is missing. People who already hold jobs in the market may control entry requirements and limit training and actual entry; the result may be effective job security and lack of competition from the outside.

OLMs have two essential structural features. One is specialized skills and knowledge that individuals can acquire only by a significant investment in education or training and practice. Training takes place in formal vocational–technical programs, in periods of informal practice lasting at least as long as formal programs, or in mixtures of the two. Entry requires prior training or apprenticeship, but we do not speak of entry ports because job ladders are generally, though not always, absent. Even though an accumulation of skill or knowledge comes with experience in an OLM, it is not by definition accompanied by movement up a ladder of jobs. The second feature is movement between jobs in the market. Typically, employees instigate the changes, but employers impose no penalty when employees do so. Movement between employers also is highly variable; therefore, we do not treat it as part of the definition or as a likely measure of this market.

The defining elements aside, other features may typify OLMs, though not all OLMs have all these features.

1. People who hold jobs in an OLM often have an occupational or market identity and organize themselves in a variety of ways. Licensing, certification, or registration are typical by-products of this feature.
2. Seniority rights according to duration of time in the market sometimes govern access to jobs, wage levels, and increases.
3. Occupants of these markets are especially vulnerable to the development and application of new skills and knowledge because their training is typically specialized and nontheoretical.

In both OLMs and OILMs employees have significant influence on work processes, but they differ in several other respects.

1. In OLMs more of the training for work is specialized. The result may be a more detailed grasp of the state of the art, craft, or service technology, or of the operation of existing machinery. But in contrast to an OILM, short

[18] This type of market was suggested in part by the notion of structure derived from skill boundaries (Kerr, 1954, p. 94; Stolzenberg, 1975, pp.647, 649).

of renewed training, jobholders in an OLM often lack the education or technical background needed to assimilate new advances.

2. For jobs in an OILM, the period of training before employment is longer, is more often a full-time activity, and typically is cumulative in that course work completed for one program can be counted toward completion of related or higher-level programs. Training for jobs in an OLM is more likely to be segregated and noncumulative with respect to certificates or degrees.[19]

3. Perhaps the greatest difference is in the contrast between job ladders in OILMs and licensing, registration, or certification programs present in some OLMs (Doeringer & Piore, 1971, p.172). In the area of health occupations, Goldstein and Horowitz (1977, pp.40, 49) have argued that "to some extent," licensing and certification have "limited upward mobility and made many entry-level positions dead-end jobs." In addition, some licensing laws make no provision for the development of new knowledge and the resulting obsolescence of previous training. In contrast to this situation typical in many health careers, Goldstein and Horowitz (1977) described an unusual "in-service training program to provide upgrading opportunities for its allied health personnel (p.46)." The program moves entry-level personnel through a five-position sequence from nursing assistant to licensed practical nurse. In effect, this hospital rearranged discrete OLMs into a FILM.

## Firm Labor Markets

Within many firms, some jobs have one common feature: Their occupants enjoy virtual tenure. They have the job security and shelter from outside competition that earlier writers have thought typical of an ILM, but the jobs lack the features of either ILMs as we have redefined them or of OLMs. These jobs are in firm labor markets (FLMs). Some holders of FLM jobs originally enter FILM job ladders but either level off or for other reasons do not progress all the way up the ladders. They leave the ladders but not the firm. Thus their jobs lack the connection between the further devel-

---

[19] For example, contrast the training of registered nurses (whose jobs we tentatively classify as an OILM) with that of either respiratory therapists and physical therapists or of respiratory therapy technicians and physical therapist assistants. In the latter two, for example, the two years of school (leading to an A.A. degree) cannot be counted toward completion of the B.S. or B.A. degrees required of therapists. The college training of registered nurses typically combines curriculums in both nursing and general education, and courses completed in either curriculum under other programs (e.g., a general B.A.) can, by and large, be counted toward an R.N. degree.

opment of firm-specific knowledge and subsequent promotion, even though either the development or the (infrequent) promotion may occur separately thereafter. Others may enter after a prolonged stay in secondary labor market jobs within the firm. Because the employer and the employee have formed an attachment, the job effectively exists in an FLM for as long as the employee holds it. FLM jobs can exist at many levels in a firm's hierarchy, but usually they concentrate in levels that parallel FILM (or OILM) job ladders (e.g., between SLAM job levels and the top management of large firms). The reason is that exit from a FILM may occur at different levels of its job ladder, and entry from SLAM-level jobs should occur at lower job levels.

Other features may typify these markets, though not all FLMs would have them.

1. Seniority rights may again govern wage levels, raises, relative position when layoffs occur, and access to better jobs reached by (infrequent) promotion.
2. Turnover usually is low, but tenure and seniority rights do not always compensate incumbents for infrequent promotions, lack of (anticipated) movement up job ladders, or lack of opportunity to develop skill or knowledge. Exit from the firm is an option; but exercising that option, unlike the situation in an OLM, is usually costly because firm-specific experience has only limited value to other employers.

## Secondary Labor Markets

All jobs in the secondary labor market lack the elements, or sources, of structure that define the other markets: job ladders, development of skill or knowledge, significant investment in training by either the employer or the employee, limited entry or notable entry requirements, and options for firm-specific tenure. Previous writers have suggested other features, associated with SLAMs:

1. Turnover is typical, expected by employer and employee alike. It is not inevitable, because some employees remain in the same jobs with the same employer for long periods of time.
2. Job training is simple and brief: More extensive training is inconsistent with the limited scope and responsibility of the job.
3. Without job ladders or opportunity to develop skill or knowledge, there is no inherent potential for orderly movement into other jobs even if some co-workers leave the market and enter others.

4. The boundaries for SLAM markets are typically geographic, either local or regional. Whether segmentation by industry exists, as Spilerman (1977) suggested it might, remains to be explored.

## The Relationship between Labor Markets and Economic Sectors

Dual labor market and dual economy theorists have written relatively little about the relationship between labor markets and economic sectors. Doeringer and Piore (1971, p.163) devoted a paragraph to the topic. Gordon (1972a, p.205) remarked that people who hold primary jobs usually work for large corporations in large plants, with salaries paid by center firms. Averitt's (1968, p.108) only comment bearing on this relationship is that center firms offer more opportunities for promotion and a greater variety of career patterns than periphery firms do.

Writers routinely assert that primary and secondary labor markets are located in center or core and periphery firms, respectively (Andrisan, 1976; Beck *et al.*, 1978). Two arguments have supported this assertion in the literature: one based on the large size of center firms; the second on other characteristics of center firms, such as capital intensity and unionization. The large size of center firms not only facilitates but may even be necessary to provide the high wages and job ladders that characterize internal labor markets (broadly defined). In a different context, Taylor and Piore (1971, pp.46–48) argued that internal promotion is more feasible in large than in small firms. For example, print firms had lines of progression; most restaurants did not. Their example shows, however, that a firm large enough to permit internal promotions is considerably smaller than the center firms described by dual economy theorists. Indeed, these consequences of firm size do not logically depend on any association with center firms, even if Averitt (as cited in the preceding paragraph) is correct about an average difference in the opportunities for promotion in center and periphery firms.

The second argument is that high wage levels and job ladders found in primary markets are a product of such characteristics as high productivity, high profits, capital intensity, unionization, and elements of monopoly (Bluestone *et al.*, 1973, pp.28–29; Edwards, 1975, pp.20–21). For some, the result is that labor markets do not affect wages net of the economic sector of firms (Beck *et al.*, 1978, p.706). Historical and theoretical questions as to the origins of primary and secondary markets become questions as to the origins of dual economic sectors. For others (Wachter, 1974, p.648), the market power of center firms together with one or more labor market features (e.g., specific training, for Wachter) jointly explain the high wages of primary market jobs.

This second argument is frequently buttressed by discussions of capitalism's history in the United States. Gordon (1972, pp.70–75); Reich, Gordon, and Edwards (1973); Edwards (1975, 1979); and Stone (1975) have argued that labor market stratification generally, and primary labor markets specifically, emerged from bureaucratic systems of control and that their purpose was to consolidate power and use the new technology available to oligopolistic or monopolistic firms. This produces a history of primary or internal labor markets only if one asserts or assumes that economic sectors shape labor markets and their location.[20] If historical studies are to enhance our theoretical understanding of the relationship between labor markets and sectors, then what is needed is a systematic collection and analysis of diverse moments in the development of capitalistic and socialistic economies. Illustrative sources of such moments might include Stone's (1975) description of the steel industry; Marglin's (1974) discussions of the long-wall system of coal mining, factory spinning and weaving, and the collectivization of Soviet agriculture under Stalin; and selected incidents from sources such as Alfred Chandler's (1977) *The Visible Hand.*[21] Taken as a whole, these sources should be sensitive to both technological and efficiency origins of oligopolies (e.g., economies of scale and speed of production) and to monopolistic motives of market control (e.g., see Gordon, 1976).

Much of the second argument also depends on the view that periphery firms are exclusively small fringe operations that experience great fluctuations in demand for production and labor, whereas center firms exclusively possess the resources, market dominance, and stability of production that engenders good jobs and high wages. This view ignores the substantive significance of those cases that produce an unknown but, we believe, substantial degree of nonoverlap between markets and firm economic sectors. Averitt's periphery firms included satellite (e.g., Whirlpool Corporation, a Sears's satellite) and loyal opposition (e.g., Maytag) firms, many of which are either large or medium sized. These firms must have enough resources

[20] Doeringer and Piore (1971, pp.52,n27) noted that ILMs antedate the widespread appearance of formalized rules structures and cited Roy Kelly's (1918) study of 30 firms, 20 of which had definite plans for internal promotions. What is more interesting is that the industries represented by the firms with or without plans do not correspond to a division between center and periphery now used and probably then current as well (see Chandler, 1977, Appendix A). There is also evidence, in Gitelman's (1966) fascinating study of internal mobility in the Waltham Watch Company between 1860 and 1890, that internal promotion predated the period when center firms and internal markets supposedly developed.

[21] Chandler's *The Visible Hand* (1977) contains some very useful analytic sections pertinent to the rise of center firms and associated industries, but there is precious little in either this work or another study by Noble (1977) that pertains to the growth of internal labor markets.

and stability of production to sustain ILMs, especially FILMs. It can be said that unions (one source of labor market control by employees) have tended to organize employees of center firms and neglect employees in periphery firms (notwithstanding the size, market, and periphery sector location of the Teamsters Union; see Averitt, 1968, pp.148–149). But large and medium-sized periphery firms must employ some people who hold jobs in OILMs and OLMs, because they require the professional and technical skills of people in these markets. In short, the market power characteristic of center firms is not required to support ILMs, any more than is their enormous size.

While supported elsewhere by Edwards (1975, p.21) and Wachter (1974, p.652),[22] Piore alone among dual labor market theorists has consistently denied the assumption that firm economic sectors and labor markets overlap perfectly. He noted (1970) that primary employers (center firms) have some secondary jobs, and secondary employers (periphery firms) have some primary jobs. Revising his position slightly, he later described in some detail how the "structure of technology" or "choice of technology" determined the distribution of upper- and lower-tier as well as secondary jobs within economic sectors (1975, pp.141–143, 146–148). The general picture is of center firms with many lower-tier jobs plus a few upper-tier management jobs and of periphery firms with mostly secondary jobs but also some upper-tier and lower-tier (craft) jobs. Of the more recent contributors to this literature, only Hodson (1978) has expressed the distinction as emphatically: "This division into capital sectors is expected to have a low to moderate correlation with the division into primary and secondary labor markets. . . . They are by no means equivalent either as constructs or as operationalizations [p.61]."

In short, the relationship between dual economic sectors and labor markets is not as straightforward as much of the literature has suggested. The theoretical issues involved have barely been joined (but see Gordon, 1976). For the most part, fundamental theoretical questions have not been addressed. Why are mobility chains or ILMs constructed as they are, and how can they be changed (Piore, 1975, p.135)? What is the relative influence of technical advances, motives or consequences of efficiency, and control over work processes in the evolution of dual sectors and various labor markets? Under what conditions can jobs change market locations (see Doeringer & Piore, 1971, pp.181–182; Kahn, 1976; Piore, 1975, pp.141–143, for a start)? What are the empirical interrelationships among economic sectors; primary, internal, or secondary labor markets; and firm size?

---

[22] "Although market power may be pervasive in the primary sector of the dualist model, this does not mean that high-wage jobs and all jobs with specific training are associated with market power [Wachter, 1974, p.652]." In effect, specific training in firms lacking market power can also produce high wages and good jobs.

There is reasoning and evidence enough to justify a framework in which labor markets represent a level of analysis distinct from economic sectors based on firm characteristics. We conclude that the structure, associated characteristics, and origins of ILMs, as well as their consequences for movement between jobs, individual careers, wage levels, or wage functions, cannot be reduced to characteristics of center and periphery firms or their consequences. We envision a theoretical model open to further specification by alternative theories, in which economic sectors have some effect on the distribution and nature of labor markets and other consequences net of markets. Similarly, labor markets have other exogenous causes and their own consequences net of those that economic sectors have. The key relationships demanding further empirical and theoretical study are between economic sectors and labor markets and between markets and their consequences.

## A Research Agenda

### Location (Measurement) of Labor Markets

An aggregated approach has dominated recent research. Researchers have used data sets that come from national samples of the civilian labor force. These samples aggregate employees who have been drawn randomly from unidentified and diverse firms, markets, and economic sectors. The sampling frames coincide with a national labor market; in effect, sociologists (Blau & Duncan, 1967, p.4) have thought this market especially suitable for the study of occupational mobility. Measurement of labor markets and economic sectors has required the classification of occupations (Osterman, 1975) and industry groups (Beck *et al.*, 1978; Bibb & Form, 1977; Hodson, 1978) as proxies for either markets or sectors. For some researchers, this procedure poses no problems. For example, referring to variables that influence the structure of career lines, Spilerman (1977) emphasizes "*industry* because it is a more useful analytic construct. Firms in the same industry are likely to have comparable technologies and organizational forms and would be subject to identical fluctuations in demand for their products [p.579]." Others (Hodson, 1978) have expressed concern with the possibility of misclassification or with the difficulty of classification (as when Osterman, 1975, following Piore, assigned individuals to secondary and upper and lower tier primary jobs according to their occupational title).[23]

---

[23] The severity of this problem has been little studied. A typical industry category assigned to the center or periphery sector aggregates employees of firms that vary in size and character.

The major advantage of this approach is that it enables analysis of the whole economy and it provides a baseline from which to assess the consequences associated with markets and sectors. But researchers should try to minimize the error likely when employees in national samples are aggregated into markets or sectors on the basis of occupational titles or industry groups, respectively. One useful procedure is to aggregate into labor markets the occupants in the cells of an occupational title–industry group matrix (Freedman, 1976). This reduces the heterogeneity within occupational titles produced by industry and firm differences and within industrial classification produced by occupational differences. When researchers interpret the findings from research that uses proxies like these, they should weigh the effects and estimate the magnitude of inaccurately assigning jobs to markets or firms and their associated industry groups to sectors. Nevertheless, we conclude that nationally aggregated data and commonly used definitions of occupations and industries are not well suited for investigations of labor market typologies.

More promising for this purpose is the second, or disaggregated, approach, whose proponents use data from sampling frames that coincide at least in part with identifiable markets and firm sectors. These include intensive samples of employees by firm and samples from many firms of people who hold jobs in one or a few occupational groups (Rees & Shultz, 1970; Talbert & Bose, 1977, for examples). The advantage of these samples is that researchers obtain qualitative knowledge about the structure of jobs and the characteristics of firms and can use that information to assign employees to labor markets and firms to economic sectors. Qualitative knowledge of a firm's employment and promotion practices would enhance the possibility

---

Parallel problems exist in the use of occupational titles. Consider the title "engineer," for example. All engineers can be disaggregated into those working in the public and private sectors, and those in the public sector work for federal, state, or local governments. Many working in the private sector, however, do not enjoy the largely noncompetitive career ladders that engineers in the public sector do.

Some writers point out other problems with this title that no doubt could be multiplied across the gamut of titles with sufficient qualitative knowledge of occupations and professions. Osterman (1975) found engineers a difficult title to classify. Some resided in the upper tier, being well educated and well paid; but most worked in an "assembly line environment, handling small, assigned pieces of a larger problem [p. 514]." Result: *All* engineers were assigned to the lower-tier category!

Cain, Freeman, and Hansen (1973) also had difficulty counting engineers. With the frequent reliance on census data, it is easy to forget the occupational self-classification of respondents. These authors found that 25% of all "engineers" had no college degree or even college training, and 60% of this 25% had no supplementary training for nondegree people. A partially overlapping 15% reported that their field of work specialization was not currently engineering. Much of the more general and continuing criticism of census occupational titles has implications for this problem as well (Scoville, 1972).

of isolating jobs or clusters of jobs that conform to our earlier definitions of labor markets.

Although few researchers have used this approach, many support its spirit (Eckaus, 1973; Spilerman, 1977, p.579). Dunlop (1966, p.37) called for an industry-by-industry study of internal labor markets. Stieber (1959) described the advantages of using individual plant data rather than industry-level figures: "Industry figures sometimes conceal what is going on at the plant level [p.327]." Kaysen (1973, pp.148–149) probably made the strongest and most direct argument for this approach. He suggests that "we are really well past the limit of what can be done on an aggregate basis," because "there is no such thing as a single labor market or mobility across all labor markets. There is not *enough* interplay among labor markets for the concept of an average return on years of educational attainment to mean much." He goes on to call for the study of "microdata with a lot of qualitative understanding."

For some researchers, this approach raises the specter of unrepresentative samples from local labor markets, single firms, and scattered occupational groups. However, if the homogeneity of a national labor market is theoretically in doubt, researchers can no longer assume that these are unrepresentative samples of that market. Rather, it is the meaning of findings from aggregate samples that await additional knowledge from disaggregated samples and their analysis.

For others, the problem with this approach is that it envisions a seemingly endless number of specific studies, an unwelcome contrast to the first approach, which has thrived on the findings of a few well-funded national surveys. However, conceptual and theoretical developments need not await a lengthy accumulation of studies. Well-done studies using theoretically selected samples will provide support for, or suggest, alternate hypotheses about the operation of labor markets and economic sectors and also provide insights about measurement and data collection. Both should prove immediately useful to those who continue to refine the aggregated approach.

## Consequences of Labor Markets

Three broad subtopics organize the diverse consequences attributed to labor markets: wage levels, wage or income functions of individual characteristics, and mobility between jobs and labor markets. Traditionally, high wage levels have been associated by definition with primary markets. There is no empirical doubt that center firms and industries pay higher wages than periphery firms and industries (Beck *et al.*, 1978; Bluestone *et al.*, 1973). The unstudied question is whether wage levels differ by labor market net of economic sector or firm size. Exploring differences in wage level by type of labor market could answer this question and illuminate the study of intraindustry wage differentials by occupations and firms. Both Rees and Shultz (1970, p.46) and Stolzenberg (1975, pp.656–657) have found that few firms are consistently high wage or low wage firms across the whole spectrum of occupations. Hypotheses about wage levels characteristic of labor markets might make sense of these and other findings. For example, Talbert and Bose (1977) found that structural differences within organizations (retail stores in city versus suburban locations) caused different wage levels even within a single occupational title. Perhaps not all retail clerks (or, more generally, employees of the same title) work in the same labor market? The result should be findings well beyond the simple discovery that wage levels in ILMs exceed those in the secondary labor markets.

Findings about wage functions have not always been consistent, and arguments have not always been consistent or testable. Dual labor market theorists supposedly believe that characteristics of human capital affect income in primary but not secondary markets (Gordon, 1972b, pp.50–51; Osterman, 1975, pp.516–517; Wachter, 1974, p.653). Yet Bluestone *et al.* (1973, pp.88–90, 103, 140) found that formal education was more important for wages in "noninstitutionalized" (periphery) than in "institutionalized" (center) industries. Future research must determine if this inconsistency is due to specific differences in studies or to more general differences between markets and sectors. Spilerman (1977) among others (Kerr, 1950, pp.282, 286) argued that wage functions are indeterminant: "The wage implication of segmented markets is principally one of a considerable variation in earnings for persons with comparable training, performing similar tasks, in different firms [p.584]." This hypothesis deserves more attention as an alternative hypothesis inconsistent with those of dual labor market theory.

Researchers also need to fill the gap between theory and the specification of wage functions. Consider two examples of rather abstract specification.

1. To paraphrase Alexander (1974, p.64), increased productivity (in manorial firms or FILMs) is of no value to other firms, so other employers ought not to bid up the wage rate. However, an employee's value to a firm increases as the length of service increases, so employers have an incentive to reduce mobility by paying employees somewhat more than they are worth to other firms.

2. To paraphrase Taylor and Piore (1971, pp.50–51), because firm-specific training is useful only to a current job, the specifically trained worker can obtain only an unskilled job on the open market. Therefore to prevent turnover, an employer would have to offer a wage above the unskilled rate but still could pay a wage below the value of a worker's marginal product.

Both theories are intriguing but difficult to relate to the coefficients in a wage function. In short, the basic structural characteristics of markets should either affect or correspond to wage structures, and appropriate functions should capture that effect. The unpleasant alternative is a conclusion that within markets, a *theoretical* indeterminacy of wages exists.

The implications for individual careers have been the hallmark of attempts by dual labor market theorists to explain the observed limitations on movement between markets (especially movement out of secondary markets). Given "backflows" between the social environments of demographic groups that congregate in secondary jobs and the environment of work in these jobs, characteristics of secondary jobs and secondary workers reinforce and interlock. This hypothesis requires more extensive, detailed, and historical study, without a priori equating labor market structure with occupational segregation by demographic characteristics. Important issues include the conditions under which varying numbers and groups of workers move into jobs or occupations. To what extent do the interests of employers coincide with, and perhaps foment, the influx? How much control do various employers actually have over the continuing location of their jobs in various markets?

Finally, under what conditions do individuals move between markets? For example, we suspect that some general principles probably describe, and perhaps explain in part, the most frequently traveled pathways between types of markets and how they differ from paths that are rarely taken. One such principle, which we call *age-pacing*, also seems related to movement up the job ladders of ILMs: "Where a job leads is very much a function of age . . . considerable importance can be expected to be attached to rate of movement and to whether or not the position one held was appropriate to one's age [Spilerman, 1977, p.563]." (See also Martin & Strauss, 1968, pp.205–206; Rosenbaum, 1978, p.6; Smigel, 1968.) The conditions under which employees are subject to or exempt from age-pacing should be explored.

We expect restrictions on movement between markets in part due to the unacceptably high cost of leaving certain markets and in part due to the existing labor market structure. Thurow associated the ILM job ladder with a training ladder that progressively developed skill and knowledge and thus tied the marginal productivity of an individual to the last job held on that ladder. The consequence, for example, is that unemployed pilots cannot switch to another airline, and unemployed aerospace engineers in New England cannot compete for the jobs of engineers who remain employed (Thurow, 1975, p.85). This example alone shows the value of studying the effects of labor market experience on patterns of unemployment and reemployment.

## Summary

In our review of literature on internal, primary, and secondary labor markets, we found the prevailing conceptualizations overly broad, multidimensional, and inconsistent with several operationalizations of these concepts. Taking an explicit departure from the broad conception of internal labor markets (ILMs), we proposed a three-part structural definition. Jobs would be in an ILM if and only if they form a ladder, with entry limited to the bottom and where movement upward is accompanied by a progressive development of skill and knowledge. Two subtypes of ILMs with this common structure were distinguished: firm internal labor markets (FILMs) and occupational internal labor markets (OILMs). Three other types of noninternal markets were suggested: firm (FLMs), occupational (OLMs), and secondary labor markets (SLAMs).

In other literature, we next found that center and periphery economic sectors completely overlapped, and hence subsumed, primary and secondary labor markets. Arguments for this included brief histories of the bureaucratic control systems emergent in U.S. capitalism and assertions that the size, capital intensity, high profit levels, and monopoly elements of center firms alone were sufficient to support ILMs. We responded that historic arguments are so far sketchy on the specific development of ILMs, that medium and large periphery firms exist with the size and market power more than sufficient to support ILMs, and that a framework where markets and sectors do not completely overlap would greatly facilitate theoretical, historical, and empirical research on fundamental questions infrequently addressed to date. An agenda for research into locating or measuring labor markets and into differences in wage levels, wage functions, and job mobility among markets has concluded our chapter.

## Acknowledgment

We thank Carolyn Mullins for her help in editing this manuscript.

## References

Abrahamson, M.
    1973   "Functionalism and the functional theory of stratification: An empirical assessment."
           *American Journal of Sociology* 78:1236–1246.
Alexander, A. J.
    1974   "Income, experience, and the structure of internal labor markets." *Quarterly Journal
           of Economics* 88:63–85.

Andrisani, P. J.
  1973   "An empirical analysis of the dual labor market theory." Unpublished doctoral dissertation, Ohio State University, Columbus.
  1976   "Discrimination, segmentation, and upward mobility: A longitudinal approach to the dual labor market theory." Unpublished manuscript, Temple University, Philadelphia, Pennsylvania.
Averitt, R. T.
  1968   *The Dual Economy: The Dynamics of American Industry Structure*. New York: Norton.
Azumi, K.
  1969   *Higher Education and Business Recruitment in Japan*. New York: Teachers College Press.
Beck, E. M., P. M. Horan, and C. M. Tolbert
  1978   "Stratification in a dual economy: A sectoral model of earnings determination." *American Sociological Review* 43:704–720.
Bibb, R., and W. H. Form
  1977   "The effects of industrial, occupational and sex stratification on wages in blue-collar markets." *Social Forces* 55:974–996.
Blau, P., and O. D. Duncan
  1967   *The American Occupational Structure*. New York: Wiley.
Bluestone, B., W. M. Murphy, and M. Stevenson
  1973   *Low Wages and the Working Poor*. Ann Arbor, Michigan: Institute of Labor and Industrial Relations, University of Michigan.
Bonacich, E.
  1972   "A theory of ethnic antagonism: The split labor market." *American Sociological Review* 37:547–559.
  1976   "Advanced capitalism and black/white race relations in the United States: A split labor market interpretation." *American Sociological Review* 41:34–51.
Broom, L., and R. G. Cushing
  1977   "A modest test of an immodest theory: The functional theory of stratification." *American Sociological Review* 42:157–169.
Cain, G. G.
  1976   "The challenge of segmented labor market theories to orthodox theory: A survey" *Journal of Economic Literature* 14:1215–1257.
Cain, G. G., R. B. Freeman, and W. L. Hansen
  1973   *Labor Market Analysis of Engineers and Technical Workers*. Baltimore: Johns Hopkins Press.
Caplow, T.
  1954   *The Sociology of Work*. New York: McGraw-Hill.
Chandler, A. D., Jr.
  1977   *The Visible Hand: The Managerial Revolution in American Business*. Cambridge, Massachusetts: Harvard Univ. Press.
Collins, R.
  1971   "Functional and conflict theories of educational stratification." *American Sociological Review* 36:1002–1019.
Doeringer, P. B.
  1967   "Determinants of the structure of industrial type internal labor markets." *Industrial and Labor Relations Review* 20:206–220.
Doeringer, P., and M. Piore
  1971   *Internal Labor Markets and Manpower Analysis*. Lexington, Massachusetts: Heath.
Dore, R. P.
  1974   "Late development—or something else? Industrial relations in Britain, Japan, Mexico,

Sri Lanka, Senegal." Brighton, England: University of Sussex, Institute of Developmental Studies.

Dunlop, J. T.
1957   "The task of contemporary wage theory." In G. W. Taylor & F. C. Pierson (eds.), *New Concepts in Wage Determination.* New York: McGraw-Hill.
1966   "Job vacancy measures and economic analysis." In National Bureau of Economic Research (ed.), *The Measurement and Interpretation of Job Vacancies.* New York: Columbia Univ. Press.

Eckaus, R. S.
1973   *Estimating the Returns to Education: A Disaggregated Approach.* Berkeley, California: Carnegie Commission on Higher Education.

Edwards, R. C.
1975   "The social relations of production in the firm and labor market structure." In R. C. Edwards, M. Reich, and D. M. Gordon (eds.), *Labor Market Segmentation.* Lexington, Massachusetts: Heath.
1979   *Contested Terrain.* New York: Basic Books.

Evans, R. Jr.
1973   "The rediscovery of the Balkans" *Keio Economic Studies* 10:33–38.

Form, W., and J. Huber
1976   "Occupational power." In R. Dubin (ed.), *Handbook of Work, Organization and Society.* Chicago: Rand McNally.

Freedman, M. K.
1976   *Labor Markets: Segments and Shelters.* Montclair, New Jersey: Allanheld, Osmun.

Gitelman, H. M.
1966   "Occupational mobility within the firm." *Industrial and Labor Relations Review* 20:50–65.

Goldstein, H. M., and M. A. Horowitz
1977   *Entry-level Health Occupations: Development and Future.* Baltimore: Johns Hopkins Press.

Gordon, D. M.
1972a   "From steam whistles to coffee breaks." *Dissent* 19:197–210.
1972b   *Theories of Poverty and Underemployment.* Lexington, Massachusetts: Heath.
1976   "Capitalist efficiency and socialist efficiency." *Monthly Review* 28:19–39.

Greenbaum, J.
1976   "Division of labor in the computer field." *Monthly Review* 28:40–55.

Hall, R. E.
1974   "Comments and discussion." *Brookings Papers on Economic Activity* 3:688–690.

Hodson, R.
1978   "Labor in the monopoly, competitive and state sectors of production." *Politics and Society* 8:429–480. Also printed as Center for Demography and Ecology Working Paper 78-2, University of Wisconsin, Madison.

Holt, C., C. D. MacRae, S. O. Schweitzer, and R. E. Smith
1971   *The Unemployment–Inflation Dilemma: A Manpower Solution.* Washington, D.C.: Urban Institute.

Kahn, L. M.
1976   "Internal labor markets: San Francisco longshoremen." *Industrial Relations* 15:333–337.

Kaysen, C.
1973   "New directions for research." In L. C. Solmon and P. J. Taubman (eds.), *Does College Matter?* New York: Academic Press.

Kelly, R. W.
1918   *Hiring the Worker.* New York: Engineering Magazine.

Kerr, C.
  1950  "Labor markets: Their character and consequences." *American Economic Review* 40:278–291.
  1954  "The Balkanization of labor markets." In E. Wight Bakke, P. M. Hauser, G. L. Palmer, C. A. Myers, D. Yoder, and C. Kerr (eds.), *Labor Mobility and Economic Opportunity.* Cambridge, Massachusetts: MIT Press.
Marglin, S. A.
  1974  "What do bosses do? The origins and functions of hierarchy in capitalist production." *Review of Radical Political Economics* 6:60–112.
Martin, N. H., and A. L. Strauss
  1968  "Patterns of mobility within industrial organizations." In B. G. Glaser (ed.), *Organizational Careers: A Sourcebook for Theory.* Chicago: Aldine.
Noble, D. F.
  1977  *America by Design: Science, Technology, and the Rise of Corporate Capitalism.* New York: Knopf.
Okamoto, H.
  1974  "Management and their organizations." In K. Okochi, B. Karsh, and S. Levine (eds.), *Workers and Employers in Japan.* Princeton: Princeton and Tokyo Univ. Press.
Osterman, P.
  1975  "An empirical study of labor market segmentation." *Industrial and Labor Relations Review* 28:508–523.
  1977  "Reply to Kruse." *Industrial and Labor Relations Review* 30:221–224.
Piore, M. J.
  1970  "Jobs and training." In S. H. Beer and R. E. Barringer (eds.), *The State and the Poor.* Boston: Winthrop.
  1975  "Notes for a theory of labor market stratification." In R. C. Edwards, M. Reich, and D. Gordon (eds.), *Labor Market Segmentation.* Lexington, Massachusetts: Heath.
Rees, A., and G. P. Shultz
  1970  *Workers and Wages in an Urban Labor Market.* Chicago: Univ. of Chicago Press.
Reich, M., D. M. Gordon, and R. C. Edwards
  1973  "A theory of labor market segmentation." *American Economic Review* 63:359–365.
Rosenbaum, J. E.
  1978  "Tournament mobility: Career patterns in a corporation." Paper presented to the Annual Meeting, American Sociological Association, San Francisco.
Scoville, J. G.
  1972  *Manpower and Occupational Analysis: Concepts and Measurements.* Lexington, Massachusetts: Heath.
Smigel, E. O.
  1968  "Weeding out lawyers." In B. G. Glaser (ed.), *Organizational Careers: A Sourcebook for Theory.* Chicago: Aldine.
Spilerman, S.
  1977  "Careers, labor market structure, and socioeconomic achievement." *American Journal of Sociology* 83:551–593.
Stieber, J.
  1959  *The Steel Industry Wage Structure.* Cambridge, Massachusetts: Harvard Univ. Press.
Stinchcombe, A. L.
  1963  "Some empirical consequences of the Davis–Moore theory of stratification." *American Sociological Review* 28:805–808.
  1965  "Social structure and organizations." In J. G. March (ed.), *Handbook of Organizations.* Chicago: Rand McNally.
  1979  "Social mobility in industrial labor markets." *Acta Sociologica* 22:217–245.

Stinchcombe, A. L., and T. R. Harris
   1969  "Interdependence and inequality: A specification of the Davis–Moore theory." *Sociometry* 32:13–23.
Stolzenberg, R. M.
   1975  "Occupations, labor markets and the process of wage attainment." *American Sociological Review* 40:645–665.
   1978  "Bringing the boss back in: Employer size, employee schooling, and socioeconomic achievement." *American Sociological Review* 43(December):813–828.
Stone, K.
   1975  "The origins of job structures in the steel industry." In R. C. Edwards, M. Reich, and D. M. Gordon (eds.), *Labor Market Segmentation*. Lexington, Massachusetts: Heath.
Talbert, J., and C. E. Bose
   1977  "Wage attainment processes: The retail clerk case." *American Journal of Sociology* 83:403–424.
Taylor, D. P., and M. J. Piore
   1971  "Issues for manpower action programs." In S. M. Jacks (ed.), *Issues in Labor Policy*. Cambridge, Massachusetts: MIT Press.
Thurow, L. C.
   1975  *Generating Inequality: Mechanisms of Distribution in the U.S. Economy*. New York: Basic Books.
Vietorisz, T., and B. Harrison
   1973  "Labor market segmentation: Positive feedback and divergent development." *American Economic Review* 63:366–376.
Wachter, M. L.
   1974  "Primary and secondary labor markets: A critique of the dual approach." *Brookings Papers on Economic Activity* 3:637–680.
Weinberg, E., and H. J. Rothberg
   1957  *A Case Study of a Modernized Petroleum Refinery*. U.S. Department of Labor, Bureau of Labor Statistics, Studies of Automatic Technology. BLS Report No. 120. Washington, D.C.: U.S. Govt Printing Office.
Williamson, O. E., M. L. Wachter, and J. E. Harris
   1975  "Understanding the employment relation: The analysis of idiosyncratic exchange." *Bell Journal of Economics* 6:250–278.
Wright, E. O.
   1976  "Class boundaries in advanced capitalist societies." *New Left Review* 98:3–41.
Wright, E. O., and L. Perrone
   1977  "Marxist class categories and income inequality." *American Sociological Review* 42:32–55.

# Part III

# EMPLOYMENT AND
# UNEMPLOYMENT

# Chapter 6

# The Structure

# of Employment

# and Unemployment[1]

*PAUL G. SCHERVISH*

The way people are employed determines the way they are unemployed. In the contemporary American economy, the structure of unemployment is segmented in accord with the segmentation of employment. Different positions of employment, determined by different means and social relations of production, produce corresponding different unemployment contingencies.

Two elements in the Marxist analysis of advanced capitalism are especially relevant to the argument of this chapter. First, economic sectors develop unevenly; as a consequence, the economy is segmented into oligopoly, competitive, and state sectors. Across and within these sectors, positions of employment have different resource pools from which to extract benefits. Because each sector is affected differently by and possesses different resources for responding to fluctuations in product demand, employment positions are associated with different forms of unemployment.

Second, employment positions are among the most salient social rela-

[1] The research reported here was supported by funds granted to the Institute for Research on Poverty at the University of Wisconsin—Madison by the Department of Health, Education, and Welfare pursuant to the provisions of the Economic Opportunity Act of 1964. The conclusions expressed are those of the author. An earlier version of this chapter was presented at the Seventy-Third Annual Meeting of the American Sociological Association, San Francisco, September 4–8, 1978.

153

tionships that embody and manifest class relations. Employment positions reflect the domination of employers over employees and the limitations on that dominance. Just as the structure of employment allows employers to subordinate labor to its requirements of profitability through market mechanisms, it also enables labor to shield itself against these mechanisms and to attain benefits from the accumulated stock of resources in the sector. Such worker capacity differs according to the extent that unionization, training requirements, or technological complexity permit employment positions to mitigate their vulnerability to market mechanisms and to attain relatively more favorable adjustments in job quitting or loss.

This research proposes that types of worker resources for obtaining benefits and types of worker capacities for resisting market forces (a) are variously attached to positions of employment; and (b) structure the type of unemployment associated with these positions. More precisely, various combinations of resources sectors and types of capacities are differentially associated with four types of unemployment: short layoffs, firings, long layoffs, and quits. The first task is to define the structure of employment as being composed of sets of positions differentiated by their resources and capacities.

## Resources

The first dimension of positions of employment, resources, is determined by the industrial sector in which the position is located. The various sectors—oligopoly (or concentrated), competitive, and state—provide different stocks of resources from which benefits may accrue to positions of employment through struggle and negotiation (Averitt, 1968; O'Connor, 1973; Poulantzas, 1975). Some traditional economic theorists and many who contribute to its literature on segmentation agree that firms in concentrated industries can extract a higher return on investment and can engage in administered pricing, enabling them to pass higher labor and capital costs on to the consumer (Beck, Horan, & Tolbert, 1978; Bluestone, 1970; R. Feinberg, 1978; Hodson, 1978; Robinson, 1969). The causal links between concentrated markets, administered pricing, economies of scale, higher profits, and higher wage rates are the subjects of much debate (cf. Scherer, 1980; pp.267–295). But despite problems of quality and comparability of data, Scherer (1980) concludes "that there is considerable statistical support for industrial organization theory's predictions of a relationship among profitability, seller concentration, and barriers to entry [pp.294–295]." Thus we argue, with some caveats, that the pool of resources available to firms in oligopolistic sector positions is large and subject to expansion in the face of labor struggles for increased job or wage benefits. In contrast, the competitive sector gains a lower return on investment being both constrained by the need to meet given prices in the product market and restricted in pricing schedules dictated by national and international competition. Consequently, the stock of resources from which positions in competitive firms may draw benefits is necessarily limited and also constrained by the inability of the firms to pass on the increased costs that result from labor struggles.

## Capacities

Employment positions differ not only in their stock of available resources but also in ability to extract benefits from resource pools. High-capacity positions are associated with social relations of production that lower a position's degree of vulnerability to market forces, whereas low-capacity positions are associated with relations of production that enforce a high degree of vulnerability to competitive market forces. More analytically, high-capacity positions are associated with what is here called *vacancy competition* ways of matching workers to jobs; low-capacity positions are those that remain tied to *wage competition* processes. For instance, high-capacity positions, such as unionized auto and steel workers, middle managers, and professional chemists, enjoy employment relations having bargaining power and job benefits that do not accrue to gas station attendants, shipping clerks, janitors, and laundry operatives.

The distinction between wage- and vacancy competition mechanisms for job attainment, wage and benefit determination,[2] and capacity for struggle derives from literature on labor market segmentation.[3] While this research often confuses attributes of workers, jobs, and labor market processes, its central insight is valid: That taken alone, traditional neoclassical theory is inadequate for explaining the relationships between characteristics of individual workers, of jobs, and of outcomes.

The present research departs from the existing literature on segmentation in its claim that, at least in the area of unemployment, so-called secondary (low-capacity) positions are vulnerable to labor market mechanisms described by neoclassical theory. Even if it can be shown that income attainment processes for workers located in such secondary positions reflect the character of their employment positions, rather than their human capital

---

[2] For an extended discussion of labor market research, see Granovetter, this volume.

[3] This literature stresses the disjunction between primary and secondary jobs (Doeringer & Piore, 1971; Edwards et al., 1975; Gordon, 1972; Piore, 1970); primary and secondary workers (Piore, 1970, 1971); and monopoly, competitive, state, and irregular sectors of the economy (Averitt, 1968; Bluestone, 1970; Edwards, 1979; O'Connor, 1973).

resources (Beck *et al.*, 1978), this does not mean necessarily that neoclassical considerations of labor supply and firm behavior are not relevant in explaining the unemployment outcomes for workers located in positions of weak bargaining power.

For these purposes, Thurow's (1975) formulation of segmentation of job positions is valuable. He distinguishes between wage and job competition labor markets as the two major arenas of exchange between employee offers and employer demands. He terms positions of employment that are subject to the market forces described by neoclassical theory *wage competition* positions. The competitive labor market associated with these positions is cleared in the short run by wage rates.

Positions that are shielded from the market relations of supply and demand are called *job competition* positions. According to Thurow (1975), "in the job competition model, instead of competing against one another based on the wages that they are willing to accept, individuals compete against one another for job opportunities based on their relative costs of being trained to fill whatever job is being considered [p.75]." Thurow offers an insightful first approximation of the forces that reduce the vulnerability of these positions to traditional market relations. Nevertheless, it has been argued elsewhere (Schervish & Sørensen, 1977; Sørensen & Kalleberg, this volume) that other job characteristics and job organizations, not just the rate of technological progress and the need for on-the-job training,[4] contribute to worker bargaining power and constrain traditional market relations. The authors just cited refer to jobs with such bargaining power as vacancy competition positions. In contrast to wage competition jobs, vacancy competition positions grant to those who hold them control over outcomes even in the technologically static sector. The basis for such protection is derived from (*a*) seniority and promotion systems needed to elicit increased productivity, creativity, or initiative; (*b*) interdependence among jobs; (*c*) difficulty in measuring output of a job; (*d*) collective organization among employees; and (*e*) other customary or legal constraints on the employment relation.

In sum, positions that make up the employment structure in the private sector are differentiated according to the stock of resources from which benefits may be won and the capacities for struggle that shield workers from market forces and thereby enhance their ability to extract benefits from the stock of resources. The location of positions in the monopoly or competitive sector, on the one hand, and the high (vacancy competition) or low (wage competition) capacities of those positions within capital sectors, on the other, structure the types of employment that workers enter

---

[4] See Granovetter (Chapter 2, this volume) for an elaboration of these issues.

and the types of unemployment that they will suffer. To this issue we now turn, examining first the structure of unemployment.

## The Structure of Unemployment

Theoretically, a job loss results from the separation of a jobholder from a position of employment (see Schervish, 1977). Unemployment is the type of job loss in which the worker is severed from one job without simultaneously reentering another one. Different combinations of outcomes for positions and outcomes for workers of these positions provide a classification of job loss and unemployment. Transfers, demotions, promotions, and voluntary retirement are modes of job loss that are not simultaneously forms of unemployment and do not necessarily entail the separation of the worker from employment; however, they do involve the loss of a specific job.

The remaining forms of job loss are concomitantly modes of unemployment. A suspension occurs when a worker is severed from a position temporarily, although the position remains unchanged. A suspension creates a temporary vacancy that may or may not be filled for the duration of the suspension. A layoff results when a position of employment is temporarily ended and the worker is temporarily severed from employment. A layoff is distinguished from a firing by the continued connection of worker and position during the period of unemployment. When the position is reopened, the worker retains priority for reentry.

A firing occurs when a worker is separated permanently and involuntarily from employment regardless of what happens to the position. A firing, as commonly understood, occurs when a position remains open but the worker is severed from employment and replaced by another worker; it may also happen when a position is ended temporarily (during a slack period in the business cycle, for instance) and the worker becomes unemployed, with little or no priority for reemployment in the temporarily ended position.

Another form of firing occurs when individual or sets of positions are ended and workers lose employment permanently. In the case of individual positions, this firing is sometimes called a dismissal or letting a worker go, but when a whole set of positions is systematically eliminated, the firings are called terminations or cutbacks.

Both voluntary retirements and quits result in the creation of a vacancy and the severance of a worker from a specific job. Retirement implies at least a temporary abandonment of the search for reemployment. Quits may coincide with the temporary or permanent ending of positions or with their reclassification. In fact, voluntary departure from a position may provoke its ending or reclassification.

## A Theory of Firings, Layoffs, and Quits

Elaborating a theory of the relationship between the structures of employment and of unemployment requires an explanation of the relationships between capacities and unemployment and between sectoral resources and unemployment. This chapter will focus on three types of unemployment that are measured in the Monthly Current Population Surveys (CPS): layoffs, quits, and involuntary job loss, which we call firings.

Whether a position of employment is located in the wage- or vacancy competition labor market determines the nature of the capacities by which workers gain relative control of property rights over their positions. In vacancy competition, the separation of workers from a position is constrained by the relatively high capacity of the workers to resist arbitrary firings and the rehiring of other workers from the labor pool. When economic downturns force firms to curtail employment, workers who are released are laid off, that is, they are separated from their positions on a temporary basis but retain a hold on them even while unemployed. Moreover, when the positions are reopened, the laid-off worker retains a prior claim to the lost position. Although workers may lose jobs permanently if positions are ended permanently, positions are usually ended only temporarily and workers are laid off.

In wage competition, workers possess low capacities for struggle and retain little or no control over the processes of unemployment and reemployment. When positions are ended permanently, workers are fired, of course. But when positions are ended temporarily or even when they are not ended, workers may be separated permanently from their jobs. This process has also been defined as a firing. Low-capacity positions do not provide workers with rights to those positions. Workers are fired and hired according to their productivity, rather than in accordance with sets of systematic constraints like those that regulate the process of unemployment in high-capacity positions. Even when production cutbacks require the temporary ending of positions, workers are said to be "let go" or "laid off" but in fact are fired and not necessarily rehired when the position is reestablished.

A similar argument applies to the relation of vacancy and wage competition capacities to quits and long layoffs. CPS data distinguish between short and long (indefinite) layoffs. Indefinite layoffs are sometimes euphemisms for firings; they represent the power of employers to separate workers from positions without the workers being able to keep track of or to ensure reentry into the lost positions. Indefinite layoffs should, therefore, relate to capacities of positions in a way similar to firings. That is, wage competition positions are expected to be associated with indefinite layoffs, as well as with firings, since persons in these positions have little resistance to or

voluntary control over the market relations that dictate employment decisions. The case of quits is more ambiguous. High-capacity, vacancy competition positions might be expected to be more regularly associated with
quits than low-capacity, wage competition positions, but this is not necessarily true.

Workers in both high and low capacity positions make decisions to quit.
Whether quits are more usual in vacancy- than in wage competition positions
depends on the size of the unemployed population, the magnitude of which
is, in turn, partly a function of the stage of the business cycle. This is
because quits represent different realities for low-capacity workers depending on labor market conditions. For low-capacity positions during periods
of high labor demand, quits tend to represent worker aspirations for better
positions, as is the case for high-capacity positions. During periods of high
unemployment and low labor demand, however, quits from low-capacity
positions represent not simply aspirations for better jobs but a reaction to
the hidden downgrading of positions as well. Workers in low-capacity positions find it difficult to resist wage cuts, because of both the inflation rates
that outstrip wage increases and the general lowering of wages induced by
market forces during periods of abundant labor. In contrast, quits associated
with high-capacity positions reflect similar worker decisions during both
high and low levels of demand for workers. Because a quit from a high-
capacity position is a decision exercised in light of a relatively high degree
of choice in the labor market, it represents across different levels of general
labor demand a dissatisfaction with existing work conditions or rewards.
Consequently, quits are expected to be associated slightly more with high-
than with low-capacity positions during periods of tight labor markets and
to be associated slightly more with low- than with high-capacity positions
during periods of relatively high unemployment.

Determining the effect of the location of positions in oligopoly or competitive sectors on types of unemployment is theoretically less straightforward than discerning the impact of capacities. While research on the so-
called monopoly or oligopoly wage premium continues to debate whether
the source of such premiums resides in the productivity of workers who
choose oligopoly employment, in union wage agreements, or in the nature
of oligopoly pricing (see Scherer, 1980, pp.358–361; Weiss, 1966), the literature does concur that imperfectly competitive firms do in fact obtain
excess income from their oligopoly product market structure (Scherer, 1980,
p.294–295). Thus, when and where income is stabilized over time, the labor
force receives wages that induce the attachment of workers to their firms
even during periods of unemployment. Because oligopoly sector positions
generally pay higher wages and require larger investments in worker benefits
and training, the oligopoly sector is faced with a dilemma during economic

downturns. On the one hand, administered pricing has resulted in greater worker benefits, which represent high levels of investment in workers that these more concentrated firms do not wish to forfeit. On the other hand, such investment directed at long-term stability or expansion undermines the range of possible responses in times of business downturn and high unemployment. Unlike competitive firms, oligopolistic ones are not as free to restructure technical relations of production in order to substitute more lower wage, ostensibly less productive, labor. Thus, they are forced to curtail production, to cut back their labor force, and to hope to weather the downturn, often by resisting relative prices, in an effort to maintain profitability. Although employment positions are decreased when demand is reduced sharply, the decrease takes the form of layoffs, both short and long term. For their part, workers benefit, at least in the short run, from an unemployment pattern of layoffs, because they receive at least some degree of enforceable guarantee of recall should the position be reestablished. Nevertheless, it should be stressed that workers, especially on long or indefinite layoffs, do not invariably return to their original jobs.

In contrast, resources available in the competitive sector induce unemployment patterns of firing and quits. Competitive firms are less capable than concentrated industries of controlling prices throughout phases of the business cycle. But at the same time, the less concentrated competitive firms are less constrained by established technical relations of production. This more flexible technology enables them to adjust to differing levels of supply, costs, and quality of labor by adding or subtracting quality and quantity of labor, rather than by temporarily ending positions as do oligopolistic industries. Free market relations of supply and demand continue to rule employment relations in the competitive sector. Thus, when product demand declines, competitive firms tend to adjust by lowering wage rates and by acquiring more productive employees. Individual capital units and individual workers adjust to structural changes in the economy through the market processes embodied in labor decisions to quit and employer decisions to fire.

## Hypotheses

The foregoing theoretical arguments here suggested the following two hypotheses: (a) that workers employed in high- rather than low-capacity positions will tend to suffer lower unemployment rates and, when unemployed, will tend to become unemployed through short layoffs and quits rather than through long layoffs and firings; and (b) that workers employed in oligopoly rather than competitive sector positions will tend to experience higher unemployment rates and, when unemployed, will tend to become unemployed through layoffs rather than through firings and quits.

A third hypothesis concerning the relation of race and unemployment is also tested in order to demonstrate the continued importance of capacities and resources in distributing workers to types of unemployment even when a personal characteristic as significant as race is taken into account.[5] If capacities and resources do exercise a strong impact on distributing workers to types of unemployment, the effect of race should be marginal or weak. However, even if weak, the effect of being black rather than white can be expected to result in forms of unemployment that reflect blacks' greater vulnerability to market relations. Thus, it is expected that the effect of being black is to increase the incidence of unemployment in general and to increase the propensity to become unemployed through firings and quits rather than through layoffs.

Moreover, a marginal effect of race can be interpreted as resulting from labor market discrimination (rather than indicating a lack of racial discrimination in unemployment) if it can be shown as well that being black increases the propensity to be employed in positions associated with high unemployment, especially unemployment through firings and quits.

## Data and Methodology

The data for testing the hypotheses are taken from the January 1973 CPS, a monthly, national random sample of households conducted by the Bureau of the Census. The January 1973 survey contains 102,374 records for members of those households 14 years and older. The subsample chosen for this research is composed of white and black males,[6] aged 20–64, who are

[5] My current research examines the relationship of sector resources and job bargaining power to unemployment types controlling not just for race but for age, education, and period in the business cycle. The findings from this research indicate that controlling for these further variables does not change significantly the major findings reported here.

[6] A number of considerations kept me from including women in the analysis despite my original predisposition to do so. First, little sociological work has been done on employment and unemployment, thus the present research was conceived of as more a theoretical argument establishing certain characteristics of the American economy than an empirical work estimating these relationships for either males or females. Second, because of the dirth of sociological literature on unemployment, the chapter was written in dialogue with economic research. This research emphasizes the importance of modeling the relationship of men and women to the labor force in different ways (cf. Cain, 1966; Mincer, 1963; Niemi, 1975; Rees, 1973; Watts & Rees, 1977). Consequently, for the sake of parsimony in this exploratory research, I tested the impact of capital sector and job segment on unemployment for males only. I believe that the independent effects of sector resources and bargaining capacity may be similar for women

employed or unemployed members of the experienced civilian labor force. Excluded are all the self-employed, those who have never worked (including those seeking their first jobs), and workers who have given up searching for work.[7]

For this research, a specific weighting procedure was designed to adjust the given CPS weights for each case so as to provide true subsample weights.[8] The deflated sample size used here is 16,571.45.

The four variables used throughout the analysis are a dependent variable (D) representing a worker's status in the employment structure, and three independent variables: capital sector resources (S), capacities for struggle (C), and race (R). Employment status comprises four categories of unemployment and the comparative category of employment. Unemployment is differentiated into short layoffs, firings, long layoffs, and quits. Short layoffs and long layoffs are derived from the CPS item that asks why a worker was absent from work the previous week. Two of the eight possible responses to the inquiry are "temporary layoff (under 30 days)" and "indefinite layoff (30 days or more or no definite recall date)." A later survey question—"Why did you start looking for work?"—is addressed to all the unemployed except those who had already indicated their unemployment status as temporary or indefinite layoff. The category of "quit" in the dependent variable is measured simply by the response of "quit job" to this

---

but to show this would entail consideration of a series of such further factors as marital status, number of children, income, and the employment status of other members of the household. Also, Hispanics were not treated as a group separate from whites for two reasons. First, the only indication of being Hispanic in the January 1973 CPS is having a Spanish surname. Such an indicator does not univocally distinguish those individuals we now consider socially important. Moreover, even if it were possible to determine the Hispanic population, there are not enough cases to properly fill the cells in a log-linear analysis dealing with unemployment. Finally, the CPS race category of "other" is excluded since groups included under that rubric, such as Japanese, are generally favorably placed in the labor market and thus data on their unemployment experience should not be allowed to confound that of blacks. Again, this group is relatively small and, even if included among the whites, would not change the results substantially.

[7] Discouraged workers are omitted from the analysis only because they are considered to be out of the labor force according to Department of Labor criteria, and thus no information is provided in the CPS survey concerning the type of unemployment by which they become severed from their last jobs.

[8] First, each case in the subsample was assigned to CPS case weight, which was calculated to inflate the total survey sample to the demographic characteristics of the national population. These assigned weights were summed over the subsample and averaged. A new subsample case weight was calculated for each subsample case by dividing the case's original CPS weight by the subsample average. Each of these adjusted subsample case weights was then deflated by a factor of .33 to adjust for the nonrandom sample design of the CPS by reducing the probability that significant statistical differences would emerge in the analysis of data.

second question. The category of "firings" cannot be so directly ascertained from the CPS data. It is derived here as those unemployed who indicated they had "lost job" but who were not explicitly among those who were unemployed because they were laid off, had quit, had left school, or had wanted temporary work. It may appear problematic to measure firings by the residual category of job loss. However, asking directly if a worker was fired would incur as much, if not more, measurement error than is incurred through deriving firings from the less threatening category of job loss. It is important to recall, also, that the category of firings includes under one rubric both disciplinary terminations as well as job loss due to labor force cutback resulting from plant closings or individual termination of positions. However, it is reasonable to assume that the majority of involuntary job losses considered firings are due to labor force cutbacks and not to disciplinary actions taken by employers against particular workers. The category of "employed" is included in the dependent variable in order to extend the analysis beyond the impact of the independent variables on the relative chances of being in one category of unemployment rather than another. Including the employed extends the comparisons to include the impact of the independent variables on the relative chance of being unemployed rather than employed and of being in any one particular type of unemployment rather than employed.

The independent variable, sector resources, is composed of four categories: oligopoly, competitive, farm, and construction sectors. These categories are derived from industry categories as described in Hodson (1978). Hodson differentiated monopoly (oligopoly) from competitive sectors of capital on the basis of four criteria: two measures of economic concentration and average weighted concentration ratios for value of shipments and employees. Farm and construction sectors, which are defined simply by the appropriate industry codes, are treated in the analysis as separate categories for the resource variable because they do not fall clearly into either oligopoly or competitive sectors.[9] Hodson defined the state sector as comprising all federal, state, and local government employment and employment in utilities. This sector is not included because preliminary analysis indicated that during the early phases of the current recession in 1973 the state sector had virtually no measurable unemployment.[10]

---

[9] The farm sector, while predominantly competitive in food production, is increasingly oligopolistic in some food lines, including fruit, lettuce, celery, and other salad products (cf. Zwerdling, 1979). Also, there is increasing concentration in grain and feed production. Similarly, the construction sector is difficult to categorize as either monopoly or competitive. The construction industry is clearly competitive on the national level, but because of the inability to transport finished products, this industry often functions as an effective monopoly on the local level. Thus this sector is sometimes referred to as a *local monopoly*.

[10] Omitting the state sector from the analysis is purely for methodological reasons and does

Ideally, the variable "capacities," separated into "high" and "low" categories, should be defined by a composite indicator constructed directly from measures of the variables that theoretically comprise vacancy- and wage competition relations. Measures of interdependence of tasks, of marginal productivity, of on-the-job training, and of unionization are available in the Michigan Quality of Employment Survey, 1972–1973; but the small sample size of this survey does not permit the scaling of the entire occupational structure. An alternate measure of capacities is available from Rosenberg's (1975) differentiation of census occupations into primary and secondary jobs on the basis of skill level, social relations on the job, and median hourly wage. The jobs Rosenberg considers secondary are listed in Appendix A.[11] In this chapter, high-capacity positions are defined by Rosenberg's primary-sector occupations, while low-capacity positions are designated by his secondary-sector occupations. It should be cautioned that dichotomizing positions into primary and secondary jobs is an oversimplification of the employment structures and as such is highly controversial (Cain, 1976), even among researchers who otherwise espouse the segmented labor market perspective (e.g., Edwards, Reich, & Gordon, 1975). In particular, Rosenberg's schema is vulnerable to criticism. First, one component that contributes to the construction of his dichotomy is hourly wage rates, which makes his schema of dubious value in research where earnings or income are the dependent variable. Second, the dichotomy fails to differentiate

---

not imply an underestimation of its theoretical or social importance. In the January 1973 CPS survey, the government sector had none of its male workers classified as either temporarily or indefinitely laid off and only 1.29 cases (weighted cell frequency) as quits. Since the focus of the present research was on the relative unemployment propensities of the oligopoly and competitive sectors, it was decided to drop the state sector from the analysis rather than allow the presence of numerous zero cells to distort the log-linear parameters for the other capital sectors. Subsequent analysis using 10 years of March CPS data (1969–1978) indicate that the state sector, as would be expected from its welfare functions and stable revenue, enjoys a much lower unemployment rate than either the oligopoly or competitive sectors.

[11] Rosenberg (1975) uses Specific Vocational Preparation (SVP) and General Educational Development (GED) as measures of the skill requirements of a job. According to the U.S. Department of Labor's *Dictionary of Occupational Titles* (1965), Specific Vocational Preparation is "the amount of time required to learn the techniques, acquire information and develop the facility needed for average performance in a specific job worker situation [p.652]." General Educational Development "embraces those aspects of education (formal and informal) which contribute to the worker's (*a*) reasoning development and ability to follow instructions and (*b*) acquisition of 'tool' knowledges, such as language and mathematical skills [p.651]." Social relations on the job are defined by a set of variables measuring the degree of independent action or judgment afforded by the job. If a position is below a certain designated level on measures of GED, SVP, and job independence, and not above certain maximum levels, and if a job has an average medium hourly wage rate that provides its incumbents with yearly wages below the Bureau of Labor Statistics' minimum support level, the job is classified in the secondary sector; all other occupations are then located in the primary sector.

between such primary jobs as managerial and professional positions, on the one hand, and traditional unionized blue-collar positions, on the other. Nevertheless, Rosenberg's classification is employed here since the dependent variable in the analysis is unemployment and not income and since even as a dichotomy it allows for a first approximation of the previously unstudied relation between employment position bargaining power and unemployment.

Log-linear techniques (Bishop, Fienberg, & Holland, 1975; Fienberg, 1977; Goodman, 1972) have proved especially suited for handling multicategory nominal variables, where the goal is to explain the observed frequency distribution of cases in a multidimensional contingency table through the specification of a theoretically relevant model.

Parameters derived from the model can be interpreted (Daymont & Kaufman, 1979; Page, 1977) so as to indicate the nature and magnitude of the association among variables. Expected odds ratios can be calculated to summarize the chances of being in one category of one variable, rather than in one or more other categories of the same variable, for observations located in specific contrasting categories of one or more other variables.

## Findings

The baseline model for the analysis (see Table 6.1) was constrained to include only the four one-way effects and the three two-way effects between the dependent and independent variables. This model is represented in Goodman notation as

$$(SC) \ (SR) \ (CR) \ (D)$$

where $(SC)$ is the interaction between sector resources and capacities, $(SR)$ is the interaction between sector resources and race, $(CR)$ is the interaction between capacities and race, and $(D)$ is the effect of employment status. Throughout, whenever two-way or higher order interactions are specified, all the lower order effects (one-way, two-way, etc.) are also included in the model and implied by the notation. Thus, Model 1 contains the three one-way effects of sector resources $(S)$, capacities $(C)$, and race $(R)$.

The three hypotheses considered here may be portrayed by either Model 2 or Model 4 as shown in Table 6.1. If the effect on labor force status $(D)$ of sector resources $(S)$ and capacities $(C)$ is thought not to vary among the different combinations of levels of $S$ and $C$, then Model 2 holds. If this three-way effect $(DSC)$ is thought to be theoretically significant, then Model 4 should adequately reflect the observed distribution. Model 2 is the most

## TABLE 6.1

Models for the Analysis of Employment Status and Independent Variables[a]

| Model | Fitted marginals | Degrees of freedom | Likelihood ratio $\chi^2$ | Index of dissimilarity | P |
|---|---|---|---|---|---|
| 1 | (CS)(CR)(SR)(D) | 63 | 384.13 | 2.167 | .000 |
| 2 | (CS)(CR)(SR)(DC)(DS) | 47 | 42.62 | .553 | > .5 |
| 3 | (CS)(CR)(SR)(DC)(DS)(DR) | 43 | 34.57 | .506 | > .5 |
| 4 | (CR)(SR)(DCS) | 35 | 33.03 | .500 | > .5 |
| 5 | (DC)(DS)(SCR) | 44 | 35.91 | .401 | > .5 |
| 6 | (DC)(DS)(SCR)(DR) | 40 | 28.13 | .373 | > .5 |
| 1 versus 2 | | 63<br>−47<br>16 | 384.13<br>− 42.62<br>341.51 | | < .001 |
| 2 versus 3 | | 47<br>−43<br>4 | 42.62<br>− 34.57<br>8.05 | | c .10 |
| 2 versus 4 | | 47<br>−35<br>12 | 42.62<br>− 33.03<br>9.59 | | > .85 |
| 2 versus 5 | | 47<br>−44<br>3 | 42.62<br>− 35.91<br>6.71 | | c .08 |
| 5 versus 6 | | 44<br>−40<br>4 | 35.91<br>− 28.13<br>7.78 | | .10 |

[a] D = Employment status (dependent variable); C = Capacities of positions; S = Sector resources; R = Race.

simply delineated expression of the theory. It states that over and above the one-way effects, racial characteristics distribute workers to the structure of employment sectors (SR) and capacities (CR). The association (SC) between sectors and capacities represents the fact that sectors have differential proportions of high- and low-capacity positions and that the relative proportion of these positions affects the long-run composition of sector resources. Finally, sectors (DS) and capacities (DC) of positions distribute workers to their status in the labor force.

Table 6.1 indicates that Model 1 must be rejected ($p$ = .000) because it fails to approximate the observed distribution. Model 2, however, dramatically reduces the disparity between the observed and expected distribution ($p$ > 5). The model reduces the likelihood ratio $\chi^2$ by 341.51 and uses up only 16 more degrees of freedom ($p$ < .001).

Comparison of Model 2 with Models 3, 5, and 6 tests for additional race effects. The interaction between race and labor force status (DR) in Model 3 means that, over and above sector and capacity, race affects the distribution of workers among labor force statuses, though the relatively high $p$ value (.1) indicates that the race effect is a marginal one. Whether we should include the DR interaction and modify the theory to take account of it is uncertain. The same is true when the interaction of sector, capacities, and race (SCR) is included, as in Model 5. One interpretation of the SCR interaction is that the relation between sectors and capacities differs for blacks and whites over different combinations of categories of sectors and capacities. The test of this interaction (row 10) indicates that the reduction of 6.71 $\chi^2$ is significant at approximately $p$ = .08. Model 6 adds the DR interaction to Model 5. The $p$ value (.10) again shows that this additional interaction involving race is only modestly significant.

Because the inclusion of the additional race interactions, DR and SCR, are not highly significant statistically and because they are theoretically excluded in the hypotheses, Model 2 serves as the basis for analyzing the effect of the structure of employment on labor force status. Nevertheless, since the DR and SCR interactions are modestly significant statistically and since it is not unreasonable to suspect some direct effect of discrimination on labor force status, we will return to Model 6 and discuss the direct effect of race on unemployment.

## Capacities and Unemployment

The first hypothesis maintains that capacities attached to positions are an important part of the structure of employment that distributes workers to the various types of unemployment. According to the hypothesis, wage competition positions suffer higher unemployment rates than vacancy com-

TABLE 6.2

Gross Unemployment Rates[a]

| Category | Percent |
|----------|---------|
| Total | 3.9 |
| Whites | 3.7 |
| Blacks | 5.7 |
| Oligopoly sector | 2.8 |
| Competitive sector | 3.0 |
| High capacity | 3.3 |
| Low capacity | 6.7 |

[a]*Data from January 1973 CPS.*

petition positions. Table 6.2 presents unemployment rates for the total sample and for selected categories within the sample. High-capacity workers have a 3.3% unemployment rate, whereas the rate for low-capacity workers is 6.7%. These unemployment rates provide one way to summarize the gross relationship between capacities and unemployment. Another representation of the relative chances of being unemployed, one that controls for race and sector, will be called the *ratio of unemployment likelihoods*. It is an odds ratio that measures the relative chances in any of the four categories of unemployment of being employed rather than unemployed. This ratio is calculated by raising the Tau parameter to the appropriate exponential level for the effect of the independent variable on the category of employment in the dependent variable.[12] In the case of capacities and labor force status, the Tau parameter (1.3027), which measures the effect of being in a high-capacity position on being employed rather than unemployed (in any of the

[12] The parameter is raised to the power of $\dfrac{ij}{(i-1)(j-1)}$

where $i$ is the number of categories of the dependent variable and $j$ is the number of categories in the independent variable. Here $i = 5$ and $j = 2$. This produces the power of 5/2.

four categories), is raised to the power of 5/2. The calculated value of this ratio of unemployment likelihood is 1.94, meaning that, as predicted by the hypothesis, the expected chance of being employed rather than unemployed (in any of the four unemployment categories) is 1.94 times greater for workers in high- compared with low-capacity positions.

Table 6.3 shows that, controlling for sector, workers in low-capacity positions are more likely to be unemployed, especially through firings and long layoffs, than workers in high-capacity positions. The first hypothesis predicted that high-capacity positions would be associated with short layoffs and quits, a prediction also confirmed by Table 6.3.

## Sector Resources and Unemployment

The second hypothesis discusses the structural effect of sector resources on the distribution of workers to the categories of unemployment or to employment (controlling for capacities). Oligopoly, competitive, farm, and construction sectors of resources are the four categories of sector resources, but only the comparative effects of oligopoly and competitive sector on unemployment are discussed here. The second hypothesis predicts that oligopoly sector unemployment rates are higher than those in the competitive sector. The ratio of unemployment likelihood[13] shows that, controlling for capacities, the chances of unemployment are greater in the oligopoly sector. Workers in this sector, as opposed to workers in the competitive sector, are on the average 1.20 times more likely to be unemployed in one of the designated categories than to be employed.

Unlike the situation with high- and low-capacity positions, however, the higher unemployment in the oligopoly sector results, not from the fact that oligopoly sector workers are more likely than competitive sector workers to be unemployed in every category, but from the fact that these positions undergo short and long layoffs at a higher rate than competitive sector positions undergo firings and quits.

As with the discussion of capacities, the odds ratios calculated in Table 6.4 formulate the degree to which workers in the oligopoly sector, as opposed to the competitive sector, are more likely to experience a particular form of unemployment.

---

[13] This ratio is calculated according to the formula:

$$\frac{\tau \text{ employment, competitive}^{5/4}}{\tau \text{ employment, oligopoly}}$$

The Tau parameters are: Tau (employment, competitive) = 1.5591; Tau (employment, oligopoly) = 1.3438. See preceding section for a discussion of the meaning and method of calculating this unemployment likelihood ratio.

TABLE 6.3

Expected Odds Ratios for Contrasting Categories
of Employment Status and Capacities[a]

| | High- versus low-capacity positions | | | | |
| | Short layoff | Firing | Long layoff | Quit | Employed |
| --- | --- | --- | --- | --- | --- |
| Short layoff | --- | 1.26 | 1.30 | 1.04 | .59 |
| Firing | .80 | --- | 1.03 | .83 | .47 |
| Long layoff | .77 | .97 | --- | .81 | .45 |
| Quit | .96 | 1.20 | 1.24 | --- | .56 |
| Employed | 1.71 | 2.14 | 2.21 | 1.78 | --- |

Low- versus high-capacity positions

[a]*In this and other tables of odds ratios, the numbers above
and below the diagonal are inverses of each other.  Also, the contrast
stated at the top of the table (here, "high- versus low-capacity positions") is reversed at the bottom (e.g., "low- versus high-capacity
positions").  When formulating a statement dealing with the contrast
stated at the top of table, begin with the category in the row at the
left side of the table and read across to the cell intersecting with the
column designating the second category of concern.  For example, within
high- versus low-capacity positions, to find the contrast between being
in a short layoff as opposed to being fired, begin with the row "short
layoff" and read across to its intersection with the column "firing."
Thus, the chances of being in a short layoff rather than being fired (in
high- as opposed to low-capacity positions) are 1.26 times greater.  To
reverse the contrast, begin with the row "firing" and read across to the
intersection with the column "short layoff."  Thus, the chances of being
fired rather than in a short layoff are simply .80, the inverse of 1.26.*

*When formulating contrasts stated at the bottom of the table, begin
with the column category and read down to the intersection with the row
category.  So for contrasts dealing with low- versus high-capacity positions, start, for instance, with the column "firing" and read down to
its point of intersection with "quit."  This gives the odds ratio of
1.20.  For the opposite contrast (i.e., for quits versus firings), start
with the column "quit" and read down to the intersection with the row
"firing."  This gives the odds ratio of .83 (the inverse of 1.20).*

*Note that because of rounding numbers above and below the diagonal
are not always exact inverses.*

TABLE 6.4

Expected Odds Ratios for Contrasting Categories of Employment Status and Sector Resources[a]

| | Oligopoly versus competitive sector positions | | | | |
| --- | --- | --- | --- | --- | --- |
| | Short layoff | Firing | Long layoff | Quit | Employed |
| Short layoff | --- | 2.30 | 1.01 | 3.21 | 1.99 |
| Firing | .43 | --- | .44 | 1.40 | .86 |
| Long layoff | .99 | 2.29 | --- | 3.19 | 1.98 |
| Quit | .31 | .72 | .31 | --- | .62 |
| Employed | .50 | 1.16 | .51 | 1.61 | --- |
| | Competitive versus oligopoly sector positions | | | | |

[a]See Table 6.3 for an explanation of how to read the table. Note that because of rounding numbers above and below the diagonal are not always exact inverses.

The hypothesis makes specific predictions about the association of oligopoly sector positions with unemploynent in the form of short and long layoffs and competitive sector positions with unemployment by firings and quits. The differences revealed in Table 6.4 are quite substantial. For instance, the expected chance of being unemployed through a short layoff, as opposed to being fired, is more than twice (2.30) as great for workers in the oligopoly than in the competitive sector, while the odds of experiencing a short layoff as opposed to a quit are strikingly high—more than three times greater—for the oligopoly sector.

Quits and firings do not evidence as similar a relationship to sector resources as do short and long layoffs (the expected chance of being fired as opposed to quitting is 1.4 times greater for workers in the oligopoly sector). Nevertheless, the contrast between sectors in the matter of quits or firings is much smaller than the sector contrasts between either type of layoffs and firings.

## Sector Resources and Capacities

An important question that remains in the analysis of the effect of resources and capacities on unemployment is whether in fact the two variables tap different aspects of the structure of employment. It can be argued that over time the transformation of positions from low to high capacities leads to concentration of an industry. This might happen, on the one hand, because high-capacity positions exert demands that lower profit and make the firm vulnerable to incorporation by a larger firm and, on the other, because workers in high-capacity positions with higher degrees of job security are willing to agree to the introduction of long-term, capital-intensive technology that permits firms to expand market shares and to concentrate resources.

It can be argued as well that over time concentrated industries produce high-capacity positions by expanded production and by the introduction of technology that requires on-the-job training, worker interdependence, and other relations that increase the preponderance of vacancy- as opposed to wage competition positions in the firm.

Such a theory of the relationship of sectors and capacities cannot be tested by the cross-sectional data considered here. Moreover, while capacities and sectors may converge over time so that high-capacity positions are located almost exclusively in the oligopoly sector and low-capacity positions in the competitive sector, this chapter argues that they do not. The impact of the employment structure on the types of unemployment must, therefore, be decomposed into the effects of capital sectors and capacities.

Table 6.5 shows that the expected chance of being employed in an oligopoly rather than a competitive sector position is 1.50 times greater for workers in high- as opposed to low-capacity positions, but the degree of association is not so high as to question the possibility that sectors and capacities actually tap different dimensions of the employment structure. Table 6.6 presents the cross-classification of the gross relationship of sectors and capacities. High-capacity positions are 85% of the total, but the oligopoly sector comprises only 40% of the positions. High-capacity, oligopoly positions are 35% of the distribution, while high-capacity, competitive positions comprise 50% of the total; oligopoly, low-capacity positions form 5% and competitive, low-capacity positions 10% of the total. Moreover, rather than finding an overwhelming congruence of oligopoly sector with high-capacity positions and competitive sector with low-capacity positions, the data show that fewer than half (45%) of the positions fall into this diagonal. This lack of convergence as well as the relatively low number of low-capacity positions is a function of the strict definition of low capacities applied in the delineation of this category. This concurs with Rosenberg's findings (1975), which show that approximately 25–32% of the work force in four major metropolitan areas is in the secondary sector.

## Race and Unemployment

We now return to Model 6, in order to assess the direct impact of race on unemployment. Assuming that the marginally significant $DR$ association merits attention, and controlling for capacities and sector resources, the ratio of unemployment likelihood is 1.12.[14] In other words, on the average, the chance of being employed rather than unemployed in any of the designated categories is 1.12 times greater for whites than for blacks.[15] But as with sector resources, the greater chance of a black's being unemployed pertains only to the categories of firings and quits. Whites are 1.10 times more likely than black workers to be unemployed through short layoffs and 1.05 times more likely to be unemployed through long layoffs. Blacks, how-

---

[14] This ratio is calculated according to the formula:

$$\frac{\tau \text{ employment, white}^{5/2}}{\tau \text{ employment, black}}$$

The Tau parameters are: Tau (employment, white) = 1.0469; Tau (employment, black) = .9552. See earlier discussion of the meaning and method of calculating this unemployment likelihood ratio.

[15] The major caveat is that this analysis has not controlled for age and education. However, my present research indicates that, even when such human capital indicators are included, the conclusions suggested here are supported (Schervish, 1980).

TABLE 6.5

Expected Odds Ratios for Contrasting Categories of Capacities and Sector Resources[a]

| | High- versus low-capacity positions | | | |
| --- | --- | --- | --- | --- |
| | Oligopoly sector | Competitive sector | Farm sector | Construction Sector |
| Oligopoly sector | --- | 1.50 | 28.10 | 1.41 |
| Competitive sector | .67 | --- | 18.77 | .94 |
| Farm sector | .04 | .05 | --- | .05 |
| Construction sector | .71 | 1.06 | 19.96 | --- |
| | low- versus high-capacity positions | | | |

[a] See Table 6.3 for an explanation of how to read the table. Note that because of rounding numbers above and below the diagonal are not always exact inverses.

TABLE 6.6

Cross-Tabulations of Monopoly and Competitive Sector Resources by High- and Low-Capacity Positions

| Capacities | Sector | | |
|---|---|---|---|
| | Oligopoly | Competitive | Total |
| **High** | | | |
| Number of cases | 5009.50[a] | 7217.95 | 12227.45 |
| Total percentage | 35 | 50 | 85 |
| Column percentage | 88 | 83 | |
| Row percentage | 41 | 59 | 100 |
| **Low** | | | |
| Number of cases | 677.08 | 1477.07 | 2154.15 |
| Total percentage | 05 | 10 | 15 |
| Column percentage | 12 | 17 | |
| Row percentage | 31 | 69 | 100 |
| **Total** | | | |
| Number of cases | 5686.58 | 8695.02 | 14381.60 |
| Total percentage | 40 | 60 | 100 |
| Column percentage | 100 | 100 | 100 |
| Row percentage | 100 | 100 | 100 |

[a] The number of cases in each cell is not an integer since the sample on which the research is based is weighted.

ever, are 1.55 times more likely than whites to be unemployed through firings and 1.18 times more likely to be unemployed through quits.

This distribution is highlighted by the odds ratio contrasts in Table 6.7, which summarize the relative chances for blacks and whites of being in one category of unemployment rather than another. The expected chance of being in a short layoff as opposed to being fired is 1.70 times greater for whites than blacks, that of being in a long layoff as opposed to being fired or quitting is, respectively, 1.62 and 1.23 times greater for whites. In contrast, the expected chances of quitting rather than receiving short or long layoffs are, respectively, 1.29 and 1.23 times greater for blacks. While blacks suffer firings and quits more than whites, blacks are still 1.32 times more likely to be fired than to quit.

## Race and the Employment Structure

As noted earlier, one interpretation of the marginal direct effect of race on unemployment is that racial discrimination as it affects unemployment is mediated by the manner in which blacks are distributed to positions of employment. It has been determined that the propensity to become un-employed is greater in low- than in high-capacity positions and in the oligopoly rather than competitive sectors. Moreover, high-capacity positions are associated with short layoffs and quits, while the oligopoly sector is associated with short and long layoffs. We have also found that blacks are more likely to be unemployed than whites and that blacks are more likely to be unemployed through quits and firings. If it is true that the marginal direct effect of race can be explained by a process of labor market discrim-ination that distributes blacks to employment positions, we would expect to find that blacks are more likely to be employed in those positions as-sociated with the least favorable unemployment propensities. Findings cal-culated from Model 2 bear out this prediction.

Controlling for capacities, the expected chance of being attached to po-sitions in the competitive rather than in the oligopoly sector is 1.08 times greater for whites than for blacks. Controlling for sectors, the association of race and capacities is more dramatic. The expected chance of being in the low-capacity position is 3.55 times greater for blacks than for whites (Table 6.8).

It is possible to compute a measure of the size of effect associated with each interaction in the model. This summary measure (see Table 6.9) is an average effect on different categories of one variable by the different categories of the second variable. Thus, the impact of race on distributing workers to positions of high- and low capacities can be compared to the impact of race on distributing workers to sector resources. Table 6.9 presents

TABLE 6.7

Expected Odds Ratios for Contrasting Categories of Employment Status and Race[a]

| | White versus black | | | | |
|---|---|---|---|---|---|
| | Short layoff | Firing | Long layoff | Quit | Employed |
| Short layoff | --- | 1.70 | 1.05 | 1.29 | 1.10 |
| Firing | .59 | --- | .62 | .76 | .65 |
| Long layoff | .95 | 1.62 | --- | 1.23 | 1.05 |
| Quit | .78 | 1.32 | .81 | --- | .85 |
| Employed | .91 | 1.55 | .96 | 1.18 | --- |
| | Black versus white | | | | |

[a]The odds ratios in this table are calculated from Model 6. See Table 6.3 for an explanation of how to read the table. Note that because of rounding numbers above and below the diagonal are not always exact inverses.

TABLE 6.8

Expected Odds Ratios for Contrasting Categories of Race and Capacities,
and Race and Sector Resources[a]

| | Race and capacities | |
|---|---|---|
| | White versus black | |
| | High capacity | Low capacity |
| High capacity | --- | 3.55 |
| Low capacity | .28 | --- |
| | Black versus white | |

| | Race and sector resource | | | |
|---|---|---|---|---|
| | White versus black | | | |
| | Oligopoly sector | Competitive sector | Farm sector | Construction sector |
| Oligopoly sector | --- | 1.08 | .74 | 1.06 |
| Competitive sector | .92 | --- | .68 | .98 |
| Farm sector | 1.36 | 1.47 | --- | 1.43 |
| Construction sector | .95 | 1.02 | .70 | --- |
| | Black versus white | | | |

[a]See Table 6.3 for an explanation of how to read the table. Note
that because of rounding numbers above and below the diagonal are not
always exact inverses.

TABLE 6.9

Summary Measures of the Relative Size of Effects of Capacities, Sector Resources, and Race on Employment Status and of Race on Capacities and Sector Resources

| Variables | Tau-parameter metric[a] | Odds-ratio metric[a] |
|---|---|---|
| Sector resources on employment status | 1.4272 | 1.8091 |
| Capacities on employment status | 1.1116 | 1.3026 |
| Race on employment status | 1.0863 | 1.2300 |
| Race on sector resources | 1.0678 | 1.1912 |
| Race on capacities | 1.3723 | 3.5466 |

[a]The summary measures were calculated according to the following formulas:

Tau-parameter metric:

$$e^{\frac{1}{IJ} \sum_{ij} |\ln \tau_{ij}|}.$$

Odds-ratio metric

$$e^{\frac{1}{(I-1)(J-1)} \sum_{ij} |\ln \tau_{ij}|},$$

where $I$ and $J$ are the number of categories in the two variables being considered and $\tau$ is the log-linear parameter that measures the association between the $i$th category of the first variable and the $j$th category of the second.

The Tau-parameter and odds-ratio metrics are simply geometric transformations of each other.

these comparisons in Tau-parameter and odds-ration metrics. The effect of race on capacities is 1.37 in the Tau-parameter metric and 3.55 in the odds-ratio metric. The effect of race on sector in the two metrics is 1.07 and 1.19. It is unclear just how to interpret the relative sizes of the effects, especially since a ratio of the effects of the two associations is partly a function of the metric that is employed. Nevertheless, it is clear that the impact of race on distributing workers to capacities is greater than its impact on distributing workers to sectors.

In view of the strong effect of race on the distribution of workers to job capacities and its weaker effect on the distribution of workers to sectors, the labor market allocation of blacks indicates that they are more likely than whites to be employed in positions associated with higher unemployment, especially long layoffs and firings, over and above the direct effect of race on the distribution of workers to firings and quits. With some caution, we can conclude that labor market discrimination complements direct discrimination in determining the unemployment experience of blacks.

## Conclusion

The findings presented in this chapter confirm the theory that the structure of employment is related to a structure of unemployment. It is considered commonplace that workers in lower status jobs receive lower job security and are subject to higher unemployment rates. An attempt has been made to demonstrate that such commonplace understandings are often misleading and, at best, present only a small part of the picture. A more complete view is generated by distinguishing different types of unemployment and by constructing arguments to explain the relationship between different positions in the employment structure and different types of unemployment.

In this chapter a series of models were tested to determine the most parsimonious, theoretically informed relationship between the independent variables of race, capacities, and sector resources, and between these variables and the dependent variable of labor force status. It was found, as predicted, that the appropriate model is one that suggests that the employment structure, rather than the personal characteristic of race, distributes workers to unemployment rather than employment and, within the unemployment structure, to particular predicted types of unemployment. Race distributes workers to capacities and sector resources but has only a marginal direct effect on distributing workers to types of unemployment once the workings of the employment structure are taken into account. Within the employment structure, sector resources have a larger effect than capacities, but capacities have a larger effect than race. This is shown by comparing the sizes of the summary measures of the average effect on different categories of the dependent variable by the different categories of the independent variables. The average effect (in the Tau-parameter metric) is 1.43 for sector resources, 1.11 for capacities, and 1.09 for race (see Table 6.9).

More specifically, the findings have shown a weak congruence of competitive sector resources with low-capacity positions. Also, as predicted, even though low-capacity positions are associated with a higher likelihood of being unemployed in all four categories, low-capacity positions distribute workers at a substantially higher rate to the least favorable forms of unemployment, such as firings and long layoffs. High-capacity positions, within this same framework, are associated with short layoffs and quits.

Controlling for capacities and race, the impact of sector of employment is smaller and different. Oligopoly sector positions are associated with short and long layoffs, while competitive sector positions are associated with firings and quits.

The effect of race on labor force status is weaker than that of sectors and capacities but parallel to that of resources. That is, for unemployed blacks, the chances relative to whites of being fired or quitting are greater than the chances of being laid off.

## Implications for Theory and Policy

On the broadest level, the aim of this chapter has been to understand the workings of unemployment in the contemporary American economy and, more particularly, to examine how different types of unemployment relate systematically to different positions of employment. Such specification is valuable, because it at once opens the study of unemployment to Marxist analysis as well as to recent theories of labor market and capital segmentation. It also questions the extent to which high black unemployment is due to direct job discrimination rather than to labor market discrimination through which blacks are allocated the least favorable employment positions. Differentiating types of unemployment and relating them to types of employment positions suggests a way to conceptualize unemployment that is more theoretically relevant for advanced capitalism than either Marx's global notions of the industrial reserve army and relative surplus population or the use in labor economics of official measures and rates of unemployment.

A number of important theoretical implications derive from the foregoing analysis. First, research must study not only the sources of economic crisis and their outcome for unemployment levels, but the way in which the segmented employment structure affects the distribution of workers to specific unemployment categories.

Second, the subordinate status of blacks in rates and types of unemployment is due, in large part, not to the direct effect of racial discrimination, although this is a factor, but to the extent to which discrimination allocates blacks to subordinate positions in the employment structure, especially to low-capacity jobs and somewhat less so to competitive sector employment. As Masters (1975) also concludes in reference to black–white income differentials, the labor market mediates the effects of racial discrimination.

Third, the evolution of the American economy creates segmented relations of production that simultaneously provide greater or fewer resources and capacities for worker control and resistance. Such resources and capacities alone do not ensure worker power. But such structural factors as workers' interdependence, on-the-job training, the low measurability of individual task, and oligopoly resources, when combined with workers' own resistance, enable workers to avoid arbitrary dismissal and to transform firings into layoffs. Thus, it is through the struggle for control over the employment structure, rather than through employer conspiracy or inevitable socialization of production, that the specific forms of social relations of work and unemployment come about and are transformed.

Clearly, the long-run solution to unemployment must provide a means to ensure a quantity and quality of employment in line with the personal desires of workers and with social need. Such a solution must ensure a decrease in the scarcity and undesirability of jobs, as well as a tempering of the cyclical economic crises and the periodic expansion of a surplus supply of workers. But until that day, one avenue for policy would be to focus not simply on creating jobs or upgrading workers but on transforming the structure of unemployment. The most straightforward policy implication of the theory considered here is that remedies for unemployment depend in part on eliminating the contingencies of firings, reducing the inadequacies of jobs that induce quits, and alleviating the duration and hardship of layoffs. Policies that simply allocate more workers to certain types of positions, or that upgrade workers to enable them to enter the employment structure under more favorable conditions, will be short-circuited unless the types of unemployment associated with these new positions or jobs are transformed also. Even within the limits of present policy options, much could be gained by distinguishing and measuring the types of unemployment discussed in this chapter, in order to develop more complex and focused policies, rather than simply by stimulating demand, lowering the aggregate rate of unemployment, or even upgrading skills of particular workers. Pursuing any of these directions, of course, entails facing many of the politically difficult issues and pitfalls of the "European solution," in which job security guarantees are extended in scope and in coverage beyond what now exists, as the consequence of union protection, government regulation, or other sources of bargaining power.

## Acknowledgment

I am grateful to Robert L. Kaufman for much helpful advice in the preparation of this chapter.

## Appendix A:
## Occupations Classified as Secondary[a,b]

| Census occupation code | Occupation | Census occupation code | Occupation |
|---|---|---|---|
| 262 | Demonstrators | 643 | Packers and wrappers, except meat and produce |
| 264 | Hucksters and peddlers | | |
| 266 | Newsboys | 661 | Sailors and deckhands |
| 310 | Cashiers | 663 | Sewers and stitchers |
| 325 | File Clerks | 670 | Carding, lapping, and combing operatives |
| 332 | Mail handlers, except post office | | |
| 333 | Messengers and office boys | 672 | Spinners, twisters, and winders |
| 374 | Shipping and receiving clerks | 674 | Textile operatives, nec[c] |
| 383 | Telegraph messengers | 711 | Parking attendants |
| 385 | Telephone operators | 740 | Animal caretakers, excluding farm |
| 391 | Typists | | |
| 501 | Millers, grain, flour, feed | 750 | Carpenter's helpers |
| 602 | Assemblers | 751 | Construction laborers, excluding carpenter's helpers |
| 611 | Clothing ironers and pressers | | |
| 623 | Garage workers and gas station attendants | 752 | Fishermen and oystermen |
| | | 754 | Garbage collectors |
| 624 | Graders and sorters, manufacturing | 755 | Gardeners and groundskeepers |
| | | 760 | Longshoremen and stevedores |
| 625 | Produce graders and packers, except factory and farm | 762 | Stock handler |
| | | 763 | Teamsters |
| 626 | Heaters, metal | 764 | Vehicle washers and equipment cleaners |
| 630 | Laundry and dry cleaning operatives, nec[c] | | |
| | | 770 | Warehousemen, nec[c] |
| 634 | Meat wrappers, retail trade | 780 | Miscellaneous laborers |
| 642 | Oilers and greasers, except auto | 785 | Not specified laborers |

[a] From Rosenberg, 1975, pp. 57–59.
[b] Rosenberg classifies all other occupations as primary.
[c] nec = not elsewhere classified.

| Census occupation code | Occupation | Census occupation code | Occupation |
|---|---|---|---|
| 822 | Farm laborers, wage workers | 933 | Attendants, personal service, nec[c] |
| 823 | Farm laborers, unpaid family workers | 934 | Baggage porters and bellhops |
| 824 | Farm service laborers, self-employed | 940 | Boarding and lodging house keepers |
| 901 | Chambermaids and maids, except private households | 941 | Bootblacks |
| 902 | Cleaners and charwomen | 942 | Child-care workers |
| 903 | Janitors and sextons | 943 | Elevator operators |
| 910 | Bartenders | 952 | School monitors |
| 911 | Busboys | 953 | Ushers, recreation and amusement |
| 913 | Dishwashers | 954 | Welfare service aides |
| 914 | Food counter and fountain workers | 960 | Crossing guards and bridge tenders |
| 915 | Waiters | 962 | Guards and watchmen |
| 916 | Food service workers, nec[c] except private household | 980 | Child-care workers, private household |
| 925 | Nursing, aides, orderlies, and attendants | 981 | Cooks, private household |
| 932 | Attendants, recreation and amusement | 982 | Housekeepers, private household |
|  |  | 983 | Laundresses, private household |
|  |  | 984 | Maids and servants, private household |

## References

Averitt, R. T.
  1965   *The Dual Economy.* New York: Norton.
Beck, E. M., P. M. Horan, and C. M. Tolbert II
  1978   "Stratification in a dual economy: A sectoral model of earnings determination." *American Sociological Review* 43(October):704–720.
Bishop, Y. M. M., S. E. Fienberg, and P. W. Holland
  1975   *Discrete Multivariate Analysis.* Cambridge, Massachusetts: MIT Press.
Bluestone, B.
  1970   "The tripartite economy: Labor markets and the working poor." *Poverty and Human Resources Abstracts* 5(March–April):14–35.
Cain, G. G.
  1966   *Married Women in the Labor Force.* Chicago: Univ. of Chicago Press.
  1976   "The challenge of segmented labor market theories to orthodox theory: A survey." *Journal of Economic Literature* 14(December):1215–1257.
Daymont, T. N., and R. L. Kaufman
  1979   "Measuring industrial variation in racial discrimination using log-linear models." *Social Science Research* 8(March): 41–62.
Doeringer, P. B., and M. J. Piore
  1971   *Internal Labor Markets and Manpower Analysis.* Lexington, Massachusetts: Heath.

Edwards, R. C.
1979   *Contested Terrain*. New York: Basic.
Edwards, R. C., M. Reich, and D. Gordon, Eds.
1975   *Labor Market Segmentation*. Lexington, Massachusetts: Heath.
Feinberg, R. M.
1978   "Employment instability, earnings, and market structures." Paper presented at the Southern Economic Association Meetings, Washington, D.C., November.
Fienberg, S. E.
1977   *The Analysis of Cross-Classified Categorical Data*. Cambridge, Massachusetts: MIT Press.
Goodman, L. A.
1972   "A modified multiple regression approach to the analysis of dichotomous variables." *American Sociological Review* 37(1):28–46.
Gordon, D. M.
1972   *Theories of Poverty and Underemployment*. Lexington, Massachusetts: Heath.
Hodson, R.
1978   "Labor in the monopoly, competitive and state sectors of production." *Politics and Society* 8:429–480.
Masters, S. H.
1975   *Black–White Income Differentials: Empirical Studies and Policy Implications*. New York: Academic Press.
Mincer, J.
1963   "Labor force participation of married women." In H. Gregg Lewis (ed.), *Aspects of Labor Economics*. Princeton, New Jersey: National Bureau of Economic Research, Princeton Univ. Press.
Niemi, B.
1975   "Geographic immobility and labor force mobility: A study of female unemployment." In C. B. Lloyd (ed.), *Sex, Discrimination, and the Division of Labor*. New York: Columbia Univ. Press.
O'Connor, J.
1973   *The Fiscal Crisis of the State*. New York: St. Martin's.
Page, W. F.
1977   "Interpretation of Goodman's Log-linear model effects: An odds ratio approach." *Sociological Methods and Research* 5(4):419–435.
Piore, M. J.
1970   "Manpower policy." In S. Beer and R. Barringer (eds.), *The State and the Poor*. Cambridge, Massachusetts: Winthrop.
1971   "The dual labor market: Theory and implications." In D. M. Gordon (ed.), *Problems in Political Economy: An Urban Perspective*. Lexington, Massachusetts: Heath.
Poulantzas, N.
1975   *Class in Contemporary Capitalism*. London: New Left Books.
Rees, A.
1973   *The Economics of Work and Pay*. New York: Harper.
Robinson, J.
1969   *The Economics of Imperfect Competition* (2nd ed.). New York: St. Martin's.
Rosenberg, S.
1975   *The Dual Labor Market: Its Existence and Consequences*. Unpublished doctoral dissertation, University of California, Berkeley.
Scherer, F. M.
1980   *Industrial Market Structure and Economic Performance* (2nd ed.). Chicago: Rand McNally.

Schervish, P. G.

1977    "A theory of the social relations of unemployment." *The Peninsular Papers* 2(2):1–14.

1980    *Vulnerability and Power in Market Relations: The Structural Determinants of Unemployment.* Unpublished doctoral dissertation, University of Wisconsin—Madison.

Schervish, P. G., and A. B. Sørensen

1977    *Alternative Theories of the Income Attainment Process.* Unpublished paper, University of Wisconsin—Madison.

Thurow, L. C.

1975    *Generating Inequality.* New York: Basic Books.

U.S. Department of Labor, Bureau of Employment Security

1965    *Dictionary of Occupational Titles* (Vols 1 and 2). Washington, D.C.: US Govt Printing Office.

Watts, H. W., and A. Rees, Eds.

1977    *The New Jersey Income Maintenance Experiment: Volume II, Labor Supply Response.* New York: Academic Press.

Weiss, L. W.

1966    "Concentration and labor earnings." *American Economic Review* 56(March):96–117.

Zwerdling, D.

1979    "The food monopolies." In J. H. Skolnick and E. Currie (eds.), *Crisis in American Institutions.* Boston: Little, Brown. (Originally published, 1974).

# Chapter 7

## The Development and Functioning of the American Urban Export Sector, 1947–1972[1]

*TOBY L. PARCEL*

Renewed sociological interest in the relationship between industrial structure and economic standing is manifest in ecological studies (Masters, 1975; Spilerman & Miller, 1976) as well as in analyses of the economic achievement of individuals (Beck, Horan, & Tolbert, 1978; Parcel, 1979). In this chapter attention is directed toward the theoretical work of urban economist Wilbur Thompson, who in *A Preface to Urban Economics* (1965) provides a rich source of hypotheses concerning the economy, which have been generally neglected by sociologists. The first two sections review some of Thompson's major ideas concerning urban economic functioning and outlines the hypotheses to be tested in this study. The third section presents empirical evidence for these propositions from an analysis of the 100 largest Standard Metropolitan Statistical Areas (SMSAs) in the United States in 1972. It provides comparable analyses of these SMSAs in 4–5-year intervals between 1947 and 1972, in order to evaluate the development of the export sector over time and to determine whether Thompson's theory is supported throughout this period. Finally, directions for future research in this area are noted.

[1] An earlier version of this chapter was presented at the American Sociological Association Meetings, August 1979, Boston.

SOCIOLOGICAL PERSPECTIVES ON
LABOR MARKETS

## The Urban Export Sector

Thompson (1965) outlines a theory of urban economic functioning that takes as its premise the operation of a local labor market that affects the local economy. One of Thompson's key concepts is that of the *export base*, a notion derived from studies of individual urban economies where the urban area is viewed as a small, industrially oriented nation that must export products to survive economically. He argues for the use of the urban area (SMSA) as the unit of analysis, seeing it as a potentially viable economic unit that devotes as much as one-half of its economic activity to the production of goods for export. Export goods are produced by the major firms in the manufacturing sector, and, of course, the productivity of this sector varies by SMSA.

Thompson argues that the wages in the dominant export sector will influence wages for other jobs in that labor market; that is, an *intra-area wage roll-out* effect will occur. This hypothesis assumes that the local labor market is autonomous and that migration between labor markets is sluggish. From this hypothesis it follows that the local service sector must offer wages that are at least partially competitive with the dominant export sector industries, or they will face problems recruiting workers. Thus, a high-wage export industry directly enriches its own workers by paying them high wages, and it indirectly enriches other workers by raising wages in the local service sector through intra-area competition (Thompson, 1965, p.73). Thompson (1965) juxtaposes the notion that wages within occupations are a function of the national market for such skills with the notion that wages will be a function of local labor demand and poses the question, "Do the wage rates of medical technologists and retail clerks in Detroit reflect more the national demand and supply for these skills or the pay scales in the nearby automobile factories [p.74–75]?" Such reasoning contrasts somewhat with sociological analyses emphasizing the importance of occupational labor markets in explaining economic achievement (Spilerman, 1977; Stolzenberg, 1975) in that Thompson allows for the influence of areal or local labor market factors as well as occupational characteristics in the prediction of earnings. To summarize, Thompson argues that the economic productivity of the manufacturing export sector of an urban area will influence wage levels in other industrial sectors of that area through competition for workers.

At the most general level, Thompson's work stresses the impact of export sector productivity on the level, distribution, and stability of income in the local labor market. The preceding discussion indicates how operation of intra-area wage roll-out effects from a productive export sector will promote heightened income levels in the local labor market. Thompson bases his income stability arguments on the notion that constant national demand for export goods will stabilize the operation of the export sector firms and thus ensure relatively continuous operation of the wage roll-out effects. He recognizes, of course, that sharp national drops in demand for these export goods in times of recession can magnify the local labor market declines to depression levels (1965, p.178). His ideas concerning income distribution involve introduction of additional concepts. He argues that specialization in manufacturing—that is, the proportion of the labor force employed in export industries—is associated with a low degree of income inequality because of increased unionization, which leads to an aggressive wage policy, and absentee ownership, which reduces the role of property income locally, thus deemphasizing a type of income disproportionately allocated to upper income groups (1965, p.183). Areas that specialize in durable manufacturing are likely to have smaller degrees of income inequality than areas that specialize in nondurable goods manufacturing. In addition, he hypothesizes a curvilinear relationship between such inequality and city size. He notes that:

> The small city, with a large share of income originating in small business "profits," has a relatively high degree of income inequality, but as this (typically) regional service center acquires factories and grows in size it probably also becomes a more egalitarian society. With further growth and true metropolitan standing, even more esoteric services are acquired and exported over greater distances (e.g., administrative, legal, financial) probably turning the income distribution back again toward greater inequality by expanding both the opportunity to express personal talents and to manipulate private property [1965, p.109].

To summarize, Thompson argues that the level, stability, and distribution of income in the local labor market is determined in part by characteristics of the export base and that income inequality is curvilinearly related to city size.

For a concrete example of some of the ideas outlined in this section, consider the case of Seattle in 1970. The Seattle labor market was heavily dependent upon employment at Boeing Aircraft in the late 1960s. When there were severe cutbacks in employment at Boeing, the economic effects of these cutbacks were felt throughout the local labor market. Auto sales fell by 30–50%, with more than 12 dealerships going out of business; the vacancy rate in some residential suburbs reached 40%, and rents actually decreased (Prager, 1971). Voters decided against tax increases and rejected expenditures for rapid transit in response to the economic downturn (O'Neil, 1970). The situations in 1979 of Detroit (due to foreign competition and recession) and of Youngstown (due to plant closings) provide analogous examples, although an article by Hayes (1979) maintains that the effects on retail sales and job loss throughout the Youngstown area have been less severe than anticipated. Certainly we expect the effects of a prosperous export sector to be positive, as in the Houston labor market in the late 1970s because of oil industry activity.

## Past Research and Current Hypotheses

Despite the obvious relevance of Thompson's (1965) ideas for sociological analysis, researchers in sociology have shown minimal interest in the theory. Studies by Reder (1955), Turner (1951), Masters (1975) and Spilerman and Miller (1976) do provide evidence that proportion manufacturing is positively associated with racial income equality, a finding of some concern to Thompson, but the theory clearly outstrips those particular investigations. Within economics, interest in export base theories in general and Thompson's ideas in particular has been more extensive, and it is worthwhile to comment on this literature. Heilburn (1974), for example, criticizes the dichotomy of basic–nonbasic economic activities as being overly simplistic. He argues that such aggregation fails to capture the complexity of relationships among industries and will probably produce inaccurate estimates concerning responses of specific industries to increases or decreases in export base activity. He suggests that attempts to calculate multiplier effects to assess the magnitude of short-run economic changes have been disappointing and that use of the basic–nonbasic analysis for making long-run economic forecasts is infeasible, in part because of the multitude of other variables that operate in the long run (Heilburn, 1974, pp.150–152). Other researchers have highlighted the difficulty of assessing what proportion of an SMSA's goods and services are consumed locally and what proportion are exported (Duncan, Scott, Lieberson, Duncan, & Winsborough, 1960; Hirsch, 1973, while additional work on specific local labor markets where the researcher has access to more detailed data concerning economic activity than is available in standard sources has provided more satisfying results (Mattila, 1973).

The issue concerning analysis of what proportion of goods and services are exported or consumed locally is a particularly important one. According to Thompson's theory, durable manufacturing goods produced for export provide the community's economic base, while service and retail activity exists to service the basic industries and their employees. While Thompson does not maintain that all durable goods prepared for export are actually exported, in order to estimate even something as basic as the size of the export sector, one must determine what proportion of goods are consumed locally. In addition, it is the case that services as well as goods can be exported, and Thompson's theory largely ignores this complication. Again one faces the problem of empirically determining what proportion of services is consumed locally and what proportion is not. In fairness to Thompson, however, it is likely that the export of services is more common beginning in the middle 1970s than in previous time periods. As an added complication, it is likely that such service exporting is disproportionately found in the larger SMSAs. These issues will be discussed again at the end of the chapter.

In view of these caveats, it is important to indicate how the focus of this chapter differs from that of the economists. The purpose of this analysis is to evaluate empirically Thompson's theory, not to provide dollar predictions concerning the impact of basic or nonbasic sector activity. The regression results to be discussed are presented as a guide to further sociological thinking and research concerning local labor market functioning. It is expected that the findings presented here will be refined by additional research. Two hypotheses will be evaluated. The first concerns export sector wages affecting wage levels in other industrial groups. If Thompson's arguments are correct, then SMSA manufacturing wage levels should directly affect wages in the retail sales, wholesale sales, and service sectors of the economy independent of sales in these respective sectors and of educational levels in the SMSA generally. The second hypothesis relates to Thompson's arguments concerning the determinants of areal income levels. If his theory is correct, then export sector wage levels should influence SMSA median family income independent of wage levels in the remaining industry groups, SMSA size, and educational level. In addition, these hypotheses will be evaluated over the time period from 1947 to 1972, in order to permit an assessment of whether Thompson's theory is equally applicable to several time periods or whether it is only supported for a limited time period. It has been argued that Thompson's model applies less well in the 1970s than in earlier time periods, primarily because of the growth of the service sector of our economy. This latter analysis will suggest whether there have been systematic changes in the functioning of the American export sector in this 25-year period.

## Empirical Evaluation of Hypotheses

### Method

This analysis uses the SMSA as the unit of analysis and defines Thompson's notion of the export sector with the 100 largest SMSAs in 1972. Such case selection allows a large enough $N$ for multivariate analysis; it avoids including the smaller SMSAs, which, although they may meet the Census

Bureau's population criteria for inclusion, may not actually contain a manufacturing sector well enough developed to qualify for Thompson's notion of *export base.* These same SMSAs in 1967, 1963, 1958, 1954, and 1947–1948, or the counties that would eventually comprise the 1972 SMSAs, are used in the second portion of the analysis. The same geographical areas are studied over time so that changes in the values in the variables will not be confounded with the changes that have occurred in the boundaries of SMSAs or with the creation of new SMSAs during this period. Hence, the study evaluates the development of the 1972 export sector from the same SMSAs in 1947–1948 through 1967 and/or from the relevant counties over that same time period.

Variables included in the analysis consist of characteristics of the export sector and of the retail trade, wholesale trade, and service sectors, as well as characteristics of the SMSA generally. Export and industrial sector variables are taken from the economic censuses for the years specified in the preceding paragraph. The economic censuses provide the best and most consistent source of economic data by SMSA throughout the time period studied.[2] The measures for the respective sectors are constructed to tap both worker outcomes (e.g., wages per employee-hour, payroll per employee) and economic functioning within the sector itself (e.g., mean establishment size, receipts per establishment). Since identical indicators are not available across sectors from this source, we are unable to evaluate, for example, the impact of retail establishment size upon retail wage levels. Several characteristics of the export sector variables are included. Wage per employee-hour, defined as the ratio of the total wage bill to number of employee-hours worked, will be used as the indicator of wage levels in the export sector and is expected to be positively associated with wages in the remaining sectors. Mean establishment size, defined as the ratio of the total number of employees divided by the number of manufacturing establishments, and value added per manufacturing worker, defined as the ratio of value added (increment in sales value of a product contributed solely by the labor needed to transform it) to the number of manufacturing workers employed, are expected to be positively related to wage per employee-hour. Characteristics of the remaining industrial sectors are similarly taken from the censuses of retail trade, wholesale trade, and services. Indicators for retail and wholesale trade include payroll per employee, defined as the ratio of the sector's payroll to the number of employees, and sales per establishment, defined as the ratio of the total sales bill to number of establishments. Indicators for the service sector include payroll per employee, defined as in the whole-

---

[2] See the 1972 Census of Manufactures (1975) for details concerning the smaller establishments excluded from the data.

sale and retail sectors, and receipts per establishment, defined as the ratio of total receipts to the number of service establishments reported. Characteristics of respective sectors are expected to be positively interrelated.

SMSA characteristics are taken from the U.S. population censuses. For the 1972 analysis, the 1970 Census of Population was used, while for the remaining years, population characteristics were derived by interpolation. The variables include median years of school completed, which is included in the equations as a control for the quality of labor supply or general skill level in the SMSA, and total population, which is included to provide a conservative test of the export sector variables in the test of the second hypothesis.

Use of these methods and measures entails several limitations. First, use of data from all manufacturing industries overestimates the extent to which manufacturing of goods represents exporting since some goods are consumed locally. Second, these measures assume that only goods are exported, whereas it was indicated in the preceding discussion that services may be exported as well. This latter limitation results in underestimation of the export base, but it cannot be argued that these biases necessarily average out to zero. Third, the model is analyzed with cross-sectional data, when in fact the theory Thompson posits is developmental. It may be that use of panel data would provide a better test of his ideas, or at least additional findings. In addition, as an SMSA grows over time and attains true metropolitan standing, reciprocal effects between the manufacturing and service and/or retail sectors may emerge. These effects cannot be estimated with the ordinary least squares analyses presented here. The findings discussed in the following section should be evaluated with these limitations in mind.

## Results and Discussion

### EXPORT SECTOR, 1972

Table 7.1 presents the results of multiple regression analyses used to evaluate the two hypotheses for 1972. In Equation 1 manufacturing wage per employee-hour is estimated as a function of the two remaining manufacturing sector characteristics as well as of SMSA educational level. All three characteristics are positive and statistically significant, with the two export sector variables exercising stronger effects than the labor supply characteristic. Equations 2, 3, and 4 evaluate the first hypothesis by describing payroll measures in the wholesale, retail, and service sectors as functions of sales or receipts in those sectors, wage per employee-hour, and SMSA educational level. Thompson's hypothesis is supported for the wholesale and service sectors, though not in retail trade. The intra-area wage roll-

## TABLE 7.1

Direct Effects (Unstandardized Coefficients) of Export Sector and SMSA Characteristics on Sector and SMSA Wage--Income Levels, 1972 (Standardized Coefficients in Parentheses)

| Independent variables | Equation 1 Dependent variable: Wage per employee hour (x1000) | Equation 2 Dependent variable: Payroll per employee (x1000) (wholesale) | Equation 3 Dependent variable: Payroll per employee (x1000) (retail) | Equation 4 Dependent variable: Payroll per employee (x10,000) (services) | Equation 5 Dependent variable: Median family income |
|---|---|---|---|---|---|
| Wage per employee hour | | 145.7*** (.396) | 21.24 (.160) | 424.8* (.141) | 515.1*** (.275) |
| Value added per manufacturing worker | 50.86*** (.469) | | | | |
| Mean establishment size | 7.609*** (.437) | | | | |
| Median year school completed | 276.4** (.222) | 43.93 (.096) | 22.12 (.134) | 504.0* (.135) | 347.9* (.150) |
| Sales per establishment (wholesale) | | .2036*** (.606) | | | |
| Sales per establishment (retail) | | | .4688* (.243) | | |
| Receipts per establishment (services) | | | | 37.46*** (.756) | |
| SMSA size | | | | | .1011* (-.166) |
| Payroll per employee (wholesale) | | | | | 2216.0*** (.436) |
| Payroll per employee (retail) | | | | | 601.0 (.043) |

Payroll per employee
(services) (÷ 10)

| | | | | | | |
|---|---|---|---|---|---|---|
| Constant | -1739.0 | 420.1 | 446.4 | -844.7 | 205.0*** | (.330) |
| | | | | | -4353.0 | |
| $R^2 =$ | .532 | .663 | .161 | .687 | .732 | |
| $\bar{R}^2 =$ | .518 | .652 | .134 | .677 | .715 | |

*** $= p \leq .001$;  ** $= p \leq .01$;  * $= p \leq .05$.

out effect is strongest from manufacturing to wholesale payroll, of modest size in the service sector, and not statistically significant in retail trade. Thus, workers in wholesale trade and services do benefit from residence in an SMSA with a productive export sector, whereas retail trade workers do not. Like those of manufacturing workers, service worker's payroll levels are sensitive to SMSA educational levels, whereas these effects are absent in the wholesale and retail sectors. In each case, positive and significant associations between sales–receipts–value added and payroll–wages in the respective sectors can be observed. The association is weakest, however, in the retail sector, where the model's explanatory power is small ($\bar{R}^2 = .134$).

To evaluate the second hypothesis, Equation 5 is estimated; it describes SMSA median family income as a function of SMSA size, SMSA educational level, manufacturing wage per employee-hour, and payroll per employee in the wholesale, retail, and service sectors. The findings suggest that wage levels in the export, wholesale, and service sectors of the urban economy contribute substantially to SMSA median family income levels, with the labor supply and population variables yielding somewhat weaker effects.[3] The payroll levels in retail trade do not significantly contribute to family income levels independent of the remaining determinants. This finding, in combination with the findings discussed earlier regarding the retail sector, suggests that in 1972 the retail sector operated largely independent of influence from the export base and, in turn, did not significantly contribute to the economic standing of families residing in the labor market. In contrast, the findings concerning the wholesale and service industries suggest that wage levels there are affected by export sector productivity and that, in turn, those wage levels do contribute substantially to resident family economic standing.[4] Hence, export sector productivity both directly and indirectly affects median family earnings. By way of explanation for this finding, one must recall the demographics of labor force participation. The retail sector is disproportionately female and disproportionately composed of low-wage jobs and of workers who are employed less than full time.

---

[3] Additional analysis not presented here was conducted to rule out tipping (Gordon, 1968) as an explanation for the signs of the regression coefficients and to eliminate the possibility that the city size variable was curvilinearly related to earnings. As used here, *tipping* refers to the situation where, because of high multicollinearity among independent variables, the resulting parameter estimates are unstable and may therefore evidence signs opposite from those predicted by theory in some cases.

[4] Additional analysis not presented here evaluated an alternative specification of the median family income equation. It is reasonable to suggest that the wage level variables in the respective sectors should be weighted by the proportion employed in these sectors. An equation based on this notion was estimated for 1972 (and for each of the earlier time periods), but the findings were comparable to those indicated in the tables. Therefore, the simpler models were included in the presentation.

Dual labor market theory would suggest that such jobs (labeled "bad" jobs) are reserved for secondary workers and thus do operate in isolation from the primary-sector (or "good") jobs and from primary-sector workers. Since these jobs are low wage and often part time, it is not surprising that wages in that sector fail to influence family earnings levels independent of the remaining predictors.

## EXPORT SECTOR FUNCTIONING, 1947–1967

The second major question of interest in this chapter concerns the development of the patterns described. Has the retail trade sector generally existed in isolation from the remaining sectors, and have the relationships among the remaining sectors become stronger or weaker or remained constant over time? Were the 1972 levels of wage roll-out effects evident in previous years?

Tables 7.2–7.6 provide equations comparable to those shown in Table 7.1. All of the dollar variables, including those on Table 7.1, have been converted to 1967 dollars to facilitate cross-year comparisons. The most consistent finding across years is the positive and substantial effect of wage per employee-hour upon payroll levels in the wholesale, retail, and service sectors. Wage levels in the export sector failed to influence payroll levels in all the remaining sectors only in 1954, and even here, the coefficients remain significant for both the wholesale and retail trade sectors. In addition, with the exception of 1947–1948, wage levels in manufacturing influence family income levels independent of the remaining predictors. These findings provide further evidence compatible with Thompson's thesis concerning intra-area wage roll-out effects and demonstrate that these effects have occurred throughout the postwar period.

These data also indicate that the influence of manufacturing wages on the retail sector between 1947–1948 and 1967 contrasts with 1972 findings concerning that relationship, which suggests that 1972 differs from the remaining years and/or that the 1972 findings are indicative of a trend that may be detected by future analysis. In contrast, the lack of impact between retail wage levels and family income observed in 1972 is replicated in each of the remaining time periods. Hence, wage increments in the retail sector are not transmitted into noticeable increments in family income independent of the remaining predictors at any point over the time period. Aside from the generally stable effects of manufacturing wage levels, the most consistent determinant of family income is payroll in services (statistically significant in every year except 1954), followed by payroll in wholesale trade (statistically significant in every year except 1947–1948 and 1963).

Concerning the relative magnitudes of these effects, however, the patterns are less clear. In only one year, 1954, is manufacturing wage levels the

## TABLE 7.2

Direct Effects (Unstandardized Coefficients) of Export Sector and SMSA Characteristics on Sector and SMSA Wage--Income Levels, 1967 (Standardized Coefficients in Parentheses)

| Independent variables | Equation 1 Dependent variable: Wage per employee hour (x1000) | Equation 2 Dependent variable: Payroll per employee (x1000) (wholesale) | Equation 3 Dependent variable: Payroll per employee (x1000) (retail) | Equation 4 Dependent variable: Payroll per employee (x10,000) (services) | Equation 5 Dependent variable: Median family income |
|---|---|---|---|---|---|
| Wage per employee hour | | 117.4*** (.315) | 56.12*** (.380) | 360.0*** (.255) | 611.6*** (.256) |
| Value added per manufacturing worker | 39.32*** (.447) | | | | |
| Mean establishment size | 5.620*** (.419) | | | | |
| Median year school completed | 246.7*** (.278) | 29.9 (.091) | 27.34* (.209) | 104.18 (.083) | 238.5 (.112) |
| Sales per establishment (wholesale) | | .1718*** (.561) | | | |
| Sales per establishment (retail) | | | .0074 (.004) | | |
| Receipts per establishment (services) | | | | 15.02*** (.698) | |
| SMSA size | | | | | - 0.0447 (-0.062) |
| Payroll per employee (wholesale) | | | | | 2360.0*** (.368) |
| Payroll per employee (retail) | | | | | 2356.0 (.145) |

Payroll per employee
(services) ($\div$ 10)

| | | | | | 433.0** ( .255) |
|---|---|---|---|---|---|
| Constant | -1121.0 | 660.6 | 447.1 | 331.8 | -3125.0 |
| $R^2$ = | .545 | .543 | .242 | .655 | .687 |
| $\bar{R}^2$ = | .531 | .528 | .218 | .644 | .667 |

*** = $p \leq .001$; ** = $p \leq .01$; * = $p \leq .05$

TABLE 7.3

Direct Effects (Unstandardized Coefficients) of Export Sector and SMSA Characteristics on Sector and SMSA Wage--Income Levels, 1963 (Standardized Coefficients in Parentheses)

| Independent variables | Equation 1 Dependent variable: Wage per employee hour (x1000) | Equation 2 Dependent variable: Payroll per employee (x1000) (wholesale) | Equation 3 Dependent variable: Payroll per employee (x1000) (retail) | Equation 4 Dependent variable: Payroll per employee (x10,000) (services) | Equation 5 Dependent variable: Median family income |
|---|---|---|---|---|---|
| Wage per employee hour | | 131.3*** (.362) | 56.91*** (.378) | 723.98*** (.297) | 582.3*** (.281) |
| Value added per manufacturing worker | 53.01*** (.498) | | | | |
| Mean establishment size | 5.775*** (.361) | | | | |
| Median year school completed | 156.8** (.226) | 20.63 (.082) | 29.55** (.284) | 283.1* (.168) | 97.5 (.068) |
| Sales per establishment (wholesale) | | .1514*** (-.404) | | | |
| Sales per establishment (retail) | | | .3443 (.151) | | |
| Receipts per establishment (services) | | | | 29.07*** (.598) | |
| SMSA size | | | | | - .0591 (-.087) |
| Payroll per employee (wholesale) | | | | | 634.1 (.111) |
| Payroll per employee (retail) | | | | | 221.8 (.016) |

| | | | | | Payroll per employee (services) (÷ 10) | |
|---|---|---|---|---|---|---|
| | | | | | 499.1*** | ( .588) |
| Constant | -326.2 | 411.5 | 140.0 | -307.6 | 1069.0 | |
| $R^2 =$ | .557 | .375 | .399 | .631 | .687 | |
| $\bar{R}^2 =$ | .543 | .356 | .380 | .619 | .666 | |

*** $= p \leq .001$; ** $= p \leq .01$; * $= p \leq .05$

TABLE 7.4

Direct Effects (Unstandardized Coefficients) of Export Sector and SMSA Characteristics on Sector and SMSA Wage--Income Levels, 1958 (Standardized Coefficients in Parentheses)

| Independent variables | Equation 1 Dependent variable: Wage per employee hour (x1000) | Equation 2 Dependent variable: Payroll per employee (x1000) (wholesale) | Equation 3 Dependent variable: Payroll per employee (x1000) (retail) | Equation 4 Dependent variable: Payroll per employee (x10,000) (services) | Equation 5 Dependent variable: Median family income |
|---|---|---|---|---|---|
| Wage per employee hour | | 148.9*** (.525) | 63.49*** (.498) | 573.7*** (.301) | 486.9*** (.244) |
| Value added per manufacturing worker | 71.50*** (.504) | | | | |
| Mean establishment size | 6.215*** (.473) | | | | |
| Median year school completed | 121.6*** (.258) | 19.53* (.146) | 19.50** (.324) | 189.7** (.212) | 21.80 (.023) |
| Sales per establishment (wholesale) | | .1250*** (.426) | | | |
| Sales per establishment (retail) | | | .0982 (.052) | | |
| Receipts per establishment (services) | | | | 21.76*** (.554) | |
| SMSA size | | | | | -.0628 (-.110) |
| Payroll per employee (wholesale) | | | | | 1868.0*** (.265) |
| Payroll per employee (retail) | | | | | 1842.0 (.118) |

| | | | | | |
|---|---|---|---|---|---|
| Payroll per employee (services) (÷ 10) | | | | | 476.5*** ( .452) |
| Constant | -233.9 | 347.7 | 213.3 | 1074.0 | -948.4 |
| $R^2 =$ | .618 | .608 | .476 | .585 | .775 |
| $\bar{R}^2 =$ | .606 | .596 | .460 | .572 | .760 |

*** $= p \leq .001$;  ** $= p \leq .01$;  * $= p \leq .05$.

TABLE 7.5

Direct Effects (Unstandardized Coefficients) of Export Sector and SMSA Characteristics on Sector and SMSA Wage-Income Levels, 1954[a] (Standardized Coefficients in Parentheses)

| Independent variables | Equation 1 Dependent variable: Wage per employee hour (x1000) | Equation 2 Dependent variable: Payroll per employee (x1000) (wholesale) | Equation 3 Dependent variable: Payroll per employee (x1000) (retail) | Equation 4 Dependent variable: Payroll per employee (x10,000) (services) | Equation 5 Dependent variable: Median family income |
|---|---|---|---|---|---|
| Wage per employee hour | | 202.2*** (.600) | 62.72** (.259) | -195.0 (-.132) | 914.3*** (.474) |
| Value added per manufacturing worker | 64.28*** (.473) | | | | |
| Mean establishment size | 4.521*** (.486) | | | | |
| Median year school completed | 101.0*** (.267) | 19.23 (.151) | 33.74** (.369) | 122.7* (.220) | 102.1 (.140) |
| Sales per establishment (wholesale) | | | | | |
| Sales per establishment (retail) | | | .0926 (.029) | | |
| Receipts per establishment (services) | | | | | |
| SMSA size | | | | 2.396 (.083) | .0518 (.108) |
| Payroll per employee (wholesale) | | | | | 1945.0*** (.340) |
| Payroll per employee (retail) | | | | | -282.5 (-.035) |

Payroll per employee
(services) (÷ 10)

| Constant | 77.51 | 372.2 | 103.6 | -347.0 | - 33.45 | (- .026) |
|---|---|---|---|---|---|---|
| $R^2$ = | .596 | .441 | .280 | .053 | 821.0 .672 | |
| $\bar{R}^2$ = | .583 | .430 | .257 | .023 | .651 | |

*** = $p \leq .001$;   ** = $p \leq .01$;   * = $p \leq .05$.

a Since wholesale figures were not available from census sources for 1954, it is difficult to compare relevant equations from 1954 with those in the other time periods.

205

TABLE 7.6

Direct Effects (Unstandardized Coefficients) of Export Sector and SMSA Characteristics on Sector and SMSA Wage--Income Levels, 1947--48[a] Standardized Coefficients in Parentheses

| Independent variables | Equation 1 Dependent variable: Wage per employee hour (x1000) | | Equation 2 Dependent variable: Payroll per employee (x1000) (wholesale) | | Equation 3 Dependent variable: Payroll per employee (x1000) (retail) | | Equation 4 Dependent variable: Payroll per employee (x10,000) (services) | | Equation 5 Dependent variable: Median family income | |
|---|---|---|---|---|---|---|---|---|---|---|
| Wage per production worker | | | 90.07** | (.280) | .3266*** | (.429) | 919.9*** | (.637) | 156.0 | ( .147) |
| Value added per manufacturing worker | .1786*** | (.533) | | | | | | | | |
| Mean establishment size | .0035*** | (.315) | | | | | | | | |
| Median year school completed | .0897 | (.176) | 11.00 | (.067) | .1301*** | (.335) | 153.6** | (.209) | 36.07 | ( .067) |
| Sales per establishment (wholesale) | | | .0239 | (.067) | | | | | | |
| Sales per establishment (retail) | | | | | .0011 | (.066) | | | | |
| Receipts per establishment (services) | | | | | | | 23.70* | (.140) | | |
| SMSA size | | | | | | | | | -.0051 | (-.013) |
| Payroll per employee (wholesale) | | | | | | | | | 279.5 | ( .085) |
| Payroll per employee (retail) | | | | | | | | | -103.6 | (-.074) |

| ...yroll per employee (services)(÷ 10) | .6530 | | .239 | | 459.7*** | ( .626) |
|---|---|---|---|---|---|---|
| Constant | 404.5 | | | 398.8 | 1188.0 | |
| $R^2$ = | .394 | .100 | .420 | .575 | .555 | |
| $\bar{R}^2$ = | .375 | .072 | .402 | .562 | .526 | |

*** $= p \le .001$;  ** $= p \le .01$;  * $= p \le .05$.

aThe data for this time period were produced from census sources that reported manufacturing data for 1947 but retail, wholesale and service data for 1948. In addition, the manufacturing wage indicator is measured as wage per production worker because of data limitations, thus hampering cross-year comparisons, and differences in the measurement of the retail payroll variable create similar difficulties.

strongest determinant, whereas service payroll is strongest in 1947–1948, 1958, and 1963. In the two most recent years, 1967 and 1972, the wholesale payroll levels are the strongest predictors. These findings suggest that, while the effects of manufacturing wage levels are consistent as predictors of family income in the post World War II period, they do not consistently provide the strongest predictors of this dependent variable.

The effects of the labor supply variable median years of school completed also differ across sectors and over time. Education consistently affects manufacturing wage levels in every year except 1947–1948 and similarly affects retail payrolls in every year except 1972; it also affects service payroll in every year except 1967. Only in 1958 does it influence wages in wholesale payrolls, and even there the effect is not strong. Similarly, only in 1972 is there an independent effect of education on family income, and again, the size of the effect is only modest. Concerning the effect of city size on median family income, in only one year, 1972, is this variable statistically significant. Such findings suggest that city size, at least within the range used in this study, does not affect family income independent of the economic status of manufacturing, service, and wholesale sectors.

One further type of comparison illuminates the role of manufacturing wages upon the economic health of the remaining sectors. While the data for 1972 indicated that sales or receipts in wholesale, retail, and service sectors influenced payrolls in their respective sectors, such findings are not duplicated in the previous time periods. Between 1947–1948 and 1967, retail sales did not affect retail payrolls independent of the remaining predictors for any time period. In contrast, manufacturing wages were important to predicting retail wage levels in all of those time periods.

## COMPARISON OF COVARIANCES, 1967 AND 1972

The data presented in Tables 7.1–7.6 are difficult to summarize succinctly. Although similarities in the data across the years have been described in the preceding section, such a summary required the analysis of a large number of regression coefficients. Since there are similarities in the magnitudes of effects across years, however, it may be that a single estimate of an effect could summarize data for several years. That is, if indeed the underlying causal processes are similar across years, variations in the magnitudes of the coefficients may be due to chance. Fortunately, a newly developed method allows evaluation of whether the causal processes discussed earlier are similar over time and, if not, where in the model the differences occur. Using principles of analysis of covariance structures (Jöreskog, 1970, 1973), Jöreskog and Sörbom have developed a computer program, LISREL IV, that accomplishes this goal (Jöreskog & Sörbom, 1978). Although the program provides for the estimation of a variety of types of models via maximum likelihood procedures, in this case the program will be used as follows. Since the goal is to provide a parsimonious model of export sector functioning across time, a common causal model implied by the results of the estimated equations in the previous tables will be reestimated.[5] That is, the covariances *implied* (expected) by the model are compared simultaneously to the *actual* (observed) covariances evident in the data for each year. A chi-square test of statistical significance is computed that indicates whether the *observed* covariances are different from the *expected* covariances by more than would be expected on the basis of chance. Thus, a large chi-square indicates what is called a poor fit between the implied and actual models and suggests the need for revisions. If the model fits the data for each year, with year-to-year deviations small enough to be due to chance, then single parameter estimates are produced. If portions of the model do not fit, then those parameters can be estimated separately, thus indicating which aspects of the model are variably operative over time. Changes that are introduced to improve the model's fit will lead to a smaller chi-square, ideally one that indicates correspondence between expected and observed covariances.

In order to render this portion of the analysis manageable, some simplifications were introduced. First, the analysis is confined to two time periods, 1967 and 1972, in order to reduce the number of parameters involved while still producing meaningful findings. Second, the model initially specified is shown in Figure 7.1. It was formulated on the basis of the findings from the ordinary least squares analysis discussed earlier and is more parsimonious than the equations estimated in those tables.

As an initial step, the model specified in Figure 7.1 was compared separately to the data for 1972 and for 1967. The models were derived by introducing additional paths ($\beta$s, $\gamma$s, and $\psi$) so as to bring them closer to being just-identified. Each change was introduced in succession in order to achieve a parsimonious solution; the derivatives associated with the paths for the respective years were evaluated on each run to determine where the next change in the model should occur.[6] The results of these analyses are

[5] As used here, *parsimonious* refers to a criterion for evaluating a theory that suggests that, all other things being equal, the simpler theory is preferred to the more complex. In the case of path analysis, the model with the fewest paths is the most parsimonious.

[6] There is currently debate concerning the most appropriate method of fitting models to data. Sörbom (1975) advises that freeing the parameter associated with the largest derivative on successive runs will result in the most parsimonious solution. Saris, dePijper, and Zegwaart (1978) argue that one must also take into account the intercorrelations among the estimates in achieving a parsimonious fit. Since the technology for using this latter method is available only for factor analysis models (Saris, personal communication), in this analysis I relied upon inspection of derivatives. For each parameter, the derivatives for each year were divided by the standard deviation on the dependent variable in order to control for the fact that variables

summarized in the first columns of Table 7.7. The findings suggest that, for both years, the models that adequately reproduce the data differ from those in Figure 7.1 and that the specifications of the models differ by year. In both years the paths $\gamma_{24}$ and $\gamma_{34}$ have been trimmed from the model. This reflects the lack of effect that median years of schooling has on wages in the service and retail sectors for both time periods. Elsewhere paths have been added. For 1972, the effects of value added and mean establishment size extend beyond affecting export sector wage levels to influencing payroll in services ($\gamma_{23}$) and retail trade ($\gamma_{32}$, $\gamma_{33}$) and median family income ($\gamma_{52}$). Though the $\gamma_{33}$ effect is comparable across years, the remaining three effects are absent in 1967.[7] These findings indicate that Thompson's theory may be extended to suggest that manufacturing sector organization affects wage levels in other sectors independent of the wage roll-out effects discussed previously. This finding is largely absent for 1967, however, which suggests that the extensions in influence of manufacturing sector organization may be a relatively recent phenomenon. Additional analysis involving data from the remaining time periods is needed to assess this hypothesis.

After deriving the models for 1967 and 1972 separately as indicated in the first columns of Table 7.7, the data for both years were simultaneously compared to a model that incorporated all the paths represented in either the 1967 or the 1972 models as listed in that table.[8] This analysis produced $\chi^2 = 87.09$, $df = 36$, $p < .001$, which suggests that there remained differences in the model by year. On the basis of analysis of derivatives and by inspection, a final model as shown in Figure 7.2 was derived where $\chi^2 = 49.55$, $df = 32$, $p = .0246$. Despite the fact that the associated probability did not quite reach the .05 level, it was decided to stop fitting in order to avoid capitalizing on chance. The final model was derived by estimating four additional parameters—$\beta_{52}$, $\gamma_{12}$, $\gamma_{21}$, and $\gamma_{45}$—separately by year. There remained eight parameters that were constrained to be equal over time. These similarities over time include the magnitudes of the wage roll-out effects from manufacturing to services and wholesale trade, though not to retail trade. There are also similarities in the effects of manufacturing and

---

were measured in different units. The parameter associated with the largest quotient was introduced into the model. Sums of parameters were similarly used when the two groups of data were compared, though the changes at this stage involved allowing such parameters to be estimated separately by year.

[7] In introducing new paths, we face the problem of how to interpret data where a path that is statistically significant for one year is not statistically significant for another. No solution to this problem is offered in the literature.

[8] In addition to the $\beta$s and $\gamma$s listed in Table 7.7, the following $\psi$s were also included in the model and estimated separately by year in the final model: $\psi_{11}$, $\psi_{22}$, $\psi_{33}$, $\psi_{44}$, $\psi_{55}$, $\psi_{32}$, $\psi_{42}$, $\psi_{43}$, $\psi_{53}$. They are statistically significant in all specifications.

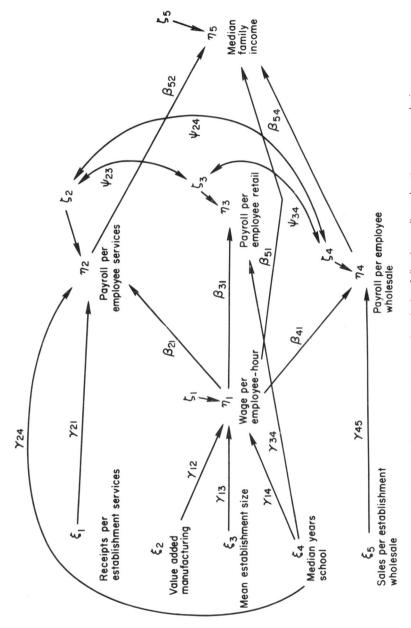

**Figure 7.1.** Specification of export sector functioning following ordinary least squares analysis.

211

wholesale wages on median family income, though not for the effects of service payrolls. Other similarities over time include the effects of mean establishment size on both manufacturing and retail wage levels, and schooling effects on manufacturing wages and on median family income. There are more differences operative among the $\gamma$s than among the $\beta$s, which suggests greater stability over time in the family income determination process than in wage attainment processes within the sectors. In particular, value added and wholesale trade sales levels evidence changing effects across the time period. In all four cases ($\gamma_{12}$, $\gamma_{32}$, $\gamma_{55}$, $\gamma_{45}$), the effects are stronger in 1972 than in 1967, though why this should be is not clear. Additional analyses of the type presented here would be useful in evaluating whether these findings extend over time periods other than between 1967 and 1972.

TABLE 7.7

Maximum Likelihood Estimates for the

$\gamma$s and $\beta$s for Several Models[a,b]

| Parameter | Final models for individual time periods | | Final model for 1967 and 1972 | | |
| | 1967 | 1972 | Constrained across years | Year specific estimates 1967 | 1972 |
|---|---|---|---|---|---|
| $\beta_{21}$ | .057*** | .083*** | .073*** | | |
| $\beta_{24}$ | -.010** | | | -.012** | -.006 |
| $\beta_{31}$ | .090*** | | | .085*** | .001 |
| $\beta_{34}$ | --- | .020*** | | -.002 | .015*** |
| $\beta_{41}$ | 1.282*** | 1.533*** | 1.401*** | | |
| $\beta_{51}$ | .071*** | .033* | .043*** | | |
| $\beta_{52}$ | .457*** | .136*** | | .461*** | .146*** |
| $\beta_{54}$ | .024*** | .031*** | .028*** | | |

*(continued)*

[a] *The estimates for the $\psi$s are not included in the table since they offer no substantive interpretation.*

[b] *In order to accommodate the precision requirements of the LISREL IV program which are relevant when analyzing covariance matrixes, the units of measurement for the input matrixes were changed from those used in Tables 7.1-7.6. Wage per employee hour (the form used as the dependent variable), wholesale sales per establishment, and retail payroll per establishment were divided by 100; service receipts and wholesale payroll per employee were divided by 10; median family income was divided by 1000; median years of schooling was multiplied by 100; services payroll per employee was multiplied by 10; and values added and mean establishment size were unchanged.*

TABLE 7.7 (continued)

| Parameter | Final models for individual time periods | | Final model for 1967 and 1972 | | |
|---|---|---|---|---|---|
| | | | Constrained | Year specific estimates | |
| | 1967 | 1972 | across years | 1967 | 1972 |
| $\gamma_{12}$ | .393*** | .509*** | | .382*** | .523*** |
| $\gamma_{13}$ | .056*** | .076*** | .064*** | | |
| $\gamma_{14}$ | .025*** | .028** | .026*** | | |
| $\gamma_{21}$ | .160*** | .319*** | | .156*** | .333*** |
| $\gamma_{23}$ | --- | -.010*** | | -.002$^\Delta$ | -.009** |
| $\gamma_{32}$ | --- | .029** | | .021* | .033** |
| $\gamma_{33}$ | -.007*** | -.009*** | -.008*** | | |
| $\gamma_{45}$ | 1.728*** | 2.148*** | | 1.668*** | 2.128*** |
| $\gamma_{52}$ | --- | .023* | | .020 | .019 |
| $\gamma_{54}$ | .003* | .003** | .003** | | |
| $\gamma_{55}$ | --- | -.037** | | -.009 | -.033** |
| | $df = 17$ | $df = 16$ | $df = 32$ | | |
| | $\chi^2 = 24.776$ | $\chi^2 = 28.564$ | $\chi^2 = 49.55$ | | |
| | $p = .0998$ | $p = .027$ | $p = .0246$ | | |

*** $= p < .001$;  ** $= p < .01$;  * $= p < .05$; $\Delta = p < .10$.

## Summary and Conclusions

This chapter has discussed Wilbur Thompson's theory concerning the role of the export sector in determining the level, stability, and distribution of income in a local labor market. Thompson argues that a manufacturing sector that produces goods for export will promote high wages in other industrial sectors through competition for workers and thus directly and indirectly contribute to higher income levels in the SMSA. Constant demand for these export goods contributes to income stability, and emphasis on manufacturing reduces income inequality through increased unionization, constriction of the skill range of occupations, and decreased role of property income. Findings were presented that are consistent with Thompson's hypotheses concerning export sector wage effects and contributions to local labor market income levels for the wholesale and service sectors in 1972, though not for retail trade. Evidence suggested that the retail trade sector

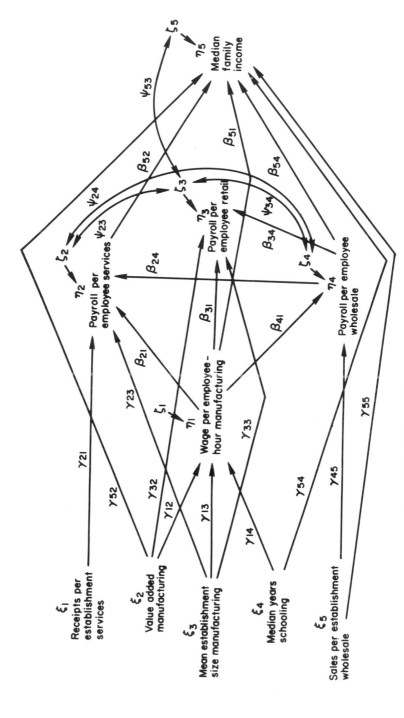

**Figure 7.2.** Final model of export sector functioning, 1967–1972.

operated largely independent of influence from the manufacturing sector and in turn did not significantly contribute to median family income level. Such isolation of the retail sector may be a partial function of its relative uniformity across local labor markets in terms of wages per employee, types of jobs, and sales levels per establishment relative to wholesale trade and services. Additional analysis for time periods between 1947 and 1967 revealed similarities in the presence of effects, particularly concerning the role of manufacturing wages, but less similarity concerning the magnitudes of the effects. This latter finding was reinforced by additional analysis comparing the covariance structures of the processes for 1967 and 1972, which produced separate parameter estimates for many paths in the model. The findings did suggest greater temporal stability in the family income attainment process than in wage attainment within respective sectors.

Two qualifications to the preceding analysis should be offered. First, it must be reiterated that local labor markets vary in their degree of specialization in manufacturing, and for some areas, a vital portion of economic activity is in retail or wholesale trade and/or services. Hence, for those areas, these sectors may be exporting goods and services, thus providing at least part of the economic base for the community. This consideration suggests that the causal ordering of the manufacturing export sector variables and those from the remaining sectors could be questioned. However, as in all correlational analyses, in this analysis the causal order is based upon theory, and the strength of Thompson's arguments regarding the role of export sector activity in the local labor market provides the justification for this assumption.

A second related qualification concerns the type of urban areas to which the models estimated here are most likely to apply. As Thompson notes, the largest urban areas, true metropolitan centers, may rely upon the export of services for a portion of their economic base. These areas also may evidence very complex interrelationships among industrial sectors. For these reasons, it may be inappropriate to include such areas as Chicago and New York City in cross-sectional analyses with such SMSAs as Youngstown or Milwaukee. Hence, the role of case studies in understanding the relevant processes for these larger areas is dramatized.

It is important to recognize that Thompson's work suggests numerous other hypotheses relevant to urban economic functioning that have not been tested in this analysis. As has been indicated, Thompson's theory covers the role of the export sector in promoting income stability and relative equality, hypotheses beyond the scope of this analysis. In addition, he analyzes the relationship of the export base and income inequality to (a) industry mix in the local labor market; (b) geographical distribution of the races; and (c) political factors in the community. Later sections of his theory deal with urban renewal, transportation, and the role of government in the growth of urban centers. At the very least, Thompson's work underscores the importance of recognizing the role of the local labor market in explaining economic achievement. Sociologists concerned with inequality, ecology, and urban development will find investigation of his theory well worth the investment.

## Acknowledgments

Helpful comments were provided by Ivar Berg, Manmohan Chaubey, Daniel Cornfield, Robert K. Miller, Jr., Charles W. Mueller, Samuel H. Preston, and Kathryn Ward. The Graduate College at the University of Iowa provided research assistance. The remaining errors are my own.

## References

Beck, E. M., P. M. Horan, and C. H. Tolbert II
  1978    "Stratification in a dual economy: A sectoral model of earnings determination." *American Sociological Review* 43:704–720.
Duncan, O. D., W. R. Scott, S. Lieberson, B. Duncan, and H. H. Winsborough
  1960    *Metropolis and Region.* Baltimore: Johns Hopkins Press.
Gordon, R.
  1968    "Issues in multiple repression." *American Journal of Sociology* 73:592–616.
Hayes, L. S.
  1979    "Youngstown bounces back." *Fortune* 100(December 17):102–104.
Heilburn, J.
  1974    *Urban Economics and Public Policy.* New York: St. Martin's.
Hirsch, W. Z.
  1973    *Urban Economic Analysis.* New York: McGraw-Hill.
Jöreskog, K. G.
  1970    "A general method for analysis of covariance structures." *Biometrika* 57:239–251.
  1973    "A general method for estimating a linear structural equation system." In A. S. Goldberger and O. D. Duncan (eds.), *Structural Equation Models in the Social Science.* New York: Seminar Press.
Jöreskog, K. G., and D. Sörbom
  1978    *LISREL IV Users Guide.* Chicago: National Educational Research.
Masters, S. H.
  1975    *Black–White Income Differentials.* New York: Academic Press.
Mattila, J. M.
  1973    "A metropolitan income determination model and the estimation of metropolitan income multipliers." *Journal of Regional Science* 13(April):1–16.
O'Neil, P.
  1970    "In the last idyllic trading post, the blight of real depression." *Life* 69(October 2):30–31.

Parcel, T. L.
 1979 "Race, regional labor markets and earnings." *American Sociological Review* 44:262–279.
Prager, K.
 1971 "Seattle under siege: The troubles of a company town." *Time* 97(January 4):28–29.
Reder, M. W.
 1955 "The theory of occupational wage differentials." *American Economic Review* 45:833–852.
Saris, W. E., W. M. dePijper, and P. Zegwaart
 1978 "Detection of specification errors in linear structural equation models." In K. F. Schuessler (ed.), *Sociological Methodology, 1979*. San Francisco: Jossey-Bass.
Sörbom, D.
 1975 "Detection of correlated errors in longitudinal data." *British Journal of Mathematical and Statistical Psychology* 28:138–151.
Spilerman, S.
 1977 "Careers, labor market structure and socioeconomic achievement." *American Journal of Sociology* 83:551–93.
Spilerman, S., and R. E. Miller
 1976 *Community and Industry Determinants of the Occupational Status of Black Males.*" Discussion Paper No. 330. Institute for Research on Poverty, University of Wisconsin—Madison.
Stolzenberg, R.
 1975 "Occupations, labor markets and the process of wage attainment." *American Sociological Review* 40:645–665.
Thompson, W. R.
 1965 *A Preface to Urban Economics.* Baltimore: Johns Hopkins Press.
Turner, R. H.
 1951 "The relative position of the Negro male in the labor force of large American cities." *American Sociological Review* 16:524–529.
U.S. Bureau of Census
 1975 Census of Manufacturers (1972). Washington, D.C.: US Govt Printing Office.
   Census of Population (various vols). Washington, D.C.: US Govt Printing Office.
   Economic Censuses (various vols). Washington, D.C.: US Govt Printing Office.

# Chapter 8

# Industrial Social

# Organization and Layoffs

# in American

# Manufacturing Industry[1]

*DANIEL B. CORNFIELD*

During the recession of 1974–1975, and throughout the 1970s, the largest single group of unemployed workers comprised those who became unemployed through losing their jobs (U.S. President, 1979, p.275). In January 1975, the manufacturing layoff rate was among the highest of any month during the post-World War II era in the United States (U.S. Bureau of Labor Statistics, 1979b, p.55).

But if layoffs have occurred frequently in recent years, they are a relatively new object of sociological inquiry (see Schervish, Chapter 6 this volume). A layoff is the termination of an employee from the payroll of a business enterprise by the employer who has deemed the job of the employee to be superfluous to the operations of the enterprise.[2] A sociological theory to explain the variation in layoff rates across firms is presented in this chapter. This theory is informed by and builds upon the work of institutional labor economists who have related unemployment and labor turnover to industrial social organization.

[1] This chapter is a revision of a paper presented at the Seventy-Fourth Annual Meeting of the American Sociological Association, Boston, August 27–31, 1979.

[2] A layoff is distinguished from a firing, which is the termination of an employee by the employer who has determined that the employee possesses personal attributes, such as incompetence, that are incompatible with the requirements of the job.

In the early decades of the twentieth century, the large corporation with its factory system and bureaucratic, hierarchical organization emerged as a major form of social organization in American industry (Berle & Means, 1932/1968; Edwards, 1975, 1979; Nelson, 1975; McNeill, 1978; Weinstein, 1969). Some economists now postulate sectoral models of a dual economy that has emerged in tandem with the large corporation (Averitt, 1968; Bluestone, Murphy, & Stevenson, 1973; Doeringer & Piore, 1971; Galbraith, 1973; O'Connor, 1973). In spite of theoretical dissension among these models, they commonly postulate two sectors that are distinguished by *sectoral dimensions*—that is, firm size, capital intensity, unionization, internalization of labor markets, and concentration. The large corporate sector is composed of large, unionized, capital-intensive firms with internally differentiated labor markets in oligopolistic or monopolistic industries, and the small-business sector comprises small, nonunion, labor-intensive firms in competitive industries.

Institutional economists maintain that a dual labor market exists and that it is associated with the dual economy. The primary labor market in the large corporate sector comprises jobs with high pay and opportunities for advancement in the firm; the secondary labor market in the small-business sector comprises low-paying jobs with little opportunity for advancement (Piore, 1975, p.126). Labor turnover in the primary labor market is characterized chiefly by planned layoffs in response to cyclical declines in demand, whereas quits, firings, and layoffs characterize labor turnover in the secondary labor market (Doeringer & Piore, 1975, pp.70–71). Some economists maintain that unemployment is generated by growth and automation in the large corporate sector and simultaneous increased competition in and the decline of the small-business sector (Braverman, 1974, p.282; O'Connor, 1973, p.25–29) or by the slow response of the educational system to higher level skill requirements in the large corporate sector (Galbraith, 1969, pp.242–245).

Although much research has been devoted to the wage and mobility differentials between the two sectors and labor markets (Alexander, 1974; Andrisani, 1973; Bibb & Form, 1977; Leigh, 1976; Osterman, 1975; Tolbert, Horan, & Beck, 1980), less research has been devoted to the difference in unemployment rates between the sectors. Sociological analyses have yielded inconclusive results. Sullivan (1978:148) finds higher unemployment rates in nonagricultural industries than in agricultural industries; but Beck, Horan, and Tolbert (1978, p.711) find no significant difference in the unemployment rates between the two sectors.

Little attention has been given to the separate effects of each sectoral dimension on the variation in layoff rates across firms, industries, or sectors (see Schervish, Chapter 6 this volume). Moreover, the effects on layoff rates of such traditional sociological components of the firm as the authority and occupational structures have only recently been examined (Cornfield, 1978, 1980).

The purpose of this chapter is to put forth a sociological theory to explain the variation in layoff rates across firms in the United States during a downturn in the business cycle and to empirically examine the variation in layoff rates across 93 American manufacturing industries during the 1975 recession.[3] In 1975, 29% of all job seekers, and 41% of blue-collar job seekers, had been laid off (Cornfield, 1978, p.1). The theory attempts to place under one sociological theoretical framework the sectoral dimensions discussed by economists and the social organizational components of the firm discussed by sociologists and to allow for the empirical examination and comparison of their separate effects on the variation in layoff rates across firms.

## Theoretical Perspective

Following Sutton, Harris, Kayser, and Tobin's (1956, pp.53–56) observation that the business enterprise occupies a central place in the American business creed, the sociological theory adopts the firm as the theoretical unit of analysis and assumes that the intrafirm labor allocation decision-making process is the primary process by which a firm implements layoffs in response to a cyclical decline in demand. This decision-making process and the outcome of the decisions are constrained and influenced by the employment relationship at the societal level of social existence and by institutional attributes and employee behavior at the firm level of social existence.

### Employment Relationship and the Legitimacy of the Layoff

An employment relationship is the set of rights and duties that accrue to employer and employee concerning employment conditions (Parsons, 1956, pp.81–82; Parsons & Smelser, 1969 pp.104–110; Vollmer, 1960, pp.7–10). A cross-cultural comparison suggests that the American employment relationship legitimizes the layoff for firms in the United States.

Employment relationships vary cross-culturally between two ideal-typical social relationships. The first is what Max Weber (1978, pp.40–41) referred

---

[3] The theoretical unit of analysis is the *firm*, but the empirical unit of analysis is the *industry*. This disparity cannot be overcome because of the absence of firm-level labor turnover data in the public domain.

to as an "associative social relationship," a social relationship that is based on a "rationally motivated adjustment of interests" between the parties of the relationship; the second is what Weber calls the "communal social relationship," a relationship that is based on a "subjective feeling of the parties, whether affectual or traditional, that they belong together [p.40]."

Cross-cultural variation in the employment relationship depends on the social institutions that define the relationship: property and ownership, laws regarding the distribution of authority between employer and employee, and culture. The effect of these social institutions on the cross-cultural variation in type of employment relationship, and hence on the legitimacy of the layoff as a labor allocation practice, is illustrated by the cases of the Israeli kibbutz, Yugoslavia, the Japanese large corporate sector, many Western European societies, and the United States.

Organized on the socialist principles of communal property, democratic decision making, and self-labor (the prohibition of hired labor), Israeli kibbutzim vest all authority in the general assembly of all adult kibbutz members, who are assigned to committees for economic production and the provision of personal services (Barkai, 1977, pp.2–7; Rosner, 1972). Kibbutz members are voluntarily bound to one another in a community, the employment relationship approximates the communal type, the involuntary expulsion of members from the kibbutz for any reason is extremely rare, and layoffs of kibbutz members never occur (Barkai, 1977, pp.4, 274).

The employment relationships of Yugoslavia and the Japanese large corporate sector are less communal than that of the Israeli kibbutz, given their formal acceptance of hired labor. Under the Yugoslav system of self-management, with the abolition of private property and decentralized decision making, the workers' council in the plant is composed of representatives elected by and from the rank and file and has authority over labor allocation and basic financial decision making (Blumberg, 1968, pp.178–180, 202–203; Tannenbaum, Kavcic, Rosner, Vianello, & Wieser, 1977, pp.27, 31). Layoffs rarely occur, Vanek claims (1977, p.75), and the normal short-run reaction to a downturn in demand is to reduce prices to induce demand. Layoffs rarely occur under the Japanese system of "permanent employment"; the employee is obliged to be loyal to the employer, who is obliged to provide the employee with a lifelong career. Permanent employment was instituted in the early twentieth century by emerging industrial enterprises to reduce labor turnover and was legitimized by values of loyalty and subordination of the individual to the group, derived from the nineteenth-century organization of Japanese familial merchant houses (Cole, 1971, pp.51, 57); Evans, 1970, pp.116–117; Hirschmeier, 1970, pp.23–25). In an empirical study controlling for age and education of workers and firm size, Cole (1979, pp.60–91) finds that voluntary and involuntary labor turnover rates are lower in Japan than in the United States.

The employment relationships of many Western European societies approach the associative type, because employer and employee are bound to one another primarily for the purpose of economic production. With the emergence of "industrial democracy" in Western Europe, however, the employer has been authorized to make decisions by virtue of private property and ownership, but the employer's authority over decisions on such issues as mergers, plant closures, automation, layoffs, and other decisions that affect the workers' livelihoods is modified by legally mandated "works councils" in many firms. The composition, rights, and duties of these councils vary across societies (King & van der Vall, 1978), but generally, the works council has the authority of prior consultation or approval of layoffs in such countries as Austria, Belgium, France, the Netherlands, and Sweden (Harrison, 1975, 1976). Under the West German system of codetermination, the works council is composed of employee representatives and has the legal right to approval of a wide variety of issues, including layoffs (Harrison, 1976, pp.39–40).

Of those thus far considered, the employment relationship in the United States most closely approximates the associative type. Private property and contract law are the main institutions upon which the employment relationship rests and by which employer and employee are related economically to one another through the "cash nexus." Under private property, ownership provides the owner of a business with broad control over the operation of the business, and the owner is accountable to no one (Selznick, 1969, p.64). With the separation of ownership from control, managers are the legal representatives of the stockholders, and therefore, managerial decisions are legitimized by private property (Berle & Means, 1932/1968). Contract law emphasizes "the high value to be placed on the freedom of individuals . . . to enter contractual relations and define for themselves the terms of the bargain [Selznick, 1969, pp.131,144]." Employer and employee enter into a relationship after an agreement is reached on work conditions, and the relationship persists as long as each party desires to be engaged in the relationship (Fox, 1974, p.189). The employer is granted authority to control the allocation of labor because the employer owns the business and is therefore granted authority to lay off employees (Sloane & Witney, 1977, p.392). Selznick (1969) writes: "The main significance of the contract at will was the contribution it made to easy layoff of employees in response to economic fluctuations [p.135]."

The percentage of the American nonagricultural labor force covered under a labor contract collectively bargained by a company management and a union has declined during the post-World War II era from 35.5% in 1945 to 26.6% in 1978 (U.S. Bureau of Labor Statistics, 1979c, p.507; 1979d,p.2). The labor union, as a legally mandated modifier of the distribution of authority between employer and employee, is relatively uncommon in American industry, especially compared to some Western European countries.[4]

The presence of a union affects the ability of the employer to unilaterally implement layoffs. In 1976, 52% of the 1570 labor agreements covering 1000 or more workers prohibited or lessened the use of subcontracting, a practice that leads to layoffs, and at least 18% of these 1570 agreements required the use of work sharing, an alternative to layoffs, instead of or before the implementation of layoffs (U.S. Bureau of Labor Statistics, 1979a, pp.73, 75). In a few instances, labor agreements prohibit layoffs and provide lifetime job guarantees to workers (U.S. Bureau of Labor Statistics, 1972, p.7).

In sum, the legitimacy of the layoff depends on the employment relationship: The layoff is more legitimate in a social setting where the employment relationship approximates the associative type than in one where the employment relationship approximates the communal type. The American employment relationship, as one that approximates the associative type, legitimizes the layoff because employer and employee are bound to one another primarily through a legal–economic bond and only secondarily through a working community organized on emotional attachments.

## Effect of Institutional and Employee Behavioral Constraints on the Firm and Layoffs

Whereas all American business enterprises operate within the framework of the employment relationship, the extent to which the layoff is used during a trough period of the business cycle varies across firms. In the early decades of the twentieth century, institutional economists John Commons and his associates (Commons, Lewisohn, Draper, & Lescohier, 1925) observed and advocated in many firms the use of alternatives to layoffs, such as work sharing. More recently, Ouchi and Jaeger (1978) observed many firms that provide job security to employees during adverse periods of the business

---

[4] The percentage of the labor forces unionized in each of the following countries is higher than that of the United States:

| | |
|---|---|
| Sweden (1972) | 87% |
| United Kingdom (1973) | 50% |
| West Germany (1972) | 37% |

See Clegg (1976, p.12) for discussion of these data.

cycle. Work sharing, reduction in hours, and attrition are alternatives to layoffs currently used by firms (Levitan & Belous, 1977; Lynton, 1975; U.S. Bureau of Labor Statistics, 1972).

The utilization of the layoff by firms is one instance of the ongoing adjustment of interests between employer and employee in the American associative type employment relationship. Institutional and employee behavioral constraints on the intrafirm labor allocation decision-making process influence the decision to implement layoffs by affecting the feasibility and costliness of layoffs for the firm. Six constraints are considered here: job structure, expectation of recall, firm size, capital intensity, concentration, and quit rate.[5]

## Job Structure

The job structure of the firm consists of two substructures: the authority structure and the occupational structure. The authority structure is the distribution of supervisory authority across jobs in the firm. Supervisory authority is the formal capacity to make decisions, such as those regarding allocation of labor into, within, and out of the firm and those regarding compensation.

Supervisory authority includes broad control over the livelihoods of employees through overall corporate policy in the firm. Such control is vested in property owners or in their legally mandated managerial agents. The vesting of such authority in these jobs is legitimized by the institution of private property, managerial ideology, and the societal system of occupational prestige (Bendix, 1974, p.312; Cornfield, 1978, p.7; Kanter, 1977, pp.20–24; Sloane & Witney, 1977, p.392).

Supervisory authority also includes immediate control over the employees' livelihoods through decisions regarding such matters as discipline and performance evaluation. Authority to make these decisions is vested in the foreman and supervisor. Jobs with no supervisory authority include technical, clerical, operative, staff professional, and other white-collar staff jobs.

Industry-level data of manufacturing employment in 1976 from the U.S.

---

[5] Unionization is another institutional constraint but is omitted from further consideration given the absence of appropriate unionization data for the empirical part of the chapter. The effect of unionization on the rate at which a firm lays off employees depends on the provisions of the labor agreement that concern job security, such as restrictions on subcontracting and the use of alternatives to layoffs. Given the variation in provisions of labor agreements, an analysis of the relationship between labor agreement provisions and layoff rates, rather than the relationship between percentage unionized and layoff rates used by Medoff (1979), is necessary for understanding the effect of unionization on the variation in layoff rates across firms.

Bureau of Labor Statistics show that the degree of centralization of authority structures—that is, the proportions of jobs endowed and unendowed with supervisory authority—varies across industries (see Table 8.1). The smaller the proportion of supervisory jobs, the more centralized is the authority structure of a firm. In Table 8.1, the transportation equipment industry, with 7.3% of jobs endowed with supervisory authority, is the most centralized industry, and the miscellaneous manufacturing industry, with 14.2% of jobs endowed with supervisory authority, is the most decentralized industry.

Employees in nonsupervisory jobs, including those in unionized settings, have tended to accept the legitimacy of the layoff as a labor allocation practice.[6] Furthermore, employees in these jobs have little formal institutional capacity to resist the implementation of layoffs by employees in jobs with the authority to implement them. Employees in jobs endowed with supervisory authority tend not to lay off one another because of self-interest, norms regarding "proper" business procedures (such as managerial ideology), and emotional cohesion, which may develop among insulated managerial elites in the firm (Blau, 1977, pp.31–47; Cornfield, 1978, p.6; Zander, 1977, pp.11–13). The first hypothesis is: In the event of a downturn in demand, centralization of authority structure is positively associated with layoff rates across firms.

The occupational substructure of the job structure is the distribution of administrative, staff, and production tasks across jobs in a firm; this is regarded by accountants as a dichotomy of indirect and direct labor. Indirect labor includes such administrative and staff tasks as managerial, financial, personnel, marketing, legal, research and development, and clerical tasks; direct labor includes tasks directly related to the production of a good, such as those associated with blue-collar jobs.

Direct exposure to fluctuations in volume of work flow from changing product demand in the marketplace is the key variable that makes a job more or less susceptible to redundancy and hence the employee in the job more or less susceptible to layoff. Indirect labor jobs experience a relatively constant flow of work, irrespective of demand fluctuations. For example, whether demand is high or low, managers continue to coordinate activities, finance analysts continue to evaluate the market, personnel employees continue to administer compensation and benefit programs, and secretaries continue to type and to answer the telephone.

The work flow of direct labor jobs varies with demand fluctuation in the marketplace. With declines in demand, the number of machines needed

---

[6] In their survey of attitudes of the unemployed, Schlozman and Verba (1979, pp.193–198) report that few respondents blame business for their job losses.

to produce output, for example, declines, and therefore the number of operatives needed to tend machines declines; or the number of craftsmen needed to fabricate a product declines.

In sum, the work flow of indirect labor jobs is not as dependent on product demand in the marketplace as is that of direct labor jobs. The second hypothesis is: In the event of a downturn in demand, proportion of direct labor jobs in the firm is positively associated with layoff rates across firms.

The authority and occupational substructures of the job structure are only analytically distinct; empirically, they are almost inextricably entangled. Their entanglement stems from the fact that positions of authority, such as managerial jobs, are simultaneously administrative jobs in the occupational structure; similarly, blue-collar jobs in the occupational structure are simultaneously nonsupervisory jobs in the authority structure. This is not the place to examine the causes of the entanglement, but the presence of blue-collar workers on the boards of directors in Western Europe, the Yugoslav workers' council, and the kibbutz general assembly suggest that the entanglement in the United States derives from the American employment relationship, with its extension of control of private property to a managerial class elected by stockholders.

The entanglement has implications for research methodology. Most American data sets, such as the U.S. Census and the Current Population Survey, utilize occupational classification schemes that do not distinguish between the authority and occupational structures and that ostensibly measure characteristics of the occupational structure. In fact, these classification schemes measure the authority and occupational structures simultaneously, and it is therefore difficult to discern which structure affects the life chances of individuals. For example, the data in Table 8.2 from the 1975 Current Population Survey show that managers and professionals experienced a lower probability of layoff than blue-collar employees in 1975. These data support the preceding discussions concerning the first and second hypotheses. Employees in jobs with no authority or employees in direct labor jobs experience higher layoff rates than employees in jobs with authority or employees in indirect labor jobs. The separate effects of the authority and occupational structures on the odds of layoff for an employee situated in these structures cannot be discerned from these data.

## Expectation of Recall

One cost incurred by firms that lay off employees during a business cycle trough is the cost of searching and hiring a work force or rehiring the laid-off work force after the trough when business picks up again. Many firms

TABLE 8.1

Percentage Distribution of Manufacturing Employment by Industry and Type of Authority, United States, 1976[a]

| | Type of authority | | | | | |
| | Jobs with supervisory authority | | | Jobs with no super- | | $N$ |
| Industry | Managers[b] | Supervisors[c] | Total with super-visory authority | visory authority[d] | Total | (in 1000) |
|---|---|---|---|---|---|---|
| All manufacturing | 6.3 | 4.1 | 10.4 | 89.6 | 100 | 19,635 |
| Durable goods | 5.9 | 3.9 | 9.8 | 90.2 | 100 | 11,410 |
| Ordnance | 5.2 | 4.1 | 9.3 | 90.7 | 100 | 296 |
| Lumber, wood products | 7.4 | 3.9 | 11.3 | 88.7 | 100 | 621 |
| Furniture, fixtures | 6.1 | 4.9 | 11.0 | 89.0 | 100 | 464 |
| Stone, clay, and glass | 7.8 | 5.4 | 13.2 | 86.8 | 100 | 644 |
| Primary metals | 3.6 | 5.4 | 9.0 | 91.0 | 100 | 1,303 |
| Fabricated metals | 6.7 | 4.8 | 11.5 | 88.5 | 100 | 1,395 |
| Machinery, excluding electrical | 6.7 | 3.3 | 10.0 | 90.0 | 100 | 1,978 |
| Electrical machinery | 5.2 | 2.6 | 7.8 | 92.2 | 100 | 1,920 |
| Transportation equipment | 4.3 | 3.0 | 7.3 | 92.7 | 100 | 1,907 |
| Instruments | 7.4 | 4.1 | 11.5 | 88.5 | 100 | 454 |

| Industry | | | | | |
|---|---|---|---|---|---|
| Nondurable goods | 6.8 | 4.5 | 11.3 | 88.7 | 100 | 8,225 |
| Food, kindred products | 7.8 | 4.7 | 12.5 | 87.5 | 100 | 1,784 |
| Tobacco manufacturing | 4.6 | 5.2 | 9.8 | 90.2 | 100 | 82 |
| Textile mill products | 4.0 | 4.8 | 8.8 | 91.2 | 100 | 978 |
| Apparel | 4.9 | 3.1 | 8.0 | 92.0 | 100 | 1,392 |
| Paper, allied products | 6.3 | 5.2 | 11.5 | 88.5 | 100 | 707 |
| Printing and publishing | 9.4 | 3.0 | 12.4 | 87.6 | 100 | 1,161 |
| Chemicals | 8.3 | 5.6 | 13.9 | 86.1 | 100 | 1,031 |
| Petroleum and coal products | 7.8 | 5.9 | 13.7 | 86.3 | 100 | 190 |
| Rubber and plastics | 6.8 | 5.9 | 12.7 | 87.3 | 100 | 578 |
| Leather products | 4.4 | 4.4 | 8.8 | 91.2 | 100 | 321 |
| Miscellaneous manufacturing | 9.7 | 4.5 | 14.2 | 85.8 | 100 | 436 |

[a] Adapted from unpublished data from the U.S. Bureau of Labor Statistics.

[b] Includes bank, financial managers, credit managers, sales managers excluding retail trade, office managers not elsewhere classified, and other managers, administrators.

[c] Includes clerical supervisors and blue-collar worker supervisors not elsewhere classified.

[d] Includes all occupations not mentioned in notes b and c.

TABLE 8.2

Layoff Rates of White- and Blue-Collar Occupations,
United States, 1975[a]

| Occupation | Layoff rate[b] |
|---|---|
| White-collar | |
| Professional -- technical | 0.4 |
| Managers | 0.5 |
| Sales | 0.6 |
| Clerical | 1.1 |
| Blue-collar | |
| Craftsmen | 4.7 |
| Laborers, nonfarm | 6.4 |
| Operatives | 8.0 |
| All occupations[c] | 2.7 |

[a]*Computed from the March 1975 Current Population Survey (CPS).*

[b]*Workers on layoff, according to the CPS definition, are people absent from work and expecting to be recalled to work. The layoff rate is computed as follows:*

$$100 \times \left[ \frac{\textit{Number workers on layoff}}{\textit{Number workers working + number workers with job but not at work + number workers on layoff}} \right]$$

[c]*Includes all farm occupations, service occupations, private household occupations, and blue- and white-collar occupations.*

have developed internal labor markets, which Doeringer and Piore (1971) define as an administratively defined bureaucratic system in the firm for the pricing, training, and allocation of labor into, within, and out of the firm. Edwards (1979, pp.145–147) maintains that internal labor markets are established by employers to stabilize the labor supply and thereby to gain control of the work force.

One aspect of the internal labor market is a layoff–recall system, whereby workers are laid off from specified job classifications, "ports of exit," and later recalled by the employer to their jobs on the basis of seniority (Doeringer & Piore, 1971, pp.49–50). Layoff–recall systems are subjects of collective bargaining and are prevalent in unionized industrial settings. In 1976, 71% of the 1570 labor agreements covering 1000 or more employees contained provisions for seniority-based, layoff–recall procedures (U.S. Bureau of Labor Statistics, 1979a, p.70).

Layoff–recall systems provide the employer with a high expectation that the laid-off work force will be easily rehired after the slack period, with a minimum of search and hiring costs, by giving employees a "right" to their jobs and, hence, encouraging employee loyalty toward the employer (Slichter, 1919, pp.269, 292–293; Slichter, Healy, & Livernash, 1960, pp.114, 167–168; Vollmer, 1960, pp.25, 108, 112). With a high expectation of relatively uncostly recall of the laid-off work force, firms with layoff–recall systems are more likely to lay off employees during a decline in demand than firms with no or less-developed layoff–recall systems and with lower expectations of recall. The third hypothesis is: In the event of a downturn in demand, a firm's expectation of recall of its laid-off work force is positively associated with layoff rates across firms.

## Firm Size

Firm size, measured financially by volume of sales, determines the extent to which firms can afford to lay off employees during a downturn in demand. Costs associated with layoffs, other than search and hiring costs, are severance pay and the employer payroll tax for unemployment insurance.

The unemployment insurance program was established under the New Deal administration in 1935 not only to compensate laid-off workers but to discourage employers from laying off employees. Based on John Commons's (1922) theory of unemployment prevention and public policy recommendations, the unemployment insurance program provides for a taxation scheme whereby the employer is taxed in direct proportion to the number of employees laid off, a procedure called experience rating (Haber & Murray, 1966, pp.337–338).

Not only can larger firms afford to operate internal labor markets (Gordon, 1974, p.49), they can also more easily afford to pay severance benefits and the unemployment insurance tax than can smaller firms.

The fourth hypothesis is: In the event of a downturn in demand, firm size is positively associated with layoff rates across firms. However, the hypothesized effect of firm size on the variation in layoff rates may be offset by smaller firms in the secondary labor market, which may hire and dismiss temporary or casual employees to avoid layoffs of full-time employees and incurring the increased payroll tax for unemployment insurance (Doeringer & Piore, 1971, pp.167–172).

## Capital Intensity

Capital intensity is the extent to which the production process of a firm is automated. The greater the degree of automation, the more buffered are jobs in the firm from changing volumes of work due to fluctuations in product demand in the marketplace.

Capital-intensive firms employ a constant number of technicians to monitor and maintain the machinery, the activity level of which corresponds to fluctuations in product demand. Labor-intensive firms employ operatives to tend semiautomatic, low-work-capacity machines, and hence, the number of operatives employed to manually produce output directly depends on, or attaches to, the level of product demand in the market. Therefore, employees of capital-intensive firms are employed in jobs less susceptible to redundancy and are therefore less susceptible to layoffs than are employees of labor-intensive firms. The fifth hypothesis is: In the event of a downturn in demand, capital intensity is negatively associated with layoff rates across firms.

## Concentration

Concentration is the proportion of business conducted by the largest firms in an industry; it is an indicator of the degree of price competition in an industry. Highly concentrated industries tend to be oligopolistic: Pricing behavior is dependent on the tacit or overt collective decision by suppliers (Blair, 1972, pp.469, 470, 477; Scherer, 1970, pp.164, 173). Competition among oligopolistic firms occurs through such nonprice mechanisms as advertising and product quality (Blair, 1972, p.308, Galbraith, 1973, p.176; Samuelson, 1973, p.511). Moreover, business custom among oligopolistic firms inhibits the lowering of prices during a downturn in demand (Blair, 1972, p.308; Galbraith, 1973, p.1976).

In low-concentration industries, no single firm or group of firms is sufficiently large to influence the price of output. Perfect competition, so-called by economists, occurs through pricing and is dependent on bargains and choices by and between suppliers and demanders. Stigler (1968, pp.16–17) maintains that a large number of firms in an industry is the one sufficient condition needed for perfect competition to exist.

In highly concentrated industries, firms respond to downturns in demand through reduction of output and employment because prices are less responsive to variation in product demand compared to the condition of perfect competition (Galbraith, 1973, pp.176–177). The sixth hypothesis is: In the event of a downturn in demand, level of concentration in an industry is positively associated with layoff rates across firms.

## Quit Rate

Quit rate is the extent to which employees terminate their participation in the employment relationship. In his extensive discussion of the turnover literature, Price (1977, p.63) finds some evidence that quit rates are higher in goods-producing than in service-producing organizations, but he does not relate quit rates to layoff rates.

Quitting, a form of natural attrition, is an alternative to layoffs (Lynton, 1975; U.S. Bureau of Labor Statistics, 1972, pp.18–19). Firms with high rates of quitting have less need to lay off employees during a trough in the business cycle and avoid incurring such costs as severance pay, the unemployment insurance tax, and search and hiring costs associated with layoffs. The seventh hypothesis is: In the event of a downturn in demand, the quit rate is negatively associated with layoff rates across firms.

## Data

### Selection of Industries

The U.S. Office of Management and Budget (1972) classifies all American manufacturing industries according to 451 4-digit industries in its 1972 Standard Industrial Classification (SIC). The U.S. Bureau of Labor Statistics (BLS) (1979b) selects, on the basis of statistical reliability (Buso & Bennett, 1978, p.9), 130 "BLS industries" from the 451 industries of the 1972 SIC and publishes their layoff rates.[7] Based on the 1972 Census of Manufactures, the 130 BLS industries accounted for 62.4% of manufacturing employment and 58.9% of the dollar value of manufacturing shipments in 1972 (U.S. Bureau of the Census, 1976, pp.3, SR2 6–49, SR2 165–240).

Although the 130 BLS industries do not constitute the universes of 4-digit manufacturing industries, manufacturing employment, and value of manufacturing shipments, they are representative of manufacturing industries with respect to the institutional constraints, except firm size, discussed in the preceding section. To detect bias with respect to the institutional con-

---

[7] This excludes multiple 4-digit industries (e.g., 3942, 4 and 3671-3) for which the BLS publishes layoff rates.

straints in the BLS industries, analysis of variance was performed on the differences of the mean scores on four of the six independent variables used in this chapter for simple random samples of BLS industries and non-BLS industries, that is, industries for which no layoff rates are published.[8] Following sampling procedures outlined by Blalock (1972, p.510–513), 150 industries were randomly selected from all 451 4-digit manufacturing industries of the 1972 SIC, yielding 43 BLS industries and 107 non-BLS industries. The analysis of variance, presented in Table 8.3, suggests that the mean scores on job structure, concentration, and capital intensity for the two samples are not significantly different but that the mean score on firm size of the BLS industries is significantly larger than that of the non-BLS industries.

Of the 130 BLS industries, 93 were selected by virtue of the similarity of their industry-specific business cycles to avoid confounding effects of these cycles on the ensuing cross-sectional analysis of the variation in layoff rates across industries. The aggregate national manufacturing layoff rate in 1973 was lower than that of any year since 1945; by 1975 it had climbed to 2.1 layoffs per 100 employees; and by 1977 it had fallen (U.S. Bureau of Labor Statistics, 1979b, p.55). The layoff rate trends of the 93 industries selected for analysis here conformed to this aggregate pattern; those of 22 other BLS industries deviated from the aggregate pattern, with highest layoff rates in 1974 instead of the aggregate high in 1975; and those of the remaining 15 BLS industries manifested no obvious pattern. The mean layoff rates between 1973 and 1977 for the 93 industries with the highest layoff rate in 1975 and the 22 industries with the highest layoff rate in 1974 are shown in Table 8.4.

The variation in timing of industry-specific business cycles across industries means that some industries experience peaks while others experience troughs. Given the sensitivity of layoff rates to business cycles (Bradshaw & Scholl, 1976, p.31), the variation in layoff rates across industries is partly a function of the variation in timing of the peaks and troughs of industry-specific business cycles across industries. To control for this effect of industry-specific business cycles on the magnitude of layoff rates, only the 93 BLS industries whose layoff rate trends conformed to the aggregate national pattern were selected for analysis here.

### Variables

The dependent variable is the 1975 layoff rate, published by the BLS (1979b). A layoff rate is the annual average of the monthly numbers of

---

[8] Data for two independent variables, recall and quit rates, are available for the 130 BLS industries only and not for non-BLS industries.

TABLE 8.3

Analysis of Variance to Test the Differences in Mean Scores on Job Structure, Concentration, Capital Intensity, and Firm Size for Samples of BLS and Non-BLS Manufacturing Industries[a]

| | Mean score | | Diff-erence | Between sum of squares | Within sum of squares | Degrees of freedom | $F$ | Probability |
|---|---|---|---|---|---|---|---|---|
| | BLS industries ($N = 43$) | Non-BLS industries ($N = 107$) | | | | | | |
| Job Structure (percent production worker) | 74.5 | 76.1 | 1.6 | 74.1 | 18,132.0 | 1/148 | .60 | $p > .05$ |
| Concentration (four-firm concentration ratio) | 40 | 38 | 2 | 208 | 62,666 | 1/148 | .49 | $p > .05$ |
| Capital intensity (ratio of total assets to value of industry shipments) | .402 | .371 | .031 | .030 | 8.196 | 1/146[b] | .54 | $p > .05$ |
| Firm size (millions of dollars of sales per company) | 19.5 | 8.5 | 11.0 | 3656.9 | 133,281.1 | 1/148 | 4.06 | $.01 < p < .05$ |

[a] Data are from U.S. Bureau of the Census, 1976, Tables 5 and 8, pp. SR 2:6-49, 165-240; 1978.

[b] Capital intensity data are unavailable for two industries.

TABLE 8.4

Mean Layoff Rates (layoffs per 100 employees) and Standard Deviations for
22 Manufacturing Industries With Highest Layoff Rate in 1974 and for
93 Manufacturing Industries With Highest Layoff Rate in 1975, United States,
1973–1977[a]

| | Mean layoff rate (LR) and standard deviation (SD) | | | | | | | | | |
|---|---|---|---|---|---|---|---|---|---|---|
| | 1973 | | 1974 | | 1975 | | 1976 | | 1977 | |
| | LR | SD | LR | SD | LR | SD | LR | SD | LR | SD |
| Industries with highest layoff rate in: | | | | | | | | | | |
| 1974 ($N = 22$) | 0.9 | 0.5 | 2.1 | 1.2 | 1.8 | 1.0 | 1.1 | 0.5 | 1.0 | 0.5 |
| 1975 ($N = 93$) | 0.6 | 0.5 | 1.1 | 0.8 | 2.0 | 1.1 | 1.0 | 0.7 | 0.9 | 0.6 |

[a] Data are from U.S. Bureau of Labor Statistics, 1979b.

layoffs per 100 employees in an industry. According to the BLS (1979b) layoffs are "suspensions without pay lasting or expected to last more than seven consecutive calendar days, initiated by the employer without prejudice to the worker [p.946]." The year 1975 was chosen not only because it was a year of high layoff rates but because, between the years 1973 and 1977, the variation in layoff rates across the 93 industries was greatest in 1975. (See the standard deviations of the mean layoff rates in Table 8.4.)

Six independent variables are used in the analysis. First, job structure is measured by the 1972 percentage of production workers in an industrial work force, computed from U.S. Bureau of the Census (BOC) (1976, pp.SR2 165–240) data. According to the BOC (1976, p.A1), production workers are all workers "up through the working foreman level," exclusive of clerical workers and "supervisory employees above the working foreman level." As with the data in Table 8.2, this measure confounds the authority and occupational structures and is the only job structure data available for 4-digit SIC industries.

Second, expectation of recall is the 1976 recall rate, published by the BLS (1979b). A recall rate is the annual average of the monthly numbers of recalls per 100 employees for a given industry. The BLS (1979b) defines recalls as "permanent or temporary additions to the employment roll of persons specifically recalled to a job in the same establishment of the company following a period of layoff lasting more than seven consecutive days [p.946]." Given that 1975 is the year of the dependent variable, the 1976 recall rate is an ex post facto measure of expectation of recall. Yet, 1976 is the first year for which the BLS publishes the recall rates of 4-digit SIC industries.

Third, firm size is the 1972 dollar value of industry shipments divided by the number of companies in a given industry, derived from BOC (1976, pp.SR2 6–49) data. Fourth, capital intensity is the 1972 ratio of the dollar values of total assets to industry shipments. These ratios are published by the BOC (1978), which advocates their use for examinations of "the differences in capital intensity among industries [p.vii]." Fifth, concentration is the 1972 four-firm concentration ratio, that is, the percentage of the dollar value of industry shipments accounted for by the four largest firms in a given industry, published by the BOC (1976, pp.SR2 6–49). Sixth, the quit rate is measured by the quit rates published by the BLS (1979b). A quit rate is the annual average of the monthly numbers of quits per 100 employees in a given industry. According to the BLS (1979b), quits are "terminations of employment initiated by employees, failure to report after being hired . . . , and unauthorized absences, if on the last day of the month the person has been absent more than seven consecutive calendar days [p.946]."

The mean scores and standard deviations on the seven variables for the 93 industries are presented in Table 8.5.

## Findings

Six multiple regression equations between the 1975 layoff rate and the six independent variables for the 93 industries are presented in Table 8.6. Equation 1 is the saturated model with all six independent variables and explains 74.3% of the variance in layoff rates across the 93 industries. The regression coefficients for expectation of recall and job structure are positive in sign and statistically significant, and lend support to the first, second, and third hypotheses. The regression coefficients for concentration, capital

TABLE 8.5

Mean Scores and Standard Deviations on the Dependent and Independent Variables for the 93 Industries[a]

| Variables | Mean | Standard deviation |
|---|---|---|
| Layoff rate (layoffs per 100 employees) | 2.0 | 1.1 |
| Job structure (percent production worker) | 75.4 | 10.6 |
| Expectation of recall (recall per 100 employees) | .9 | .7 |
| Firm size (millions of dollars of sales per company) | 10.8 | 16.5 |
| Capital intensity (ratio of total assets to value of industry shipments) | .393 | .260 |
| Concentration (four-firm concentration ratio) | 36 | 20 |
| Quit rate (quits per 100 employees) | 1.2 | 0.8 |

[a]See Tables 8.3 and 8.4 for sources.

TABLE 8.6

Six Multiple Regression Equations Between Selected Independent Variables
and 1975 Layoff Rate for 93 American Manufacturing Industries[a]

| Independent variables | Equation 1 | Equation 2 | Equation 3 | Equation 4 | Equation 5 | Equation 6 |
|---|---|---|---|---|---|---|
| Expectation of recall | 1.308 ( .797) | 1.302 ( .794) | 1.264 ( .770) | 1.324 ( .807) | 1.265 ( .771) | 1.262 ( .770) |
| Job structure | .021 ( .204) | .017 ( .167) | .019 ( .185) | .017 ( .169) | .018 ( .180) | .019 ( .189) |
| Concentration | -.004* (-.079) | -.005* (-.091) | --- | --- | --- | --- |
| Capital intensity | -.303* (-.072) | --- | -.265* (-.064) | --- | --- | --- |
| Firm size | -.003* (-.053) | --- | --- | -.007* (-.102) | --- | --- |
| Quit rate | -.096* (-.074) | --- | --- | --- | -.013* (-.010) | --- |
| Constant | -.268 | -.228 | -.410 | -.366 | -.489 | -.516 |
| $R^2$ | .743 | .735 | .732 | .737 | .728 | .728 |

[a]See Tables 8.3 and 8.4 for sources.

*$p > .05$; unstarred coefficients are significant at the .05 level.

intensity, firm size, and quit rate are statistically insignificant and provide no support for the fourth, fifth, sixth, and seventh hypotheses.

To test for some of the possible suppressor effects among the variables whose coefficients are insignificant in Equation 1, each of Equations 2–5 include three variables: expectation of recall, job structure, and one of the four variables whose coefficients are insignificant in Equation 1. The coefficients of each of these four variables—concentration, capital intensity, firm size, and quit rate—are insignificant in Equations 2–5, and those for expectation of recall and job structure are positive and significant.

Equation 6 is the most parsimonious of the six models, includes only expectation of recall and job structure, and explains 72.8% of the variance in layoff rates—slightly less than the saturated model. The coefficients are positive and significant, and the magnitude of the association between expectation of recall and layoff rate is greater than that between job structure and layoff rate.

In summary, the hypothesized separate effects of expectation of recall and job structure on the variation in layoff rates across firms, controlling all other hypothesized effects, are supported by these findings. Those of concentration, capital intensity, firm size, and quit rate receive no support from the findings. Further, the effects of expectation of recall and job structure account for almost three-quarters of the variance in layoff rates across the 93 industries.


## Discussion

The findings suggest that expectation of recall and job structure are the most influential constraints, of those examined here, on the intrafirm labor allocation decision-making process whereby layoffs are implemented. Whereas the layoff is a legitimate labor allocation practice in the United States by virtue of the societal employment relationship, expectation of recall and job structure constrain the intrafirm decision to implement layoffs by affecting the costliness and feasibility of laying off employees and, therefore, the variation in layoff rates across firms.

The creation of internal labor markets with layoff–recall systems may be seen in light of a broader historical process in the twentieth century of internalization by firms, especially those of the large corporate sector, of markets and functions formerly external to the firm to reduce instability in these markets (McNeill, 1978, pp.65–71; Williamson, 1975). In 1904, Thorstein Veblen (1904/1932, pp.14–15) noted in *The Theory of Business Enterprise* that industries were intimately connected to one another via supplier–demander relationships and that a disruption in any one of these connections sent unstable reverberations throughout American industry, thereby bringing "derangement to the industrial process at large." Since the early decades of the twentieth century, firms, especially in heavy manufacturing, have gone through a series of mergers and acquisitions, as well as conglomerations, to stabilize their supplier, distribution, and consumer markets (Blair, 1972, pp.257–296; Pfeffer, 1972). Chandler (1969, pp.24–37) shows that some firms underwent backward and forward vertical integration to stabilize supplier and distributor markets. Blair (1972, pp.308–310) and Galbraith (1973, pp.139–141) maintain advertising provides the firm with control over consumer markets.

John Commons (1922) advocated the internalization of labor markets to reduce instability that derives from involuntary and voluntary labor turnover—turnover that, Commons and his associates (1925, pp.108–109) claimed, cost employers "hundreds of millions of dollars annually" (see also Slichter, 1919, pp.107–109). Internalization of labor by the firm was to occur through the use of alternatives to layoffs, such as training workers for diversified work, so that employers would not have to lay off employees who would be loyal to the employer and would refrain from quitting (Commons, 1919, pp.25–27; 1922; Slichter, 1919, p.269).

Ironically, Commons's expectation of the dampening effect internalization would have on the utilization of layoffs seems to have been reversed, since the internal labor market with its layoff–recall system appears to encourage layoffs by reducing instability in the supply of labor, by reducing costs incurred by firms in their procurement of labor, and by raising the managerial expectation of easy recall of the laid-off work force. However, the preceding cross-sectional analysis is no substitute for a longitudinal, historical one required to examine the relationship between the process of internalization and labor turnover.

Indeed, internalization may have contributed to the secular decline in aggregate, manufacturing layoff rates that has occurred since the 1930s (U.S. Bureau of Labor Statistics, 1979b, p.55). Two dimensions of internalization, the use of overtime and the provision of fringe benefits, may have lowered the layoff rate. Firms that provide large fringe benefit packages are less likely to hire and fire employees during the peaks and troughs of the business cycle than they are to vary the overtime of their employees. Although the average number of weekly hours of work has remained stable in the post-World War II era, the percentage of overtime and the provision of fringe benefits have increased in a secular manner (Galenson & Smith, 1978, pp.22, 59–60; U.S. Bureau of Labor Statistics, 1979c, pp.219, 221).

The empirical entanglement of the authority and occupational structures in the composite job structure measure suggests a twofold intepretation of the consequences job structure has on the layoff process. First, as a proxy for authority structure, job structure is the institutional arena within which employees in jobs endowed with different amounts and types of authority to make labor allocation decisions adjust the interests of one another in the process by which layoffs are implemented. The more centralized the authority structure, the greater is the rate at which a firm implements layoffs during a cyclical trough. In firms with centralized authority structures, a large proportion of employees are in jobs unendowed with the authority to make labor allocation decisions and hence have no formal institutional capacity to govern their own life chances, other than their right to quit; moreover, the small proportion of employees in the jobs endowed with the authority to allocate labor tend not to lay themselves off and are confronted with little authorized and unauthorized resistance to the implementation of layoffs from nonsupervisory employees, except in unionized settings. The centralized authority structure, then, facilitates the implementation of layoffs through the vesting of managerial authority in a small proportion of jobs, in a broader societal and normative context that has primarily condoned the use of layoffs.

Firms with decentralized authority structures comprise a large proportion of employees in jobs endowed with the authority to participate in labor allocation decision making and hence to govern their life chances in a more collective manner than in the centralized firm. In decentralized settings, one may hypothesize, following the work of Zander (1977, pp.11–13), that emotional cohesion may develop among members of work groups with shared decision making that effectively reduces the legitimacy of the layoff.

Second, as a proxy for occupational structure, job structure determines the extent to which jobs are exposed to and buffered from changing volumes of work from fluctuations in product demand in the marketplace. Firms with large proportions of direct labor jobs comprise many employees whose jobs are susceptible to declining volumes of work from declining product demand in the market and who are therefore susceptible to redundancy and layoff. More bureaucratized firms with large proportions of administrative jobs comprise many employees whose jobs receive a constant flow of work independent of fluctuations in product demand and who are therefore buffered from redundancy and layoff.

In summary, internalization of labor markets, as one dimension that defines the two sectors of what institutional economists call a dual economy, influences the variation in layoff rates across firms by virtue more of the layoff–recall system than of the other sectoral dimensions considered here. With the exception of internalization of labor markets, the sociological authority and occupational structures, as measured by job structure, have more impact on the variation in layoff rates across firms than do the sectoral dimensions.

## Conclusion: The Future of the Layoff and Implications for Further Research

The variation in layoff rates across firms during a downturn in demand in the United States is influenced by industrial social organization at two levels of social existence. At the societal level, the American associative-type employment relationship legitimizes the layoff as a labor allocation practice available to firms. At the level of the firm, institutional and employee behavioral constraints influence the costliness and feasibility of layoffs for the firm. The foregoing cross-sectional analysis suggests that variation in the degree of bureaucratization of internal labor market layoff–recall systems, centralization of authority structures, and extent of direct labor jobs in the occupational structure affect the variation in layoff rates across firms during a downturn in demand.

The two-level social organizational impact on this pattern of layoff rates suggests that change in this pattern may be affected by change either at the level of the societal employment relationship or at the level of the job structure in the firm. Unionization and collective bargaining may affect the employment relationship and hence the utilization of the layoff. The secular decline in the percentage unionized of the American labor force, partly attributable to the decline in blue-collar jobs, may become reversed given that unions of white-collar employees are among the fastest growing unions (Sloane & Witney, 1977, p.9; U.S. Bureau of Labor Statistics, 1979d, p.6). Recent experiments in the United States of worker participation in managerial decision making and discussion of the legitimacy of unilateral managerial authority in the American labor movement are indicators of the awareness by management and labor of Western European models of industrial democracy and may affect the distribution of authority between employer and employee (Kamber, 1980; Serrin, 1980; Shaw, 1977). The potential for the redistribution of authority could affect the legitimacy and utilization of the layoff in the United States, especially in unionized industrial settings.

The importance of firm-level industrial social organization (Baron & Bielby, 1980) for the variation in layoff rates in the 1975 recession suggests that change in industrial social organization is related to the secular decline in aggregate manufacturing layoff rates. Longitudinal case studies of firms, as well as longitudinal studies based on comprehensive firm-level survey data, should be done to examine the effect of the historical processes of internalization of labor markets, centralization–decentralization of industrial authority structures, and bureaucratization of business enterprises on the decline in layoff rates and on the historical variation in layoff rates across firms.

## Acknowledgments

I am indebted to the following people who provided useful comments: Ivar Berg, Lawton Burns, Mark Granovetter, Eric Hirsch, Edward Laumann, Susan Mason, Robert Miller, Jr., James Price, Teresa Sullivan, and Roy Young. I am solely responsible for the contents herein.

## References

Alexander, A,
    1974  "Income, experience, and the structure of internal labor markets." *The Quarterly Journal of Economics* 88(1):63–85.
Andrisani, P.
    1973  *An Empirical Analysis of the Dual Labor Market Theory.* Columbus: Center for Human Resource Research, The Ohio State University.
Averitt, R.
    1968  *The Dual Economy.* New York: Norton.
Barkai, H.
    1977  *Growth Patterns of the Kibbutz Economy.* Amsterdam: North-Holland Publ.
Baron, J., and W. Bielby
    1980  "Bringing the firms back in: Stratification, segmentation, and the organization of work." *American Sociological Review* 45(5):737–765.
Beck, E., P. Horan, and C. Tolbert
    1978  "Stratification in a dual economy: A sectoral model of earnings determination." *American Sociological Review* 43(5):704–720.
Bendix, R.
    1974  *Work and Authority in Industry.* Berkeley: Univ. of California Press.
Berle, A., and G. Means
    1968  *The Modern Corporation and Private Property.* New York: Harcourt. (Originally published, 1932.)
Bibb, R., and W. Form
    1977  "The effects of industrial, occupational, and sex stratification on wages in blue-collar markets." *Social Forces* 55(June):974–996.
Blair, J.
    1972  *Economic Concentration.* New York: Harcourt Brace Jovanovich.
Blalock, H.
    1972  *Social Statistics* (2nd ed.). New York: McGraw-Hill.
Blau, P.
    1977  *Inequality and Heterogeneity.* New York: The Free Press.
Bluestone, B., W. Murphy, and M. Stevenson
    1973  *Low Wages and the Working Poor.* Policy Papers in Human Resources and Industrial Relations 22. Ann Arbor: The Institute of Labor and Industrial Relations, The University of Michigan and Wayne State University.
Blumberg, P.
    1968  *Industrial Democracy.* New York: Schocken.
Bradshaw, T., and J. Scholl
    1976  "Workers on layoff: A comparison of two data series." *Monthly Labor Review* 99(11):29–33.

Braverman, H.
1974   *Labor and Monopoly Capital.* New York: Monthly Review Press.

Buso, M., and W. Bennett
1978   "BLS establishment estimates revised to reflect new benchmark levels and 1972 SIC." *Employment and Earnings* 25(10):8–32.

Chandler, A.
1969   *Strategy and Structure.* Cambridge, Massachusetts: MIT Press.

Clegg, H.
1976   *Trade Unionism under Collective Bargaining.* Oxford: Basil Blackwell.

Cole, R.
1971   "The theory of institutionalization: Permanent employment and tradition in Japan." *Economic Development and Cultural Change* 20(October):47–70.

1979   *Work, Mobility, and Participation: A Comparative Study of American and Japanese Industry.* Berkeley: Univ. of California Press.

Commons, J.
1919   *Industrial Goodwill.* New York: McGraw-Hill.

1922   "Unemployment Prevention." *American Association for Labor Legislation Review* 12(1):15–24.

Commons, J., S. Lewisohon, E. Draper, and D. Lescohier
1925   *Can Business Prevent Unemployment?* New York: Knopf.

Cornfield, D.
1978   *Organizational Influences on the American Employment Relationship: Occupations and Layoffs.* Paper presented at the Seventy-third Annual Convention of the American Sociological Association, San Francisco, September 4–8.

1980   *Layoffs: An Inquiry into the Social Causes of Separations from the Firm.* Unpublished doctoral dissertation. Department of Sociology, University of Chicago.

Doeringer, P., and M. Piore
1971   *Internal Labor Markets and Manpower Analysis.* Lexington, Massachusetts: Heath.

1975   "Unemployment and the 'dual labor market.'" *The Public Interest* 38(Winter):67–79.

Edwards, R.
1975   "The social relations of production in the firm and labor market structure." In R. Edwards, M. Reich, and D. Gordon (eds.), *Labor Market Segmentation.* Lexington, Massachusetts: Heath.

1979   *Contested Terrain.* New York: Basic.

Evans, R.
1970   "Evolution of the Japanese system of employer–employee relations, 1868–1945." *Business History Review* 44(1):110–125.

Fox, A.
1974   *Beyond Contract.* London: Faber and Faber.

Galbraith, J.
1969   *The New Industrial State.* Boston: Houghton.

1973   *Economics and the Public Purpose.* New York: Signet.

Galenson, W., and R. Smith
1978   "The United States." In J. Dunlop and W. Galenson (eds.), *Labor in the Twentieth Century.* New York: Academic Press.

Gordon, D.
1974   *Theories of Poverty and Underemployment.* Lexington, Massachusetts: Heath.

Haber, W., and M. Murray
1966   *Unemployment Insurance in the American Economy.* Homewood, Illinois: Irwin.

Harrison, R.
1975    *Redundancy in Western Europe.* London: Institute of Personnel Management.
1976    *Workers' Participation in Western Europe, 1976.* London: Institute of Personnel Management.
Hirschmeier, J.
1970    "The Japanese spirit of enterprise, 1867–1970." *Business History Review* 44(1):13–38.
Kamber, V.
1980    "Protecting workers' rights." *New York Times,* January 5, p.21.
Kanter, R.
1977    *Men and Women of the Corporation.* New York: Basic.
King, C., and M. van der Vall
1978    *Models of Industrial Democracy.* New York: Mouton.
Leigh, D.
1976    "Occupational advancement in the late 1960's: An indirect test of the dual labor market hypothesis." *The Journal of Human Resources* 11(2):155–171.
Levitan, S., and R. Belous
1977    *Shorter Hours, Shorter Weeks: Spreading the Work to Reduce Unemployment.* Baltimore: Johns Hopkins Press.
Lynton, E.
1975    *Alternatives to Layoffs.* Based on conferences held by the New York City Commission on Human Rights, April 3–4. New York: Commission on Human Rights.
McNeill, K.
1978    "Understanding organizational power: Building on the Weberian legacy." *Administrative Science Quarterly* 23(1):65–90.
Medoff, J.
1979    "Layoffs and alternatives under trade unions in U.S. manufacturing." *American Economic Review* 69(3):380–395.
Nelson, D.
1975    *Managers and Workers: Origins of the New Factory System in the United States, 1880–1920.* Madison: Univ. of Wisconsin Press.
O'Connor, J.
1973    *The Fiscal Crisis of the State.* New York: St. Martin's.
Osterman, P.
1975    "An empirical study of labor market segmentation." *Industrial and Labor Relations Review* 28(4):508–521.
Ouchi, W., and A. Jaeger
1978    "Social structure and organization type." In M. Meyer and associates (eds.), *Environments and Organizations.* San Francisco: Jossey-Bass.
Parsons, T.
1956    "Suggestions for a sociological approach to the theory of organizations—I." *Administrative Science Quarterly* 1(January):63–85.
Parsons, T., and N. Smelser
1969    *Economy and Society.* New York: The Free Press.
Pfeffer, J.
1972    "Mergers as a response to organization interdependence." *Administrative Science Quarterly* 17(3):382–394.
Piore, M.
1975    "Notes for a theory of labor market stratification." In R. Edwards, M. Reich, and M. Piore (eds.), *Labor Market Segmentation.* Lexington, Massachusetts: Heath.

Price, J.
    1977    *The Study of Turnover.* Ames: Iowa State Univ. Press.
Rosner, M.
    1972    *Self-Management in Kibbutz–Industry–Organizational Patterns and Psychological Effects.* Paper presented at the First International Sociological Conference on Participation and Self-Management, Dubrovnik, Yugoslavia, December 13–17.
Samuelson, P.
    1973    *Economics* (9th ed.). New York: McGraw-Hill.
Scherer, F.
    1970    *Industrial Market Structure and Economic Performance.* Chicago: Rand McNally
Schlozman, K., and S. Verba
    1979    *Injury to Insult: Unemployment, Class, and Political Response.* Cambridge, Massachusetts: Harvard Univ. Press.
Selznick, P.
    1969    *Law, Society and Industrial Justice.* New York: Russell Sage Foundation.
Serrin, G.
    1980    "Coalition forming for a 1980's drive against business." *New York Times,* January 19, p.19.
Shaw, P.
    1977    "Worker participation—American style." *Employee Relations Law Journal* 3(2):38–48.
Slichter, S.
    1919    *The Turnover of Factory Labor.* New York: Appleton.
Slichter, S., J. Healy, and E. R. Livernash
    1960    *The Impact of Collective Bargaining on Management.* Washington, D.C.: The Brookings Institution.
Sloane, A., and F. Witney
    1977    *Labor Relations* (3rd ed.). Englewood Cliffs, New Jersey: Prentice-Hall.
Stigler, G.
    1968    *The Organization of Industry.* Homewood, Illinois: Irwin.
Sullivan, T.
    1978    *Marginal Workers, Marginal Jobs.* Austin: Univ. of Texas Press.
Sutton, F., S. Harris, C. Kaysen, and J. Tobin
    1956    *The American Business Creed.* Cambridge, Massachusetts: Harvard Univ. Press.
Tannenbaum, A., B. Kavcic, M. Rosner, M. Vianello, and G. Wieser
    1977    *Hierarchy in Organizations.* San Francisco: Jossey-Bass.
Tolbert, C., P. Horan, and E. M. Beck
    1980    The structure of economic segmentation: A dual economy approach." *American Journal of Sociology* 85(5):1095–1116.
U.S. Bureau of Labor Statistics
    1972    *Layoff, Recall, and Worksharing Procedures.* Bulletin #1425-13. Washington, D.C.: US Govt Printing Office.
    1979a    *Characteristics of Major Collective Bargaining Agreements, July 1, 1976.* Bulletin #2013. Washington, D.C.: US Govt Printing Office.
    1979b    *Employment and Earnings, United States, 1909–78.* Bulletin #1312–11. Washington, D.C.: US Govt Printing Office.
    1979c    *Handbook of Labor Statistics, 1978.* Bulletin #2000. Washington, D.C.: US Govt Printing Office.
    1979d    "Labor union and employee association membership—1978." News release, September 3.

U.S. Bureau of the Census
  1976   Census of Manufacturers, 1972. *Vol. I., Subject and Special Statistics*. Washington, D.C.: US Govt Printing Office.
  1978   Annual Survey of Manufacturers, 1976. *Industry Profiles*. M76(AS)-7. Washington, D.C.: US Govt Printing Office.
U.S. Office of Management and Budget
  1972   *Standard Industrial Classification Manual, 1972*. Washington, D.C.: US Govt Printing Office.
U.S. President
  1979   *Employment and Training Report of the President*. Washington, D.C.: US Govt Printing Office.
Vanek, J.
  1977   *The Labor-Managed Economy*. Ithaca: Cornell Univ. Press.
Veblen, T.
  1932   *The Theory of Business Enterprise*. New York: Mentor. (Originally published, 1904.)
Vollmer, H.
  1960   *Employee Rights and the Employment Relationship*. Berkeley: Univ. of California Press.
Weber, M.
  1978   *Economy and Society* (Vol. 1, E. Fishoff *et al.*, Trans., G. Roth and C. Wittich, Eds.). Berkeley: Univ. of California Press. (Originally published, 1922)
Weinstein, J.
  1969   *The Corporate Ideal in the Liberal State: 1900–1919*. Boston: Beacon Press.
Williamson, O.
  1975   *Markets and Hierarchies*. New York: The Free Press.
Zander, A.
  1977   *Groups at Work*. San Francisco: Jossey-Bass.

# Part IV

# DISCRIMINATION IN
# LABOR MARKETS

# Chapter 9

# Female Underemployment in Urban Labor Markets[1]

*ALICE ABEL KEMP*

*E. M. BECK*

Much of the research on the differential unemployment rates between males and females tends to focus on individual characteristics and, too often, neglects the organization of the industrial economy, features of the local labor market, and other factors that may also affect unemployment. An understanding of organizational as well as individual factors as they relate to female unemployment seems necessary before development of a more complete explanation of the structure of sex differentials in labor market rewards is possible. In this chapter we focus on whether the organization of industry affects female unemployment, and we explore approaches from human capital theory as well as the dual economy approach to inequality to derive a model for an analysis of female labor force participants in urban labor markets.

The official definition of unemployment states that a person must be out of work and actively looking for a job within the previous 4 weeks (U.S. Department of Labor, 1976). While most analyses of unemployment are based on this definition, some economists recognize that such a narrow behavioral specification is incapable of assessing the extent of contemporary

[1] Partial support for this project was provided by a grant to E. M. Beck and Patrick M. Horan from the Small Grants Research Program, Office of General Research, Boyd Graduate Studies Research Center, University of Georgia.

SOCIOLOGICAL PERSPECTIVES ON
LABOR MARKETS

employment problems (Cain, 1978; Gordon, 1977; Harrison, 1972; Levitan & Taggart, 1974; Miller, 1973). Indexes of subemployment (Miller, 1973) and underemployment (Gordon, 1977; Harrison, 1972) have been proposed to better capture the true employment picture. These indexes include measures of the unemployed; the involuntary part-time worker who wants, but cannot find, full-time work; the discouraged worker who has given up the job search; and the working poor who are full-time, year-round workers with earnings below some poverty threshold.

While all of these reflect somewhat different dimensions of employment problems, empirical constraints dictate we focus on the unemployed and the involuntary part-time worker.[2] For these workers we define underemployment as the amount of time employed relative to the amount of time the worker desires to work. While this approach ignores discouraged workers and the working poor, it does capture more fully the employment problems of females than does the more restricted definition of unemployment.

Before considering the effect of the organization of production on underemployment in an industrial economy, it will be useful to explore some of the more traditional explanations of individual-level underemployment. In this regard, human capital theory is particularly relevant.

## Human Capital Theory

While macroeconomic theory has explained aggregate unemployment as being produced by such market forces as inadequate product demand, seasonal business fluctuations, technological advances, and normal job turnover,[3] we look to human capital theory for an explanation of individual-level underemployment. Human capital theory stresses the importance of the quality of labor in determining labor market outcomes, in particular the role of the "skills and knowledge of the individual [Thurow, 1969, p.66]" in influencing wages and employment stability. The basic argument is that workers with minimal stocks of human capital have low individual productivity and therefore receive the low wages and experience the high job turnover that is commensurate with their human capital (Thurow, 1969). More skilled and experienced labor, on the other hand, are the beneficiaries of higher wages and stability in employment. From this perspective, un-

---

[2] There are two reasons for this restriction: (a) discouraged workers are difficult to identify because of the latitude that exists in definitions of this group (Gordon, 1977); and (b) defining the working poor requires the establishment of a meaningful poverty line, a task sufficiently complex to warrant separate analysis (e.g., Bluestone et al., 1973).

[3] For a discussion of the macroeconomic approach to unemployment, see Rees, 1979.

deremployment of females can be seen as resulting from their human capital deficits.

Although men and women have parity in average levels of schooling, it has been argued that the discontinuous work history of many females results in less human capital. Since females spend fewer years in the labor force, and have more employment disruptions, their human capital accumulation is less; therefore, they receive lower wages and less stable jobs (Blau & Jusenius, 1976). Furthermore, if the notion of human capital is broadened to encompass such factors as motivation, on-the-job performance, ability and willingness to migrate, health, and job location information, then even more powerful arguments can be presented to explain female underemployment (Gordon, 1972; Mincer & Polachek, 1974; Rees & Shultz, 1970).

Polachek (1975) argues that females do not expect or intend to work continuously over their lifetimes and therefore select employment in occupations where labor force interruptions are not penalized.[4] Thus, the long-range "intentions" of females becomes an explanation for the crowding of females into a relatively few female-dominated occupations. And it has been argued (Blau & Jusenius, 1976; Ferber & Lowry, 1976a, 1976b; Stevenson, 1975, 1978) that the crowding of females into gender-typed occupations tends to produce an oversupply of females to these occupations. The result is a larger supply of female labor for the limited demand in the "female" occupations, and thus higher underemployment and lower earnings than would be expected if females were evenly distributed across occupations.[5]

We note, however, that whether this crowding of females really produces higher underemployment depends, in part, on how strongly females are affected by the discouraged worker phenomenon. If crowding reduces the number of available jobs for females, this may be so completely discouraging as to cause workers to drop out of the labor force altogether, thus removing them from the pool of the unemployed. In this instance, crowding would have the effect of reducing labor force participation rates among females while leaving female underemployment unaffected. Therefore, not only are

---

[4] See England (1981) for evidence against Polachek's view. England demonstrates with the National Longitudinal Survey (NLS) data that women are not penalized less for being out of the labor force when they are in female-dominated occupations.

[5] The fact of sex segregation in occupations is well documented in Oppenheimer (1970). She shows, for example, that over 48% of the female labor force in 1960 were in occupations that were 80% or more female. Our calculations from the 1970 census, elaborated in Appendix A, show that, of the 420 detailed occupational categories used by the census, 21.4% have 50% or more female incumbents.

The crowding hypothesis was first proposed by Fawcett (1918) and Edgeworth (1922). The modern, updated elaboration is presented in Bergmann (1971).

the personal characteristics of years of schooling and work experience important for female underemployment, but also whether or not she is in a female-dominated occupation.

Yet this reliance on individual characteristics creates a one-sided approach to labor market outcomes. Although human capital theory has made a significant contribution through emphasizing differences in the quality of labor, the allocation of females to jobs is taken as either voluntary or due to individual characteristics, and no account is taken of structural factors, such as the organization of industries, that may impinge or set limits upon the choices and opportunities of individuals. These structural factors are explicit in the dual economy theory.

## Dual Economy Theory

From traditional perspectives, much of the female underemployment problem has been seen as due to the failure of women workers to migrate, or to retrain for job vacancies, or to have a strong attachment to the labor force (Feldstein, 1977; Rees, 1979). There is renewed interest, however, in the structure of the industrial economy as an important determinant of labor market rewards (Averitt, 1968; Beck, Horan, & Tolbert, 1978; Bibb & Form, 1977; Bluestone, Murphy, & Stevenson, 1973; Edwards, Reich, & Gordon, 1975; Gordon, 1972, 1977; Harrison, 1972; Horan, Beck, & Tolbert, 1980; Tolbert, Horan, & Beck, 1980). While much of the more recent research in this approach has concentrated on worker earnings, the general framework can be applied to the problems of female underemployment as well. In particular the conceptualization of the industrial economy being divisable into two ideal-type sectors, with one being organized on the basis of competitive capitalism and the other on oligopolistic capitalism, is particularly relevant for labor market outcomes of minority workers and females (Beck, Horan, & Tolbert, 1980).

Edwards and colleagues (Edwards et al., 1975) argue that the origins of this dualistic industrial structure can be found in the growth and evolution of monopolistic capitalism in the late nineteenth and early twentieth centuries in the United States. In this era there was a strong growth in the oligopolistic control over certain basic industries, such as steel manufacturing, petroleum production and distribution, and railroad transportation. The expansion of this trend in the later twentieth century led to the formation of an oligopolistic industrial sector concentrated in the extractive, construction, petrochemical, transportation, durable manufacturing, and wholesale trade industries (Tolbert et al., 1980). In this sector firms tend to be large, unionized, and relatively insensitive to fluctuations in product demand and to control large shares of the product market. They have high capital-to-labor ratios and higher profit margins. These characteristics have produced in this sector demand for a stable, trainable work force with a strong labor force commitment.

In juxtaposition to the oligopolistic sector, a second sector of the economy exists that is based on a somewhat different mode of organization. Organized around the principle of competitive capitalism, this sector is concentrated in the agricultural, nondurable manufacturing, retail trade, and service industries. The firms in the competitive sector are smaller, have few unions, utilize more antiquated physical capital, and have relatively low profit margins, low capital-to-labor ratios, and a greater sensitivity to fluctuations in product demand. In contrast to the oligopolistic sector, the competitive sector requires a work force that will tolerate inferior, if not adverse, working conditions, arbitrary and often harsh discipline, lower pay, and greater odds of job instability (Beck *et al.*, 1980; Edwards, 1979; Hall, 1970). As a result, those with the weakest position in the labor force, women and racial minorities, are often disproportionately represented within the competitive sector (Beck *et al.*, 1980).[6]

In brief, dual economy theory would suggest that part of the explanation of female underemployment involves the differential location of females within the structure of industrial capitalism. Specifically, females within the competitive sector of the economy will experience higher underemployment, as well as lower pay, than females in the oligopolistic sector. This does not mean, however, that the labor supply factors identified by human capital theory are unimportant, just that they are incomplete. This suggests that, even after controlling for many of the individual-level variables normally considered to be important determinants of labor supply and labor quality, females in the competitive sector of the industrial economy will experience higher underemployment, reflecting a disadvantaged position for females that is independent of human capital factors.

## Data

Data used in this analysis come from the Bureau of the Census, Survey of Income and Education. This 1976 survey contains 151,170 household interviews selected independently from the 50 states, the District of Columbia, and 119 of the larger Standard Metropolitan Statistical Areas (SMSA)

---

[6] It is important to emphasize that, while minorities and females are overrepresented in the competitive sector, race and gender are not suitable proxies for sectoral location (Beck *et al.*, 1980).

(U.S. Department of Commerce, 1977a). The interview schedule is similar in content to the Current Population Survey (March Supplement) and contains information of the previous year's employment and earnings as well as information on the worker's schooling attainment. From the Survey of Income and Education (SIE), we selected all females who met four criteria: (a) were aged 18 years or older in 1975; (b) resided within a Standard Metropolitan Statistical Area that contained a central city; (c) were employed or experienced unemployed in 1975;[7] and (d) were either the head of a household or the wife of a head of household.[8] These restrictions produced a sample of 21,252 females located in 47 metropolitan areas. These unweighted cases represent approximately 16 million urban female workers. All analyses were done with the weighted sample.

In Table 9.1 we present the means for selected characteristics of this sample by sector of the industrial economy and race.[9] As indicated by the $t$ ratios on the right side of the table, there are statistically significant sectoral differences for both races for all but one of the characteristics tabulated. Especially notable are the striking sector differences in annual earnings and incidence of poverty. For both white and nonwhite females, being in the oligopolistic sector is associated with higher earnings and lower incidence of poverty.

## Analysis of Underemployment

The dependent variable, the percentage of underemployment, is defined as the ratio (times 100) of the weeks unemployed in 1975 to weeks in the

---

[7] The experienced unemployed refers to those persons who were not working in 1975 but who sought work and had worked full-time 2 weeks or more between 1971 and 1975.

[8] This restriction is necessary to permit use of the information on number of children. The presence of children is probably the most frequently cited factor for lower female labor force participation (Sweet, 1973). In the Survey of Income and Education data, this question is asked only at the household level, of the head and his wife when the head is a male. Therefore, we can include in our analysis only females who are heads themselves or the wives of heads. Other adult females who are both in the labor force and have children could easily be in the same household, but we have no information on the number of children they may have. Restricting our sample in this way eliminated 12.4% of the 24,256 ECLF females in the 47 SMSAs. We examined the employment status for these excluded females and found the mean underemployment to be slightly higher, but we felt the misspecification from ignoring number of children would be more serious than the exclusion of this small proportion.

[9] The sectoral classification employed here was developed by Tolbert and colleagues (Tolbert et al., 1980).

TABLE 9.1

Descriptive Statistics by Race and Industrial Sector of 21,252 Females in 47 Metropolitan Areas, 1976

| | Means | | | | Absolute t-ratios for between sectors contrasts[a] | |
| | Oligopoly sector | | Competitive sector | | | |
| Variable | White | Nonwhite | White | Nonwhite | White | Nonwhite |
|---|---|---|---|---|---|---|
| Proportion head of household | .2952 | .4333 | .2673 | .4064 | 3.95* | 1.53 |
| Age | 38.91 | 34.82 | 40.32 | 39.57 | 6.59* | 11.21* |
| Years of schooling completed | 12.54 | 12.37 | 12.72 | 11.73 | 4.70* | 7.20* |
| Estimated years of work experience | 12.40 | 11.03 | 12.94 | 14.37 | 4.12* | 11.86* |
| Proportion in female dominated occupations | .6127 | .5956 | .7317 | .8096 | 16.12* | 13.07* |
| Occupational prestige | 42.80 | 39.40 | 39.81 | 34.35 | 15.47* | 10.89* |
| Annual earnings | $7488.63 | $7680.30 | $5440.87 | $5504.69 | 27.17* | 13.29* |
| Imputed hourly wages[b] | $ 4.68 | $ 4.41 | $ 4.03 | $ 3.64 | 6.14* | 7.11* |
| Proportion with poverty earnings[c] | .1624 | .1409 | .3518 | .3156 | 29.40* | 12.57* |

*Statistically significant from zero at the .05 level.

[a]Absolute value of t ratio based on approximate standard errors under simple random sampling.

[b]Imputed wage rate computed from annual earnings divided by hours worked per year where hours per year is con- structed from the product of hours worked per week times weeks worked per year.

[c]Poverty threshold based on weighted average thresholds for unrelated individuals in 1975 by sex and age for nonfarm residents (U.S. Department of Commerce, 1977b, p. 199).

TABLE 9.2

Unadjusted and Adjusted Mean Female Underemployment in Urban Labor
Markets by Sector and Race

| Statistic | Oligopoly sector | | Competitive sector | |
|---|---|---|---|---|
| | White | Nonwhite | White | Nonwhite |
| **Unadjusted** | | | | |
| Mean underemployment | 6.237 | 9.296 | 7.480 | 10.057 |
| Approximate standard error[a] | .226 | .656 | .177 | .472 |
| **Adjusted for covariates** | | | | |
| Mean underemployment | 6.622 | 5.750 | 7.468 | 8.826 |
| Approximate standard error[a] | .254 | .763 | .182 | .557 |

[a]*Approximate standard errors based on simple random sampling.*

labor force in 1975.[10] It expresses the amount of time working relative to
the amount of time the individual wants to work. The index ranges from
zero for women who were continuously employed while in the labor force
to 100 for those who were totally unemployed while a labor force participant.
It should be noted that the index is a conservative measure of underemployment, because it does not differentiate between those truly out of the
labor force and those who are simply discouraged workers. With present
data we are unable to distinguish adequately between females who choose
not to work and those who were unable to find work, because both groups
are defined as out of the labor force.

The top panel of Table 9.2 presents the means and approximate standard

[10] The involuntary part-time workers are counted as one-half unemployed for all weeks in
the labor force in 1975. This is based on an assumption that part-time work (voluntary or
involuntary) is equal to one-half of full-time work, and this assumption is supported by the
fact that the ratio of average hours worked for part-time workers (nonagricultural) is .502
in 1977 (U.S. Department of Labor, 1977, Table A-26). Therefore, weeks in the labor force
is the sum of weeks worked and weeks unemployed, and this will not equal 52 for any
individual out of the labor force any time in 1975.

TABLE 9.3

t Ratios for Contrasts in Female Underemployment in Urban Labor Markets
by Sector and Race[a]

| Comparison group | Oligopoly sector | | Competitive sector | |
|---|---|---|---|---|
| | White | Nonwhite | White | Nonwhite |
| **Oligopoly industrial sector** | | | | |
| White females | --- | 1.08 | 2.71* | 3.60* |
| Nonwhite females | 4.41* | --- | 2.19* | 3.26* |
| **Competitive industrial sector** | | | | |
| White females | 4.33* | 2.67* | --- | 2.32* |
| Nonwhite females | 7.30* | .94 | 5.11* | --- |

*Statistically significant from zero at .05 level.

[a]Absolute value of t ratio based on approximate standard errors
under simple random sampling. Contrasts among unadjusted means below
the main diagonal. Contrasts among least squares adjusted means above
the main diagonal.

errors of the underemployment index by race and industrial sector.[11] Not
surprisingly, there is greater underemployment in the competitive sector of
the urban economy than in the olgipolistic sector, and there is greater
underemployment among nonwhite females than white females. While the
directions of these findings are not unanticipated, the relatively small magnitudes of underemployment experienced by both nonwhite and white urban
females is noteworthy, and we shall return to this point somewhat later
in the analysis.

To facilitate specific comparisons among these means, the absolute value
of the *t* ratios for the six possible race–sector contrasts in the top panel of
Table 9.2 are presented below the main diagonal in Table 9.3. These show
that there are statistically significant differences in mean underemployment
between whites and nonwhites within each of the industrial sectors. Within

[11] The standard errors from the weighted analysis were inflated proportionally to the ratio
of the number of weighted to unweighted cases. These inflated standard errors are reported
in Tables 9.2 and were used to compute the *t* ratios in Tables 9.1, 9.3, and 9.4.

each race, however, the sector difference is statistically significant for white females, but there is little evidence that sectoral placement has any noticeable effect on the level of underemployment among nonwhite urban females.

While summary data in Tables 9.2 and 9.3 reveal important race and sector differences in levels of underemployment, these data shed no light on how particular explanatory variables affect underemployment, nor on whether the differences observed in Table 9.2 would remain intact if other factors were controlled. To address this question, we regressed, within each race and industrial sector combination, the degree of underemployment on labor supply factors, human capital, occupational and employment variables, and features of the local urban labor market.

In particular, we control for two individual characteristics thought to affect labor supply: (a) whether the female was the head of a household or the wife of the head;[12] and (b) the number of the female's own children (Feldstein, 1977; Sweet, 1973). Next we include two measures of human capital: (a) number of years of schooling completed; and (b) estimated number of years of work experience.[13] As for the occupational–employment variables, we control for: (a) the occupational prestige of the longest held job in 1975 or the last job;[14] (b) whether the female's 1975 or last job was

[12] While definitionally none of the females who are heads of a household are married with a husband present, 64% of the nonheads are married with a husband present. We elected not to utilize marital status in this analysis, not only because we feel that measuring the effect of being the head of a household on underemployment better captures the economic situation for females than would marital status, but also because marital status seems to be more properly a polytomous variable with as many as six mutually exclusive categories, which would make interpretation difficult.

[13] The measure of years of work experience is an estimate for these females. While the usual formula (Age − Schooling − 5) works fairly well for males, it may result in an overestimate for females, since their time in the labor force since leaving school may have been interrupted by childbirth and child rearing. A different proxy has been proposed for females and is described in more detail in Beck et al. (1980) and Tolbert et al. (1980). This proxy was constructed from a regression of working females' years of work experience (from the NLS data) on the usual proxy for experience by race and marital status. The following four equations resulted, and these represent the work experience proxy used in this analysis:

White ever-married females: experience = .5483 (Age − Schooling − 5)

Nonwhite ever-married females: experience = .6164 (Age − Schooling − 5)

White never-married females: experience = .8757 (Age − Schooling − 5)

Nonwhite never-married females: experience = .7731 (Age − Schooling − 5)

As these formulas indicate, age cannot be used as a separate independent variable because of its use in this construction. The overall correlation between age and experience is .957.

[14] For those females who were not employed during 1975, we used the occupation and industry for the last job held prior to 1975.

in a predominantly female occupation;[15] and (c) the number of employers worked for in 1975. In order to avoid confounding of regional and residential factors, we also include a binary variable indicating whether the female was located in the South and a binary variable for either central city or noncentral city residence.

In addition to these individual-level variables, we also included a set of variables reflecting the socioeconomic context of the urban metropolitan labor market. The theoretical work of Thompson (1965), Fusfeld (1973), and Parcel and Mueller (1980), as well as the empirical work of Harrison (1972), Rees and Shultz (1970), Parcel (1979), and Hanuskek (1973), have suggested that socioeconomic outcomes can be affected by the nature of the local economy. Of prime consideration here are the local aggregate demand for labor and the composition of the industrial base. Large urban environments characterized by a tight labor market, high average prices of labor, an expanding population size, and a high proportion of the labor force in the oligopolistic sector would have lower average levels of underemployment.

In this regard we entered six aggregate-level variables into the regressions: (a) the population size of the metropolitan area in 1975; (b) the percentage population growth rate between 1970 and 1975; (c) the percentage of the labor force that was white; (d) the percentage of the labor force in the oligopolistic industrial sector; (e) the mean weeks unemployed for the labor force, an indicator of the local aggregate demand for labor; and (f) the mean imputed hourly wage rate, a measure of the local price of labor.[16] The metric coefficients for these regressions are presented in Table 9.4.

Most of the personal and residential characteristics of these urban female workers have little direct effect on underemployment once the other explanatory variables are controlled. There is, however, one set of findings that merit discussion. Being a head of a household has a significant effect only for nonwhite females in the competitive sector, where being a head of a household is associated with greater underemployment. Similarly, the number of children has an exacerbating effect on underemployment only for this same group. Taken together, these two findings would seem to suggest that having responsibility for a large family tends to produce higher

---

[15] The "female" occupations, defined as those with 50% or more of the incumbents being female, were identified from the detailed occupation sex distributions in the 1970 census. In Appendix A, we list all these female occupations and the percentage of female incumbents.

[16] The aggregate measures population size and percentage growth were taken from census materials for the 47 SMSAs in our sample, whereas the remaining aggregate measures were estimated from the Survey of Income and Education data.

TABLE 9.4

Metric Coefficients from Regression of Percent
Unemployment for Females in Urban Labor Market by Sector and Race

| Term in regression | Oligopoly sector | | Competitive sector | |
| --- | --- | --- | --- | --- |
| | White | Nonwhite | White | Nonwhite |
| Intercept | - 3.833 | 25.219 | 4.727 | .457 |
| **Individual-level characteristics** | | | | |
| Head of household (yes = 1) | - .304 | - .848 | .345 | 5.099* |
| Number of own children | .180 | .395 | - .074 | 1.017* |
| Years of schooling | - .256* | - .558 | - .342* | - .513* |
| Years of work experience | - .171* | - .593* | - .178* | - .562* |
| Occupational prestige | - .192* | - .411* | - .145* | - .243* |
| Female occupation (yes = 1) | - 1.985* | - 5.485* | - 1.408* | - 1.651 |
| Number of employers | 1.950* | - 9.835* | 2.878* | - 3.394* |
| Residence (central city = 1) | .412 | 2.966* | - .016 | - .024 |
| Region of country (south = 1) | .849 | - 2.727 | 1.773* | 1.425 |
| **Aggregate-level factors** | | | | |
| Population size (1000s) | - .000 | .000 | .000 | .000 |
| Percentage growth rate | - .021 | .152 | - .081* | - .069 |
| Racial composition (% white) | 8.586 | 2.221 | 6.465 | 25.544* |
| Sectoral composition (% oligopoly sector) | 4.826 | 27.747 | - 9.569 | 15.195 |
| Mean weeks unemployed | 1.765* | 1.526 | 2.121* | 2.209* |
| Mean hourly wage | 1.153* | .558 | .798* | - .787 |
| $R^2$ x 100 | 3.22* | 11.82* | 4.14* | 8.50* |

*Statistically significant from zero at the .05 level.  Based on approximate standard errors under simple random sampling.*

underemployment for these nonwhite females. This may result because these females have less access to day-care centers and other mechanisms for coping with child rearing. While some economists use both these characteristics as explanations for the higher unemployment of females in general (e.g., Feldstein, 1977), finding this effect only for this one group suggests not only that sectoral placement is important for individual outcomes (i.e., there is an advantage to being employed in the oligopolistic sector) but also that race discrimination exists against nonwhite females within the competitive sector.

In general, the human capital variables of schooling and work experience have a negative effect on underemployment such that those females with the most human capital tend to have the least underemployment. This is in accordance with the general theoretical expectation that greater human capital places a worker in a stronger position in the labor market and produces greater employment stability as well as higher wages.

The occupational and employment variables show a somewhat more complex relationship with underemployment. For whites and nonwhites in both industrial sectors, having a job with high occupational prestige is associated with less underemployment. Again, this is consistent with general labor market theory, in that high-prestige jobs tend to have greater training costs thus providing an incentive for both the employer and the employee to minimize job instability.

Being in a predominantely female occupation also tends to reduce underemployment. There is no effect, however, for the nonwhite females in the competitive sector. This finding fits with the expectation about the discouraged-worker effect. Crowding may cause more females to become discouraged workers and thus drop out of the labor force. Because of this, the employment situation of the working females left in these female occupations is improved. However, Oppenheimer (1970) shows that female-dominated occupations are the lower paying ones; thus, the only advantage for these females may be in less underemployment. The lack of an effect for the nonwhites in the competitive sector may suggest that there is a limit to any advantage from female occupations.

The last employment variable, the number of employers, has an important interaction with race in its effect on underemployment: For white females, changing employers produces greater underemployment; but for nonwhites, this is reversed. For nonwhite females, changing employers has a negative relationship with underemployment. This could indicate a pattern where nonwhite females leave one employer only when another job is available, whereas white females may have more discontinuous employment, with longer periods of unemployment interwoven among periods of working. It has been argued that it is job turnover or instability that creates more underemployment for females, but these results indicate this may only apply to white females. The finding that more job changing means less underemployment for nonwhite females suggests that a very different process is operating for them.

As for the aggregate-level characteristics of the local urban labor market, the results in Table 9.4 show minimal effect on individual-level underemployment. There is some evidence, however, that declines in the local demand for labor increase the amount of underemployment, especially among those in the competitive industrial sector. This is consistent with the general dual economy perspective that argues that competitively organized industries are more susceptible to change in aggregate product demand and therefore produce greater job instability for their workers. As for the price of labor, for nonwhite females the local price of labor has no effect on underemployment, yet for white females higher priced urban labor markets tend to be associated with higher underemployment. This could reflect an oversupply of white female labor in those markets characterized by high wages.

In sum, while the results presented in Table 9.4 demonstrate considerable heterogeneity across race groups and industrial sectors, the human capital and occupational and employment variables have important effects on the level of underemployment for all females. Yet, as reflected by the small percentage of explained variance, the explanatory variables entered into the regressions do not have a strong effect on underemployment for any of the race–sector groups. Even though these variables explain only a small fraction of the variance in underemployment, we may still ask whether the significant differences in the level of underemployment by race and industrial sector observed in Table 9.2 are due to differences in the explanatory variables.

That is, it remains to be discovered whether controlling for the explanatory variables in Table 9.4 would effectively eliminate the observed differences in the average levels of underemployment. In order to explore this question, we computed a revised mean level of underemployment for each race–sector group by adjusting through least squares the observed means for the effects of the covariates presented in Table 9.4.[17] These adjusted means and their approximate standard errors are given in the bottom panel of Table 9.2. The adjusted means show that when the covariates are statistically controlled, the degree of underemployment is substantially reduced for nonwhite females in both sectors, yet has essentially no effect on the underemployment of white females in the competitive sector, and actually increases slightly the underemployment for white females in the oligopolistic industrial sector.

In order to make specific comparisons among the adjusted means, the absolute value of the $t$ ratios for the six contrasts are given above the main diagonal in Table 9.3. These show that even after controlling for the explanatory variables, there is a significant race effect within the competitive sector, although no such effect exists in the oligopolistic sector. There are, however, statistically significant sectoral differences in underemployment for both white and nonwhite females such that females in the competitive sector have greater underemployment even after controlling for the explanatory variables. Thus, the sectoral difference cannot be attributed exclusively to differences in the explanatory variables given in Table 9.4.

---

[17] For a discussion of the adjustment procedure, see Winer (1971, pp.752–812).

## Conclusions

In this chapter we sought to explore the effects of the organization of industrial economy on female underemployment, as an area for investigation logically prior to the development of an explanation of sex differentials in labor market rewards. One widely accepted theory for differential underemployment is human capital theory. This theory emphasizes the role of the "quality" of labor in determining labor market outcomes and, for women, the effect of discontinuous labor force participation on reducing their human capital accumulation. In contrast to this individually focused theory, a theory of industrial segmentation, the dual economy theory, predicts that the organization of production will exert an influence on underemployment that is over and above that produced by the quality of labor.

When we inspected the mean levels of underemployment by race and industrial sector, we found that white females in the competitive sector had significantly greater underemployment than white females in the oligopolistic sector. This is consistent with the expectations from the dual economy literature. However, no such significant sectoral effects could be found for nonwhite females. In both sectors, however, nonwhite females had significantly higher underemployment than did white females. These findings suggest that white females pay an additional cost for being in the competitive sector, but the cost of being nonwhite is constant across sectors of the industrial economy.

After controlling for many personal, residential, regional, human capital, employment and occupational, and aggregate-level contextual variables, we found that the race effect was eliminated within the oligopolistic sector, but not within the competitive sector. This suggests that when the quality of labor is held constant, there is no racial differential in underemployment among those women located in the oligopolistic sector of the economy. Yet, the disadvantaged position of white females persists in the competitive sector even after controlling for labor quality. More importantly, however, we found that after controlling for the quality of labor, both white and nonwhite females had significantly higher underemployment if they were within the competitive sector. This certainly suggests that, independent of many individual characteristics, the organization of production within the structure of industrial capitalism has a definite impact on the degree of underemployment experienced by female workers. Placement in the competitive sector of the industrial economy, we found, has important negative consequences for women workers, especially if they are nonwhite.

We do need, however, to address directly the low explained variance we obtained with our model. Explanations for this include the fact that we omitted all the experienced civilian labor force (ECLF) females between 16 and 18 years old, a group whose unemployment rate is always higher than that of older workers. We also excluded females who were not heads of a household or the wife of a head, another group with higher underemployment. And most important, the amount of underemployment we found was low because of the very nature of the definition of unemployment. The fact that the definition requires an individual to be currently and actively looking for a job defines all the discouraged workers as out of the labor force. A more reasonable definition of unemployment will be necessary in order to gain a clearer picture of the labor market situation for all workers.

Understanding inequality is, in our opinion, the major goal of stratification research. Often, inequality is measured and studied by comparing dollar earnings or wage rates, yet to have earnings, one must have a job. But jobs do not exist in the abstract; they exist within a particular firm, which is within a particular industry. Partly because of the structure of that industry, the job carries with it not only a wage rate but also a time-worked component and a certain risk of unemployment. Consistent sectoral differences in underemployment illustrate how inequality can be embedded in the organization of production and have an effect on individual labor market outcomes over and above the effect of the characteristics of the individual worker. This analysis emphasizes the necessity of examining the organization and structure of industries, as well as the individual characteristics of workers, in order more fully to understand inequalities in labor market rewards.

## Acknowledgments

We acknowledge the helpful comments of James J. Dowd, David Gartrell, and Patrick M. Horan on earlier drafts of this chapter.

# Appendix A

Female Occupations --- Those in 1970 That Were 50% or More Female[a]

| Three digit code | Occupation | Percent female | Total in occupation 1000s |
|---|---|---|---|
| | Professional, technical, and kindred | | |
| 026 | Home management advisors | 95.9 | 5393 |
| 032 | Librarians | 81.9 | 121852 |
| 074 | Dietitians | 92.0 | 40131 |
| 075 | Registered nurses | 97.3 | 829691 |
| 076 | Therapists | 63.3 | 75161 |
| 080 | Clinical laboratory technicians and technologists | 72.0 | 117606 |
| 081 | Dental hygienists | 94.0 | 15805 |
| 082 | Health record technicians and technologists | 92.1 | 11164 |
| 083 | Radiologic technicians and technologists | 67.9 | 52230 |
| 084 | Therapy assistants | 66.0 | 3211 |
| 085 | Health technicians and technologists, n.e.c.[b] | 56.0 | 59823 |
| 090 | Religious workers, n.e.c. | 55.7 | 35609 |
| 100 | Social workers | 62.7 | 216623 |
| 142 | Elementary school teachers | 83.7 | 1413915 |
| 143 | Pre-kindergarten and kindergarten teachers | 97.9 | 124996 |
| 145 | Teachers, except college and university, n.e.c. | 70.3 | 151362 |
| | Sales workers | | |
| 262 | Demonstrators | 91.0 | 37854 |
| 264 | Hucksters and peddlers | 79.2 | 117562 |
| 283 | Salesclerks, retail trade | 64.7 | 2272019 |
| | Clerical and kindred | | |
| 301 | Bank tellers | 86.2 | 249243 |
| 303 | Billing clerks | 82.3 | 106001 |
| 305 | Bookkeepers | 82.0 | 1534768 |
| 310 | Cashiers | 83.7 | 823512 |

*(continued)*

| Three digit code | Occupation | Percent female | Total in occupation 1000s |
|---|---|---|---|
| 311 | Clerical assistants, social welfare | 78.2 | 1198 |
| 314 | Counter clerks, except food | 66.6 | 227530 |
| 320 | Enumerators and interviewers | 77.6 | 64568 |
| 325 | File clerks | 81.9 | 356660 |
| 330 | Library attendants and assistants | 78.9 | 123327 |
| 341 | Bookkeeping and billing machine operators | 89.4 | 63268 |
| 342 | Calculating machine operators | 91.3 | 34896 |
| 344 | Duplicating machine operators | 56.9 | 20265 |
| 345 | Keypunch machine operators | 89.8 | 272570 |
| 355 | Office machine operators, n.e.c. | 67.8 | 36199 |
| 360 | Payroll and time-keeping clerks | 68.8 | 155807 |
| 362 | Proofreaders | 74.8 | 28099 |
| 364 | Receptionists | 94.8 | 302912 |
| 370-372 | Secretaries | 97.6 | 2702099 |
| 375 | Statistical clerks | 64.3 | 249322 |
| 376 | Stenographers | 93.7 | 127957 |
| 382 | Teacher aides, except school monitors | 90.3 | 130005 |
| 385 | Telephone operators | 94.5 | 407001 |
| 391 | Typists | 94.2 | 977446 |
| 394 | Miscellaneous clerical workers | 63.7 | 474840 |
| 395 | Not specified clerical workers | 75.2 | 807244 |
| 396 | Clerical and kindred, allocated[c] | 72.6 | 757209 |
| | Craftsmen and kindred | | |
| 405 | Bookbinders | 57.1 | 34034 |
| 425 | Decorators and window dressers | 57.5 | 69960 |
| | Operatives, except transport | | |
| 611 | Clothing ironers and pressers | 75.3 | 181200 |
| 613 | Dressmakers and seamstresses, except factory | 95.1 | 96820 |
| 624 | Graders and sorters, mfg. | 64.1 | 38008 |

*(continued)*

| Three digit code | Occupation | Percent female | Total in occupation 1000s |
|---|---|---|---|
| 625 | Produce graders and packers, except factory and farm | 73.0 | 26530 |
| 630 | Laundry and drycleaning operatives, n.e.c. | 63.8 | 169375 |
| 634 | Meat wrappers, retail trade | 93.2 | 44095 |
| 636 | Milliners | 91.0 | 2038 |
| 643 | Packers and wrappers, except meat and produce, n.e.c. | 60.9 | 515516 |
| 663 | Sewers and stitchers | 93.7 | 867402 |
| 664 | Shoemaking machine operatives | 60.2 | 60483 |
| 665 | Solderers | 81.6 | 40251 |
| 671 | Knitters, loopers and toppers | 63.7 | 28406 |
| 672 | Spinners, twisters and winders | 63.6 | 156089 |
| 673 | Weavers | 53.2 | 50141 |
| 681 | Winding operatives, n.e.c. | 50.9 | 60739 |
| | Service workers, except private household | | |
| 901 | Chambermaids and maids | 94.9 | 196767 |
| 902 | Cleaners and charwoman | 57.5 | 439063 |
| 912 | Cooks | 63.1 | 828977 |
| 914 | Food counter and fountain workers | 76.3 | 151381 |
| 915 | Waiters | 89.0 | 1019400 |
| 916 | Food service workers, n.e.c. | 75.9 | 324524 |
| 921 | Dental assistants | 97.9 | 88175 |
| 922 | Health aides, except nursing | 84.6 | 118907 |
| 923 | Health trainees | 93.7 | 17655 |
| 924 | Lay midwives | 79.6 | 675 |
| 925 | Nursing aides, orderlies, and attendants | 84.8 | 717968 |
| 926 | Practical nurses | 96.4 | 237133 |
| 931 | Airline stewardess | 95.8 | 32654 |
| 933 | Attendants, personal service, n.e.c. | 62.3 | 59792 |
| 940 | Boarding and lodging housekeepers | 71.7 | 7371 |

*(continued)*

**Appendix A (Cont'd)**

| Three digit code | Occupation | Precent female | Total in occupation 1000s |
|---|---|---|---|
| 942 | Child-care workers | 93.0 | 131258 |
| 944 | Hairdressers and cosmetologists | 90.1 | 471536 |
| 950 | Housekeepers | 71.9 | 103332 |
| 952 | School monitors | 90.2 | 26007 |
| 954 | Welfare service aides | 76.5 | 51304 |
| 960 | Crossing guards and bridge tenders | 57.4 | 41645 |
| 976 | Service workers, allocated | 59.0 | 705327 |
| | Private household workers | | |
| 980 | Child-care workers | 98.1 | 212187 |
| 981 | Cooks | 94.2 | 31297 |
| 982 | Housekeepers | 96.3 | 100695 |
| 983 | Laundresses | 95.4 | 11751 |
| 984 | Maids and servants | 96.6 | 666864 |
| 986 | Private household workers, allocated | 97.4 | 123097 |

[a]*Data are from 1970 Census of the Population Vol. 1, Characteristics of the Population, U.S. Summary, Part 1, Detailed Characteristics, PC(1)-D1. Washington, D.C.: U.S. Government Printing Office Table 223.*

[b]*n.e.c. = not elsewhere classified.*

[c]*allocated = a category to which those respondents not giving an occupational response are allocated on the basis of the other information and characteristics of the respondent.*

# References

Averitt, R. T.
    1968    *The Dual Economy.* New York: Norton.
Beck, E. M., P. M. Horan, and C. M. Tolbert II.
    1978    "Stratification in a dual economy: A sectoral model of earnings determination." *American Sociological Review* 43:704–720.
    1980    "Industrial segmentation and labor market discrimination." *Social Problems*, 28:113–130.

Bergmann, B. R.
  1971  "The effect on white incomes of discrimination in employment." *Journal of Political Economy* 79:294–313.
Bibb, R., and W. H. Form
  1977  "The effects of industrial, occupational, and sex stratification on wages in blue-collar markets." *Social Forces* 55:947–996.
Blau, F. D., and C. L. Jusenius
  1976  "Economists' approaches to sex segregation in the labor market: An appraisal." In M. Blaxall and B. Reagan (eds.), *Women and the Workplace*. Chicago: Univ. of Chicago Press.
Bluestone, B., W. M. Murphy, and M. Stevenson
  1973  *Low Wages and the Working Poor*. Ann Arbor: Institute of Labor and Industrial Relations, University of Michigan.
Cain, G. G.
  1978  *Labor Force Concepts and Definitions in View of Their Purposes*. Special Report SR20. Institute for Research on Poverty, University of Wisconsin.
Edgeworth, F. Y.
  1922  "Equal pay to men and women for equal work." *Economic Journal* 32:431–457.
Edwards, R. C.
  1979  *Contested Terrain*. New York: Basic.
Edwards, R. C., M. Reich, and D. M. Gordon, Eds.
  1975  *Labor Market Segmentation*. Lexington, Massachusetts: Heath.
England, P.
  1981  "The failure of human capital theory to explain occupational sex segregation." *Journal of Human Resources*, in press.
Fawcett, M.
  1918  "Equal pay for equal work." *Economic Journal* 28 (March):1–6.
Feldstein, M.
  1977  "The economics of the new unemployment." In D. M. Gordon (ed.), *Problems in Political Economy* (2nd ed.). Lexington, Massachusetts: Heath.
Ferber, M. A., and H. M. Lowry
  1976a  "The sex differential in earnings: A reappraisal." *Industrial and Labor Relations Review* 29:377–387.
  1976b  "Women: The new reserve army of the unemployed." In M. Blaxall and B. Reagan (eds.), *Women and the Workplace*. Chicago: Univ. of Chicago Press.
Fusfeld, D. R.
  1973  *The Basic Economics of the Urban Racial Crisis*. New York: Holt.
Gordon, D. M.
  1972  *Theories of Poverty and Underemployment*. Lexington, Massachusetts: Heath.
  1977  "Counting the underemployed." In D. M. Gordon (ed.), *Problems in Political Economy: An Urban Perspective* (2nd ed.). Lexington, Massachusetts: Heath.
Hall, R. E.
  1970  "Why is the unemployment rate so high at full employment?" *Brookings Papers on Economic Activity* 1:339–402.
Hanuskek, E. A.
  1973  "Regional differences in the structure of earnings." *Review of Economics and Statistics* 55:204–213.
Harrison, B.
  1972  *Education, Training, and the Urban Ghetto*. Baltimore: Johns Hopkins Press.
Horan, P. M., E. M. Beck, and C. M. Tolbert II
  1980  "The market homogeneity assumption: On the theoretical foundations of empirical knowledge." *Social Science Quarterly*, 61(September):278–292.

Levitan, S. A., and R. Taggart III
    1974    *Employment and Earnings Inadequacy: A New Social Indicator.* Baltimore: Johns
            Hopkins Press.
Miller, H. P.
    1973    "Measuring subemployment in poverty areas of large U.S. cities." *Monthly Labor
            Review* 96 (October):10–18.
Mincer, J., and S. Polachek
    1974    "Family investments in human capital: Earnings of women." *Journal of Political
            Economy* 82:S76–S110.
Oppenheimer, V. K.
    1970    *The Female Labor Force in the United States.* Westport, Connecticut: Greenwood Press.
Parcel, T. L.
    1979    "Race, regional labor markets and earnings." *American Sociological Review* 44:262–279.
Parcel, T. L., and C. W. Mueller
    1980    "Interrelationships among areal, industrial and occupational labor markets as de-
            terminants of labor earnings." Paper presented at the National Science Foundation
            sponsored Conference on Labor Market Structure and Socioeconomic Stratification,
            Athens, Georgia, March 3–5.
Polachek, S.
    1975    "Discontinuous labor force participationa and its effect on women's market earnings."
            In C. B. Lloyd (ed.), *Sex Discrimination, and the Division of Labor.* New York:
            Columbia Univ. Press.
Rees, A.
    1979    *The Economics of Work and Pay* (2nd ed.). New York: Harper.
Rees, A., and G. P. Shultz
    1970    *Workers and Wages in an Urban Labor Market.* Chicago: Univ. of Chicago Press.
Stevenson, M. H.
    1975    "Relative wages and sex segregation by occupation." In C. B. Lloyd (ed.), *Sex Dis-
            crimination and the Division of Labor.* New York: Columbia Univ. Press.
    1978    "Wage differences between men and women: Economic theories." In A. H. Stromberg
            and S. Harkess (eds.), *Women Working.* Palo Alto: Mayfield Publishing.
Sweet, J.
    1973    *Women in the Labor Force.* New York: Seminar Press.
Thomson, W. R.
    1965    *A Preface to Urban Economics.* Baltimore: Johns Hopkins Press.
Thurow, L. C.
    1969    *Poverty and Discrimination.* Washington, D.C.: The Brookings Institution.
Tolbert, C., P. M. Horan, and E. M. Beck
    1980    "The structure of economic segmentation: A dual economy approach." *American
            Journal of Sociology* 85:1095–1116.
U.S. Department of Commerce, Bureau of the Census
    1977a   *Technical Documentation of the 1976 Survey of Income and Education.* Washington,
            D.C.: Bureau of the Census.
    1977b   *Current Population Reports.* Series P-60, no. 106. Washington, D.C.: Govt Printing
            Office.
U.S. Department of Labor, Bureau of Labor Statistics
    1976    *Concepts and Methods Used in Labor Force Statistics Derived from the Current Pop-
            ulation Survey.* Report No. 463. Washington, D.C.: Govt Printing Office.
    1977    *Employment and Earnings, February, 1977.* (Vol. 24, no. 2) Washington, D.C.: Govt
            Printing Office.
Winer, B. J.
    1971    *Statistical Principles in Experimental Design.* New York: McGraw-Hill.

# Chapter 10

## Assessing Trends in

## Occupational Sex

## Segregation, 1900–1976[1]

*PAULA ENGLAND*

The assessment of trends in occupational sex segregation is plagued with methodological dilemmas. Yet, monitoring change in segregation is important because of the demonstrated link between segregation and male–female earning differentials. Reductions in segregation may be a prerequisite to equalizing the earnings of men and women. This chapter discusses (*a*) past research on sex differences in earnings, highlighting the explanatory importance of occupational sex segregation; (*b*) methodological problems involved in using the index of dissimilarity to assess change in the amount of such segregation; and (*c*) conclusions about the timing and amount of decline in occupational sex segregation that occurred between 1900 and 1976 in the United States.

### The Importance of Occupational Sex Segregation in Explaining Sex Differences in Earnings

The following review shows that, to understand the processes generating sex differences in earnings, one must recognize occupational sex segregation.

[1] Part of the research for this chapter was done on NIMH grant ST 32 MH 14670 03 while the author was a postdoctoral fellow at Duke University Medical Center. The chapter was prepared as a paper for the March 1980 annual meeting of the Southern Sociological Society.

SOCIOLOGICAL PERSPECTIVES ON
LABOR MARKETS

ISBN: 0-12-089650-8

Early literature identified influences on women's propensity to be employed (Cain, 1966; McNally, 1968; Sweet,1973) and sought to explain the dramatic increase in female labor force participation since 1940 (Oppenheimer, 1970). As the influx of women into paid employment continued, attention turned to the status of employed women.

Quantitative sociologists began the study of socioeconomic sex stratification using the models and prestige scales that had proved useful in mapping the ways males convert socioeconomic family background and educational attainment into occupational status (on males, see Blau & Duncan, 1967). Both the Duncan scale (Duncan, 1961) and the Hodge–Siegel–Rossi scale (Siegel, 1971) give occupations scores that correlate highly with the earnings, education, and prestige of the males employed in the occupations. The same relationships hold for females, taken separately (U.S. Department of Labor, 1970, Appendix D). Since they were viewed as general indicators of socioeconomic status, these scales seemed a natural dependent variable for research on sex differences.

To most researchers' surprise, when prestige scales were taken as the dependent variable, there were no sex differences in socioeconomic attainment to be explained. Women and men in the labor force have nearly identical mean scores on prestige scales and on years of education completed. In addition, the process through which men and women convert socioeconomic background and education into occupational prestige is very similar (Bose, 1973; DeJong, 1972; Featherman & Hauser, 1976; Treiman & Terrell, 1975a). The use of prestige scales draws attention away from occupational sex segregation, since almost every prestige level contains some male and some female occupations. Prestige levels are more integrated by sex than are occupations (England, 1979).

Sex equality of occupational prestige does not imply socioeconomic equality between the sexes, despite the claims of prestige scales to be general socioeconomic indicators (England, 1979, Appendix). The median earnings of women who work full time are less than 60% of male earnings (U.S. Department of Labor, 1976). Women receive a lower payoff than do men in earnings (Featherman & Hauser, 1976; Suter & Miller, 1973; Treiman & Terrell, 1975a) and in job authority (Wolf & Fligstein, 1979) for each increment of occupational prestige they gain. Though these findings were revealing, many sociologists still did not pose the question of whether women earn less primarily because women are paid less than men within occupations or because women are segregated in lower paying occupations within each level of education and occupational prestige.

Although women are usually paid less than men in the same occupation, more of the aggregate sex gap in earnings results, because of pervasive occupational sex segregation, from women's concentration in lower paying occupations. Labor economists who had not been sidetracked by prestige scales were the first to point this out (Cohen, 1971; Fuchs, 1971; Sanborn, 1964). Even human capital theorists came to realize that a theory that explains women's low earnings has also to explain the sex segregation of occupations (compare Polachek, 1975 with Polachek, 1979).

Once it was established that segregation was a cause of sex differences in earnings, research forked in two directions. One set of inquiries asks why women and men end up in the sex-segregated occupations they do. Quite diverse hypotheses of both self-selection and discrimination have some support (for a review, see England, 1981). A second literature by sociologists and economists asks what it is about predominantly female-held jobs that determines their lower pay (Bergmann, 1971; Blau, 1977; Bluestone, 1974; England, Chassie, & McCormack, 1978; England & McLaughlin, 1979; Gottfredson, 1977; Hodge & Hodge, 1965; McLaughlin, 1978; McLaughlin & Spykerman, 1979; Snyder & Hudis, 1976; Stevenson, 1975; Treiman & Terrell, 1975b). One consistent finding is that, for any given amount of skill or training, male-dominated occupations are better remunerated. Authors advance various explanations of this fact. The lower pay for female-dominated occupations may result from sexist devaluation of the kinds of skills traditionally acquired by women; from the greater capital intensiveness and market power of industries in which men predominate; from the higher ratio of potential supply to demand for labor in female-dominated occupations, owing to the crowding of women into few jobs and to the "reserve army" of housewives; or from the fact that men have bargained harder about wages, developing occupational power through such institutions as unions.

The importance of segregation in maintaining sex differences in earnings has been established mainly through cross-sectional research. What are the trends in segregation over time? If segregation facilitates income inequalities between men and women, is the decline of segregation a necessary or sufficient condition for a reduction in the earning differential between men and women? This chapter cannot answer that question. But assessing trends over time in the extent of occupational sex segregation is a prerequisite to testing the hypothesis that declines in segregation are correlated with reductions in the earnings gap between the sexes. It is with this theoretical rationale that I proceed to discuss methodological problems and findings on trends in occupational sex segregation.

## Methodological Problems in Assessing Trends in Occupational Sex Segregation

Most analyses of trends in occupational sex segregation have used the index of dissimilarity that Duncan and Duncan (1955a, 1955b) proposed to measure residential race segregation (Blau, 1977; Blau & Hendricks, 1979; Gross, 1968; U.S. Commission on Civil Rights, 1978; U.S. President's Council, 1973; Williams, 1976). When computed across occupational categories, the value of the index tells the percentage of either men or women who would need to change occupation in order to make every occupation contain the same sex mix exhibited by the labor force as a whole. Thus, the index can take on values from 0 (maximum integration) to 100 (maximum segregation). Other authors have assessed trends in occupational sex segregation with a panel model in which changes over time in the autoregression coefficients of percentage female across occupations indicate changes in segregation (Snyder & Hudis, 1976; Treiman & Terrell, 1975b). For example, if the correlation between percentage female across occupations at Time 1 and Time 2 is larger than the same correlation between Time 2 and Time 3, then a decline in segregation is indicated. Since the index of dissimilarity is easy to interpret intuitively and has been used extensively, it will be the focus of the methodological discussion to follow. (Hereafter, the index of dissimilarity will be referred to as simply "the index.") The appendix presents illustrative computations of the index.

Two major methodological problems are encountered when the index is used to assess change in occupational segregation:

1. Comparability must be achieved between the occupational categories used for the different points in time over which change is to be assessed;
2. One must decide whether occupational categories are to be treated as if each employs the same number of persons or whether larger occupations should contribute to the index value in proportion to the number of people who are employed in them.

These two issues of method will be discussed in turn.

## Comparability of Occupational Categories

Occupational data for any two decennial census years appear in different categories; each decade, the Census Bureau has increased the number of titles that form the most detailed occupational classification. Researchers using the index have responded to this in three ways:

1. *All current occupations:* Gross (1968) computed the index over whatever detailed occupational titles were provided by the Census Bureau for each decennial census year between 1900 and 1960. He then compared the index values for various years, despite the fact that each successive year's index was computed on a more detailed occupational classification. He does not discuss problems with this procedure or alternate methods of forming occupational categories.

2. *Constant subset of occupations:* Blau (1977) criticizes Gross's (1968) method because the occupational categories used in the various years are not comparable. She computes the index over just that subset of occupational titles that appeared in every decennial census year to which her analysis pertains (1950–1970). Occupations that later branched into more detailed categories are excluded from the analysis, as are the detailed categories into which they branched.

3. *All occupations back-aggregated for comparability:* Williams (1976, 1979) advocates backward aggregation of occupational categories for comparability (although he also presents a replication of Gross's method, which he criticizes). For occupational categories that branched over time, dividing into two or more titles, Williams used the earlier, more inclusive category, collapsing data for the later years into the earlier category. These occupations formed by back-aggregating were then combined with the subset of occupations that retained the same title in every year. This combination comprises almost all occuaptions,[2] allowing one to compute the index over the same occupational categories for each year without leaving out data from virtually any occupations.

Unfortunately, each of these three methods of forming occupational categories over which to compute the index introduces distinct biases. Blau's use of only a subset of occupations is misleading if trends in segregation differ between occupations included in and omitted from the analysis. The direction of this bias is not clear a priori. Blau's (1977; also Blau & Hendricks, 1979) analysis covers only 1950–1970. The constant subset of occupations on which the index was computed employed about 65% of the labor force in each of the three decennial census years during that period. Her method would be misleading for an analysis over the entire century, however, because many more occupations would be omitted to pare down to constant titles. Leaving out additional occupations would increase the unrepresentativity of findings on segregation.

Gross's method of computing the index over all current occupations for each census year is biased toward understating declines in segregation

---

[2] Two types of occupations, those that kept a constant title over time and those that branched, include most all occupations. However, there are two other types of occupations, comprising just a few each, that Williams had to deal with in his strategy to form comparable categories. A few occupations (e.g., airline pilot, radio operator) appeared because of technological change and were not derived by branching some previous occupational category. These he dropped from the analysis. A few occupations were collapsed by the Census Bureau into a broader category when they declined in size. For these few occupations, data were aggregated forward to the more recent, broader category in Williams's strategy to make occupational categories comparable. Nonetheless, I have labeled his method of achieving comparability *back-aggregating occupations,* since back-aggregating was the strategy used on most occupations that changed.

(Williams, 1976). The same real pattern of segregation will show up as a larger index value when computed over more detailed categories, since broader categories mask some of the segregation in the more detailed categories within them. Thus, since census categories have become more detailed over time, Gross's method of using the increasingly detailed current titles may overestimate increases and underestimate decreases in segregation. However, what Williams's critique of Gross fails to recognize is that, insofar as the increasing detail of available occupational categories accurately reflects the increasing division of labor, using current occupations does not bias the index toward understating declines in segregation. That is, if the occupational classification is apace with the differentiation of new jobs, no more segregation is masked by the earlier broader occupational categories than by the later more detailed titles. Thus, the critique of Gross's method hinges on the assumption that detail has been added to census occupational categories faster than genuine job differentiation has proceeded. It is virtually impossible to estimate the extent to which this is true.

In contrast, Williams's method of back-aggregating occupations biases the index toward overestimating declines in segregation to the extent that increasing detail in the census occupational classification reflects a real job differentiation rather than simply a change in labeling. When occupations differentiate, one newly emergent occupation may become "male," while another becomes "female," but Williams's method for insuring comparability of occupations by back-aggregating newly branched occupations into the earlier undifferentiated title causes the index to ignore such new segregation that occurs with differentiation. Thus, using back-aggregated occupations for comparability may cause the index to mask an increasing amount of segregation over time. This critique of Williams's method hinges on the assumption that the increased detail in the occupational classification is not primarily a change in labeling; but rather represents a real increase in differentiation. Again, the extent of truth in the assumption is virtually impossible to assess.

Let us take stock of the criticisms of each method of choosing occupational categories on which to compute the index over time. Blau's method of using only that subset of occupational titles that were not reclassified over time is not feasible for analyses over many decades, since a high proportion of occupations would have to be omitted from the computation. The greater the number of occupations omitted, the less representative the findings. Gross's method of using current occupational categories underestimates decline in segregation to the extent that the increased detail in the census categories is merely a change in labeling. Williams's method of back-aggregating occupations to achieve comparable categories overestimates decline in segregation to the extent that increased detail in census occupational categories reflects real job differentiation rather than merely increased detail in labeling. Since we do not know the extent to which increases in detail in the census occupational classification may have outstripped trends in real job differentiation, our tentative conclusion should be that the real level of segregation is midway between the readings from these latter two methods.

## Weighting Occupations

The second methodological question that must be decided is whether occupational categories are to be treated as if they all employ the same number of people or whether occupations are to contribute to the value of the index in proportion to the number of people they employ. The index that is affected more by larger than by smaller occupations, I will call *weighted*. The version of the index that is affected equally by each occupation, regardless of its size, I will call *size-standardized*.[3] (Illustrative computations of both versions of the index are presented in the Appendix.) The weighted version of the index gives the actual percentage of men or women who would have to change occupations in order for each occupation to contain men and women in proportion to the sex mix in the labor force at large. The size-standardized index reveals the proportion who would have to change occupation to achieve integration if all occupations employed the same number of persons.

To grasp the consequence of choosing between the weighted and size-standardized version of the segregation index, consider the following illustrations. Suppose first that the work world contains two very populated occupations, one all male and one all female, and a large number of sex-integrated occupations employing very few people. In this case, the size-standardized index would take on a much smaller value (indicating less segregation) than would the weighted index. Suppose, on the other hand, that there were two very populated occupations, each sex-integrated, and a large number of small occupations, each sex-segregated. In this second case, the weighted index would take on a smaller value than would the size-standardized index.

Using the index to assess trends, if the proportion male and female in each occupation remained constant over time but integrated occupations grew fastest, the size-standardized index would take a constant value, whereas the weighted index would show a decrease in segregation. The two

---

[3] What I call the weighted index is called the *index of segregation* by Gross and the *crude measure of differentiation* by Williams. What I call the size-standardized index is called *standardized measure of differentiation* by Gross and *absolute standardized measure of differentiation* by Williams.

indexes are telling us different things. The size-standardized index controls or adjusts for changes in the relative sizes of occupations. It does not let such changes affect the value the index takes on, even though such structural changes may mean an increase or decrease in the proportion of employed persons who are working in segregated occupations. Whereas the size-standardized index tells what change in amount of segregation would have occurred had there been no change in the relative size of occupations, the weighted index reveals change in the extent of segregation of the job the average person worked in and, thus, in the proportion who would have had to change occupations to achieve integration.

The weighted index has more intuitive appeal. Suppose that occupations that segregate more (or less) grow faster over time, putting a greater (or lesser) number of persons into segregated work. I prefer an index that reveals this increase (or decrease) in segregation over one that adjusts the change out because it resulted from a change in the relative size of occupations that segregate to different extents. Yet one might want to know how much of a given change in the weighted index value arose from changes in the sex composition of specific occupational categories and how much arose from changes in the relative size of occupations with different sex compositions. Blau and Hendricks (1979) have presented a method for decomposing the weighted index into these two components, plus a residual that represents interaction between the two factors. (See the Appendix for the formula for the decomposition.) Given the availability of this decomposition technique, the use of the size-standardized index seems superfluous.

Based on this reasoning, I would favor disregarding findings from the size-standardized index were it not for Williams's (1976) argument that using the size-standardized index compensates somewhat for the bias toward exaggerating decline in segregation introduced by back-aggregating occupations. Recall that back-aggregating titles to form comparable occupational categories may lead to overstating declines in segregation, since segregation within newly differentiated occupations will appear as integration within the newly back-aggregated category. Since categories formed by back-aggregating are greater in number in the later years, even the size-standardized index may overestimate declines in segregation. But Williams is pointing out that the overestimation of segregation decline will be greater with the weighted index. Occupations formed through back-aggregating will represent an increasing number of persons over time, since emergent occupations are continually aggregated into them. Thus, these back-aggregated occupations that may mask segregation will each get more weight in the later years when the weighted index is used; this is not so for the size-standardized index. Williams (1976) therefore thinks the size-standardized index computed over back-aggregated occupations gives the most accurate reading of trends. He is correct that, overall, the size-standardized index will overstate declines in segregation less than the weighted index when back-aggregated occupations are used, but some (probably smaller) amount of bias in the opposite direction will occur, because growing, consistently segregated occupations do not receive their proportionate weight using the size-standardized index. Though Williams does not mention it, the size-standardized index should also lessen any bias toward understating decline in segregation inherent in Gross's method of using all current occupational titles for each year. The reasons are analogous to those regarding back-aggregated categories. Thus, despite its own problems of bias, the size-standardized index can be advocated for its attenuation of the biases inherent in either Gross's or Williams's method of forming occupational categories. Like Gross and Williams, I will consider results from both the weighted and size-standardized indexes.

## Empirical Findings on Trends in Occupational Sex Segregation

Tables 10.1 and 10.2 catalog the findings from all published uses of the index of dissimilarity to assess trends in occupational sex segregation. For each published analysis, the tables give the author, the procedure used to form occupational categories, the number of occupations over which the index was computed, whether the weighted or size-standardized index was used, the index values in each year for which the author computed them, and the change in the index between each consecutive pair of years. (Note that authors using total current occupations do not agree on the level of detail in occupational categories available from the Census Bureau for any given year. This is because government publications vary in the number of occupations that they disaggregate by industry and self-employment status.)

### Effects of Methods on Findings

Tables 10.1 and 10.2 show that the methods' results generally differ in the directions predicted by the preceding methodological discussion. Aggregating backward to achieve comparable occupational categories makes the index show more decline than using total current occupations for each year, whether the weighted or size-standardized index is used. The difference in findings between the two methods of forming occupational categories is greater using the weighted index; the size-standardized index attenuates the opposite biases involved in using current and back-aggregated occupational categories. The size-standardized index shows more decline than the weighted index when total current occupations are used, but the weighted index shows more decline when occupations are back-aggregated.

TABLE 10.1

Trends in Segregation, 1900--1976, Measured by the Weighted index of Dissimilarity[a]

| Citation | Occupational categories used | Year | 1900 | 1910 | 1920 | 1930 | 1940 | 1950 | 1960 | 1970 | 1976 |
|---|---|---|---|---|---|---|---|---|---|---|---|
| Gross, 1968 | Total current occupations,[b] N = 300--400,[c] varying by year. | Index | 66.9 | 69.0 | 65.7 | 68.4 | 69.0 | 65.6 | 68.4 | d | d |
| | | Change | | +2.1 | -3.3 | +2.7 | +.6 | -3.4 | +2.8 | | |
| Williams, 1979 | Total current occupations, N varies. | Index | 64.3 | 66.4 | 65.7 | 68.4 | 68.9 | 67.3 | 64.9 | 61.6 | d |
| | | Change | | +2.1 | -.7 | +2.7 | +.5 | -1.6 | -2.4 | -3.3 | |
| | | N | 252 | 307 | 311 | 315 | 370 | 434 | 470 | 670 | |
| Blau, 1977 | Constant subset of occupations, N = 183. | Index | d | d | d | d | d | 71.9 | 74.1 | 70.7 | d |
| | | Change | | | | | | | +2.2 | -3.4 | |
| Williams, 1979 | Back-aggregated occupations to 1900, N = 246. | Index | 64.2 | 60.1 | 57.9 | 59.1 | 43.9 | 34.2 | 32.7 | 32.0 | d |
| | | Change | | -4.1 | -2.2 | +1.2 | -15.2 | -9.7 | -1.5 | -.7 | |
| Williams, 1979 | Back-aggregated occupations to 1960 Technical Paper 26 Segments, N = 1980 | Index | d | d | d | d | d | d | 65.0 | 63.8 | d |
| | | Change | | | | | | | | -1.2 | |

| U.S. Presidents Council, 1973 | Back-aggregated occupations to 1960 categories, N = 197. | Index | $d$ | $d$ | $d$ | $d$ | $d$ | $d$ | $d$ | $d$ | 62.9 | 59.8 | $d$ |
|---|---|---|---|---|---|---|---|---|---|---|---|---|---|
| | | Change | | | | | | | | | | -3.1 | |
| U.S. Commission on Civil Rights, 1978 | 1970 categories, N = 441. Data for whites only. | Index | $d$ | $d$ | $d$ | $d$ | $d$ | $d$ | $d$ | $d$ | 65.8 | 66.1 | |
| | | Change | | | | | | | | | | + .3 | |

[a] Data are from Gross, 1968, Table 2; Williams, 1979, Table 2; Blau, 1977, Chap. 4; U.S. President's Council, 1973, p. 155; U.S. Commission on Civil Rights, 1978, p. 42.

[b] Gross dropped a few very small occupations.

[c] Gross does not give exact N for each year.

[d] Not computed for this year.

TABLE 10.2

Trends in Segregation, 1900--1970, Measured by the Size-Standardized Index of Dissimilarity[a]

| Citation | Occupational categories used | Year | 1900 | 1910 | 1920 | 1930 | 1940 | 1950 | 1960 | 1970 |
|---|---|---|---|---|---|---|---|---|---|---|
| Gross, 1968 | Total current occupations,[b][c] N = 300--400, varying by year. | Index | 70.3 | 68.1 | 65.9 | 66.6 | 63.8 | 59.3 | 62.2 | d |
| | | Change | | -2.2 | -2.2 | + .7 | -2.8 | -4.5 | +2.9 | |
| Williams, 1979 | Total current occupations, N varies. | Index | 70.5 | 68.5 | 66.2 | 66.9 | 64.1 | 61.3 | 62.2 | 54.9 |
| | | Change | | -2.0 | -2.3 | + .7 | -2.8 | -2.8 | + .9 | -7.3 |
| | | N | 252 | 307 | 311 | 315 | 370 | 434 | 470 | 670 |
| Williams, 1979 | Back-aggregated occupations to 1900, N = 246. | Index | 70.2 | 64.9 | 62.7 | 63.2 | 55.3 | 46.7 | 48.1 | 44.8 |
| | | Change | | -5.3 | -2.2 | + .5 | -7.9 | -8.6 | +1.4 | -3.3 |
| Williams, 1979 | Back-aggregated occupation's to 1960 Technical paper 26 Segments, N = 1980. | Index | d | d | d | d | d | d | 76.0 | 73.0 |
| | | Change | | | | | | | | -3.0 |

[a] Data are from Gross, 1968, Table 3; Williams, 1979, Table 3.
[b] Gross dropped a few very small occupations.
[c] Gross does not give exact N for each year.
[d] Not computed for the year.

Blau's method of using the constant subset of occupations that did not branch shows trends similar to those found over total current occupations, using the weighted index. (Blau did not use the size-standardized index, so this comparison cannot be made.) Blau's analysis pertains only to 1950–1970. However, though he does not give the specific numbers, Williams (1976) reports having also computed the weighted index on the subset of occupations that did not change title from 1900 to 1960. The results were similar to those for total current occupations, showing little decline in segregation between 1900 and 1960. Thus, using either total current or the constant subset of nonchanging occupational categories shows much more stability in segregation than when back-aggregated occupations are used.

Holding other aspects of method constant, a more detailed occupational classification yields a larger index, since more of the existent segregation can be revealed. But it is surprising and instructive to note that using a less detailed version of one year's occupational classification reduces the amount of segregation the index detects to a much lesser degree than a smaller reduction of detail accomplished by back-aggregating to the occupational titles used by the Census Bureau in an earlier year.

Although the effects of methods on results are generally as predicted, there are a few instances where methods' results differ in the direction opposite the prediction. All such deviations of at least two index points occur in the change of the index between 1960 and 1970, perhaps because of the unusually large increase in the number of occupational categories during that decade. Williams shows more decline between 1960 and 1970 when the weighted index is computed on total current occupations than on back-aggregated occupations. The opposite is true when the size-standardized index is used. Related to this is the fact that Williams's computations show a much greater decline on the size-standardized than on the weighted index for the 1960s. Finally, Williams's back-aggregated occupations show less decline in the weighted index over the 1960s than does Blau's subset of constant occupational titles. In short, the three-factor interaction of occupational category formation, use of the weighted or size-standardized index, and change in the index is different for the 1960s than was predicted and found for other decades. Each of these divergences from prediction is at least two index points in magnitude. The fact that all these anomalies pertain to the 1960s makes substantive conclusions especially hard to draw for that decade.

## Trends for Specific Decades

Since the preceding methodological discussions conclude that we cannot choose one best method of calculating the index, findings on trends from all methods will be discussed. We should trust most conclusions reached by all methods. When methods' results differ in the hypothesized directions of bias, I conclude that the magnitude of change is between the high and low estimates. Given the methodological dilemmas of this analysis, further precision in estimation is not possible. The following discussion of trends for specific decades follows Tables 10.1 and 10.2.

The decade between 1900 and 1910 shows a decrease in segregation, according to four of the six published findings. Estimates of the size of the decrease vary from 2.0 to 5.3. However, the weighted index over total current occupations actually shows an increase in segregation of 2.1 points. (Recall that the index can take on values from 0 to 100.) The true amount of change in segregation between 1900 and 1910 was probably between these estimates, perhaps a decline of 3 or 4 points. All methods of computation find a small decrease in segregation between 1910 and 1920 as well. Estimates of the magnitude of the change range from .7 to 3.3. All methods find a small increase in segregation in the 1920s, with estimates ranging from .5 to 2.7. In none of these three decades do the estimates of the magnitude of change fall perfectly into the order predicted by the preceding methodological discussion, though the deviations are minute.

The computations for the 1930s show the least consensus between methods of any decade, although the differences in results between methods are in the predicted direction. The major change in occupational classification between 1930 and 1940 and the switch to asking respondents for their current rather than usual occupation (Hauser, 1964) may explain this messiness. Estimates of change in segregation during the 1930s range from less than a point of increase to 15.2 points of decrease. Thus, conclusions for the 1930s are extremely difficult to draw.

All methods show some decrease in segregation during the 1940s. Estimates range from a decrease of 1.6 to 9.7, with methods' results ranking in the predicted order. The true drop in segregation during the 1940s was probably somewhere between these two estimates, perhaps about 6 points, and it was probably larger than the decreases occuring in any of the three decades between 1900 and 1930. The need for women to fill traditionally male-dominated jobs during the war undoubtedly explains this decline in segregation; apparently some women kept nontraditional jobs after the war was over.

Segregation increased in the 1950s, according to five of seven readings. The other two readings show a small decrease of less than 2.5 points, and they are from the methods most biased toward exaggerating decrease in segregation. The conclusion that segregation increased slightly during the 1950s is also consistent with Treiman and Terrell's (1975b) findings from panel autoregression. They show a larger correlation across occupations between percentage female in 1950 and 1960 than for 1940 and 1950 ($R^2$ = .83 for 1940, 1950; $R^2$ = .98 for 1950, 1960). The increase in the size of the correlation for the latter pair of years is indicative of an increase in segregation in the 1950s. Blau and Hendrick's (1979) decomposition of the change in the index between 1950 and 1960 indicates that most of this small increase in segregation resulted from a disproportionate growth in female-dominated clerical occupations, rather than from a change in the sex composition of specific occupations.

All readings show some decrease in segregation during the 1960s; however, estimates vary in size from .7 to 7.3. Since different methods' results do not order as predicted, it is hard to compare the magnitude of decline in segregation to that found in other decades. Blau and Hendricks's (1979) decomposition of the change in the index for this decade shows most of the decrease to have occurred because of a shift in the sex composition of particular occupations, rather than as a result of a difference in the amount of growth in employment between more segregated and less segregated occupations. They link the small decline in segregation during the 1960s to the entry of men into the traditionally female professions of teaching and social work and to women becoming real estate salespersons, door-to-door peddlers, postal clerks, and ticket agents.

Only one estimate of the trend in occupational sex segregation since 1970 exists (U.S. Commission on Civil Rights, 1978). The weighted index is computed over 441 occupational categories that form a version of the 1970 occupational classification. A negligible change of less than 1 point is found. The women's movement has not yet had a dramatic impact on occupational sex segregation. Even if there has been a decline in discrimination against applicants for sex-atypical jobs and in traditionalism of occupational choices, change in the overall magnitude of segregation will be glacial. This is because new hires constitute only a small share of those employed in any given year, and of those hired, it is only recent cohorts who have experienced somewhat less traditional regimes of sex-role socialization. Yet it is telling that the combined forces of changing sex roles, the women's movement, and affirmative action should have less imact on segregation during the 1970s than a war did in the 1940s. This contrast supports Lipman-Blumen's (1973) contention that sex-role dedifferentiation has occurred primarily as a response to crises.

## Overall Trends in Segregation, 1900–1976

Undoubtedly there has been some decrease in occupational sex segregation in this century, although it has occurred sporadically. The difficult question is whether to conclude that the magnitude of decline has been small or substantial. The divergence in amounts of decline shown by the various methods is great. The largest estimate of decline between 1900 and 1970 is 32.2 and was found by Williams, who used the weighted index on back-aggregated occuaptions. Declines of less than 3 points are found by Gross and Williams using the weighted index over total current occupations for each year. The size-standardized index attentuates the opposite biases entailed in using back-aggregated or current occupations. Yet even these intermediate estimates from the size-standardized index vary greatly according to whether back-aggregated or current occupations are used. Current occupations show a decline of 8.0 or 8.3 between 1900 and 1960 and of 15.6 between 1900 and 1970. Back-aggregated occupations show a much larger decline of 22.1 between 1900 and 1960 and 25.4 between 1900 and 1970. While we can conclude that some decline in occupational sex segregation has occurred, it is difficult to estimate the magnitude of the decline. As a ballpark figure, perhaps the decline has been between 10 and 20 points.

## Conclusions

Cross-sectional research shows occupational sex segregation to play an important role in generating sex differences in earnings. Before we can determine whether this relationship between segregation and income differences holds over time, we need analyses of trends in occupational sex segregation. With this rationale, I have explored the methodological dilemmas entailed in using the index of dissimilarity to assess change in occupational sex segregation. Unfortunately, each method of forming and weighting occupational categories introduces distinct biases. After examining all published analyses using various methods of computing the index, I conclude that there has been a sporadic decline in occupational sex segregation over the century but that the magnitude of the decline is impossible to estimate. My guess is that it has been somewhere between 10 and 20 points. The 1920s and the 1950s brought small increases in segregation. The 1970s brought negligible change. Other decades brought small amounts of decrease, with the largest decline in the 1940s.

## Prospects

This assessment of trends in occupational sex segregation was justified as a prerequisite to analyses exploring the links between change in segregation and change in male–female earning differentials. Such analyses will not be possible for the period before 1939, since the first questions on earnings were asked in the 1940 census. A cursory look at data on earnings indicates that the ratio of white women's to white men's earnings (for full-time workers) has declined since 1939, despite the declines in occupational segregation discussed earlier (U.S. Bureau of Census, 1975, p.305). Future research should monitor the links between movements in these two indicators.

## Acknowledgments

I am grateful to Gregory Williams, Teresa Sullivan, E. M. Beck, Ivar Berg, Robert K. Miller, Diane Miller, and Daniel Cornfield for comments and suggestions.

## Appendix

The weighted index of dissimilarity is calculated as follows. Suppose the labor force contained only three occupations; Table 10.A1 provides an example of such a labor force. The index is calculated by dividing $D$ (the sum of the percentage differences, each expressed as an absolute value) by 2. In the example in Table 10.1 $D/2 = 25$.

To compute the size-standardized index for the same hypothetical data, one preserves the proportions of male and female in each occupation but changes the absolute numbers to treat all occupations as if they were the same size. Suppose that the labor force on which the example in Table 10.A1 was calculated consisted of 60 males and 40 females. Then we can calculate the proportion of each occupation that is male and female from Table A-1 (see Table 10.A2).

To size-standardize the index, one changes the size of occupations so that each contains the same number of persons. Suppose 100 is the size for each occupation. Using the percentage in Table 10.A2, one adjusts the number of males and females in each occupation, preserving

TABLE 10.A1

Calculation of the Weighted Index of Dissimilarity
on a Hypothetical Labor Force

| Occupation | A<br>Percentage of<br>all males in<br>occupation | B<br>Percentage of<br>all females in<br>occupation | C<br>Absolute value<br>of difference<br>between A and B |
|---|---|---|---|
| 1 | 35 | 50 | 15 |
| 2 | 40 | 15 | 25 |
| 3 | 25 | 35 | 10 |
| TOTAL | 100 | 100 | $D = 50$ |

TABLE 10.A2

Calculation of the Sex Composition of Each Occupation in Table 10.A1 for a Labor Force of 60 Men and 40 Women

| Occupation | Number of males in occupation | Percentage male of those in occupation $(q)$ | Number of females in occupation | Percentage female of those in occupation $(p)$ | Total number of persons in occupation $(\hat{T})$ |
|---|---|---|---|---|---|
| 1 | 21 | 51.2 | 20 | 48.8 | 41 |
| 2 | 24 | 80.0 | 6 | 20.0 | 30 |
| 3 | 15 | 51.7 | 14 | 48.3 | 29 |
| TOTAL | 60 | --- | 40 | --- | 100 |

TABLE 10.A3

Calculation of the Size-Standardized Index of Dissimilarity on a Hypothetical Labor Force

| Occupation | Adjusted number of males | Adjusted number of females | A Adjusted percentage of all males in occupation | B Adjusted percentage of all females in occupation | C Absolute value of difference between A and B |
|---|---|---|---|---|---|
| 1 | 51 | 49 | 27.9 | 41.9 | 14.0 |
| 2 | 80 | 20 | 43.7 | 17.1 | 26.6 |
| 3 | 52 | 48 | 28.4 | 41.0 | 12.6 |
| TOTAL | 183 | 117 | 100.0 | 100.0 | $D = 53.2$ |

the proportion male and female in each occupation but changing the numbers of men and women in each occupation to correspond with the adjusted size of the occupation. From these adjusted numbers of males and females, one can calculate analogs to columns A, B, and C in Table 10.A1 and thus compute the size-standardized index (see Table 10.A3). The size-standardized index = $D/2$. In this example, $53.2/2 = 26.6$.

Blau and Hendricks (1979) provide the following formula for the decomposition of changes in the weighted index of dissimilarity into the component due to shift in the relative size of occupations (called OCMIX) and due to shifts in sex composition within occupations (called SEXCOMP).

$$ \text{OCMIX} = \frac{1}{2}\left[ \sum_i \left| \frac{q_{i1}T_{i2}}{\Sigma_i q_{i1}T_{i2}} \geqslant \frac{p_{i1}T_{i2}}{\Sigma_i p_{i1}T_{i2}} \right| - \sum_i \left| \frac{q_{i1}T_{i1}}{\Sigma_i q_{i1}T_{i1}} \geqslant \frac{p_{i1}T_{i1}}{\Sigma_i p_{i1}T_{i1}} \right| \right] $$

$$ \text{SEXCOMP} = \frac{1}{2}\left[ \sum_i \left| \frac{q_{i2}T_{i1}}{\Sigma_i q_{i2}T_{i1}} \geqslant \frac{p_{i2}T_{i1}}{\Sigma_i p_{i2}T_{i1}} \right| - \sum_i \left| \frac{q_{i1}T_{i1}}{\Sigma_i p_{i1}T_{i1}} \geqslant \frac{p_{i1}T_{i1}}{\Sigma_i p_{i1}T_{i1}} \right| \right] $$

where $p_{it}$ = the proportion of all those in occupation $i$ who are female in year $t$; $q_{it}$ = the proportion of all those in occupation $i$ who are male in year $t$; $T_{it}$ = the total number of persons employed in occupation $i$ in year $t$. If the sum of OCMIX and SEXCOMP is subtracted from the change in the weighted index between 2 years, the difference is a result of the interaction of OCMIX and SEXCOMP.

# References

Bergmann, B.
   1971   "The effect on white incomes of discrimination in employment." *Journal of Political Economy* 79:294–313.
Blau, F.
   1977   *Equal Pay in the Office.* Lexington, Massachusetts: Heath.
Blau, F., and W. Hendricks
   1979   "Occupational segregation by sex: Trends and prospects." *Journal of Human Resources* 12:197–210.
Blau, P., and C. D. Duncan
   1967   *The American Occupational Structure.* New York: Wiley.
Bluestone, B.
   1974   *The Personal Earnings Distribution: Individual and Institutional Determinants.* Unpublished doctoral dissertation, Department of Economics, University of Michigan, Ann Arbor.
Bose, C.
   1973   *Jobs and Gender: Sex and Occupational Prestige.* Baltimore: Johns Hopkins Center for Metropolitan Planning and Research.
Cain, G.
   1966   *Married Women in the Labor Force: An Economic Analysis.* Chicago: Univ. of Chicago Press.

Cohen, M.
  1971   "Sex differences in compensation." *Journal of Human Resources* 6:434–447.
DeJong, P.
  1972   *Factors Instrumental in Female Occupational Status: A Comparison to Factors Instrumental in Male Occupational Status.* Unpublished doctoral dissertation, Department of Sociology, Western Michigan University.
Duncan, O. D.
  1961   "A socioeconomic index for all occupations," and "Properties and characteristics of the socioeconomic index." In A. Reiss (ed.), *Occupations and Social Status.* New York: Free Press.
Duncan, O. D., and B. Duncan
  1955a  "A methodological analysis of segregation indices." *American Sociological Review* 20:200–217.
  1955b  "Residential distribution and occupation stratification." *American Journal of Sociology* 60:493–503.
England, P.
  1979   "Women and occupational prestige: A case of vacuous sex equality." *Signs* 5:252–265.
  1981   "Explanations of occupational sex segregation: A review." *Paper presented at The annual meetings of the Southwest Social Science Association,* Dallas, Texas.
England, P., M. Chassie, and L. McCormack
  1981   "Skill demands of female and male occupations." *Sociology and Social Research,* in press.
England, P., and S. McLaughlin
  1979   "Sex segregation of jobs and male–female income differentials." In R. Alvarez, K. Lutterman, and Associates (eds.), *Discrimination in Organizations.* San Francisco: Jossey-Bass.
Featherman, D., and R. Hauser
  1976   "Sexual inequalities and socioeconomic achievement in the U.S., 1962–1973." *American Sociological Review* 41:462–483.
Fuchs, V.
  1971   "Differences in hourly earnings between men and women." *Monthly Labor Review* 94(5):9–15.
Gottfredson, L.
  1977   *A Multiple-Labor Market Model of Occupational Achievement.* Report No. 225. Baltimore: Center for Social Organization of Schools, Johns Hopkins University.
Gross, E.
  1968   "Plus ça change . . . ? The sexual structure of occupations over time." *Social Problems* 16:198–208.
Hauser, P.
  1964   "Labor force." In R. E. L. Faris (ed.), *Handbook of Modern Sociology.* Chicago: Rand McNally.
Hodge, R., and P. Hodge
  1965   "Occupational assimilation as a competitive process." *American Journal of Sociology* 61:249–264.
Lipman-Blumen, J.
  1973   "Role de-differentiation as a system response to crisis: Occupational and political roles of women." *Sociological Inquiry* 43:105–129.

McLaughlin, S.
  1978   "Occupational sex identification and the assessment of male and female earnings inequality." *American Sociological Review* 43:909–921.
McLaughlin, S., and B. Spykerman
  1979   "Occupational labor market segmentation and the male/female wage differential." Unpublished manuscript.
McNally, G. B.
  1968   "Patterns of female labor force activity." *Industrial Relations* 7:204–218.
Oppenheimer, V.
  1970   *The Female Labor Force in the United States.* Population Monograph Series, No. 5. Berkeley: Univ. of California Press.
Polachek, S.
  1975   "Discontinuous labor force participation and its effect on women's market earnings." In C. Lloyd (ed.), *Sex, Discrimination, and the Division of Labor.* New York: Columbia Univ. Press.
  1979   "Occupational segregation among women: Theory, evidence and a prognosis." In C. Lloyd, E. Andrews, and C. Gilroy (eds.), *Women in the Labor Market.* New York: Columbia Univ. Press.
Sanborn, H.
  1964   "Pay differences between women and men." *Industrial and Labor Relations Review* 17:534–550.
Siegel, P.
  1971   *Prestige in the American Occupational Structure.* Unpublished doctoral dissertation, Department of Sociology, University of Chicago.
Snyder, D., and P. Hudis
  1976   "Occupational income and the effects of minority competition and segregation." *American Sociological Review* 41:209–234.
Stevenson, M.
  1975   "Relative wages and sex segregation by occupation." In C. Lloyd (ed.), *Sex Discrimination and the Division of Labor.* New York: Columbia Univ. Press.
Suter, L., and H. Miller
  1973   "Income differences between men and career women." *American Journal of Sociology* 78:962–974.
Sweet, J.
  1973   *Women in the Labor Force.* New York: Seminar Press.
Treiman, D., and K. Terrell
  1975a   "Sex differences in the process of status attainment: A comparison of working women and men." *American Sociological Review* 40:174–200.
  1975b   "Women, work, and wages—trends in the female occupational structure since 1940." In K. Land and S. Spilerman (eds.), *Social Indicator Models.* New York: Russell Sage Foundation.
U.S. Bureau of Census
  1975   *Historical Statistics of the United States* (P. 1). Washington, D.C.: US Govt Printing Office.
U.S. Commission on Civil Rights
  1978   *Social Indicators of Equality for Minorities and Women.* Washington, D.C.: US Govt Printing Office.
U.S. Department of Labor
  1970   *Dual Careers* (Vol. 1). Manpower Research Monograph No. 21. Washington, D.C.: US Govt Printing Office.

1976   *The Earnings Gap between Women and Men.* Washington, D.C.: US Govt Printing Office.

U.S. President's Council of Economic Advisors

1973   *Economic Report of the President.* Washington, D.C.: US Govt Printing Office.

Williams, G.

1976   "Trends in occupational differentiation by sex." *Sociology of Work and Occupations* 3(1):38–62.

1979   "The changing U.S. labor force and occupational differentiation by sex." *Demography* 16(1):73–88.

Wolf, W., and N. Fligstein

1979   "Sex and authority in the workplace." *American Sociological Review* 44:235–261.

# Chapter 11

# Patterns of Employment Difficulty among European Immigrant Industrial Workers during the Great Depression: Local Opportunity and Cultural Heritage

*ROBERT K. MILLER, JR.*

The work behavior of immigrants to the United States has been the object of both popular interest and social scientific study for most of this century. One major aspect of this interest in immigrant work behavior has been with immigrants' job mobility and, particularly, with the effects of employment difficulty on the patterns of their mobility. It is commonly understood that at any given time from the 1870s to the 1920s, the period of massive immigration from Europe, a sizable proportion of the newly arrived immigrants experienced employment difficulty. "Immigrants . . . faced not only constant changes in the locations of their work, but also frequent spells of unemployment [Ward, 1971, p.107]." One generic explanation of these purported difficulties focuses on immigrants' cultural heritage or, more specifically, on the appropriateness of their cultural heritage (Handlin, 1973, p.55).

SOCIOLOGICAL PERSPECTIVES ON
LABOR MARKETS

Among sociologists, the notion that immigrants experienced more employment difficulty than did similarly skilled native-born workers, and that this difference was largely due to immigrant cultural heritages, is common. Of the cultural explanations that account for variations in employment difficulty, perhaps the most widely known and completely formulated is assimilationist theory (cf. Gordon, 1964; Park, 1950). One major variant of assimilationist theory suggests that immigrants, socialized in other sociocultural systems, exhibited behaviors that were not only different from those of the native-born population but often inappropriate or maladaptive in the new sociocultural context. As time passed, moreover, immigrants gradually came to learn the culture of their new home. This reduction or attenuation of other cultural ways and their replacement with the culture of American society was presumed to occur in all aspects or categories of social behavior and to continue inexorably until the last vestiges of the old were extinguished.

With respect to work behavior, assimilationists make few explicit statements. However, the assimilationist perspective strongly suggests that the cultures that emerged from the work structures in the immigrants' native lands contributed in important ways to employment difficulty in American society, particularly in urban industrial settings. Immigrants brought with them different definitions of work, including definitions of what was proper and desirable work; different work and achievement motivations and values; different orientations toward time, the future, and productivity; and an integrated set of meanings and dispositions toward work—that is, a work culture—that was completely different. These work cultures not only were different from those emerging into dominance in urban industrial American society but were inappropriate and not conducive to occupational success (Banfield, 1958; Handlin, 1957; Schooler, 1976; U.S. Immigration Commission, 1911).[1]

Application of assimilationist theory to the explanation of native and immigrant patterns of employment difficulty led to the development of the

---

[1] Similar arguments are also commonly employed in American cultural anthropological literature on economic development and sociocultural change in industrializing societies, especially in examinations of the work experiences of rural-to-urban migrants (cf. Lewis, 1966). A similar perspective has been common in the literature that sought explanations for the causes of disproportionately high poverty levels of racial minorities in American society. Until recently, there was some currency to the notion that the cultures of minority groups, particularly of blacks and Puerto Ricans, explained their high levels of poverty, low occupational status, and high job instability and employment difficulty (cf. Banfield, 1970; Glazer & Moynihan, 1963; Moynihan, 1965). Modified "class cultural" arguments have been devised in efforts to account for class differences in work behavior, particularly for the work behavior of members of the lower class. Gutman (1973) has suggested a similar class cultural explanation for the work behavior of intrasocietal rural-to-urban migrants. Finally, a large segment of the literature on the labor force participation of women has had a cultural explanation at its base.

following set of hypotheses, the critical evaluation of which is one aim of this chapter. First, as immigrants gain job experience in this society, their levels of employment difficulty should progressively become more similar to those of native-born workers. In other words, accumulated postmigration job experience results in attenuation of initial immigrant–native differences in employment difficulty. Second, the more extensive the exposure to and experience in other sociocultural systems, the slower this process of attenuation or assimilation. In other words, the rate of attenuation of differences in levels of employment difficulty between immigrant and native-born workers varies inversely with the amount of other sociocultural experience of the former group. Third, the following should contribute, separately and in combination, to postmigration employment difficulty: foreign birth, foreign education, foreign apprenticeship, extensive work experience in a foreign society (both in terms of time and number of jobs), short period of time in this society before first job here, and migration as an adult. The patterns of employment difficulty of immigrants who received all their education in this society, were apprenticed here, had no work experience abroad, lived in this society for several years before their first job, and migrated as children should be highly similar to that of native-born workers. Fourth, immigrants will exhibit greater employment difficulty than native-born workers in situations of declining opportunity.[2]

An alternative explanation of immigrant employment difficulty, suggested by conventional or neoclassical labor market theory, is also critically evaluated. A review of the literature on the economics of labor force participation and labor mobility makes it clear that structures external to workers have important effects on their patterns of employment difficulty. While conventional or neoclassical labor market theory does not directly address the issue of employment difficulty, it suggests that the occupational and industrial structures of an area may be thought of as markets within which wages, labor allocation, and job training decisions are determined largely through undifferentiated competition among employers for the relatively changeable skills of workers and that the outcome of this competition is determined by the simple interaction of supply and demand for labor. For the worker, these markets constitute structures of occupational and industrial opportunity, which determine to a large extent whether the worker is employed or unemployed, mobile or stable.

Other subsystems or institutions of society, in interaction with the productive subsystem, generate workers equipped with job skills demanded. Given imperfect subsystem integration, there is usually a set of occupational

---

[2] The patterns of employment difficulty for native migrants and nonmigrants should be very similar, but both should differ significantly from those of the immigrants.

and industrial slots for which opportunity is high because demand exceeds the supply of suitably skilled workers, as well as a set of low-opportunity slots in which supply exceeds demand.

In situations in which workers possess job skills for which the opportunities are expanding, they should exhibit relatively fewer periods of unemployment (most of which should be short term), little part-time employment, and mobility that is voluntary rather than involuntary. By comparison, in situations in which workers possess job skills for which opportunities are declining, they should exhibit more periods of unemployment (some of which may be long term), more part-time employment, and mobility that is more likely to be involuntary than voluntary. In situations of declining opportunity, the total volume of mobility may be expected to be slightly greater than in situations of high or expanding opportunity, because involuntary mobility generally constitutes the larger of the two components of total mobility, regardless of variations in opportunity (Parnes, 1968). Furthermore, involuntary mobility varies more closely with changes in opportunity than does voluntary mobility. Workers employed in slack or declining sectors of the labor market may voluntarily shift into expanding sectors of the labor market, if skills and experience are transferable. When opportunities are expanding, the incidence of involuntary shifting should be low. However, the incidence of voluntary shifting may be lower than expected because of employers' efforts to retain employees, workers' lack of information about alternative opportunities, and low interchangeability of job skills. The net result of this is that the ratio of voluntary to involuntary job shifts may be expected to be higher in situations of expanding opportunities than in situations of declining opportunities.

There is much evidence of the importance of demand levels for job skills in the determination of amounts and patterns of worker mobility. Palmer reports (1954) that one-third of the time workers change employers because of economic conditions having nothing to do with their work performance or work preferences. In a later study, she states that "rates of mobility . . . in this country vary with the business cycle [1960, p.521]." And noting the effects of fluctuations in economic activity, she argues that a cyclical downswing can, in the short run, increase the number of layoffs per man and the amount of involuntary mobility (1962, p.113).[3] Swerdloff and Bluestone (1952), in summarizing a study of the mobility of tool and die makers, state

> The extent to which tool and die makers change employers, go from one industry to another, transfer into other occupations, or move to different areas, is influenced by the nature of the occupation *and by the economic circumstances which affect it in a particular period* [p.605; italics added].

[3] Essentially the same argument is presented by Miller and Form (1964, pp.601–603).

They also note that, during periods of favorable employment opportunities, involuntary job mobility was low and voluntary mobility increased; they conclude that the growth of occupational opportunities is directly related to low involuntary job mobility and increased voluntary mobility (1952; pp.605–609). Parnes (1968) notes that "the proportion of the total [mobility] that results from layoff is very sensitive to the level of aggregate demand for labor [p.484]." Burton and Parker (1969) note that "the volume of voluntary mobility . . . depends on the workers' opportunities to move [pp.201–204]." In slack markets, voluntary job mobility decreases and involuntary mobility increases.

> The short run supply of labor adjusts to changes in the volume and pattern of labor requirements by movements of workers into and out of the labor force, between employment and unemployment, and among firms, occupations, industries, or localities [Parnes, 1968; pp.482–483].

In sum, conventional or neoclassical labor market theory applied to the study of employment difficulty suggests that such difficulty varies by opportunities, which in turn are a function of the supply and demand for labor. Thus, variation in immigrant employment difficulty is not attributable to cultural heritage per se but rather to variations in local occupational and industrial opportunity structures. Controls for individual worker characteristics, or human capital variables (education, occupational training, skills, and experience), as well as for local occupational and industrial opportunity structures should eliminate any native–immigrant differences in patterns of employment difficulty.

## Research Design

To evaluate these competing hypotheses, two major data sets were used. Two samples of 10-year work histories were located, one consisting of 682 skilled manual workers customarily attached to one of four occupations in the metal-working industries in Philadelphia, and a second sample consisting of 420 manual workers customarily attached to the radio industry in Philadelphia.[4] These histories were gathered by Gladys L. Palmer and her associates in 1936 for a study that was part of the Works Progress Administration's National Research Project. The original work history questionnaires were recoded for this analysis. Each work history contains sociodemographic information, a detailed work history for the 10-year period

---

[4] I thank William L. Yancey and Eugene P. Ericksen for informing me of the existence and availability of these data and for procuring them for my use from Ann R. Miller, Department of Sociology, University of Pennsylvania.

from 1926 to 1935, and similar information for work experience prior to 1926 for those workers who had such experience.[5]

These samples are not representative of the population of skilled and semiskilled manual workers in Philadelphia, either for 1935 or for any prior date. However, they are representative of important occupational groups within the skilled and semiskilled manual occupational categories, and over 200 occupations are represented in the work histories. The workers in these samples were employed in major industries in the Philadelphia area. The metal-working industry had long been a large and important industry in the city. Two-thirds of the workers in this sample were employed as machinists, millwrights, tool and die makers, or apprentices to these trades. Generally, opportunities for machinists declined from 1926 to the onset of the Great Depression, and by 1930, the number of machinists had fallen almost to the 1910 level. Herrmann (1938) notes that machinists' opportunities are determined primarily by the industry in which they are employed. There was considerable interindustrial variation in opportunity from 1899 to 1929 among 16 specific metal products industries, but the two dominant patterns were either continuous decline in opportunities or expansion followed by decline (Welch, 1933).

The radio industry was relatively new. It began in the mid-1920s, expanded rapidly, and had become an important industry in the area by the end of the 1920s. More than 150 industries are represented in these two samples. The metal workers were employed in 271 different firms in the Philadelphia industrial area, while the radio workers were employed in three large firms, one of which was located in Camden, New Jersey.

Both samples contain a large proportion of foreign-born workers. The metal-worker sample contains approximately one-third foreign-born, and the radio-worker sample contains approximately 30% foreign-born. At the time, the employable population of Philadelphia included about 24% foreign-born. These workers arrived in Philadelphia at widely different times, at different ages, and with varying amounts and kinds of European occupational and industrial experience. Within the native-born group, a sizable proportion had migrated from other cities and regions of the United States.

A large proportion of the immigrants in these samples had experience in and exposure to the educational, apprenticeship, and work structures of the sociocultural systems from which they migrated. On one hand, few

---

[5] In addition to a detailed work history, each questionnaire contained the following information: name, residential address, age (in 1936), sex, race, birthplace, years in Philadelphia, years in the United States, marital status, school grade completed, age leaving school, and age beginning full-time employment. Using this information, society of first job, society in which educated, age at migration, and other variables were derived (see Miller, 1978, 1979). For a copy of the work history questionnaire, see Herrmann (1938) or Palmer and Stoflet (1938).

were peasants who had come from rural areas where they had little or no contact with or experience in urban-industrial occupational structures. Rather, their work experiences before coming to Philadelphia were, in many cases, extensive and included jobs at the skilled and semiskilled manual levels in the manufacturing sectors of the industrial structures of the societies they left behind. For example, about two-thirds had begun work before migration and continued by taking their first postmigration job soon after their arrival.

On the other hand, some immigrants were very young, had little or no premigration occupational experience, industrial or otherwise, and were educated, apprenticed, and took their first jobs in America. Thus, three-tenths of the workers migrated before their sixteenth birthday, and about one-third of the immigrants in these samples took their first jobs in this society. About two-fifths had no premigration industrial work experience, and one-fifth had only 1 to 6 years of such experience.

Data on the occupational and industrial macrostructures of Philadelphia, needed to reconstruct worker-specific occupational and industrial opportunity structures, were gathered from the U.S. Censuses of Manufactures and the U.S. Censuses of Population (Occupations). Using these data, indexes of opportunity change for a set of specific occupations and industries represented in the work history sample were constructed.[6] Each change index represents the increase or decrease in the number of workers employed in that specific occupation or industry during the 1931–1935 period.

## 1931–1935: The Great Depression

It would be difficult to overemphasize the magnitude and generality of the declines in occupational and industrial opportunity that occurred during the Great Depression. Industrial employment declined sharply, then expanded from 1933 to 1935. However, industrial employment in 1935 was only 106% of the 1931 level and 82% of the 1925 level, which itself was lower than that of the years immediately preceding World War I. The number of skilled and semiskilled manual workers continued to decline during this period. There was a sharp decline in employment in the radio

---

[6] I constructed indexes of opportunity change for a set of 94 specific occupations represented in the work histories and a similar set of opportunity change indexes for a set of 67 industries represented in the sample. The specific index employed was:

$$[(n_{t2} - n_{t1})/n_{t1}] + 1 = \Delta$$

where $n$ = number of workers in a specific occupational or industrial category, $t1$ = beginning of the period, and $t2$ = end of the period. Delta > 100 indicates increasing or expanding opportunities, and $\Delta$ < 100 indicates decreasing or declining opportunities.

industry from 1931 to 1933. Beginning at the end of 1933 and continuing until the time of the interviews in 1936, this industry increased activities, but the levels of the earlier years were not attained. Next, there were seasonal variations in opportunity. Significant interfirm variations in opportunity also occurred, partially because one of the three firms discontinued production of radios in the middle of the period. Opportunities for machinists, furthermore, declined from 1931 to 1935, and although they began to increase by the end of 1933, they had not risen above 1926 levels by 1935. Finally, although there was variation among the metal products industries in opportunity during the period, the most typical pattern was one of severe decline. Another pattern, far less common, was decline followed by partial recovery from 1933 to 1935.

## Employment Difficulty

Of primary concern in this research is job mobility that indicates employment difficulty. I classified all job shifts into two types: voluntary and involuntary. Voluntary shifts are defined as those that are the consequence of worker-initiated decisions and for which evidence of external compulsion is absent. Involuntary shifts are those for which there is evidence of external compulsion and are divided into two categories: labor market and other. The former comprises all shifts that are explicitly the consequence of demand changes in the labor market and includes plant closings and layoffs due to seasonal, cyclical, or secular declines in demand for the worker's skills. In the tables, this variable is indicated by NVLM. The latter, a residual category, includes all other involuntary shifts that are not explicitly the consequence of demand changes in labor markets. Analysis is limited to the former category of involuntary shifts.

The other indicators of employment difficulty used for this analysis include two related measures of unemployment—total amount of unemployment in months (TMUN) and average length of unemployed periods in months (LUNE)—and a measure of average length of service in months per job at jobs defined as the usual occupation (LSPJ) (see Table 11.1).

This analysis is primarily concerned with examining the employment difficulty of experienced workers for whom 1931–1935 was not their first period of employment in Philadelphia. During this period, as expected, the incidence of involuntary job shifting was high. Periods of unemployment were common: 55.7% of the experienced workers were unemployed for more than a month, and 28.4% were unemployed for 19 or more months. The average length of unemployed periods was also high: 36.2% averaged seven or more months, and a larger proportion experienced some unem-

TABLE 11.1

Indicators of Employment Difficulty, Experienced and New Workers,
1931--1935 (percents)

| Indicator of employment difficulty[a] | Experienced workers | New or beginning workers[b] |
|---|---|---|
| NVLM | | |
| None | 34.8 | 23.5 |
| ≥ 1 | 65.2 | 76.5 |
| TMUN | | |
| None | 44.3 | 28.4 |
| 1--18 | 27.3 | 59.3 |
| ≥ 19 | 28.4 | 12.3 |
| LUNE | | |
| None | 44.3 | 28.4 |
| 1--6 | 19.5 | 44.4 |
| ≥ 7 | 36.2 | 27.2 |
| LSPJ | | |
| 0--6 | 21.6 | 40.7 |
| 7--24 | 30.5 | 40.7 |
| 25--59 | 18.2 | 17.3 |
| 60 | 29.7 | 1.2 |

[a]*NVLM = number of involuntary job shifts; TMUN = total amount of unemployment in months; LUNE = average length of unemployed periods in months; LSPJ = average length of service in months per job at jobs defined as the usual occupation.*

[b]*New or beginning workers are those for whom 1931--1935 was the initial period of Philadelphia employment (N = 81).*

[c]*The frequencies presented in this table are adjusted, that is, they exclude missing cases.*

ployment. Finally, only 47.9% of the workers averaged more than 2 years at jobs defined as the usual occupation.

In sum, experienced workers exhibited considerable employment difficulty during the period. Interestingly, these findings hold without exception for new or beginning workers. Of equal importance, employment difficulty was greater among the new or beginning workers than among the experienced workers. Workers tend to be least skilled at the beginnings of their careers, to have less training and experience investments, and to be more likely to have occupations that offer less job security. The comparison of levels of employment difficulty between experienced and beginning workers during the period also clearly shows the effects of differences in occupational and industrial opportunity.

## Occupational and Industrial Opportunity and Employment Difficulty

It has been suggested that employment difficulty is affected by occupational and industrial structures within which workers are employed. Application and extension of conventional or neoclassical labor market theory to the explanation of amounts and patterns of employment difficulty generated a set of hypotheses examined later in the chapter. Before discussing the findings, it is useful to present one-way frequency distributions for the indicators of job opportunity and to discuss several data problems that compel one to qualify the conclusions (see Table 11.2).

TABLE 11.2

Industrial and Occupational Opportunity, 1931--1935

| | Relative percent | Adjusted percent | *N* |
|---|---|---|---|
| Industrial opportunity | | | |
| Decreasing | 35.5 | 85.5 | 354 |
| Increasing | 6.0 | 14.5 | 60 |
| Unknown | 58.5 | --- | 583 |
| Number | --- | --- | 997 |
| Occupational opportunity | | | |
| Decreasing | 56.2 | 86.0 | 560 |
| Increasing | 9.1 | 14.0 | 91 |
| Unknown | 34.7 | --- | 346 |
| Number | --- | --- | 997 |

The analysis of the effects of occupational and industrial opportunity on employment difficulty during this period is complicated by three related data problems: missing opportunity data, occupational and industrial homogeneity, and correlation between occupations and opportunities. Industrial opportunity data are missing for 58.5% of the cases, and occupational opportunity data are missing for 34.7% of the cases. Thus, complete occupational and industrial opportunity data are available for only 29.9% of the cases (see Table 11.3). During the period, 84.6% of the workers had occupations in which opportunities were declining. Of the small proportion of workers who had occupations in which opportunities were expanding, 83% were tool and die makers (see Table 11.4). Similar problems complicate the analysis of the effects of industrial opportunity: 83.2% of the workers were employed in industries in which opportunities were declining (see Table 11.5). Furthermore, there is industrial homogeneity within categories of industrial opportunity. During this period, 30% of the workers in the decreasing-opportunities category were employed in the radio industry, 57% were employed in only two industries, and 87% were employed in only four industries. Thirty percent of the workers in the increasing-opportunities category were employed in one industry, 48% were employed in only two industries, and 74% of the workers were employed in only four industries. Evaluation of the effects of occupational opportunity essentially involves comparison of employment difficulty patterns of machinists and toolmakers, both occupations that are in declining industries. Evaluation of the effects of industrial opportunity involves comparison of skilled workers (70% machinists) in expanding industries with that of a much larger group consisting primarily of skilled workers in declining industries. I now turn to an examination of the relationships between indicators of employment difficulty and occupational and industrial opportunity.

TABLE 11.3

Industrial Opportunity by Occupational Opportunity, 1931--1935

| Industrial opportunity | Occupational opportunity | | |
| --- | --- | --- | --- |
| | Decreasing (N) | Increasing (N) | Total |
| Decreasing | 209 | 39 | 248 |
| Increasing | 43 | 7 | 50 |
| | 252 | 46 | 298 |

TABLE 11.4

Occupation, 1931, by Occupational Opportunity, 1931--1935

| Occupation, 1931 | Occupational opportunity, 1931--1935 | | | |
|---|---|---|---|---|
| | Decreasing (%) | N | Increasing (%) | N |
| Tool and die maker | --- | --- | 83 | 38 |
| Machinist | 59 | 148 | --- | --- |
| Cabinetmaker | 6 | 16 | --- | --- |
| Foreman | 7 | 18 | --- | --- |
| Other skilled manual | 7 | 18 | 4 | 2 |
| Cabinet and furniture[a] | 11 | 27 | --- | --- |
| Apprentice | 5 | 13 | --- | --- |
| Other semi-skilled manual | --- | --- | 9 | 4 |
| All other | 5 | 12 | 4 | 2 |
| | 100 | 252 | 100 | 46 |

[a]*Semi-skilled.*

## Industrial Opportunity and Employment Difficulty

In her original analysis of the job mobility of the workers that constitute the machinist subsample, Herrmann found that "the outstanding differences in the recent employment experience of Philadelphia machinists arise not from differences in their personal or occupational characteristics but from changes in the business activity of the industries to which the men have become customarily attached [1938; pp.72–73]." Thus, job mobility was found to vary with industry of customary employment, and I attribute this variation to interindustrial variation in opportunities. In industries in which opportunities were declining, unemployment was higher than in industries in which opportunities were expanding. Since there was little variation in occupation, Herrmann could not directly address the issue of the relationship between employment difficulty and occupational opportunity. However, I found evidence of intraoccupation variation in job mobility not completely explained by interindustrial variation in opportunity. Herrmann suggests that these variations are accounted for, in part, by intraoccupation variation

TABLE 11.5

Industry, 1931, by Industrial Opportunity, 1931--1935

| Industry, 1931 | Industrial opportunity, 1931--1935 | | | |
|---|---|---|---|---|
| | Decreasing (%) | N | Increasing (%) | N |
| Food products | --- | --- | 18 | 9 |
| Textiles and clothing | 3 | 8 | 14 | 7 |
| Chemicals | --- | --- | 30 | 15 |
| Transportation equipment | 17 | 41 | 12 | 6 |
| Metal products | 10 | 26 | --- | --- |
| Machinery | 27 | 66 | --- | --- |
| Radio | 30 | 74 | --- | --- |
| Other | 13 | 33 | 26 | 13 |
| | 100 | 248 | 100 | 50 |

in skills and differential demand for these skills. Specifically, she found that production machinists were more mobile and experienced more unemployment than maintenance machinists. The latter, as a group, were more highly skilled: "Each factory employs one maintenance machinist or, at most, a small group of them. These men are needed even when work is very slack. . . . Maintenance machinists in these industries experienced less unemployment in the years under review [Herrmann, 1938; p.72]." Additionally, she found interindustrial variation in the transferability of occupational skills. Interindustrial transferability of machinists' skills were more limited than generally assumed, and still more limited by experience in some industries than others:

> Machinists customarily attached to these [transportation equipment] industries faced an additional problem with regard to employment. Work required of them is less exacting than that required of machinists in other industries. Consequently it has been harder for men attached to these industries to make a transfer to precision work [Herrmann, 1938, p.72].

This lack of transferability of skill operates to reduce industrial shifting and increases chances of unemployment and part-time employment in situations of declining opportunity.

Similarly, in their original anslysis of the job mobility of the workers who constitute the radio subsample, Palmer and Stoflet (1938) found that job mobility is dependent upon job opportunities:

> It is recognized that the mobility of a worker is dependent upon two important economic factors: first, the diversity of industries and employers offering employment in the labor market in which he lives or with which he has contact and second, the activity of the industry to which he is attached in relation to that of other industries. . . . But if few jobs are available, it is more difficult for a worker to shift his employer, industry, or occupation [Palmer & Stoflet, 1938, p.45].

Since theirs was a study of the job mobility of workers in one industry, there is obviously no evidence concerning interindustrial variation in opportunity or its relationship to employment difficulty. However, Palmer and Stoflet found that variation in job mobility was related to variation in opportunity within the industry. While their study did not directly address the issue of the relationship between employment difficulty and occupational opportunity, considerable evidence was presented that indicated that occupational opportunity varied within the industry, both temporally and by skill level, and that these variations in occupational opportunity were related to variation in employment difficulty.

Skilled workers entered the industry first, followed by semiskilled and unskilled workers. Thus, the opportunities for skilled workers occurred earliest and were greater during the entire period. Furthermore, there was evidence of variation in opportunity within occupational skill level that was related to variation in employment difficulty. For example, cabinetmaker, machinist, toolmaker, and millwright were all skilled manual occupations. However, at any given time, opportunities in these occupations varied and so consequently did the levels of employment difficulty of workers in these occupations. Cabinetmakers were more likely to be production workers than were those in other occupations in the radio industry. A larger proportion of the latter were maintenance workers, and their opportunities were more constant. Put another way, these workers were needed even during slack periods, so their levels of employment difficulty were only weakly related to variations in opportunity of the general occupation and the entire industry. Finally, Palmer and Stoflet noted that this industry was characterized by seasonal variations in opportunity, but that "the periodicity of the industry's operation . . . is not reflected in so great amplitude in the unemployment experience of the radio workers selected for study [1938, p.32]."

I found that variation in employment difficulty is not large for any of the indicators. Examination of the differences in patterns of employment difficulty under different conditions of industrial opportunity during the 1931–1935 period reveals findings that are generally supportive of conventional labor market theory: The incidence of involuntary job shifting was higher in situations of declining opportunity than expanding opportunity; the proportion of workers who experienced unemployment was larger in situations of declining than expanding opportunity; the proportion of workers who had high average lengths of unemployed periods was greater in situations of declining than expanding opportunity; the proportion of workers who had high average lengths of service per job at jobs defined as the usual occupation was larger in situations of expanding than declining opportunity; and the ratio of voluntary to involuntary job shifting was higher in situations of expanding opportunity (.47) than in situations of declining opportunity (.25) (see Table 11.6).

## Occupational Opportunity and Employment Difficulty

In turning our attention now to examination of the relationship between occupational opportunity and employment difficulty during the period, we

TABLE 11.6

Employment Difficulty by Industrial Opportunity, 1931--1935

| Indicator of employment difficulty[a] | Industrial opportunity | | | | |
| | Decreasing (%) | Increase (%) | Total (%) | Gamma | $p$ |
|---|---|---|---|---|---|
| NVLM ($\geq$ 1) | 67.2 | 56.7 | 65.7 | -.21 | ns[b] |
| TMUN ($\geq$ 19) | 21.8 | 21.7 | 21.7 | -.14 | ns |
| LUNE ($\geq$ 7) | 27.7 | 25.0 | 27.3 | -.15 | ns |
| LSPJ ($\geq$ 25) | 52.5 | 53.0 | 52.6 | +.08 | ns |
| Number of cases | 354 | 60 | 414 | | |

[a]For explanation of indicators, see Table 11.1.

[b]ns = not statistically significant.

find that while the data are not strongly supportive of conventional labor market theory, they do support the most basic predictions: The incidence of involuntary job shifting was higher in situations of declining opportunity than in situations of expanding opportunity; the proportion of workers who experienced unemployment was larger in situations of declining than expanding opportunity; the proportion of workers who had high average lengths of unemployed periods was larger in situations of declining than expanding opportunity; and the ratio of voluntary to involuntary job shifting was higher in situations of expanding opportunity (.52) than in situations of declining opportunity (.28) (see Table 11.7).

In sum, the relationships between indicators of employment difficulty and industrial and occupational opportunity support conventional labor market theory. Of the eight relationships, seven are in the predicted direction. Nevertheless, most of the relationships were weak and only one was statistically significant. One observes a general lack of large variation in employment difficulty, a lack due in part to similarity of conditions of occupational and industrial opportunity generated by the Great Depression and in part to the occupational and industrial homogeneity of the samples. The findings suggest that industrial opportunity is more important in its

TABLE 11.7

Employment Difficulty by Occupational Opportunity, 1931--1935

| Indicator of employment difficulty[a] | Occupational opportunity | | | | |
|---|---|---|---|---|---|
| | Decrease (%) | Increase (%) | Total (%) | Gamma | $p$ |
| NVLM ($\geq$ 1) | 62.6 | 56.0 | 61.7 | -.02 | .09 |
| TMUN ($\geq$ 19) | 19.5 | 12.2 | 18.5 | -.16 | ns[b] |
| LUNE ($\geq$ 7) | 28.4 | 20.0 | 27.2 | -.15 | ns |
| LSPJ ($\geq$ 25) | 57.3 | 54.5 | 56.9 | -.06 | ns |
| Number of cases | 560 | 90 | 650 | | |

[a]For explanation of indicators, see Table 11.1.

[b]ns = not statistically significant.

effect on employment difficulty than is occupational opportunity, a finding that is consistent with those of both Herrmann (1938) and Palmer and Stoflet (1938).

The effects of occupational and industrial opportunity may not be additive. If the effects of these variables were not additive, patterns of employment difficulty in situations of increasing occupational opportunity–decreasing industrial opportunity would be different from those in situations of decreasing occupational opportunity–increasing industrial opportunity. The ability to test for interaction was jeopardized by the joint distribution of cases on these variables. Nevertheless, analyses of variance were conducted, and statistically significant interactions were found for number of involuntary separations and length of service per jobs defined as usual, but not for amount of unemployment and average lengths of unemployed periods. I believe that these interactions are simply artifacts of the joint distribution of cases on occupational and industrial opportunity variables and the fact that most (87%) of the workers in the increasing occupational opportunities–decreasing industrial opportunities category were toolmakers, whereas most (81%) of the workers in the decreasing occupational opportunities–increasing industrial opportunities category were machinists. Regardless, I made no predictions concerning interaction between occupational and industrial opportunity, because I could find no compelling theoretical basis for positing an interaction effect. Therefore, any interpretation for these findings is essentially post hoc.

## Excursus: Human Capital and Employment Difficulty

No assessment of the effects of cultural heritage and opportunity structural factors in the explanation of patterns of employment difficulty would be complete without consideration of possible effects of individual worker characteristics, or human capital variables, on patterns of employment difficulty. What follows is a brief summary of such effects.[7] This summary is brief for several reasons. First, the major focuses of the analysis are on the effects of occupational and industrial opportunity structural conditions and cultural heritage variables. Second, most of the individual worker characteristics for which I had data do not appear to significantly modify the relationships between opportunity conditions and employment difficulty. Those that do, such as occupational skill level, are substantively unsurprising. Finally, and most importantly, those individual worker character-

---

[7] For a more detailed discussion of this issue, see Miller (1978, 1979).

istics that do appear to be related to patterns of employment difficulty show essentially the same relationships for immigrant and native workers. This suggests that human capital payoffs, at least in terms of vulnerability to employment difficulty, were highly similar for immigrant and native workers.

Several individual worker characteristics were not related to patterns of employment difficulty: school grade completed, age leaving school, age beginning full-time employment, skill level of first Philadelphia occupation, and industry of first Philadelphia job. Among the individual characteristics that were related to employment difficulty, the associations were statistically significant and constitute a logically consistent set, although of only moderate strength. This means that workers in a category of an individual characteristic for which employment difficulty was high were also likely to be in categories of other individual characteristics variables in which levels of employment difficulty were high. Thus, the younger workers were more likely to have entered the labor force at the beginning of the Great Depression, to have had no formal apprenticeship, to have held few jobs prior to the period, to have had few years of industrial employment prior to the period, and to have had semiskilled or lesser skilled occupations.

Furthermore, the individual characteristics that were related to employment difficulty were also related to occupational and industrial opportunity conditions. These relationships were generally weak and statistically insignificant; taken as a set, however, they suggest that an assessment of the effects of individual characteristics on patterns of employment difficulty must include controls for the effects of opportunity conditions.

The general relationships between opportunity structures and levels of employment difficulty appear to be modified by individual worker characteristics. This interpretation is supported by both Palmer and Stoflet's (1938) and Herrmann's (1938) original analyses.

The rank-ordering of the importance of these individual worker characteristics to the modification of the general relationships between employment opportunities and patterns of employment difficulty is fairly clear. Occupational skill level appears to be the most important factor. Large proportions of the relationships between occupational skill level at the beginning of the period, as well as skill level of the longest occupation prior to the onset of the Great Depression, remained statistically significant when opportunity was held constant. Next in importance were industry of employment at the beginning of the period and longest industry of attachment prior to 1931. These relationships are partially attributable to differences in occupational skill level distributions among the industries. Less important individual worker characteristics were year of first Philadelphia job and apprenticeship status. Although apprenticeship status and occupational skill level were related, that association was only moderate: Many workers who never took formal apprenticeships acquired skills that afforded them access to skilled manual occupations due to the extent and variety of their work experiences. Some workers who had served formal apprenticeships nevertheless held semiskilled manual occupations. Individual characteristics of still lesser importance were number of jobs held prior to the beginning of the period, number of years of industrial work experience prior to 1931, and surprisingly, age at the beginning of the period. Age per se was not directly related to levels of employment difficulty: The younger workers were generally less skilled and more likely, at least in these samples, to be employed in industries in which opportunities were declining.

Finally, several individual worker characteristics were unrelated to patterns of employment difficulty: school grade completed, age leaving school, age beginning full-time employment, skill level of first Philadelphia occupation, and industry of first Philadelphia job. Because of their zero-order lack of relationships with patterns of employment difficulty, they were excluded from the elaboration.

## Cultural Heritage and Employment Difficulty

Having determined that structures of occupational and industrial opportunity are related to patterns of employment difficulty, I now turn to an examination of the possibility that cultural heritage may also affect patterns of employment difficulty.[8] This involves evaluation of the following hypotheses, which have been derived from assimilationist theory. First, as immigrants gain job experience in this society, their levels of employment difficulty should become progressively more similar to those of native-born workers. In other words, accumulated postmigration job experience results in attenuation of initial immigrant–native differences in employment dif-

[8] The following are indicators of culture or cultural heritage of immigrants. These indicators directly measure time spent outside this society and include character of occupational training and kinds and extent of work experience during the premigration period. They indirectly measure variation in cultural heritage by indicating differences in amounts of influence, experience, or exposure to cultures or systems of information other than those of urban American society: BIRTHPLC (birthplace), APRNTSHP (apprenticeship status), SOCAPRNT (society of apprenticeship), AGEMIGTP (age at migration to Philadelphia), SOCJOB1 (society of first job), YRSINDPP (number of years of industrial work experience before first Philadelphia job), NPPHLJBS (number of jobs held before first Philadelphia job), LPPHLOCC (longest occupation before first Philadelphia job), LPRPHLOC (last occupation before first Philadelphia job), LINDPPHL (longest industry before first Philadelphia job), LPPHLIND (last industry before first Philadelphia job), SOCED (society of education), and FAMPHIL (number of years living in Philadelphia before first Philadelphia job).

ficulty. Second, the more extensive the exposure to and experience in other sociocultural systems, the slower this process of attenuation or assimilation. In other words, the rate of attenuation of differences in patterns of employment difficulty between immigrant and native-born workers varies inversely with the immigrants' nonnative sociocultural experience. Third, immigrants will exhibit greater employment difficulty in situations of declining opportunity than will native-born workers.

In Herrmann's original analysis (1938) of the job mobility of the workers who constitute the machinist subsample, these issues were only tangential to her major research purposes. Although she reported that there was little, if any, relationship between immigrant–native status and job mobility, her treatment of the problem does not exclude the possibility that a relationship did exist. While relationships were reported between immigrant–native status and unemployment, few controls were introduced. Herrmann did present some tantalizing textual material:

> Many of those who were born abroad did not feel that foreign birth was the handicap that some unskilled workers find it. On the contrary many told of the eagerness of shops to secure machinists with foreign training, but there were also cases in which it was evident that less skilled work had to be accepted while the language was being learned [1938, p.67].

However, data presented in the text and appendixes were inadequate for proper evaluation of the hypothesis. Thus, reexamination of the original data was required to determine the extent to which they support the hypothesis that variation in occupational training and experience, and the demand for these in local labor markets, and not cultural heritage per se account for variation in patterns of employment difficulty for native-born and immigrant workers.

Palmer and Stoflet's original analysis of the job mobility of workers who constitute the radio-worker subsample did not address this issue directly either, although almost 3 in 10 workers in the male portion of the sample were foreign-born. Data presented in the text and appendixes did not enable an independent evaluation of the hypotheses, necessitating reexamination of the original data.

As already noted, for the most part, immigrants in the sample had experience in and exposure to educational, apprenticeship, and work structures of the sociocultural systems from which they migrated. For many, work experience before migration to Philadelphia was extensive and included jobs at skilled and semiskilled manual levels in manufacturing sectors in the industrial structures of the societies from which they migrated. A large proportion had begun work before migration, a sizable proportion had served apprenticeships prior to migration, some had been upwardly mobile in terms of occupational skill level, and most continued their careers with a minimal amount of disruption by taking their first postmigration jobs within a short time after their arrival.

However, some immigrants were young, had little or no premigration occupational experience (industrial or otherwise), and were educated and apprenticed and took their first job in this society. For example, about one-third of the immigrants took their first job in this society, about two-fifths had no industrial work experience before coming to Philadelphia, and almost one-fourth migrated to this society at age 15 or younger. I now turn to an examination of the relationships between cultural heritage and employment difficulty and the evaluation of the hypotheses presented at the beginning of this section.

None of the hypotheses derived from assimilationist theory are supported. First, Table 11.8 shows that the foreign-born did not exhibit greater employment difficulty during this period than did native migrants and nonmigrants.

Second, there is no convincing evidence that levels of employment difficulty vary inversely with extent of other sociocultural experience (see Table 11.9). Regardless of the indicator of extent of other sociocultural experience, it is simply not the case that the more experienced exhibit greater postmigration employment difficulty than the less experienced. As often as not, the relationships are in the opposite, contradictory direction.

Birthplace is not significantly related to mobility responses to occupational and industrial opportunity (see Table 11.10). Immigrants do not exhibit greater employment difficulty in situations of declining opportunity than do native migrants and nonmigrants.

If differences in employment difficulty attenuate, then there should be a systematic reduction in both the strength and significance of relationships between birthplace and employment difficulty as the number of years of Philadelphia employment increases. Conversely, the shorter the period of Philadelphia employment, the larger the native–foreign differences in employment difficulty should be. The data in Table 11.11 show that native–foreign differences in employment difficulty are consistently small and generally not statistically significant. Importantly, the sizes of these differences do not systematically decline as the number of years of employment in Philadelphia increases.

The need to reformulate the assimilationist argument to allow for the view that employment difficulty of immigrants during the period varies, not by extent of other sociocultural experience, but by kinds of occupational experience and by local demand for that experience is commended by the analysis conducted so far. It is clear that immigrant employment difficulty during the period varies by skill level of the occupation held at the outset

TABLE 11.8

Employment Difficulty, 1931–1935, by Birthplace

| Indicator of employment difficulty[a] | Birthplace | | | Total (%) | Gamma | p |
| | Philadelphia (and SMSA) (%) | United States (except Philadelphia) (%) | Foreign (%) | | | |
|---|---|---|---|---|---|---|
| NVLM ($\geq$ 1) | 64.3 | 66.9 | 66.1 | 65.3 | .06 | .02[b] |
| TMUN ($\geq$ 19) | 27.3 | 26.8 | 31.1 | 28.5 | .05 | ns[c] |
| LUNE ($\geq$ 7) | 37.2 | 34.0 | 36.0 | 36.3 | .02 | ns |
| LSPJ ($\geq$ 25) | 49.3 | 46.4 | 46.1 | 47.8 | -.05 | ns |
| Number of cases | 513 | 153 | 328 | 994 | --- | --- |

[a]For explanation of indicators, see Table 11.1.

[b]A significance level reported as .00 indicates that the probability of chance occurrence is < .001.

[c]ns = not statistically significant.

TABLE 11.9

Employment Difficulty, 1931--1935, by Indicators of Extent of Other Sociocultural Experience (Immigrants Only)

| Indicator of other socio-cultural experience[a] | Indicators of employment difficulty 1931--1935 | | | | | | | | Number of cases |
| | NVLM (≥ 1) | | TMUN (≥ 19) | | LUNE (≥ 7) | | LSPJ (≥ 25) | | |
| | G[b] | p[c] | G | p | G | p | G | p | |
|---|---|---|---|---|---|---|---|---|---|
| SOCED | -.05 | ns | .06 | ns | .05 | ns | .06 | ns | 319 |
| SOCJOB1 | -.11 | ns | -.06 | ns | -.05 | ns | .09 | ns | 309 |
| SOCAPRNT | .08 | ns | .00 | ns | -.14 | ns | -.08 | ns | 206 |
| APRNTSHP | -.30 | .01 | -.27 | .01 | -.09 | .00 | .15 | ns | 328 |
| AGEMIGTP | -.12 | ns | -.09 | ns | -.08 | ns | -.08 | ns | 330 |
| NPPHLJBS | -.01 | ns | -.06 | ns | -.02 | ns | .03 | ns | 286 |
| YRSINDPP | -.01 | ns | -.02 | ns | .00 | ns | -.01 | ns | 296 |
| LPPHLOCC | -.07 | ns | .00 | ns | -.06 | ns | .09 | ns | 220 |
| LPRPHLOC | -.13 | ns | .01 | ns | -.07 | ns | .04 | ns | 214 |
| LINDPPHL | .03 | ns | .05 | ns | .06 | ns | .09 | ns | 295 |
| LPPHLIND | .04 | ns | .06 | ns | .07 | ns | .08 | ns | 290 |
| FAMPHIL | -.12 | ns | .01 | ns | .05 | ns | .15 | ns | 330 |

[a]For explanation of indicators, see text footnote 8.

[b]G = Gamma, a measure for bivariate associations using ordinal level data.

[c]p = probability of chance occurrence; ns = not statistically significant, that is, probability of chance occurrence > .10.

[d]A negatively signed association indicates that native nonmigrants exhibited greater employment difficulty than immigrants; a positively signed association indicates that immigrants exhibited greater employment difficulty than native nonmigrants.

TABLE 11.10

Employment Difficulty, 1931--1935, by Industrial Opportunity and Occupational Opportunity by Birthplace

| Indicator of employment difficulty[a] | Industrial opportunity | | | Occupational opportunity | | |
|---|---|---|---|---|---|---|
| | Gamma | p | $N$[b] | Gamma | p | $N$[b] |
| NVLM | | | | | | |
| Decreasing | .05[b] | ns | 352 | .08 | .04 | 558 |
| Increasing | .31 | ns | 60 | .17 | ns | 90 |
| TMUN | | | | | | |
| Decreasing | -.01[c] | ns | | .04 | ns | |
| Increasing | .10 | ns | | .02 | ns | |
| LUNE | | | | | | |
| Decreasing | -.05 | ns | | .02 | ns | |
| Increasing | .12 | ns | | .00 | ns | |
| LSPJ | | | | | | |
| Decreasing | .04 | ns | | .00 | ns | |
| Increasing | .18 | ns | | -.18 | ns | |

[a] For explanation of indicators, see Table 11.10.

[b] Number of cases in each column is same as listed in the first two rows of each column.

[c] ns = not statistically significant.

[d] A negatively signed association indicates that native nonmigrants exhibited greater employment difficulty than immigrants; a positively signed association indicates that immigrants exhibited greater employment difficulty than native nonmigrants.

TABLE 11.11

Employment Difficulty, 1931--1935, by Birthplace by Year of First Philadelphia Job[a]

| Indicator of employment difficulty[b] | Year of first Philadelphia job | | | | | | |
|---|---|---|---|---|---|---|---|
| | 1926-1930 | 1921-1925 | 1916-1920 | 1911-1915 | 1905-1910 | 1899-1904 | Before 1899 |
| NVLM | | | | | | | |
| Gamma | .07[c] | .04 | .08 | .04 | .15 | .04 | -.16 |
| p | ns[d] | ns | ns | ns | ns | ns | ns |
| TMUN | | | | | | | |
| Gamma | .06 | -.10 | -.01 | -.06 | .12 | .39 | .07 |
| p | ns | ns | ns | ns | ns | .04 | ns |
| LUNE | | | | | | | |
| Gamma | -.02 | -.09 | .00 | -.18 | .05 | .32 | .11 |
| p | ns | ns | ns | ns | ns | ns | ns |
| LSPJ | | | | | | | |
| Gamma | -.04 | -.02 | .00 | .05 | -.10 | -.11 | -.25 |
| p | ns | ns | ns | ns | ns | ns | ns |
| Philadelphia born (N) | 90 | 71 | 56 | 70 | 75 | 69 | 81 |
| Foreign born (N) | 43 | 70 | 40 | 57 | 56 | 38 | 24 |

[a]Philadelphia born (native nonmigrants) and immigrants are the two groups compared. Native migrants are not included in the comparison because of the small number of cases in several of the "year of first Philadelphia job" categories.

[b]For explanation of indicators, see Table 11.1.

[c]A negatively signed association indicates that native nonmigrants exhibited greater employment difficulty; a positively signed association indicates that immigrants exhibited greater employment-difficulty.

[d]ns = not statistically significant.

of the period, industry in which the worker was employed at the outset of the period, and occupational and industrial opportunity. There is little, if any, convincing evidence that cultural heritage has an independent effect on levels of employment difficulty or that immigrants exhibit greater employment difficulty than native migrants and nonmigrants that can be attributed to cultural heritage.

This failure to find differences in levels of employment difficulty between immigrant and native workers may be partially attributable to the characteristics of the sample. As noted earlier, this sample represents only two industries in which skilled and semiskilled manual occupations predominate. Perhaps one might not expect to find large differences when occupational skill level is held constant. Yet, this is precisely a major point of my theory. That is, once skill level effects are controlled, purported immigrant–native differences in levels of employment difficulty, often attributed to cultural heritage effects, disappear as predicted.

It may be the case that a sample more representative of major industries and occupational skill levels would have shown a stratification of groups across the local labor markets and hence across industries and occupational skill levels. But again, if this were the case, my hypothesis would nevertheless be consistent with the facts. For if one were to assume that such a sample would show greater immigrant employment difficulty, my theory would attribute it to concentration of some immigrant groups in industries and occupations characterized by declining or unstable opportunity. Furthermore, these concentrations would be due not to cultural heritage per se, but to premigration occupational experience and skill levels and the opportunities in local postmigration job markets for workers exhibiting these skills and experience.

## Discussion and Conclusions

Obtaining a job and keeping it are central problems that must be confronted by a large proportion of the adults in industrial society, and immigrants are certainly no exception. The findings presented here indicate that culturally based work behaviors did not manifest themselves in differentially greater employment difficulty among immigrants. Either the cultural basis of work behavior has been exaggerated in the literature or immigrants rapidly abandoned culturally based work behaviors that jeopardized their chances of successfully finding and keeping jobs.

Nevertheless, variations in cultural heritage may well be related to other kinds of work behavior not examined in this research or to a wide variety of other forms of social behavior. In other realms of social life, particularly those less central to survival, greater variation in social behavior may be tolerated, accepted, or even encouraged. In these areas of social life, such as gestural styles, familial sex roles involving power relations and task allocation, food styles, dress styles, leisure time activities, and religious activity, to suggest but a few possibilities, cultural heritage effects may be substantial and may attenuate in the manner suggested by assimilationist theory.

I have not argued that immigrants do not bring a cultural heritage with them. To the contrary, I would argue strongly that they do. Nevertheless, I conclude that it is not variations in these transported cultural heritages that account for variation in patterns of employment difficulty. These findings are consistent with research that indicates that immigrants were not only culturally heterogeneous, but also were heterogeneous in terms of occupational and industrial skills and experience. I suggest that variations in these factors, together with intercity and interregional differences in occupational and industrial opportunity structures, account for most of the variation in immigrant employment difficulty.

I am convinced that this is a more elegant, parsimonious, and general explanation than those relying on the notion of cultural heritage and that it can account for a wide variety of facts that the cultural heritage orientation either cannot explain or can explain only with great difficulty. This explanation accounts for intercity variation in the representation of particular immigrant groups as well as intercity variation in occupational concentrations of particular immigrant groups.

Assimilationist theory, although not uncritically accepted, remains a widely held orientation. I certainly do not claim that these findings are a critical and definitive contradiction of assimilationist theory, for no one piece of research could be. However, this research does cast considerable doubt on two of assimilation theory's underlying assumptions and its central thesis: that there are important immigrant–native differences in major forms of social behavior, that these differences attenuate, and that the rate of this attenuation varies inversely with the extent of other sociocultural experience. The findings of this research suggest a critical and systematic reexamination of the premises of assimilationist theory.

My findings that occupational skill level is associated with patterns of employment difficulty suggest that job competition is not as undifferentiated, nor are job skills as transferable among occupational skill levels and industries, as neoclassical theory suggests. These findings offer some support to the Balkanization theory of Kerr (1954) as well as to the more contemporary theories of labor market and industrial segmentation. Unfortunately, the work histories and census data did not include information necessary to evaluate these theories.

Finally, these findings contradict several commonly held notions about postmigration job experiences and opportunities of immigrants relative to those of native migrants and nonmigrants. Immigrants were not a homogeneous group in terms of occupational skills and experience, even within specific nationality groups. They certainly did not all start at the bottom of the occupational hierarchy, regardless of occupational skill. Most immigrants in this sample who had skilled manual occupations before leaving Europe obtained their first jobs here at the skilled manual level. Additionally, many immigrants whose last and/or longest premigration occupations had been semiskilled obtained their first jobs here at skilled manual occupations. In short, immigrants in this sample did not appear to have been systematically denied the "better" job opportunities. As a result, immigrant job experiences, at least in terms of patterns of employment difficulty, did not appear to be significantly different from those of native migrants and nonmigrants, even during the Great Depression.

## References

Banfield, E. C.
  1958   *The Moral Basis of a Backward Society*. Glencoe: Free Press.
  1970   *The Unheavenly City: The Nature and Future of Our Urban Crisis*. Boston: Little, Brown.
Burton, J. F., and J. E. Parker
  1969   "Inter-industry variations in voluntary labor mobility." *Industrial and Labor Relations Review* 22 (January):199–216.
Glazer, N., and D. P. Moynihan
  1963   *Beyond the Melting Pot*. Cambridge, Massachusetts: MIT Press and Harvard Univ. Press.
Gordon, M. M.
  1964   *Assimilation in American Life: The Role of Race, Religion and Natural Origins*. London and New York: Oxford Univ. Press.
Gutman, H. C.
  1977   *Work, Culture, and Society in Industrializing America: Essays in American Working-Class and Social History*. New York: Vintage.
Handlin, O.
  1957   *Race and Nationality in American Life*. Boston: Little, Brown.
  1973   *The Uprooted* (2nd ed.). Boston: Little, Brown.
Herrmann, H.
  1938   *Ten Years of Work Experience of Philadelphia Machinists*. Philadelphia: WPA National Research Project and Industrial Research Department, University of Pennsylvania.
Kerr, C.
  1954   "The Balkanization of labor markets." In E. W. Bakke *et al.*, (eds.), *Labor Mobility and Economic Opportunity*. New York: Wiley.
Lewis, O.
  1966   "The culture of poverty." *Scientific American* 215(4):19–25.

Miller, D. C., and W. H. Form
   1964   *Industrial Sociology: The Sociology of Work Organizations* (2nd ed.). New York: Harper.
Miller, R. K.
   1978   *Job Mobility and Employment Difficulty: Social Structural and Cultural Heritage Bases.* Unpublished doctoral dissertation, Department of Sociology, Temple University.
   1979   *Postmigration Employment Difficulty among European Immigrants: A Test of Assimilationist Theory.* Paper presented at the Forty-ninth Annual Meeting of the Eastern Sociological Society, New York City.
Moynihan, D. P.
   1965   *The Negro Family: The Case for National Action.* Washington, D.C.: US Govt Printing Office.
Palmer, G. L.
   1954   *Labor Mobility in Six Cities: A Report on the Survey of Patterns and Factors in Labor Mobility, 1940–1950.* New York: Social Science Research Council.
   1960   "Contrasts in labor market behavior in northern Europe and the United States." *Industrial and Labor Relations Review* 13:519–532.
   1962   *The Reluctant Job Changer: Studies in Work Attachments and Aspirations.* Philadelphia: Univ. of Pennsylvania Press.
Palmer, G. L., and A. M. Stoflet
   1938   *The Labor Force of the Philadelphia Radio Industry in 1936.* Philadelphia: WPA National Research Project and Industrial Research Department, University of Pennsylvania.
Park, R. E.
   1950   *Race and Culture.* Glencoe: Free Press.
Parnes, H. S.
   1968   "Labor force: Markets and mobility." In D. L. Sills (ed.), *Encyclopedia of the Social Sciences.* New York: Cromwell-Collier.
Schooler, C.
   1976   "Serfdom's legacy: An ethnic continuum." *American Journal of Sociology* 81:1265–1286.
Swerdloff, S., and A. Bluestone
   1952   "The mobility of tool and die makers." *Monthly Labor Review* 75:605–610.
U. S. Bureau of the Census
   1890–   *Censuses of the United States Population, (Occupations) and Manufactures.* Wash-
   1940   ington, D.C.: US Govt Printing Office.
U. S. Senate
   1911   *United States Immigration Commission Reports.* (Dillingham Commission Reports, 42 volumes.) Washington, D.C.: US Govt Printing Office.
Ward, D.
   1971   *Cities and Immigrants: A Geography of Change in Nineteenth Century America.* London and New York: Oxford Univ. Press.
Welch, E. H.
   1933   *Employment Trends in Philadelphia.* Philadelphia: Univ. of Pennsylvania Press.

# Part V

# ALTERNATIVES TO HUMAN CAPITAL AND STATUS ATTAINMENT RESEARCH MODELS: TWO VIEWS

# Chapter 12

# Sociological Views of

# Labor Markets:

# Some Missed

# Opportunities and

# Neglected Directions

*TERESA A. SULLIVAN*

Even a cursory glance at recent sociology journals and monographs shows the resurgence of sociologists' interests in labor markets.[1] An emphasis on economic structure distinguishes this new work from older research themes in industrial sociology or occupations and professions. The substantive impetus for the studies has often been labor market segmentation theory; secondary analysis of large data sets has usually provided the empirical base.

New or hybrid subfields tend to grow in lopsided, irregular patterns, and the sociology of labor markets is no exception.[2] Many of the authors in this area see themselves in a conscious dialogue with students of status attainment and human capital formulations. (Granovetter juxtaposes these research traditions in his chapter in this volume. See also Beck, Horan, & Tolbert, 1978; Bibb & Form, 1977; Horan, 1978; Stolzenberg, 1975.)[3] This

---

[1] Volume 85 (1979–1980) of the *American Journal of Sociology* carried 16 articles on topics related to labor force or labor market, compared with 5 in Volume 80 (1974–1975). For the *American Sociological Review*, the comparable numbers were 10 in Volume 44 (1979) and 7 in Volume 37 (1974).

[2] Fields may become "hot" and attract talented researchers as a result of new discoveries or ideas; "cold" fields tend to lose researchers (Merton, 1973, p. 331).

[3] Arguably, however, the findings are not inconsistent with human capital theory (Kalleberg & Sørenson, 1979, pp.363–364).

SOCIOLOGICAL PERSPECTIVES ON
LABOR MARKETS

dialogue tends to dictate the research agenda. For example, despite the explicit choice of independent variables that reflect aspects of economic structure, dependent variables concentrate on such individual-level attributes as annual earnings (Beck, *et al.*, 1978; Stolzenberg, 1975; Talbert & Bose, 1977). Moreover, secondary analysis of large data sets poses its own constraints. The terms of the dialogue suggest the need to reanalyze data sets previously used in status attainment or human capital studies. But these data sets rarely contain the variables needed for convincing tests of labor market segmentation (see Edwards, 1975, p.18; Harrison & Sum, 1979; Piore, 1975, p.125).

These constraints have not prevented a flow of interesting and stimulating literature.[4] Nevertheless, the potential contribution of sociologists to labor market studies is much larger. The continued development of a sociology of labor markets requires a broad intellectual base that reflects dialogue with a variety of intellectual predecessors and that sets an affirmative, not a reactive, research agenda. From these dialogues, sociologists can construct a more comprehensive and coherent theory of labor markets. This is obviously an ambitious undertaking. This chapter undertakes to do no more than to sketch three potential lines of development: (*a*) a sharper articulation of the concepts used in defining economic structure; (*b*) a broader set of hypothesized consequences of labor market segmentation; and (*c*) anomalies and contradictions that require explanation in any broader theory.

## Market Differentiation—An Exegesis

Social scientists have a long history of approaching market structure in terms of differentiation.[5] The most elementary differentiation was that of market production from nonmarket production. As market production became organized into firms, this distinction implied two others. The first was the separation of commodity markets, in which goods and services were bought and sold, from labor markets, in which employment contracts and wages were exchanged for workers' time and skills. A further distinction could be made between the economically active population, or the labor force, and the economically inactive population.[6]

---

[4] For recent reviews of the literature by sociologists, see Kalleberg and Sørenson (1979) and Wilson (1978, pp.96 ff.).

[5] For a capsule description of some of the concepts discussed within this section, see Edwards, Reich, and Gordon (1975).

[6] On the development of the labor force concept, see Hauser (1949).

In economically less developed countries, it became common to divide both the commodity markets and the labor markets into "modern" and "traditional" sectors (see Form, 1979, pp.8–10). The distinction is based partly on organization and partly on technology. The modern sector tends to use the advanced technology and to be part of (or to imitate) the organizational structure of producers in the advanced economies. It is not necessarily the case that all parts of the modern sector are integrated into a world capitalist economy—for example, in some socialist states, modern-sector industries are state owned. Nor is the commodity market for the modern sector necessarily integrated into a world economy. However, the products of the modern sector are often, although not inevitably, produced for export, and the producer goods bought by the modern sector are often imported. Frequently, demand in the local consumer market is very limited.

The traditional sector tends to produce consumer goods and services on a small scale, usually with traditional technologies and many producers. Except for craft items, which might be exported, most production is for a local commodity market with many consumers, each of whom buys very little.

The modern and traditional commodity markets correspond to a similar division in the labor market. Because the modern sector is more likely to be capital-intensive, the modern-sector labor force is likely to remain relatively small. Workers in the modern sector tend to be better educated, somewhat younger, and more urbanized than their counterparts in the traditional sector. Both sectors of the labor market may be integrated into a wider world labor market. The geographic mobility of workers, like the destination of commodities, may be partly analyzed in terms of the export–import analogy. Well-trained and educated workers, instead of remaining in the developing economy, may join a "brain drain" to a developed country. Similarly, managers and technicians may move to a developing country to supervise production. For workers in the traditional labor market, opportunities are more limited, although some receiving countries admit unskilled workers, at least on a temporary basis (see Buroway, 1976; Castells, 1975; Piore, 1979).

The description of modern and traditional sectors in developing countries has its counterpart in the distinction of primary from secondary sectors in advanced economies. The production of a commodity or service in the primary sector is characterized by relatively few, large-scale producers and by considerable insulation from market forces in both the commodity and the labor markets. The secondary sector is more likely to have many small-scale producers who are vulnerable to business cycle fluctuations and whose commodity markets are limited in terms of competition, geographic extent, and possibly the perishability of the product (Edwards, 1975, p.47). Primary-sector industries may have a near-oligopoly as well as an oligopsony. In the secondary sector, as in the traditional sector of developing countries, producers are likely to rely on numerous buyers.

The labor market in advanced economies can similarly be partitioned into primary and secondary sectors.[7] Primary and secondary workers can be distinguished on the basis of personal attributes (sex, race, age, educational attainment), and also on the basis of work career, but there is no one-to-one correspondence between primary workers and incumbents of jobs in the primary sector (Gordon, 1972, pp.51–52). Some analysts would even argue that no designation of primary workers is possible apart from their jobs, whereas others (Sullivan, 1978a, pp.20–21) would argue that there are plausible grounds for an a priori probabilistic differentiation.

## Market Concepts—A Critique

Many of the concepts just outlined are so familiar that they are used unreflectively. Unfortunately, this series of dichotomous concepts may mislead researchers in two important ways. First, a false or premature closure of categories may distract attention from significant work phenomena whose analysis could importantly modify current theory. Second, false isomorphisms may be assumed and false analogies drawn between work situations that vary in important ways.

### Market versus Nonmarket Production

Consider first the categories market and nonmarket production. Most historical treatments have regarded the development of markets as a historical *process;* in some cases, it is assumed to be an inevitable process. It is tempting to the researcher, who is faced with the problem of coding data, to neglect the processual aspects of market development and so to freeze the two categories. It is even more tempting to assume that more and more economic activities will be drawn into the market economy and not to look for reversals. It is, however, in studying the occasional reversals as well as the process of broadening markets that we can learn most about the dynamics of the market.

---

[7] "Primary" workers here are not to be understood in the older sense of being the principal wage earner in the household.

A few examples will suffice. There is a renewed interest in the extent and value of nonmarket work, especially do-it-yourself or self-sufficiency projects (see Burns, 1975, pp.12–29). Sociologists, if they have been aware of this trend at all, have viewed it as a form of leisure activity. Sociologists of the labor market might also view it, with equal logic, as decreased demand for certain skills in paid market work and a return to nonmarket production. A related issue is the growth of barter. Barter usually functions in an ad hoc manner among kin groups and neighbors. In some areas, workers willing to barter are organized into formal exchanges, which function much like labor markets but without contracts or wages; time and skills are exchanged directly. Although it would require ingenuity in research designs and methods, a careful study of a barter exchange could tell us much about what is or is not essential to the functioning of labor markets. Other fuzzy areas between market and nonmarket production are occupied by consumer cooperatives, talented small-scale hobbyists, and some family enterprises.

A second set of examples consists of nonmarket activities that are moving into the market. Although this may be relatively more common in developing countries, it also occurs in advanced economies. An important group of such activities is household services. In some activities, such as housecleaning, the work is being rationalized and reorganized by cleaning teams equipped with the tools and chemicals of industrial cleaners. Each team makes a number of house calls every day. In other activities, such as day care of children or the elderly, errand services, specialized catering, and carry-out foods, the work place has moved from the household. These services, usually small scale but often encountering only nonmarket competition, provide a new outlet for entrepreneurship. On the surface, these new jobs may appear to be secondary or dead end. But merely to label them so is to overlook what is intrinsically most interesting about them.

In advanced economies, both kinds of examples given are sensitive to the business cycle. Just as a recession will differentially benefit some parts of the commodity market (e.g., used goods and repair services), it may also result in more nonmarket production. Many new services appear in the market only in times of prosperity.[8]

If such nonmarket production could be considered variable, there is also a relatively fixed "shadow market" between market and nonmarket production. This area consists of illicit goods and services, and the workers who provide them, as well as licit but unreported exchanges. Although this

---

[8] To be sure, many new services have resulted from increased female labor force participation rates.

shadow market is not reported in the usual data sources, many observers believe that it is an important arena of economic activity. I have referred to it as "relatively fixed" because it exists regardless of the business cycle, but many believe that this underground economy is growing.

Illicit goods include those whose possession is prohibited or limited by some requirement other than offering the sale price. Some firearms, most narcotics, syringes, pelts of endangered species, some archeological treasures, and stolen goods are obvious examples. Goods that are legal in one context may be illegal in another—for example, homemade alcoholic beverages and bootlegged cigarettes. Workers in illicit industries—drugs, gambling, prostitution, organized and street crime—may or may not participate simultaneously in the licit labor market. "Scuffling" or hustling constitutes a kind of entrepreneurship in the shadow labor market. Also in the gray area—although not illegal—are unreported cash transactions, such as those from the innocuous garage sale. Such exchanges have their unique occupations in the form of small liquidators and brokers.

Unlike nonmarket production, the shadow market is monetized, although most transactions are cash only. However, unlike the usual market production, the shadow market goes undetected in the conventional social science data sets. Workers in the shadow market are unlikely to give accurate reports of their occupation, industry, or even labor force status, let alone income.

Although almost by definition we do not know the magnitude of nonmarket production or of the shadow economy, these examples suggest that our approach to market activity may be too severely limited by our reliance on conventional data and concepts. The market–nonmarket concepts have fuzzy edges, as do many of the other commonly used concepts.

### Commodity versus Labor Markets

The conventional distinction between markets for goods and services and labor markets can mislead in two ways: (a) it assumes an employer–employee relationship; and (b) it misses much in the transformation of an economy from goods to service production.[9]

Most workers participate simultaneously in both markets. As employees, they earn wages within the labor market context. As consumers, they spend their wages for goods and services within the commodity market. They are buyers of goods and sellers of labor.[10] But not all workers function in this

[9] On the transformation of the economy, see Singelmann and Browning (1978).

[10] The classic discussion of this case lies in Marx's description of commodities and money and of the expropriation of small farmers from the land (Marx, 1887/1967, especially Vol. 1, Pts. I and VIII).

way: The self-employed are buyers and sellers of goods and possibly buyers of labor.[11] Industries that are dominated by small-scale entrepreneurs or family-run businesses participate in the labor market in a limited way, and workers in these industries really must be considered in relation to their ownership of the means of production.

The development of a service sector, and the growth of the service occupations, amplifies this point. Service workers in self-owned or very small enterprises simultaneously sell their labor (in the labor market) and their service (in the commodity market). The services rendered and the characteristics of the workers cannot be distinguished. To some extent, then, analysts cannot study the labor market without also considering the commodity market.

## In or Out of the Labor Force

The commonly used definition of the labor force avoids some of these pitfalls by specifying a minimum number of hours that must be worked by unpaid family workers and by including those who work for profit as well as for pay (U.S. Bureau of the Census, 1976, pp.3–4). It is customary to assume that the persons in the labor force are those in the labor market.

Once again the dichotomy has fuzzy edges. Leaving aside the question of whether housewives or volunteer workers should be considered part of the labor force, [12] or whether students and the military should be excluded, the most vexing issue has been whether to include discouraged workers as labor force members (National Commission, 1979, pp.43–53; see also Finegan, 1978).[13] Discouraged workers are those who, for one reason or another, have given up the search for employment. By definition they are able and available to work, but behaviorally they have withdrawn from the labor market, at least as we now measure it.

It is customary to divide the labor force further into the employed and the unemployed. For a number of years, in both developing and advanced economies, the argument has been made that the employed category lumps together too many workers, masking a variety of inadequate employment

[11] We set aside for the time being the function of corporate actors in the labor market; corporate actors are certainly buyers and sellers in the commodity market and because of their relative size usually command more market power than the individual buyer–seller. This implies a stratification in the commodity market that has important similarities to that in the labor market (see the discussion later in the chapter).

[12] This change was considered and rejected by the National Commission on Employment and Unemployment Statistics.

[13] Over the dissent of four commissioners, the National Commission on Employment and Unemployment Statistics recommended that discouraged workers not be counted in the labor force.

situations (Clogg, 1979; Sullivan, 1978a). The symptoms of this underemployment are generally recognized to be multidimensional, and a worker may be affected by one or all of them. Concern with the underemployed is obviously closely allied to the interest in secondary labor markets.

## Primary and Secondary Markets

Because both commodity and labor markets diverge from the model of perfect competition, the concept of market segmentation has provided insight and understanding. Market segments are relatively homogeneous in the degree of insulation they provide from competitive forces. To a much lesser extent, depending on the elasticity of demand for the product or service, the primary sector is also buffered against the business cycle. The number of segments hypothesized has varied from two or three to an indefinite many,[14] depending on the theory or research method of the researcher. Knowing the actual number is perhaps less important than understanding the processes by which segmentation occurs. Sociologists have occasionally been negligent in this latter task, assuming that their job is done when the data analysis confirms a finite number of segments. The story that is waiting to be told is how and why market segments emerge. In developing countries, the issue might be phrased in terms of the mechanisms creating the modern and the traditional sectors.

The literature contains a number of hints about the origins of primary sectors in commodity markets. The primary sector or sectors have the highest degree of insulation from competition. The insulation is hypothesized to come about in several ways.

1. The creation or conferral of a monopoly. State-owned industries, "natural monopolies," and other monopolies, when appropriately licensed, are the major examples. Most government agencies also fall into this category.
2. Innovation in an economy that cannot generate competition. This is a variation of the monopoly. However, whereas the monopoly usually enjoys at least tacit government approval, the innovator-industry need not. The most familiar example is the industry that establishes itself in the modern sector in a less developed economy by introducing new capital, new organization, and new techniques. The motive for the innovator may be an improved competitive position in the advanced economies. The controversial issue is whether this investment induces

---

[14] For a two-sector argument, see Tolbert, Horan, and Beck (1980). For three sectors, see Hodson (1978) and O'Connor (1973). For an analysis of multiple segments, see Freedman (1976).

local development or merely local dependence on the advanced countries.[15]

3. The evolution of an oligopoly. In certain key industries,[16] especially those marked by a high degree of technology and need for capital, only large firms are efficient enough to survive. Economies of scale, especially in capital-intensive industries, may provide the initial impetus to oligopolistic competition. Continued survival depends on further insulating the firm from market shocks—unreliable suppliers, shaky product demand, scarce capital, and labor turnover.

The secondary sector, by contrast, is vulnerable to competitive pressures and fluctuates with the business cycle. Primary-sector firms may subcontract extra work to the secondary sector during peak periods; thus, part of the secondary sector serves as an overflow production mechanism. In recessions, the impact on the secondary sector is correspondingly severe (Doeringer & Piore, 1971).

Segmented production structure is significant for the labor market, because it implies a corresponding segmentation of the structure of labor demand. Insulation against market pressures includes recruiting high-quality workers and minimizing labor turnover. Research on internal labor markets—career ladders within a single economic organization—has dealt with this mechanism for recruiting and retaining workers in the primary sector.

But labor markets are also hypothesized to be segmented on the supply side (see, e.g., Kerr, 1954; Stinchcombe, 1979; Stolzenberg, 1975). Craft union membership, occupational licensing, and professional certification constitute a first level of insulation from market pressures and a segmentation of labor supply by occupation. A second level of occupational insulation comes from specialized training and previous work experience. Entrepreneurs are an interesting and neglected case. Especially in service industries, they could be said to create their own labor demand by creating a product or service demand. (See my earlier discussion of the commodity–labor market distinction.) The secondary workers, then, are those without certified skills (including entrepreneurial skills). From this perspective, the secondary labor market can be defined in reference both to the structure of demand and to the structure of supply. The protected position of the primary worker can be explained by the partially competing and partially complementary mechanisms of the internal labor market and of employee associations and unions. But the two sets of explanations deserve further comparison and research.

---

[15] A discussion of the dependency argument may be found in Szentes (1976).
[16] Key industries are defined in Averitt (1968).

Labor market regulations deserve investigation as a source of segmentation that affects both demand and supply. These include legal protection of groups of workers. For example, United States age discrimination legislation now constitutes additional insulation against job loss for workers between the ages of 50 and 70. Affirmative action requirements or quotas both in the United States and in some developing countries (e.g., Malaysia) can insulate some ethnic, religious, or racial groups from full market competition. Immigration regulations and guest worker provisions can intensify competition with native-born workers in some parts of the labor market while eliminating it in others. Legislation that is ostensibly benevolent, such as protection codes for women and youths, may create more intense competition. And it is not always possible to predict beforehand what the consequences of legislation will be: Witness the continuing debate over the minimum wage and the growing new debate over the differential minimum wage.

These considerations form partly competing and partly complementary explanations of the secondary labor market. It soon becomes clear that the secondary labor market is best defined by the *via negativa*, for it contains so many heterogeneous work situations. Workers as disparate as the owners of small retail establishments and the occasional day laborer can be counted as secondary workers. As with the dichotomous concepts discussed earlier, many fruitful investigations are waiting to be conducted around the edges of our concepts.

## False Isomorphisms and Analogies

The significance of these conceptual distinctions can be dealt with on two levels. Empirically, their significance can be estimated. Theoretically, they can caution the researcher who seeks broader application of results. It is tempting to allow incomplete conceptualization to become the forerunner of misleading generalizations. For example, it is convenient to use surveys of the labor force to make inferences about the structure of jobs. This must be done with care, for some members of the labor force have more than one job and others (the unemployed) have none. The self-employed literally create their own jobs; several part-time workers may share a single full-time job. Some jobs are vacant.

A second pitfall is assuming that similar structures are identical. This is an obvious danger in comparing the segmentation of production with the segmentation of labor. For example, the relationship between primary jobs and primary workers may be simply tautologous in one study and the source of important, competing alternative explanations in another.

A third danger lies in assuming that concepts and findings in one context are or are not easily translated to a different context. It is probably as false to assert that underemployment does not exist in advanced economies as to assert that it is a function only of advanced capitalism. Although we have been warned about the exportability of the labor force concept (Moore, 1953), few inquiries have been made about the possible importability of the concepts of economic dependency, peripheral development, marginalization, and the informal urban sector.

There are obvious parallels between the modern and traditional sectors of developing countries and the primary and secondary sectors of advanced countries, but the relations between the two are problematic. Does the export of industrial jobs from the United States to Mexico expand Mexico's modern sector while contracting our primary sector? Does it at the same time induce immigration of traditional Mexican workers and expand our secondary market?[17] Or does it create new primary jobs for U.S. workers to coordinate and report on international operations? Does Mexico's modern sector serve the same functions as the United States's primary sector, or does it merely induce the export of profits to capitalize non-Mexican firms and the export of wages to buy imported consumer goods? Theoretical inquiries into the international labor market are an important area for labor market sociologists, but the assumptions of the inquiries must be carefully scrutinized. We know far too little about the criteria for importing or exporting concepts (see Form, 1979, p.3); it is in itself an area that deserves reflection.

## Hypothesized Consequences of Segmented Markets

While the conceptual background of market segmentation theory offers fruitful research grounds to sociologists, the theory in its current articulation suggests a variety of additional studies. One strategy for these studies is to move away from the usual dependent variables (e.g., annual earnings, career mobility) to consider the additional consequences of segmentation.

### The Mechanics of Market Insulation

Stability of market segments is an obvious issue to consider. Firms in the primary sector will want to maintain or improve their competitive positions. Sociologists of the labor market have been principally interested in the internal labor market,[18] with its differentiated entry ports and career ladders,

---

[17] Portes (1979) argues that Mexican illegal immigration comes from "groups already modernized, already living in cities and having above-average education [p.432]."

[18] An important discussion of internal labor markets as a device for inducing stability is given in Stone (1975).

as a technique for assuring a stable and well-trained work force—certainly a factor in maintaining a stable competitive position.

An additional mechanism that deserves more sociological attention is the job equity workers establish in primary-sector firms. The most common form of equity is the pension plan, but profit-sharing, stock options, and lucrative fringe benefits may also make leaving a firm a substantial hardship (see Stone, 1975). This is particularly true if benefits are not vested. Job security is one of the principal attractions of the primary-sector job; the reverse side of this coin is the greater cost of losing the primary-sector job. Compared with a secondary job, which is often merely an exchange of wages for 8 hours' work, the primary-sector job can buy into a worker's health, home, family's education, and plans for retirement and leisure. A worker's investment in a primary-sector firm may thus go well beyond the inducements of a steady job and a chance for promotion.

It is also important to note, however, the limited nature of the firm's investment. It extends to the worker and only derivatively to the worker's family. The worker can leave to his or her family only money and what money will buy. The firm accepts no responsibility for the worker's children; the child of the corporation president, as a rule, can no longer inherit his parent's position. Every member of top management, almost by definition, is a self-made man or woman.

Besides these rather obvious consequences in the labor market, maintaining a competitive edge involves strategies with less obvious consequences for the labor market. One of these is vertical or horizontal integration and the sharing of resources across several subsidiaries. Integrated firms may be able to assure more reliable supply and shipping; conglomerates may be better able to withstand shifts in consumer demand or the business cycle. The labor market effects of these organizational shifts may be difficult to discern, in part because the firm, occupation, or industry are inappropriate units of analysis.[19] But several kinds of consequences could be envisioned: the export of jobs to an international subsidiary; lateral career movement between subsidiaries; or more centralized decision making on appointments and promotions. All these areas would contribute substantially to our understanding of the effects of segmentation.

## The Structure of Demand

In the development of labor market segmentation theory, authors have stressed the desire of the firm for a stable work force and of the worker

[19] For an argument for the importance of employer size, see Stolzenberg (1978); for an argument about the importance of new organizational forms, see Cornfield and Sullivan (1979).

for a stable job. This suggests a kind of queue of both employers and workers, in which the most preferred worker takes the most preferred job. A great deal of work has been done on workers' standing in the queue,[20] or in queues within segments, but we have spent far less time examining the origin and maintenance of the employers' queue. One aspect of the structure of labor demand is the stratification of employers.

To oversimplify, there are two kinds of employers—corporate actors and natural persons (Coleman, 1974)—and these have very different characteristics in terms of their ability to provide job security. Corporations are legally immortal, although they may fail financially or become part of larger corporations. Natural persons may die, get sick, or retire, as well as go bankrupt. On this basis alone, we might expect corporate actors to go to the head of the queue in labor recruitment. Naturally, corporate actors can be distinguished again in terms of elasticity of product demand, profitability, employment policies, and so on. But the fact remains: Working for a corporation is, on its face, more secure than working for an individual person.[21]

Individual employers may also be internally stratified in terms of their personal and financial assets. In general, job security correlates with the size and stability of the employer's business.

Some employers may be able to offer only 1 day's work a week. A good example would be the person who can afford 1 day of paid housework every week. The housekeeper who wishes to work full time must then find five such employers. Is this an example of five employers or of five consumers? The housekeeper could also be considered a self-employed entrepreneur with five customers. This example suggests that fragmented labor demand is at the very bottom of the employment queue (although self-employment is probably not).

The empirical question then lies in assessing the rank-order correlation between worker queues and employer queues. We would expect the employers who are natural persons to employ disproportionate numbers of minority, female, or uneducated workers; in cases of fragmented labor demand, the workers are even more likely to display these characteristics.

How does the volume of labor demand shift within the employer queue? Although it is difficult to be sure, the existence of a large, gainfully employed illegal alien population in the United States argues for unmet demand at the lower end of the employer queue. It is not just an issue of who does

---

[20] On racial queues, see Hodge (1973).

[21] Two intermediate organizational forms should be noted. The *corporation sole*, which is almost obsolete, is an employer as the incumbent of a position; at his death, another person takes the position. Employment by the corporation sole is thus more likely to be unstable. The other is the partnership, which may be easily dissolved and reformed, with subsequent loss of positions.

the dirty work—all primary industries have some dirty work to be done—but rather of how the dirty work is organized or packaged into discrete jobs.

## Anomalies and Contradictions

Running like a thread through this discussion are several phenomena that do not fit neatly into the idea of labor market segmentation. One is entrepreneurship, an anomaly that is especially tantalizing because of its significance in business ideology. Labor market segmentation theory seems to leave little room for the positive values of risk taking. Yet the persistence of entrepreneurship and self-employment, which is especially striking in some racial–ethnic groups, surely deserves more attention.[22] This is true a fortiori when entrepreneurship spawns an ethnic enclave that has characteristics of both primary and secondary markets (see Wilson & Portes, 1980).

A second anomaly is the crosscutting effect of some structural aspects of segmentation, such as occupation and industry. The classification of services is an example. The service sector in advanced economies is growing rapidly, yet its role in segmentation is protean. Service industries are likely to have local markets, because services cannot be stockpiled or shipped, and where services are licensed, they often cannot be offered outside a given geographic jurisdiction. Yet service workers may be easily integrated into firms of all types, and monopolies on services (e.g., telephones) are prototype primary-sector firms.

Legal services are a good example. Lawyers are licensed, but the license is geographically limited. Occupationally, lawyers are buffered from competition, but to look at them only in terms of their occupational labor market, apart from their industry and firm location, is to misunderstand the circumstances of their economic competition. As part of their vertical integration, most large corporations have house counsel. But they also are likely to retain a large corporate law firm, which is itself a corporate employer. The services of the large law firm may approach the position of producer goods in the commodity market, in the sense that relatively few buyers demand the service and very few individual buyers could afford it. There is also a variety of medium and small law firms and a goodly number of solo practitioners (many of whom are also small-scale employers). The difficulty for the sociologist is not only the specification of the structural

---

[22] Some of these "ethnic niches" are discussed in Bonacich (1972), Loewen (1971), and Sullivan (1978b).

attributes of a labor market but also the confluence of attributes that may modify the formulation of segmentation theory. Obviously, a single classification of law as an occupation or of legal services as an industry is likely to mislead.

## Conclusion

Labor markets were once considered the unique province of economists. Sociologists, who stressed the importance of social organization and stratification, have contributed much to the understanding of the market. Recent work in labor market segmentation theory has been especially helpful. This chapter sketches a few areas of missed opportunities and neglected directions, no doubt missing and neglecting a few on the way. For the sociology of labor markets to remain fruitful, it will need to undertake a vigorous research program that encompasses all forms of economic activity and retains an open mind about the significance of economic organizations of all types.

## References

Averitt, R. T.
   1968   *The Dual Economy: The Dynamics of American Industry Structure.* New York: Norton.
Beck, E. M., P. M. Horan, and C. M. Tolbert II
   1978   "Stratification in a dual economy: A sectoral model of earnings determination."
         *American Sociological Review* 43(October):704–720.
Bibb, R., and W. H. Form
   1977   "The effects of industrial, occupational, and sex stratification on wages in blue-collar
         markets." *Social Forces* 55(June):974–996.
Bonacich, E.
   1972   "A theory of middleman minorities." *American Sociological Review* 38(October):583–594.
Burns, S.
   1975   *Home, Inc.* Garden City, New Jersey: Doubleday.
Buroway, M.
   1976   "The functions and reproduction of migrant labor: Comparative material from South-
         ern Africa and the United States." *American Journal of Sociology* 81(March):1050–1087.
Castells, M.
   1975   "Immigrant workers and class struggle in advanced capitalism: The Western European
         experience." *Politics and Society* 5(1):33–66.
Clogg, C. C.
   1979   *Measuring Underemployment.* New York: Academic Press.
Coleman, J. S.
   1974   *Power and the Structure of Society.* New York: Norton.
Cornfield, D., and T. A. Sullivan
   1979   *The Sociologist and the Oligopolist: Protecting the Corporate Subject.* Paper presented
         at the annual meeting of the American Sociological Association, Boston.

Doeringer, P. B., and M. J Piore
   1971   *Internal Labor Markets and Manpower Analysis*. Lexington, Massachusetts: Heath.
Edwards, R. C.
   1975   "The social relations of production in the firm and the labor market structure." In
           R. C. Edwards, M. Reich, and D. M. Gordon (eds.), *Labor Market Segmentation*.
           Lexington, Massachusetts: Heath.
Edwards, R. C., M. Reich, and D. M. Gordon (eds.)
   1975   *Labor Market Segmentation*. Lexington, Massachusetts: Heath.
Finegan, T. A.
   1978   *The Measurement, Behavior, and Classification of Discouraged Workers*. Background
           Paper No. 12. Washington, D.C.: National Commission on Employment and Un-
           employment Statistics.
Form, W.
   1979   "Comparative industrial sociology and the convergence hypothesis." *Annual Review
           of Sociology* 5:1–25.
Form, W., and F. C. Pampel
   1978   "Social stratification and the development of urban labor markets in India." *Social
           Forces* 51(September):119–135.
Freedman, M. K.
   1976   *Labor Markets: Segments and Shelters*. Montclair, New Jersey: Allanheld, Osmun.
Gordon, D. M.
   1972   *Theories of Poverty and Underemployment*. Lexington, Massachusetts: Heath.
Harrison, B., and A. Sum
   1979   *Labor Market Data Needs from the Perspective of "Dual" or "Segmented" Labor Market
           Research*. Background Paper No. 29. Washington, D.C.: National Commission on
           Employment and Unemployment Statistics.
Hauser, P. M.
   1949   "The labor force and gainful workers—Concept, measurement, and comparability."
           *American Journal of Sociology* 54(January):338–354.
Hodge, R. W.
   1973   "Toward a theory of racial differences in employment." *Social Forces*
           52(September):16–31.
Hodson, R.
   1978   "Labor in the monopoly, competitive and state sectors of production." *Politics and
           Society* 8(3–4):429–480.
Horan, P. M.
   1978   "Is status attainment research atheoretical?" *American Sociological Review*
           43(August):534–541.
Kalleberg, A. L., and A. B. Sørenson
   1979   "The sociology of labor markets." *Annual Review of Sociology* 5:351–379.
Kerr, C.
   1954   "The Balkanization of labor markets." In E. Wight Bakke *et al.* (eds.), *Labor Mobility
           and Economic Opportunity*. Cambridge, Massachusetts: MIT Press.
Light, I. H.
   1972   *Ethnic Enterprise in America*. Berkeley: Univ. of California Press.
Loewen, J. W.
   1971   *The Mississippi Chinese: Between Black and White*. Cambridge, Massachusetts: Har-
           vard Univ. Press.
Marx, K.
   1967   *Capital* (3 vols.). New York: International Publishers. (Originally published, 1887.)

Merton, R. K.

1973 "Behavior patterns of scientists." In N. W. Storer (ed.), *The Sociology of Science.* Chicago: Univ. of Chicago Press.

Moore, W. E.

1953 "The exportability of the labor force concept." *American Sociological Review* 18(February):68–72.

National Commission on Employment and Unemployment Statistics

1979 *Counting the Labor Force.* Washington, D.C.: US Govt Printing Office.

O'Connor, J.

1973 *The Fiscal Crisis of the State.* New York: St. Martin's.

Piore, M. J.

1975 "Notes for a theory of labor market stratification." In R. C. Edwards, M. Reich, and D. M. Gordon (eds.), *Labor Market Segmentation.* Lexington, Massachusetts: Heath.

1979 *Birds of Passage.* London and New York: Cambridge Univ. Press.

Portes, A.

1979 "Illegal immigration and the international system: Lessons from recent legal Mexican immigrants to the United States." *Social Problems* 26(April):425–438.

Singelmann, J., and H. L. Browning

1978 "The transformation of the U. S. labor force: The interaction of industry and occupation." *Politics and Society* 8(3–4):481–509.

Spilerman, S.

1977 "Careers, labor market structure, and socioeconomic achievement." *American Journal of Sociology* 83(November):551–593.

Stinchcombe, A. L.

1979 "Social mobility in industrial labor markets." *Acta Sociologica* 22(2):217–245.

Stolzenberg, R. M.

1975 "Occupations, labor markets and the process of wage attainment." *American Sociological Review* 40(October):645–665.

1978 "Bringing the boss back in: Employer size, employee schooling, and socioeconomic achievement." *American Sociological Review* 43(December):813–828.

Stone, K.

1975 "The origins of job structure in the steel industry." In R. C. Edwards, M. Reich, and D. M. Gordon (eds.), *Labor Market Segmentation.* Lexington, Massachusetts: Heath.

Sullivan, T. A.

1978a *Marginal Workers, Marginal Jobs.* Austin: Univ. of Texas Press.

1978b "Racial–ethnic differences in labor force participation: An ethnic stratification perspective." In F. D. Bean and W. P. Frisbie (eds.), *The Demography of Racial and Ethnic Groups.* New York: Academic Press.

Szentes, T.

1976 "Structural roots of the employment problem." *International Social Science Journal* 28(4):789–807.

Talbert, J., and C. E. Bose

1977 "Wage attainment processes: The retail clerk case." *American Journal of Sociology* 83(September):404–424.

Tolbert, C., P. M. Horan, and E. M. Beck

1980 "The structure of economic segmentation: A dual economy approach." *American Journal of Sociology* 85(March):1095–1116.

U. S. Bureau of the Census

1976 "Concepts and methods used in labor force statistics derived from the Current Population Survey." *Current Population Reports.* Special Studies, Series P-23, No. 62. (October):3–4.

Wilson, K. L., and A. Portes

1980    "Immigrant enclaves: An analysis of the labor market experiences of Cubans in Miami." *American Journal of Sociology* 8(2):295–319.

Wilson, W. J.

1978    *The Declining Significance of Race.* Chicago: Univ. of Chicago Press.

# Chapter 13

# Toward Model

# Specification in

# the Structural

# Unemployment Thesis:

# Issues and Prospects[1]

*IVAR BERG*   *T. ALDRICH FINEGAN*

*ROBERT BIBB*   *MICHAEL SWAFFORD*

There has been increasingly wide acceptance over the past decade of the proposition that the unhappy circumstances of a great many unemployed persons are beyond the reach of expansionist economic policies except at the cost of increased inflation. Even many of those social scientists and policymakers who assert the need for public interventions targeted on economic growth are far less optimistic about the straightforward and noninflationary unemployment-shrinking powers of increases in aggregate demand in the late 1970s than they were, for example, in the late 1950s.[2]

Increasingly, attention has come to focus on so-called structural conditions that contribute to the apparent fact that "successive increments of effective

[1] This chapter, as described in chapter 1, which also serves as this chapter's preface, is taken directly from a research proposal for a project funded by NIMH commencing August 1, 1980. It appears here in lieu of the customary summary of research and policy implications in volumes of the present one's genre.

[2] For three slightly different versions, see Moses Abramovitz "In Pursuit of Full Employment," Robert M. Solow "Macro-policy and Full Employment," Arthur Okun "Conflicting National Goals," and Lloyd Ulman "Manpower-Policies and Demand Management," in Ginzberg (1976). All these scholars were more optimistic about the noninflationary implications of expansionist policies targeted on unemployment in the 1950s and early 1960s than they are today. For an earlier detailed assessment, see Bergmann and Kaun (1966).

SOCIOLOGICAL PERSPECTIVES ON
LABOR MARKETS

demand [ultimately for labor] will buy successively smaller increases in productivity and output and successively greater increases in unit costs and prices" as unemployed persons line up "before the hiring gates of the economy in order of their skill and efficiency, with the most skilled and efficient at the head of the line [Ginzberg, 1976, p.87]." Inflation, it is argued thereupon, increases in proportion to the larger numbers of less productive workers (and less productive capital equipment) who are called into use in the wake of the applications of stimuli aimed at economic growth by increasing capital investments or, more generally, by expanding demand. Put differently, inflation increases measurably in proportion to the gaps between successive waves of workers' productivity and workers' earnings, as one moves down the labor queue, in diverse industries. The deficient productive capacities of the less efficient workers, finally, are held to be the result of a variety of structural factors having to do (a) with the education, training exposure, work experience, and mobility (or rather the immobility), and knowledgeability about labor markets of the unemployed; and (b) with ever-changing (i.e., short-run) shifts in the precise skill demands of employers who are regularly obliged to adapt their production methods to shifts in market and related conditions.[3] The resulting labor supply and demand mismatches, meanwhile, have increased in magnitude as baby-boom offspring have entered the labor force and as the labor force participation rates of women have bolted upward (Bergmann & Kaun, 1966; Gordon, 1972), so sounds a familiar theme.

These formulations have not, of course, been derived hastily. Indeed, discussions about unemployment have undergone a series of transmutations in both social science and public policy circles over the past 40 years, reflecting major changes both in economic circumstances and in the theoretical apparatus for understanding the changes.

Prior to Keynes, unemployment was conceived to be essentially voluntary: The unemployed were seen to be withholding their services from the labor market pending more favorable working conditions, especially better wages (Keynes, 1936). Protracted, cyclical periods of unemployment occurred when they did because employers would not pay going rates for the marginally

---

[3] Deficient and therefore problematical attitudes toward work—resistance to low-wage, low-skill jobs among "unrealistic" youths, for example—are also assigned some weight by many of the proponents of this thesis. As time passes, however, the causes of these deficient attitudes are understood by some to be the residues of wider social developments well beyond the control of those holding the problematical attitudes. For empirical evidence suggesting, for example, that many welfare recipients' work attitudes become as cynical, hopeless, or psychologically despairing as they often do only *after* innumerable disappointments in the workaday world, see Goodwin (1972).

less productive workers in unemployment queues; unemployment rates would decline when new wage levels came to reflect the marginal product— the economic benefits to employers—of unutilized but work-willing job candidates.[4]

Though some early attention was given to structural unemployment, it was, as Abramovitz writes, "Keynes and the Great Depression [that] changed the unemployment map [Ginzberg, 1976, p.45]." It was a central point in Keynes's analysis that involuntary unemployment was both real and remediable: though many unemployed were willing to work for wages lower than prevailing rates, they were unable to find jobs "because the increment of aggregate real demand which their employment would create would be insufficient to absorb the goods which their work would produce [Ginzberg, 1976, p.45]."[5] The prescription for this economic malady, Keynes theorized, was not improved market information systems, reforms in the labor market's organization, or what we now term *manpower programs*, but support for higher aggregate demand—for *demand management*, in the current phrase, for policy on the demand side, rather than programs targeted on labor supply.[6]

## Demand and Inflation

While liberals and conservatives have haggled over the details of demand management policies and of the business investment incentives in question, and over the degree of inflationary threat associated with different policies, few after Keynes categorically rejected the idea that a good deal of unemployment could be characterized as involuntary. The liberal version of the problem made visible progress anew in the early 1960s as high unemployment gave way before the expansionist policies in the period 1961–1969. These liberal economists were not unaware, of course, of the

[4] We mention cyclical unemployment here, and bypass unemployment in its seasonal and frictional (i.e., its more clearly voluntary) manifestations, in the interest only of parsimonious discussion. For four slightly different but current constructions of the evolution of what we may here call unemployment theory, see the works cited in Footnote 2.

[5] A similar argument could be made about joblessness attributable to deficiencies or shortages in capital for investment in job-producing enterprises.

[6] As we have noted, we leave aside here those conceptions of unemployment, not unlike the Keynsian ones, that emphasize shortages of capital and the consequent shortages of jobs. Though these conceptions do not focus upon workers' traits, they do involve notions of labor queues and labor redundancy like those stressed in the structural unemployment thesis. For Keynes's discussion of the demand–supply question, see Keynes (1936). For a radical critique, see Sherman (1976).

possibility that a considerable portion of the great surges of job growth in the years 1966–1969 could be linked to the business confidence-building (i.e., noninflationary) expectations that took form during the long preceding period of joblessness and stagnation.

As we moved into the 1970s, the inflationary spiral following the excess demand sparked by the fighting in Vietnam (and following changes in price expectations) began to concern theorists and policymakers of all stripes.[7] When well into the 1970s, mounting inflation rates—energy and food prices aside—were not slowed by mounting unemployment rates, attention increasingly focused on discovering the reasons why the tradeoff between unemployment and inflation no longer assumed the character of what many had come to regard as fixed proportionality, in accordance with the logic of economists' Phillips Curve calculations, calculations that have been effectively shown to be among the most primitive calculations ever to be taken seriously by social scientists (Wheeler, 1979).

By 1976 there was nearly a consensus: While aggregate demand might still need some stimulus, most observers strongly suspected that increasing numbers of unemployed were the victims of circumstances that would be linked once again, but in greater numbers, along with the expectation factor, to the factors stressed in the structural unemployment thesis and, in related contexts, in human capital and status attainment theorists' efforts to account for occupational successes as well as failures. The fate of the victims, the majority of unemployed, it was widely believed, would not likely be reversed by expansionist, investment-, or demand-oriented policies. Expansionist policies targeted on the structurally unemployed, furthermore, would aggravate inflation, because the lower productivity of workers whose attributes placed them toward the end of the labor queue could only fuel inflation, a finding that enjoys the fullest measure of support in the work of human capital and status attainment theorists.

There have been a few technical disputes, of course, over the precise numbers of unemployed whose pitiable circumstances inhere in intractably personal but necessarily job-relevant traits or attributes for which job seekers could in greater or lesser degree themselves be held accountable.[8] A con-

---

[7] For a relatively early, lucid, and apparently prescient theoretical discussion of the impendent greater importance of inflationary expectations in inflation-generating processes, especially in the U.S. economy, see Morley (1971).

[8] The implicit distinction here is between well-intentioned, hard-working but structurally unemployable job seekers, on one side, and members of the "underclass," the *lumpenproletariat*, the "disreputable poor," the shiftless, the welfare "freeloaders," the "discouraged workers," and workers with wildly unrealistic job expectations, on the other side. The issue is an important one because, we suggest, the question whether persons with unstable work histories become discouraged and depressed in consequence of their experience or whether their psychological

siderable body of literature in support of the proposition, however, suggests that the number of structurally unemployed is a very large proportion of the total number of unemployed persons. The emphasis in this literature is upon the seeming irony that, for a given technology, higher skilled, higher wage labor is ultimately less costly, whereas lower priced labor is more expensive. The apparent paradox is dissolved, allegedly, by recognizing the "fact" that, while the structurally unemployed—mostly youths and women—are less well paid than "higher quality" workers, they would assertedly be paid rather more in a tight labor market and in an inflation-ridden economy than, by economic standards, they are worth.[9]

While all of the economically deficient and therefore maladaptive traits of the structurally unemployed we have listed are assigned some weight in popular social science theories, educational achievements and deficiencies in experience and training, so-called human capital attributes, come in for extraordinary attention. Their maladaptiveness is imputed to less fortunate job seekers as a corollary of five fundamental and interrelated assumptions (a) that managers are constantly alert to (and prepared to act with alacrity upon) opportunities to modify productive techniques; (b) that managers make economically rational estimates of the traits and attributes their employees actually need for effective performance; (c) that employers construct the operational wage–skill formulas in their personnel policies on the basis of thoughtfully and imaginatively disaggregated cost analysis; (d) that employers regularly make reliable estimates and forecasts of the personnel implications, as they do other implications, of their business decisions in all realms of their firms' policies that have staffing implications; and, finally, (e) that employers otherwise behave approximately in accordance with the standard model of managers contemplated in textbooks.

The unemployment that results is, in the view of the majority of investigators, held to occur systematically, with allowances only for idiosyncratic and very short-run developments, across essentially all labor markets, industries, occupations, and technologies. The behavior of managers, given the perception of the constraints perceived to govern them, must necessarily be productive of employment and unemployment patterns among citizens of measurably different traits. In the long run, it is assumed, employers' behavior must approximate the model lest their firms simply be frozen out by the chill winds in a competitive marketplace; only in a few deviant cases,

---

circumstances contribute in some meaningful way to their unhappy work histories should be regarded as an empirical one, to be left open to inquiry, a matter to which we return in a brief description, later, of what we identify as the sixth prong of our research design.

[9] For discussions of a variety of estimates of the "actual" inflation–unemployment trade-off and the logics of their derivation, see Perry (1971, 1977), Alban (1976), and Wheeler (1979). For a summary, see Solow and Ginzberg (1976).

in which a few employers (and their employees) are protected by market-neutralizing imperfections, can the implicit imperatives be ignored, even for a relatively short time. Our own and the research of a very few others, creates considerable doubts about this highly simplified view of managers' decision making (Albrecht, 1978; Berg, 1970, 1978; Brown, 1978; Piore, 1979).

Consider, first, that the implications of technological changes for jobs are, like managers' economically rational responses, not nearly as demonstrable as the structural unemploymemt, human capital, or status attainment theses would have us believe, in terms of either the numbers of changes that occur, the speed with which they occur, the manner in which they occur, or their precise effects on jobs. Thus, it is the case that the untoward effects of automation and computerization on employmemt, loudly proclaimed in the mid- and late 1950s, failed to materialize (see Horowitz & Herrenstadt, 1966; Jaffee & Froomkin, 1968); in the aggregate and in balance, newfangled technology has affected economic agents slowly and steadily, as technology always has, rather than in radically discontinuous ways.

The report of the National Commission on Technology, Automation and Economic Progress provides apposite data (1966); while the pace of technological change had increased after World War II, the increase in the rate of productivity and productivity growth—perfectly useful indirect measures of the hard-to-measure rate of technological change—was not consistent with the assumption that "a veritable technological revolution has occurred. . . . The notion that the product of an hour of work can double in 24 years—not much more than half a working lifetime—is quite enough to justify the feeling of continuous change that is so much a part of the contemporary environment [p.2]." To be sure, "the time scale has shrunk visibly," but, according to the commission, "it has by no means contracted to the vanishing point [p.2]." While the time frame from discovery to commercial application has indeed shortened, "major technological studies may wait as long as 14 years before they reach commercial application even on a small scale, and perhaps another 5 years before their impact on the economy becomes large [p.4]." Thus, the connventional wisdom that a great many occupational shifts are almost immediately the result of technological changes—a judgment the structural unemployment thesis conceives to be an axiom—does not square well with the commission's detailed findings.[10]

Further evidence supporting the contention, the validity of which we are currently testing, that the occupational correlates of technological changes

---

[10] Technology and the American Report of the National Commission on Technology, Automation and Economic Progress (1966). For an empirically well-informed discussion, including a careful review of 17 extant studies of the nearly incoherent processes by which technology is created, developed, and used in firms, see Utterback (1974).

are less dramatically conspicuous than those contemplated in the currently popular theories of unemployment, human capital, and status attainment comes in a 1969 report on the effects of technological changes on the organizational and occupational experiences perceived by a national probability sample of 2662 labor force participants. Mueller and her colleagues at Ann Arbor (1969) discovered that the jobs of about 1.5–2 million members of the work force—2–3%—changed to a significant degree by technological changes in the course of a year.[11] There is not a shred of evidence from these survey respondents, meanwhile, that, though these changes were "significant" in their eyes, they were actually of the types that made either their jobs too difficult or their skills obsolete, though such issues as conflicting jurisdictional claims to jobs raised by respondents undoubtedly had to be joined by employers and employees.

None of the foregoing denies that the labor force's members are often buffeted, or even staggered, by changes in organizations or that jobs, job classifications, skill hierarchies, disciplinary and supervisory arrangements, work group membership patterns, and organizational rules, for example, are not infrequently subject to substantial revisions by employers. Nor need we deny that the typographers' and coal miners' occupations, to take two glaring examples, have not been substantially affected by new printing and coal-cutting techniques. We simply point out that many of the putatively untoward labor market effects of technological changes are selective in their incidence, generally slow moving, and almost always caught up together with parallel and intervening forces, such as those in collective bargaining, that may temper or even traduce what might otherwise be more predictable, unsettling correlates of changes observed in labor markets and in aggregated employment data of the type favored by the advocates of human capital, status attainment, and structural unemployment theses.

Among the reasons why technological changes are often handled in ways that leave relatively modest marks on organizations are those reported in the organizational literature that bear upon the operations of internal labor markets. In these internal markets, one discerns the applications by employers of employment criteria other than those putatively dictated by the

---

[11] One possible reason for the basically modest amount and slow rate of technological changes is that nearly two-thirds of all dollars expended in the United States in 1976 for research and development were spent for development, not research, activities (see NSF, 1976). It is worth noting, in this context, that fully 36% of the respondents to the third national Labor Department-sponsored survey by colleagues at Ann Arbor of a national probability sample of employed Americans & Quinn & Staines, (1977) report that their skills are "underutilized," while 32% report that they are "overeducated." For detailed analyses of the relevant and, in this project, the important difficulties in identifying *real* as contrasted with *subjectively* perceived "underutilization of education," see Berg, Freedman, and Freeman (1978).

narrow economic logics emphasized in studies of structural unemployment. Thus employers often retrain their workers and others modify the work methods in their enterprises, suiting them to workers' capabilities. Such adaptations are reported in a 1971 study of technological changes in 75 firms; these adaptations are remarkably like those reported by industrial sociologists for over 40 years. These scientists' studies show (a) that employers very often balance economic and noneconomic criteria in efforts to stabilize their operations; (b) that the costs of alternative mixes of labor skills are barely estimated at all; and (c) that job demands are basically adjusted with an eye to the skills possessed by extant members of the firms' internal labor force (Doeringer & Piore, 1971, see especially pp.119–132).[12]

The results reported in these studies of internal labor market operations suggest that more refined analysis of the effects of technological changes are prerequisite to orderly revisions in the relevant lines of the social science theories that aspire to deal with these changes. Such refined analyses as are presently available point us in the same direction as those by Doeringer and Piore (1971). Thus Horowitz and Hernstadt (1966) compared the trait requirements and the detailed job requirements for five industries over the period 1940–1965 and have reported that the net change in the skill requirements in those industries was remarkably small, especially considering that their study covered a quarter century.

## The Demand for Education

The view, meantime, that technological and other changes account in large measures for the extraordinary increase in the educational achievements of labor force participants, by putting long-term pressures on job aspirants to achieve more education and training, does not accord well with one of the few efforts to study directly, rather than indirectly, the relationship between education and jobs (Berg, 1970). There was virtually no evidence, from 1950 to 1960, in support of the argument that better-educated workers performed better than less-educated workers in the same jobs and that the income differences of these differentially educated workers were attributable to the empirically founded recognition by employers of the specific economic advantages of hiring larger numbers of better educated persons. And when the actual job requirements of Americans were compared with their edu-

[12] For earlier versions of the adjustment-making process in internal labor markets in which collective bargaining contracts apply, see Kuhn and Berg (1964, pp.466–481), Kuhn (1961), and Dalton (1959). For classic sociological and related analyses of intraorganizational adjustment process, with or without unions, see Commons (1904) and Lieserson's and Roy's introductions in Mathewson (1931, 1969).

cational achievements, either in aggregate terms or at the level of employment settings, we reported, there were increasingly large numbers of Americans whose educations were being underutilized by managers who believe in, but can in no wise demonstrate, the empirical validity of the logic in their use of educational credentials for jobs (Berg, 1970). The latter portion of the analysis has been brought up to 1970 and indicates that the underutilization of education reported in 1970, for the period 1950–1960, has worsened by an appreciable margin (Berg *et al.*, 1978, pp.75–97). These results square not at all well with the widely shared assumptions either about managers' personnel requirements in general or about personnel practices that are specifically basic to the structural unemployment hypothesis.

In addition to our own findings, consider Diamond and Bedrosian's (1970) findings, in a study of hiring standards and labor market imbalances, from data on 10 entry-level and near-entry-level jobs in each of five white-collar and four blue-collar occupations, together with one service occupation, in the New York and St. Louis Standard Metropolitan Statistical Areas and those obtained by Heneman and Seltzer, designed to gain a sense of the approaches to personnel planning and forecasting, and the techniques applied, by the managers of 69 Minnesota firms employing 500 or more workers (Henneman & Seltzer, 1970). The Minnesota study showed that:

1. Forecasts of personnel requirements were not undertaken at all in 50% of the firms; forecasting efforts were undertaken by nearly one-quarter of these firms for the first time only 1 year before the study; only one-third sought to forecast personnel supplies.
2. About 90% of the firms used forecasts for recruiting but only one-third related personnel forecasts to budget plans, training, or transfer and promotion programs; only one-tenth of the firms used the forecasts in plans for production, space, and facilities. The use of such forecasts in plans for acquisition and expansion or in product pricing was reported even less frequently.
3. Twenty percent of the firms were able to produce no employment data breakdowns; 30% had none on separations and hires; 60% had none on the ages of their employees. "In brief," report the investigators, "manpower seemed to be almost completely isolated from other types of planning."[13]

[13] After 1974, all but small firms in the United States have been obliged to track such information in order to comply with equal opportunity and affirmative action requirements. It is of immediate interest that government regulations, not the need to respond to market forces, will induce people in business to act, far more than they did before, in accordance with textbook images of personnel management inherent in the theory of the firm. Given the generally critical attitudes toward government among neoclassicists, it is not a small irony

A third study, targeted on the deficiencies in national data on absenteeism, uncovered substantially the same (perhaps understandable) tendencies in the personnel analyses of managers (Hedges, 1973). We may remind ourselves, in this specific context, that background circumstances of labor force participants regularly seen, in statistical terms, to contribute to precisely these deficient work habits are strongly emphasized in the axioms of the structural unemployment thesis about employability and unemployability, especially of youths and black workers.

One gets an additional sense of the complexities in the logics applied to personnel by employers from another highly relevant study, this time of subcontracting decisions, by Chandler and Sayles (1959). They reported that "complex cost calculations were not employed universally in determining whether it is cheaper to contract-out or to do the work inside, but rather were limited to about three-fifths of the group [p.36]." Finally, two critics of Berg (1970) were admittedly unable to develop either empirical or theoretical arguments that could successfully contradict his 1970 results (Albrecht, 1978; Brown, 1978).

The point in reviewing these findings is to underscore the need (a) for updated analyses anchored in macro-type aggregate data giving evidence of the character of labor market processes regarding the match-up of the credentials of labor force participants and the actual job requirements of employers overall, a suggestion like that by Granovetter elsewhere in this volume; and (b) for elaborating upon disparate but relevant studies of particular labor markets, employment settings, and managers' practices as, in fact, most of our fellow authors have done and reported on in this volume.

Such analyses will afford us opportunities to gain a firmer grip on the realities of the boundary-like exchanges between the labor market writ large and its constituent, internal labor markets within regions, industries, and employers' organizations. Properly executed, such explorations would be productive of aggregated and disaggregated macroscopic-, "meso-," and microscopic-level data that are indispensible in efforts to adequately specify the numbers of job seekers to whom the terms of the structural unemployment thesis apply.

Such explorations would, in turn, be productive of scientifically creditable guidelines for the assessment of a variety of public policy initiatives. We may mention, in passing, for example, that in addition to policies having to do with skill acquisition, educational programs, and the financing of both are oft-heard urges that the United States embark upon programs that

---

that government actions oblige employers to act in the fashion prescribed for them by conventional theory.

would aid unemployed persons to relocate to areas in which jobs are plentiful. Preliminary studies suggest that such programs should be drafted with a weather eye to the processes not only by which workers find jobs but by which they become "attached" to occupations and jobs.[14]

In the next section, we describe some of the work we and others have performed that bear upon a research strategy we outline later.

## Structural Unemployment: Pros, Cons, and Prospects

The structural unemployment thesis, in its general outline, has been specifically informed by four types of studies. The first type is demographic and ecological in character; studies under this rubric show unmistakably enough, as we noted earlier, that unemployment is more concentrated in some population and occupational groups than in others. The use of these studies exclusively, of data that are basic to discovering the structure of unemployment, leads to imprecise and even to tautological conclusions and formulations about structural unemployment and the causes of and relevant policies for dealing with unemployment.

The second type of study, deriving from human capital and status attainment, shows indirectly (by use of data on income and education) that workers with more developed skills and higher educational achievements earn higher incomes, on the average, and must therefore, according to the logic that employers operate at the margins at which labor costs overtake productivity, be more productive than their less-skilled, less-educated peers (Becker, 1964; Mincer, 1970). Though very few detailed (i.e., disaggregated) studies have been made to prove the point, it is argued, for example, that the lower wages of workers in the South make economically possible the employment of innumerable workers in that section of the country. Human capital investments are decidedly lower in the South, however, than those made in the health, education, and training of workers in the West, the Northeast, and the Midwest (Flain & Schwab, 1970; Fuchs, 1967; Kalachek & Goering, 1970).

The third body of evidence shows that the attitudes of large numbers of unemployed persons toward work may be distributed on a continuous scale ranging from "unrealistic" to "alienated," with stops in-between for "discouraged," "negative," and "hostile." Though his point is quite different

---

[14] A preliminary investigation of publicly guaranteed loan programs for education and training indicate that they are uninformed by any of the aforementioned findings regarding the utilization of education and training investments (see Berg & Freedman, 1978).

from that made by the structural unemployment and kindred theorists, Goodwin (1972) documents such attitudes.

The fourth body of evidence, regarding the pace of technological change, is not properly speaking a body of evidence at all: Rather than assessing it empirically, the pace of technological change is inferred to be rapid and its character discontinuous (*a*) tautologically, from the mounting educational achievements of the work force that employers have been putatively obliged by changing technical circumstances to hire; (*b*) from dollar amounts of investment in physical capital; and (*c*) from evidence concerning dollar investments in research and development.

There is contravening evidence, however, in our and others' studies, from which one learns:

1. Substantially large numbers of particular members from high-unemployment parent groups are, in fact, regularly employed, while other large numbers are intermittently but fairly regularly employed; not by any means are all youths, reentering women, or black Americans from inner-city precincts, for example, essentially unemployed.

2. Nearly all the ranks in nearly all the occupations of employed Americans are populated with persons of very varied educational backgrounds, skills, and experiences; correlations between ability and occupations are far from perfect, as Taubman and Wales (1971) have shown. Indeed, variations in the educational backgrounds and abilities of employed Americans within the overriding numbers of occupations are as wide as the variations in those between workers in higher and lower level occupations.

3. Wage and salary differences between male and female and between black and white blue-collar workers in different Standard Metropolitan Statistical Areas (SMSAs), and in a number of particular cities, are attributable far less to human capital-type investment differences than to clusters of differences reflecting different mixes of occupations, which are related, in turn, to the industrial composition of these different SMSAs and cities (Bibb, 1977; Bibb & Form, 1978). These differences in structure give rise to different racial and sex differences in the composition of labor markets; wage differences, thereupon, may be readily attributed to discriminatory wage and hiring policies, however, and not, as in the structural unemployment thesis, to employers' demonstrated and empirically well-informed sensitivities about differences in the productivity of different classes of workers.[15]

---

[15] This analysis has been performed by Robert Bibb, one of the senior associates on the project from which the proposal for this chapter derived. By comparing data for 1950 with those he analyzed for 1970, we can perform an analysis, as we note later, that will afford

4. Patterns of utilization of differentially educated Americans in the work force represent efforts on the part of employers to screen job applicants in essentially superficial ways, not reasonably sophisticated efforts to utilize workers' background exposures in accordance with the model contemplated in the theory of the firm favored in the structural unemployment thesis.

5. The variations in the detailed attitudes toward work of respondents to three cross-sectional surveys and to a panel survey, between 1969 and 1977, of stably employed Americans are very nearly as wide as those expressed by workers who are unemployed or intermittantly employed (Quinn & Staines, 1978). The intragroup variations and intergroup similarities, here only adumbrated, are sufficiently large and small, respectively, that they simply must be considered by theorists who offer models that assertedly have explanatory value and predictive powers.

These five bodies of findings, based on disaggregated analyses, do not, of course, necessarily contradict the thrust of findings derived from demographic accountings and from indirect studies of job requirements based on aggregated data on the economic returns to persons of different educations. They point most emphatically, however, to the usefulness of (a) analyses based on disaggregated data that permit detailed comparisons of individual workers with similar traits but with different employment histories in different markets, in order that the numerous possible "causes" of these different histories can be disentangled one from another; (b) analyses based on aggregated and on highly disaggregated data on educational achievements and actual job requirements, data that permit direct rather than indirect measures of employers' practices; and (c) analyses based on disaggregated data on labor demand schedules of the types so well represented by the contributors to the present volume.

Indeed, the five sets of findings discussed may be combined (a) with additional evidence that at least one-third, and perhaps as many as one-half, of all employed Americans obtain their jobs "particularistically," through family, friends, and other personal contacts;[16] and (b) with

---

somewhat crude but highly suggestive estimates of the occurrence of technological change in the SMSAs and cities under discussion in the cross-sectional analysis that Bibb has already completed (see also Getz & Huang, 1978). For examples of the highly differentiated character of the effect of technological change in different industries and occupations otherwise, see Carey (1976), and Carey and Otto (1977).

[16] We have no reason to doubt that friends and associates will be reasonably discriminating on behalf of economically rational employers when they commend workers to these employers from their family and friendship circles. But, we need not assume, by that token, that personal contacts are *totally* objective, in accordance with what sociologists call "universalistic" rather

Doeringer's and Piore's (1971) evidence, cited earlier, that employers regularly adapt their changing requirements for differential skills, after introducing changes in their productive methods, by adopting specific work techniques such that they are able to juggle personnel in their internal labor markets. By doing so, moreover, these employers avoid competition from skilled workers in the larger external labor market while they impart specific skills to their workers that are not likely to be highly valued by competing employers.

From a third body of data, we learn that, while access to public higher education has improved, the enrollment rates of high-ability, low-income youths in postsecondary training and educational institutions are 22 percentage points lower than those of high-ability, high-income youths. Indeed, the third highest of four ability groups among the highest income families has the same enrollment rate as the highest ability youths in the lowest income groups (64%) (Berg, 1970, p.102; 1978, p.107; Peng & Dunteman, 1975).[17] There is accordingly a much larger number of "able" youths situated toward the back of the so-called labor queue than prevailing social science theories have made clear in their emphases on human capital differences.

When these eight discrete but immediately relevant bodies of data are considered together, they suggest substantial reasons for conducting analyses of demand-side issues to balance the alternative supply-side approaches based almost exclusively upon simple ecological–demographic comparisons of successful, unsuccessful, unemployed, and employed Americans. The analyses we commend would permit one:

1. To compare and conflate data on individuals who possess similar abilities, demographic traits, attitudes, and preemployment experi-

---

than "particularistic" standards, in their efforts on behalf of employers and prospective employees. For evidence regarding job placements, see Employment and Training Administration (1974) and Granovetter (1974). It could very well be, meantime, that comparably educated or comparably talented job seekers with grossly different career experiences simply have or use more or have or use fewer personal contacts in their job-seeking efforts.

[17] Clearly, the educational selection picture is improving, a fact that, when taken together with facts about increasing educational underutilization, suggests that one might derive another version, or specification, of the structural unemployment thesis applicable to workers whose formal education and school-linked training are in *excess* of labor market demands. This modified version of the current version of the structural unemployment thesis, with its emphasis upon "insufficiently trained" and "insufficiently educated" workers, would be designed to treat the two extremes. Excess formal education may obviously be as much a handicap in the labor market as insufficient education in some occupations, a fact that is neglected in both the structural unemployment thesis and the status attainment and human capital literature. We contend, meanwhile, that it is far easier, in concretely scientific terms, to prove that better educated workers are underutilized than that lesser-educated workers are, for that reason, deficient.

ences, but who have had qualitatively different employment experiences. These souls are lost in the large residuals in human capital and status attainment studies, which emphasize the high correlations among variables in discussions of the explained variance. Often "luck" or "chance" rather than differences in demand in different labor markets, for example, are offered as explanations for the different experiences of similar persons (Jencks *et al.*, 1976, 1979).

2. To isolate the pragmatically adaptive from the more genuinely technologically constrained practices of employers in dealing with personnel issues under different labor market conditions.[18]

3. To isolate the roles of discriminatory behavior of employers from the productivity of workers in determining wage contours and employment patterns in different labor markets, industries, and occupations. It is important to isolate these, one from the other, in order to separate the real as contrasted with the putative contribution to inflation of workers deemed less unemployable in the structural unemployment thesis.

4. To understand the actual operation of the labor markets in which the demands for given types of labor skills and worker attributes are observably different.

## Model Specifications in the Structural Employment Thesis

The investigators whose empirical work is reported in the selections in the present volume have clearly joined in a movement toward more carefully specified studies of demand, studies that carry us into labor markets in different sectors, regions, occupations, and communities, and even within distinguishable organizations. In doing so they have joined with a larger number of researchers whose work, though far less celebrated than that in the human capital and status attainment traditions, gives one hope that the assumptions about demand in those traditions' approaches to employment, mobility, and stratification will be constructively reformulated in both theoretically and empirically well-informed ways. This larger body of

---

[18] The adaptations of employers to labor market offerings during World War II are well known. The argument that employers were enabled by "cost plus" contracts and wage controls, in that period, to dip to the bottom of the human resources apple barrel surely helps explain some of the differences between wartime and peacetime practices, but this argument cannot contend adequately with the fact that productivity (i.e., output per person-hour) was far higher in the wartime period than it is now when employers are less pressed to hire many of the putatively unemployable.

work is helpfully reviewed and usefully juxtaposed with the more simplified indirect conceptualization of demand in Kalleberg and Sørensen's (1979) summary of labor market research.

Our own current research, for which the discussion in the preceding sections of this chapter serves as the background and research rationale, moves along most of the lines staked out by our collaborators in this volume and is responsive to the same urges. This investigation is proceeding along what, for lack of a better designation, we term *prongs*, as follows.

First, we are making comparisons of three large longitudinal panel-type samples of individual labor force participants designed to give us a better purchase on the proportions of the variances in the different types of employment histories they have experienced that are "attributable" to the respondents' demographic traits, personal attributes, abilities, backgrounds, attitudes, and mental health, on one side, and the labor market conditions they faced over time, on the other. The thrust of this prong, in a broad sense, is to model workers' careers with eyes to the frequency and duration of bouts of unemployment, to the industry composition and labor market conditions they have faced, and to observable stabilities and changes in their individual perspectives, health, and attitudes. The analysis will accordingly permit us to make differentiated estimates of (a) the contributing effects of human capital and other attributes to the most and least agreeable types of labor market experiences; (b) the correlates, if not the effects, of variations in the differentiated demands of labor markets of different structures; and (c) the ways in which labor market and non-labor-market factors interact.

Second, we will analyze data relevant to the hypothesis that differential unemployment rates among youths across a variety of urban labor markets have attended changes in urban industrial composition rather than shifts in different qualifications among young job seekers of the type stressed in human capital and status attainment research. In investigating industry compositional effects on youth unemployment, we are entering an uncharted area. Nevertheless, we expect to discover that intermetropolitan differences in increases in youth unemployment over a 20-year period are essentially unrelated to the technological obsolescence of skills or differences in educational attainment among youths variously situated in differing labor markets. Conversely, we place our bets or changes in the sheer availability of employment subsequent to (a) increased factor substitution and capital utilization in goods-producing industries; and (b) firm out-migration from labor market areas.

Declining enrollment opportunities in affected labor markets, we argue, have been paralleled by the allocation of the onus of unemployment to new labor force entrants and erstwhile employed youths, many if not most of whose educational qualifications are nevertheless concordant with those of older workers and of fully employed youths in unaffected metropolises. We anticipate, furthermore, that, within the stratum of youthful workers and job seekers, increased unemployment generated by changes in industry composition in local markets will be disporportionately visited upon black youths, even after controls for education have been introduced. This portion of the research will thus help us understand far more clearly than we now do the consequences for workers' employment experiences of secular changes in production technologies, industrial composition, and occupational structures at the level of local labor markets.

The third prong of our project entails a systematic comparison of the frequency distributions of jobs according to their educational requirements with frequency distributions of employed Americans according to their educational achievements. We have already published results of this type of analysis, comparing 1966 with 1971, based on the use of bridgetapes that link the Department of Labor's *Dictionary of Occupational Titles'* educational requirements for 40,000 jobs, with the Current Population Survey's 440 occupations for Americans of different educational achievements (Berg *et al.*, 1978, pp.75–110). In this portion of the research, trait analyses by the Department of Labor's job analysts will be used once again, for developing "actual" educational requirements for jobs. Our method permits us to examine the relationship between education and jobs directly, avoiding the indirect method familiar in the human capital approach, in which job requirements are inferred from data on education and income. As we pointed out earlier, the latter method tautologically imputes management needs to management practices without an empirical demonstration that the needs exist.

The fourth prong of our project involves secondary analysis (*a*) of survey data concerning recruitment and job search efforts in 1974 (Camil, 1976); and (*b*) of relevant data on job acquisition. In this fourth segment of our research, we will sort the samples examined in our first prong according to the groupings derived in our study of labor markets (prong two).

In this prong we will seek to determine whether stable jobholders have more personal contacts for getting jobs than do other labor force participants, while holding constant the other traits and attributes of persons with different employment histories and controlling for relevant local labor market characteristics (Granovetter, 1974; Mortenson, 1970).

The fifth prong of our research involves interviews and archival research with employers and labor leaders in 40 Midwest firms. This effort is designed to enable us to reconstruct the responses of employers and union leaders to events occurring in their external and internal labor markets from 1948 to 1979.

In the sixth prong of our study, we will use mental health-related items from the data files used in connection with the first prong of our research, in order to observe (a) relationships between self-reported mental health indicators (attitudes, feelings, job satisfactions, and health symptoms) and personal traits, family background exposures, and schooling experiences prior to full-time labor market exposures, while controlling for differences in labor market conditions among 50 large SMSAs; (b) relationships between (changing) mental health indicators, reported in what are successive panel surveys, and longitudinal changes in employment experiences, again in 50 large SMSAs with their specific labor market conditions; and (c) possible interactions among data on personal, familial, and demographic traits, and among labor market conditions and personal employment experiences, vis-à-vis the self-reported mental health indicators in the files.

In all, these six prongs will permit us to test the axioms of the structural employment thesis and a number of those of human capital and status attainment theories; to specify the terms of these axioms regarding employer needs, employer behavior, employee attributes, and the role of human capital variables; and to state somewhat more precisely the relevance of supply and demand factors in shaping employment and unemployment trends and the structure of unemployment. The fifth prong permits us to compare and contrast the results of analyses of aggregated data on individuals and of aggregated ecological data with data at the organizational level of analysis.

While our research will not answer all the scientific or policy questions that are coming to the fore regarding the demand and supply of labor in the next two decades, the foregoing discussion and description is offered in substitution of a more abstract statement of research agendas and policy prospects at the conclusion of a volume whose authors' completed work has so usefully and reassuringly shown the way to those who suspect that questions about demand deserve more scholarly attention than they have received in the 1960s and 1970s.

## Acknowledgments

We are grateful to Samuel Morley, William Rushing, Frank Sloan, and Stanley Black for critical comments on an earlier draft of this chapter.

## References

Albrecht, J.
1978    "Interpreting the returns to education." *Discussion Paper 77–7811.* New York: Columbia University Department of Economics. (Mimeo)

Becker, G. S.
   1964   *Human Capital.* Chicago: Univ. of Chicago Press.
Berg, I.
   1970   *Education and Jobs: The Great Training Robbery.* New York: Praeger.
Berg, I., and M. Freedman
   1978   "Manpower requirements and student finances." New York: Columbia University Conservation of Human Resources. (Mimeo)
Berg, I., M. Freeman, and M. Freedman
   1978   *Managers and Work Reform: A Limited Engagement.* New York: Free Press.
Bergmann, B. R., and D. E. Kaun
   1966   *Structural Unemployment in the United States.* Washington, D. C.: US Govt Printing Office.
Bibb, R.
   1977   *Sex Earnings Inequality in Metropolitan Workingclass Labor Markets.* Unpublished doctoral dissertation, University of Illinois, Urbana–Champaign.
Bibb, R., and W. Form
   1977   "The effects of industrial, occupational and sex stratification on wages in blue-collar markets." *Social Forces* 55(June):991 ff.
Brown, C.
   1978   "Education and jobs: An interpretation." *Journal of Human Resources* 12(3):417–420.
Carey, M. L.
   1976   "Revised occupational projections to 1985." *Monthly Labor Review* 99(November):10–12.
Carey, J. L., and P. F. Otto
   1977   "Output per unit of labor input in the retail food store industry." *Monthly Labor Review* 100(January):42–47.
Chandler, M., and L. Sayles
   1959   *Contracting Out: A Study of Management Decision Making.* New York: Columbia University Graduate School of Business.
Common, J. R.
   1904   *Regulation and the Restriction of Output: Report of the Department of Labor and Commerce.* Washington, D. C.: US Govt Printing Office.
Dalton, M.
   1959   *Men Who Manage.* New York: Wiley.
Diamond, D. E., and H. Bedrosian
   1970   *Hiring Standards and Jobs Performance.* Manpower Research Monograph No. 18. Washington, D. C.: US Govt Printing Office.
Doeringer, P., and M. J. Piore
   1971   *Internal Labor Markets and Manpower Analysis.* Lexington, Massachusetts: Heath.
Flaim, P. O., and P. M. Schwab
   1970   "Employment and unemployment developments in 1969." *Monthly Labor Review* 93(February):40–53.
Fuchs, V.
   1967   *Differentials in Hourly Earnings by Region and City Size.* Occasional Paper 101. Washington, D. C.: National Bureau of Economic Research.
Getz, M., and Y-C. Huang
   1977   "Consumer preferences for environmental goods." *Review of Economics and Statistics* 60(October):446–449.
Ginzberg, E., ed.
   1976   *Jobs for Americans.* Englewood Cliffs, New Jersey: Prentice-Hall.
Goodwin, L.
   1972   *Do the Poor Want to Work?* Washington, D. C.: Brookings Institution.

Gordon, D. M.
  1972  *Theories of Poverty and Underemployment.* Lexington, Massachusetts: Heath.
Granovetter, M.
  1974  *Getting a Job: A Study of Contacts and Careers.* Cambridge, Massachusetts: Harvard Univ. Press.
Hedges, A.
  1973  "Absence from work: A look at national data." *Monthly Labor Review* 96(April):24–25.
Henneman, H. G., and G. Seltzer
  1970  *Employee Manpower Planning and Forecasting.* Manpower Research Monograph, No. 19. Washington, D. C.: US Govt Printing Office.
Horowitz, M. A., and I. L. Herrenstadt
  1966  "Changes in the skill requirements and occupations in selected industries." *Report of the National Commission on Technology* (2):Appendix.
  1969  "An evaluation of the training of tool and die makers." Boston: Northeastern University.
Jaffe, A. J., and J. Froomkin
  1968  *Technology and Jobs: Automation in Perspective.* New York: Praeger.
Jencks, C., S. Bartlett, M. Corcoran, J. Crouse, D. Eaglesfield, G. Jackson, K. McClelland, P. Mueser, M. Olneck, J. Schwartz, S. Ward, and J. Williams
  1979  *Who Gets Ahead?* New York: Basic.
Kalachek, E., and J. M. Goering
  1970  *Transportation and Central City Unemployment.* Working Paper No. 5. St. Louis: Institute for Urban and Regional Studies, Washington University.
Kalleberg, A., and A. Sørensen
  1979  "The sociology of labor markets." *Annual Review of Sociology* 5:351–379.
Keynes, J. M.
  1936  *General Theory of Employment, Interest and Money.* New York: Harcourt Brace.
Kuhn, J.
  1961  *Bargaining in the Grievance Process.* New York: Columbia Univ. Press.
Kuhn, J., and I. Berg
  1964  "Bargaining in work rule disputes." *Social Research* 31(Winter):466–481.
Mathewson, S. B.
  1931  *Restriction of Output Among Unorganized Workers.* Carbondale, Illinois: Southern Illinois Univ. Press.
Mueller, E.
  1969  *Technological Advance in an Expanding Economy: Its Impact on a Cross-Section of the Labor Force.* Ann Arbor: Univ. of Michigan.
Mincer, J.
  1961  "On the job training: Costs, returns and some implications." *Journal of Political Economy* 70(October):50–79.
  1966  "Labor force participation and unemployment: A review of recent evidence." In R. A. Gordon (ed.), *Prosperity and Unemployment.* Lexington, Massachusetts: Heath.
Morley, S.
  1971  *The Economics of Inflation.* Hinsdale, Illinois: Dryden.
Mortenson, D.
  1970  "Job search, duration of unemployment, and the Phillips Curve." *American Economic Review* 65(December):560–580.
National Committee on Technology, Automation and Economic Progress
  1966  Report of the National Committee on Technology, Automation and Economic Progress. Washington, D. C.: US Govt Printing Office.

Peng, S. S.
   1977   *The National Longitudinal Study: Review and Annotation of Reports.* Research Triangle Park, North Carolina: Research Triangle Institute.
Priore, M. J. (Ed.)
   1979   *Unemployment and Inflation: Institutionalist and Structuralist Views.* White Plains, New York: Sharpe.
Perry, C. R.
   1975   *The Impact of Manpower Training Programs.* Philadelphia: The Wharton School, University of Pennsylvania.
Perry, G. L.
   1971   *Changing Labor Markets and Inflation.* Brookings Papers on Economic Activity No. 3. Washington, D. C.: Brookings Institution.
   1977   *Potential Output and Productivity.* Brookings Papers on Economic Activity No. 1. Washington, D. C.: Brookings Institution.
Quinn, R. P., and G. L. Staines
   1978   *The 1977 Quality of Employment: Descriptive Statistics.* Ann Arbor: Institute for Survey Research.
Sherman, H. J.
   1976   *Stagflation: A Radical Theory of Unemployment and Inflation.* New York: Harper.
Taubman, P., and T. Wales
   1961   "Education as an investment and screening device." Philadelphia: University of Pennsylvania and University of British Columbia. (Mimeo)
Wheeler, D.
   1979   "Is there a Phillips Curve?" In M. J. Piore (ed.), *Unemployment and Inflation: Institutionalist and Structuralist Views.* White Plains, New York: Sharpe.

# Subject Index

# QUANTITATIVE STUDIES IN SOCIAL RELATIONS

*Consulting Editor: Peter H. Rossi*

UNIVERSITY OF MASSACHUSETTS
AMHERST, MASSACHUSETTS

Richard F. Curtis and Elton F. Jackson, INEQUALITY IN AMERICAN COMMUNITIES

Richard A. Berk, Harold Brackman, and Selma Lesser, A MEASURE OF JUSTICE: An Empirical Study of Changes in the California Penal Code, 1955–1971

Samuel Leinhardt (Ed.), SOCIAL NETWORKS: A Developing Paradigm

Donald J. Treiman, OCCUPATIONAL PRESTIGE IN COMPARATIVE PERSPECTIVE

Beverly Duncan and Otis Dudley Duncan, SEX TYPING AND SOCIAL ROLES: A Research Report

N. Krishnan Namboodiri (Ed.), SURVEY SAMPLING AND MEASUREMENT

Robert M. Groves and Robert L. Kahn, SURVEYS BY TELEPHONE: A National Comparison with Personal Interviews

Peter H. Rossi, Richard A. Berk, and Kenneth J. Lenihan, MONEY, WORK, AND CRIME: Experimental Evidence

Walter Williams, GOVERNMENT BY AGENCY: Lessons from the Social Program Grants-in-Aid Experience

Juan E. Mezzich and Herbert Solomon, TAXONOMY AND BEHAVIORAL SCIENCE

Zev Klein and Yohanan Eshel, INTEGRATING JERUSALEM SCHOOLS

Philip K. Robins, Robert G. Spiegelman, Samuel Weiner, and Joseph G. Bell (Eds.), A GUARANTEED ANNUAL INCOME: Evidence from a Social Experiment

James Alan Fox (Ed.), MODELS IN QUANTITATIVE CRIMINOLOGY

James Alan Fox (Ed.), METHODS IN QUANTITATIVE CRIMINOLOGY

Ivar Berg (Ed.), SOCIOLOGICAL PERSPECTIVES ON LABOR MARKETS

*In Preparation*

Ronald C. Kessler and David F. Greenberg, LINEAR PANEL ANALYSIS: Quantitative Models of Change

Bruce Jacobs, THE POLITICAL ECONOMY OF ORGANIZATIONAL CHANGE: Urban Institutional Response to the War on Poverty

Michael E. Sobel, LIFESTYLE AND SOCIAL STRUCTURE: Concepts, Definitions, Analyses

Howard Schuman and Stanley Presser, QUESTIONS AND ANSWERS IN ATTITUDE SURVEYS: Experiments on Question Form, Wording, and Context